PACIFIC
CURRENTS

THE RESPONSES OF U.S. ALLIES AND SECURITY
PARTNERS IN EAST ASIA TO CHINA'S RISE

Evan S. Medeiros

Keith Crane | Eric Heginbotham

Norman D. Levin | Julia F. Lowell

Angel Rabasa | Somi Seong

Prepared for the United States Air Force

Approved for public release; distribution unlimited

 PROJECT AIR FORCE

The research described in this report was sponsored by the United States Air Force under Contract FA7014-06-C-0001. Further information may be obtained from the Strategic Planning Division, Directorate of Plans, Hq USAF.

Library of Congress Cataloging-in-Publication Data

Is Available For This Publication

ISBN 978-0-8330-4464-8

The RAND Corporation is a nonprofit research organization providing objective analysis and effective solutions that address the challenges facing the public and private sectors around the world. RAND's publications do not necessarily reflect the opinions of its research clients and sponsors.

RAND® is a registered trademark.

Cover Design by Peter Soriano

Published 2008 by the RAND Corporation
1776 Main Street, P.O. Box 2138, Santa Monica, CA 90407-2138
1200 South Hayes Street, Arlington, VA 22202-5050
4570 Fifth Avenue, Suite 600, Pittsburgh, PA 15213-2665
RAND URL: http://www.rand.org/
To order RAND documents or to obtain additional information, contact
Distribution Services: Telephone: (310) 451-7002;
Fax: (310) 451-6915; Email: order@rand.org

Preface

The rise of the People's Republic of China in Asian economic and security affairs is one of the most consequential developments in the 21st century. China's regional power and influence are growing at the very time that U.S. strategic equities in Asia are increasing. China's rise raises the prospect of intensifying security competition in East Asia both between the United States and China and between China and Japan. These developments have prompted some American and Asian commentators to question whether China will eventually displace the United States as the predominant power in East Asia by gradually chipping away at the foundation of the U.S. network of defense alliances and security partnerships in the region.

To address these potential challenges, this book analyzes how U.S. allies and major security partners have responded to the rise of China in the last decade in their domestic political, economic, diplomatic, and military policymaking. This book assesses the reactions of the five U.S. defense allies in Asia plus Singapore. Documenting and assessing these responses are critical for U.S. policymakers and military planners for several reasons. First, China is the big, new, and uncertain variable affecting the foreign policies and, in some cases, the domestic affairs of countries throughout East Asia. Second, understanding whether and how China's rise will alter the content or operation of U.S. relationships in the region will help the United States maintain a robust network of alliances and security partnerships. Third, limited systematic research on East Asian responses to China has been done to date.

This document is directly relevant to policymakers and military planners who are focused on ensuring that the United States maintains maximum access to the region and maximum freedom of maneuver in conducting U.S. diplomacy and military affairs. This book's results will help policymakers and defense planners calibrate the tone and substance of U.S. regional diplomacy and military policies to ensure that U.S. alliances and security partnerships remain highly effective in shaping the strategic landscape in East Asia as China's regional power and influence grow.

This book is part of a substantial and growing body of RAND Corporation research—now spanning a decade—that examines the changing regional security environment in Asia and, specifically, China's improving diplomatic and military capabilities. Recent RAND Project AIR FORCE work on Asia includes the following:

- Roger Cliff and David A. Shlapak, *U.S.–China Relations After Resolution of Taiwan's Status*, MG-567-AF, 2007.
- Roger Cliff, Mark Burles, Michael Chase, Derek Eaton, and Kevin Pollpeter, *Entering the Dragon's Lair: Chinese Anti-Access Strategies and Their Implications for the United States*, MG-524-AF, 2007.
- Evan S. Medeiros, Roger Cliff, Keith Crane, and James C. Mulvenon, *A New Direction for China's Defense Industry*, MG-334-AF, 2005.
- Keith Crane, Roger Cliff, Evan S. Medeiros, James C. Mulvenon, and William H. Overholt, *Modernizing China's Military: Opportunities and Constraints*, MG-260-AF, 2005.

This research was sponsored by the Commander of the Pacific Air Forces and was conducted within the Strategy and Doctrine Program of RAND Project AIR FORCE for a fiscal year 2006 study, "China's Rise Through the Eyes of U.S. Allies and Security Partners in Asia."

RAND Project AIR FORCE

RAND Project AIR FORCE (PAF), a division of the RAND Corporation, is the U.S. Air Force's federally funded research and development center for studies and analyses. PAF provides the Air Force with independent analyses of policy alternatives affecting the development, employment, combat readiness, and support of current and future aerospace forces. Research is conducted in four programs: Aerospace Force Development; Manpower, Personnel, and Training; Resource Management; and Strategy and Doctrine.

Additional information about PAF is available on our Web site:
http://www.rand.org/paf/

Contents

Preface iii

Figures xi

Tables xiii

Summary xv

Acknowledgments xxv

Abbreviations xxvii

CHAPTER ONE

Introduction 1

Scope and Methodology 2

Organization 4

CHAPTER TWO

China's Changing Economic Relations with Asia 5

Trade Flows 5

   China as a Key Export Market 5

   Declining Importance to China 8

   China as an Assembly Hub for East Asian Electronics 9

Trade in Services 11

   Chinese Payments for Services, Factor Incomes, and Transfers 13

   Chinese Earnings from Services, Factor Incomes, and Transfers 14

Foreign Direct Investment: Competitors or Collaborators? 15

   Patterns of Foreign Direct Investment into China 15

   Chinese Investment in the Six Nations 17

   Competition for FDI 18

Winners and Losers from Trade with China 19

   Winners 19

   Losers 21

Net Assessment 21

CHAPTER THREE

Japan 23
National Conditions 24
Domestic Politics and Public Opinion 25
    The History Question and Yasukuni 26
    Popular Perceptions of China 28
    The LDP's China Posture 30
    The Opposition 31
Economic Responses 32
    Trade with China 33
    Foreign Direct Investment Flows 34
    The Economic Ministries' Position 37
    Japanese Businesses Embrace China 39
Diplomatic and Foreign Policy Responses 40
    Tighter Embrace of the United States 41
    Strategic Relations with India, Taiwan, and Australia 42
    Reengaging Southeast Asia 45
    Democracy, History, and Asian Leadership 45
    Bilateral Relations with China 46
Defense Policy Responses 49
    Military Planning and Guidance 50
    New Missions, Old Budgets 51
    Strengthening the Coast Guard 55
Conclusions and Implications 55
    Policy Integration 56
    Domestic and International Variables 58
    Indicators of Change 59

CHAPTER FOUR

South Korea 63
National Conditions 65
Domestic Politics and Public Opinion 68
    Domestic Politics 68
    Popular Views and Public Opinion 72
Economic Responses 73
    Fading Optimism and Growing Concerns 77
    Assessing Winners and Losers 80
Diplomatic and Foreign Policy Responses 82
Defense Policy Responses 85
    Defense Policy 85
    Military Relations with China 89

Conclusions and Implications 90
  Driving Forces and Likely Futures..91
  The Strength of U.S.–South Korean Security Relations 93
  Potential Tests of Will.. 94

CHAPTER FIVE

The Philippines... 97
National Conditions... 98
Domestic Politics and Public Opinion 100
Economic Responses.. 102
  Winners and Losers from Trade with China 104
  Trade in Services.. 107
  Foreign Direct Investment.. 108
  Role of the Ethnic Chinese Business Community......................... 109
Diplomatic and Foreign Policy Responses 110
  Bilateral Relations with China 110
  Philippine-ASEAN Interactions 112
  Relations with the United States.. 114
  Taiwan Policy... 115
Defense Policy Responses 116
  Rebuilding of U.S.–Philippine Military Ties............................. 118
  Defense Cooperation with Other Countries 119
  Military Exchanges with China.. 120
Conclusions and Implications 120
  Key Findings 120
  Future Responses and the Implications for the United States........... 122

CHAPTER SIX

Thailand.. 125
National Conditions.. 126
Domestic Politics and Public Opinion 128
  A Pro-China Tilt?.. 129
  Party Differences... 130
Economic Responses.. 132
  Chinese-Thai Trade.. 132
  Thailand and China in Regional Production Chains..................... 133
  Thailand's Chinese Business Groups 136
  Interlocking FTAs and Thailand as Hub 137
  Chinese Investment in Thailand 139
Diplomatic and Foreign Policy Responses 141
  Bilateral Relations with China and the United States................... 141
  Improving Relations with Burma, India, and China..................... 143

Multilateralism and Regional Politics 145
Defense Policy Responses 147
    Force Modernization Plans 147
    Threat Perceptions and China 149
    Strategic Relations and Military Diplomacy with China 150
    Security Cooperation with the United States 152
    Cultivating New Security Partners 153
Conclusions and Implications 155
    Policy Integration 155
    Variables and Indicators 156

CHAPTER SEVEN
Singapore 159
National Conditions 160
    The Ethnic Dimension 162
    Domestic Politics and Public Opinion 162
    Public Perceptions of China 163
Economic Responses 164
    Singapore's Stake in Regional Economic Integration 165
    Merchandise Trade 167
    Foreign Direct Investment 171
    Economic Winners and Losers 175
Diplomatic and Foreign Policy Responses 176
    Regional Policy 176
    Taiwan Policy 178
Defense Policy Responses 180
    Defense Cooperation with the United States 181
    Importance of Technology Cooperation 183
    Defense Relations with ASEAN States and China 184
Conclusions and Implications 185

CHAPTER EIGHT
Australia 189
National Conditions 190
Domestic Politics and Public Opinion 195
    Domestic Politics 195
    Public Opinion 196
Economic Responses 197
    Trade 198
    The Composition of Trade 201
    Foreign Direct Investment 204

Winners and Losers... 205
Diplomatic and Foreign Policy Responses 208
Perceptions of China in Regional Security Affairs............................. 209
Australia's Embrace of China.. 210
Australia's Asia Diplomacy... 213
The U.S. Factor in Australian-Chinese Relations............................. 215
Interpreting Australian-Chinese Relations 217
Defense Policy Responses 219
Defense Community Perceptions of China...................................... 220
Defense Planning and Procurement.. 222
Military-to-Military Relations with China 224
Conclusions and Implications 226
Key Findings 226
Future Trends and Indicators.. 228

CHAPTER NINE

Conclusions.. 231
Overall Conclusions 231
Evaluating Regional Responses to China 234
Australia, Japan, and Singapore... 234
The Philippines and Thailand 235
South Korea 236
Understanding Regional Responses to China 237
Domestic Politics and Public Opinion 237
Economic Relations.. 239
Diplomacy and Foreign Policy 240
Defense Policy Responses.. 242
Implications for U.S. Regional Security Policy................................. 244
Implications for the U.S. Air Force 247
Prospects for Future Security Cooperation 249
Australia.. 249
Japan... 251
The Philippines... 252
Singapore... 253
South Korea 254
Thailand.. 255

Bibliography.. 257

Figures

2.1.	Exports to China, 1996 and 2006	6
2.2.	Top Exports of the Six Case-Study Nations to China, 1996 and 2006	7
2.3.	China's Exports, by Country and Region, 1996 and 2006	8
2.4.	Composition of China's Exports to the Six Case-Study Nations and to the World, 1996 and 2006	10
2.5.	China's Top Exports to the Six Nations, 1996 and 2006	11
2.6.	Services, Factor Incomes, and Transfers as a Share of Exports in China, Hong Kong, and the Six Nations, 2006	12
2.7.	Chinese Expenditures on Services, Factor Incomes, and Transfers, 2005	13
2.8.	Inflows of FDI into China, 1994, 2000, and 2005	16
2.9.	Cumulative FDI in China from the Six Nations, 1994–2005	17
2.10.	FDI in China, the Six Nations, a Subset, and Five ASEAN Countries	19
3.1.	Japanese Perceptions of China	28
3.2.	Japanese Imports, by Country of Origin, Selected Years	34
3.3.	Japanese Exports, by Country of Destination, Selected Years	35
3.4.	Composition of Japan's Imports from China, 2006	35
3.5.	Composition of Japan's Exports to China, 2006	36
3.6.	Japanese FDI in China and the United States	36
4.1.	South Korea's Major Export Markets, Selected Years	74
4.2.	Composition of South Korean Exports to China, 2006	75
4.3.	Composition of South Korean Imports from China, 2006	75
4.4.	South Korea's Annual FDI in the United States and China, 1995–2005	76
4.5.	South Korea's Cumulative FDI, by Destination, 2006	77
4.6.	FDI from the United States, Japan, and China, 1995–2005	78
5.1.	Philippine Exports, by Country of Destination, Selected Years	102
5.2.	Composition of Philippine Exports to China, 2006	103
5.3.	Composition of Philippine Imports from China, 2006	105
5.4.	Total Philippine Exports of Clothing, Textiles, and Shoes, 1995–2006	106
6.1.	Thai Imports, by Country of Origin, Selected Years	133
6.2.	Thai Exports, by Country of Destination, Selected Years	134
6.3.	Composition of Thailand's Imports from China, 2006	134
6.4.	Composition of Thailand's Exports to China, 2006	135

7.1.   Singapore's Major Exports, by Country of Destination, Selected Years......... 168
7.2.   Singapore's Major Imports, by Country of Origin, Selected Years 169
7.3.   Singapore's Imports from China as a Share of Worldwide Imports, 2006...... 169
7.4.   Singapore's Exports to China as a Share of Worldwide Exports, 2006 170
7.5.   Distances to Taiwan.. 184
8.1.   Australian Exports, by Country of Destination, Selected Years 199
8.2.   Australian Imports, by Country of Origin, Selected Years 199
8.3.   Composition of Australian Exports to China, 2006 202
8.4.   Composition of Australian Imports from China, 2006......................... 202
8.5.   Trends in Australian Winning World Exports, 1996–2006.................... 205

Tables

3.1. Japanese Defense Expenditures 52
6.1. Thailand's Free Trade Agreements 138
6.2. Thailand's Defense Budget 148
7.1. Top Five Singaporean Imports from China, 2006 170
7.2. Top Five Singaporean Exports to China, 2006 171
7.3. Singapore's Stock of Inward and Outward Direct Investment,
Selected Countries, Year-End 2005 172

Summary

China's growing involvement and influence in East Asian economic and security affairs are not fundamentally eroding the foundation of U.S. alliances and security partnerships in the region. None of the six nations covered in this book—Australia, Japan, the Philippines, Singapore, South Korea, and Thailand—see China as a viable strategic alternative to the United States. The United States remains the security partner of choice in the region. But consistent U.S. efforts are needed to ensure this situation continues in perpetuity.

China, however, is changing some U.S. alliances and security partnerships in Asia. In many cases, China makes U.S. security commitments even more relevant: Nations can confidently engage China precisely because U.S. security commitments endure. However, America's Asian allies and partners are increasingly seeking to maximize their maneuvering room by positioning themselves to benefit from ties with both China and the United States. On balance, America's Asian allies and security partners want continued U.S. involvement in the region, but sometimes only in certain ways, at certain times, and on particular issues.

What is *not* occurring in Asia in response to China's rise is as important as what is occurring. Contrary to media reporting, East Asia is not gradually falling under China's hegemony, at least not the six nations addressed here. China is not gradually and surreptitiously pushing the United States out of the region or otherwise making it irrelevant. Regional states are not climbing on a Chinese bandwagon in expectation of its eventual hegemony. The United States and China are jockeying for power and influence, but not in a zero-sum manner.

The six East Asian nations are also not modernizing their militaries in an effort to balance Chinese power. Regional governments are watching Chinese military modernization with varying degrees of attention and concern. But China's military modernization has not sparked a regional rush to expand military budgets or force structures (i.e., internal balancing). Rather, regional responses have been to tighten existing alliance links and diversify security ties with other regional states (i.e., external balancing).

As China's role in Asian affairs has expanded, the desire of our six nations to have the United States remain engaged in the region has not diminished and, in some important cases, has grown. Most East Asian nations welcome positive and mutually beneficial interactions with both the United States and China on a range of traditional and nontraditional security issues. China is undoubtedly gaining influence among all six East Asian nations but in a limited way and of a certain type. China looms larger in the policy decisions of them all. These nations have become more sensitive to Chinese preferences and interests, often on sovereignty-related questions that already resonate. Also, many countries are more frequently self-censoring their China policy. However, the influence China is gaining is most effective at precluding the development of an "anti-China" containment effort. It is a passive variety of influence that involves nations not taking certain actions deemed to be provocative to China. We assess that China has not gained "offensive" influence, with which it could attenuate alliance relationships or otherwise marginalize U.S. influence. When China has tried to assert itself in such ways, its efforts have often been counterproductive, alienating its Asian interlocutors instead.

All six nations uniformly view China as a source of economic opportunity and are rapidly expanding their economic links with China. There is a pervasive and compelling economic logic to these bilateral relationships. However, for some, trade with China is not an unqualified good; it has damaged certain sectors of their economies, producing both economic winners and losers. Nevertheless, there is little sign that these nations will come to see trade with China as a net loss any time in the foreseeable future. In fact, most regional leaders see China as key to their nation's future prosperity, a perception that is often out of step with the realities of their bilateral economic interactions with China.

Several East Asian nations are now moving out of the honeymoon phase with China. They recognize the costs and complexities involved in managing multidimensional relationships with China. While, on balance, many view stable relations with China as central to their economic livelihood, China is not uniformly seen as reliable or predictable.

None of America's East Asian allies want to have to choose between the United States and China, not even the United States' closest Asian security partners in the region. They all see such a choice as a worst-case scenario, to be avoided at all costs. In fact, most reject the idea that such a choice exists, often arguing that they do not view interactions between the United States and China in Asia in zero-sum terms. Thus, the Taiwan issue, and the possibility of a U.S.–Chinese conflict over it, is an issue of unique sensitivity because it could force such an unwanted choice.

The six East Asian nations are uniformly expanding their bilateral interactions with China. To varying degrees, they are accommodating some Chinese interests, such as those relating to Taiwan and human rights, in both bilateral interactions and multilateral forums. None are in favor of appeasing China, and most are cognizant of the dangers of appearing to do so. While these nations are more sensitive to China's preferences and increasingly calculate China's reactions in their policymaking, they have not demonstrated a willingness to capitulate to China's demands on issues deemed of core national interest, which specifically includes their security ties with the United States. In fact, there is little evidence that the growing economic links between China and U.S. allies have translated into direct political influence that China could effectively leverage to shape their policy choices. China would face difficulties translating economic ties into direct influence over other nations' foreign policy or military affairs. There is some self-censorship and self-restraint in areas of key interest to China, commonly on Taiwan or human-rights-related questions. Yet, these countries remain highly sensitive and resistant to Chinese actions that appear to be open attempts at manipulation from Beijing.

U.S. allies in Asia expressed differing levels of concern about the uncertainty of China's future and its potential influence on regional stability and prosperity. The six nations in this book fear both a strong and a weak China because both possibilities could threaten regional security and development.

All the countries we assessed support a robust role for the United States in regional security affairs. To varying degrees, they have strengthened their security relationships with the United States at the same time as they have engaged China—although often for reasons having little to do with China. While they need to expand economic interactions with China to foster economic development, these nations want to ensure that the United States remains a principal security guarantor in the region as insurance against a destabilizing China. None of the six East Asian nations favor or expect China to supplant the United States as the predominant power in Asia. At the same time, none of them support an explicit or implicit U.S.–led effort to contain China's rise. None of these nations consider such a strategy desirable or feasible because it would precipitate unnecessary strategic rivalry.

The nations we surveyed all believe that U.S. policy toward China, and Asia as a whole, will have a strong and determining influence on whether China's rise is stabilizing or destabilizing. In short, U.S. policy remains a key variable in how these nations react to China's growing regional influence. As long as the United States remains a major economic actor and security guarantor to the region, the regional responses to the rise of China will be taken with confidence and moderation.

On balance, the responses of U.S. allies and security partners to China reflect relative optimism about China's current and potential contributions to Asian and global economic affairs. This reaction is, in part, an indication of these nations' desire for Washington to remain a key economic actor and security guarantor in East Asia; it also reflects a general satisfaction with the role the United States plays, albeit with differing levels of dissatisfaction about U.S. international and regional diplomacy. These views are coupled with complaints that Washington is not engaged sufficiently on issues of primary interest to East Asian nations and that U.S. Asia policy is insensitive to the diplomacy nations in the region extend toward China.

Japan

The rise of China has clearly stirred Japan's competitive impulses, but its posture toward China remains characterized by considerable ambivalence marked by growing anxiety. Many Japanese leaders are more willing than in the past to cite China explicitly as a potential military threat, and the two countries have engaged in heated disputes over territorial boundaries, historical issues, and regional leadership. These three sets of issues will, in large measure, drive regional competition between China and Japan in the coming years. Japan has edged closer to the United States and strengthened ties with other regional partners, from India to Australia to Taiwan, moves that are increasingly justified with reference to China. Tokyo has also demonstrated a new willingness to use its military forces, for example, to patrol ocean areas disputed with Beijing.

At the same time, Japan's businessmen and economic planners remain convinced that the nation's economic well-being remains tied to continued trade and investment with China. A broad alliance of business, political, and media actors appealed for and supported the post-Koizumi outreach to China, and Beijing has reciprocated by taking a more-conciliatory posture. Many strategists and politicians also foresee damage to Japan's position in Asia should a cold war develop between Tokyo and Beijing.

The long-term prognosis is highly uncertain for Sino-Japanese relations, and there are certainly grounds for concern. For the first time, both China and Japan are unified internally, powerful in economic and military terms, and capable of influencing events beyond their borders. At the same time, the United States is pushing for Japan to assume a larger regional and global role. Domestically, the demise of the Socialist Party during the mid-1990s nudged the political center of domestic politics to the right. Japan's emergence from 15 years of sluggish economic growth has helped usher in the rise of nationalist sentiments. At the same time, a new breed of popular politicians has challenged the long-dominant bureaucracy for control of national policy, including foreign policy.

South Korea (Republic of Korea)

The simplest—but not the most complete—answer to the question of what is driving South Korea's response to China is a generally benign view of China and the perceived economic benefits of stable relations between South Korea and China. Given these conditions, there is considerable sensitivity toward China in South Korea today and reluctance either to challenge major Chinese interests or to needlessly stimulate Chinese sensitivities. At the same time, growing concerns and anxieties about Chinese economic policymaking and diplomacy show that the honeymoon in Chinese–South Korean relations is decidedly over. The forces holding the relationship back, if not driving it in the opposite direction, include uncertainties about China's prospects and long-term intentions (especially regarding China's growing influence in North Korea), awareness of potential South Korean vulnerability to Chinese economic or other pressures, continuing irritants in the bilateral relationship, a widely shared awareness of the importance of the United States, and a continuing gap between South Korean aspirations and capabilities.

These cross pressures suggest that, first, South Korea will continue to try to expand ties with China, with the economic side of the relationship remaining dominant. South Korea is likely to emphasize solving actual problems between the two countries, such as the need for a maritime security agreement, and to try to use the relationship to discuss confidence and security-building measures and other steps that could improve prospects for peace on the peninsula. By geography alone, sensitivity toward Chinese interests will remain a characteristic of South Korean policies.

Second, the irritants in and constraints on the relationship will also continue, and an occasional spike in tensions is to be expected. As China continues to ensconce itself in North Korea, issues pertaining to the North could come to have as many negatives as positives for South Korean–Chinese relations. Even short of this, a new strategic alignment between South Korea and China is not likely in the absence of some major external event. South Korea will likely seek to maintain good relations with China on the basis of—rather than instead of—a continued close alliance with the United States. Another North Korean nuclear test, and/or clear Chinese unwillingness or inability to bring the North to resolve the nuclear issue peacefully, would reinforce this inclination.

This mixed picture suggests that, barring unexpected developments, South Korea will stick with the United States, even at critical decision points that test the U.S.–South Korean alliance, as was the case in Iraq. But China's rise will continue to challenge U.S. efforts to *expand* U.S.–South Korean security cooperation. South Korean agreement to participate in U.S. military operations out of its homeland will be particularly difficult to obtain, although this will depend heavily on the context in Korean domestic politics, bilateral relations, and international relations. The key to the future of the relationship will be reconfiguring the alliance correctly.

The Philippines

The main factor affecting the Philippines' response to China is the country's fundamental and myriad weaknesses. Chronic political instability, debilitating domestic insurgencies, and deteriorating military capabilities have left the Philippines unable to ensure peace and order even within the main islands, let alone defend its offshore territorial and natural resource claims vis-à-vis China. This weakness has spurred Filipino efforts to reestablish close defense ties with the United States, mainly to cope with its severe internal security challenges. Philippine leaders have increasingly come to view

China not as a major security threat but as a relatively benign power. This is reflected in current Philippine military modernization plans, which do not appear to be informed by considerations relating to China—or, really, any external threats.

The Philippine economy is less dependent on trade with China (and international trade, more generally) than are the economies of its Asian neighbors. Like other Asian economies, however, China has become an increasingly important target for Philippine exports, with the burgeoning trade relationship becoming an important force for the Philippines' own economic growth. The broad consensus in the Philippines over China's importance as an economic partner bolsters support for efforts to strengthen bilateral ties. Yet, the view that China is an important future economic partner is mixed with an incipient sense that China is also a potential competitive economic threat.

While these are the major forces driving the Philippines' response to China, it is important to stress that the forces are not "driving" Filipino policy anywhere in particular. The leadership is heavily focused on internal challenges. And the public is relatively inattentive to China and, for that matter, most other foreign-policy issues. Chinese-Philippine tensions have certainly decreased in recent years, and the relationship has assumed a more-affable and -productive tenor.

Thailand

Thailand has a long tradition of "bending with the wind." In today's East Asia, that means accommodating—and seeking advantage from—both China and the United States. Thaksin Shinawatra, the former Prime Minister, modified Thailand's recent approach by trying to "blow the wind," as well as bend with it. He strengthened political and military, as well as economic, ties with China at the same time he was taking bold new steps to buttress Bangkok's alliance with the United States. His successor, however, is likely to return to a more-muted style of foreign policy. A post-Thaksin government may de-emphasize bold initiatives, particularly on the strategic or military front, and refocus Bangkok's diplomatic efforts on the Association of Southeast Asian Nations. But assuming China continues to grow economically without exhibiting manifestly aggressive behaviors in Southeast Asia, Bangkok is likely to continue deepening its economic; political; and, to a lesser extent, military relationships with Beijing.

While the direction of movement in Thai foreign policy has not been all in one direction, several long-term trends suggest that relations with China have become more important to Thais. China's importance as a trade and investment partner has grown substantially. With the Thai military budget growing after a decade of stagnation, it has acquired some military hardware from China but has made major purchases from Western suppliers. Despite Thailand's past efforts to engage Burma (which removed a source of tension with Beijing), Burma's recent instability has once again made it an issue between Beijing and Bangkok.

There are also limits to the magnitude of the growing Thai-Chinese relationship. Thai leaders are committed to a balanced posture between China and the United States because Thai policymakers recognize the long-standing material and symbolic benefits of the alliance with the United States. Bangkok is also working to develop options with other countries. Economically, it has moved to strengthen ties with India, Australia, New Zealand, and Japan. Politically and militarily, it cooperates with India, Singapore, Malaysia, and Indonesia, as well as with the United States and China. China's regional behavior will be the largest variable in the evolution of Thai attitudes toward the rise of China. Events in Burma, the success or failure of ongoing negotiations with the United States and Japan for free trade agreements, and the future of political reform in Thailand are also important variables, albeit less widely appreciated ones.

Singapore

Singapore shows less ambivalence in its response to the rise of China than do most other Southeast Asian countries addressed in this book. The country's small size, geostrategic vulnerability, and continuing concerns about long-term Chinese intentions propel it toward a close, *strategic* relationship with the United States—despite its close ethnic links to China. Singaporean leaders see the United States as both the principal stabilizer in the event of internal Chinese unrest and the only realistic counterweight to potential Chinese external assertiveness. Keeping the United States actively engaged and forward deployed in the region has thus been a central Singaporean foreign policy objective. China's rise and the spread of Islamic extremism and heightened concerns about stability in neighboring countries have prompted Singapore to further strengthen security cooperation with the United States. At the same time, Singapore has sought to expand security ties with the United Kingdom, Japan, Australia, and other nations with stakes in regional stability.

This core component of Singapore's response to the rise of China is coupled with efforts to further develop Singaporean-Chinese economic relations, as with other nations in this book. The benefits Singapore receives from increasing trade and investment with China, as well as from China's broader economic integration in the region, underpin efforts to expand bilateral economic ties. These efforts are balanced, however, by an attempt to diversify Singapore's economic relationships to avoid excessive dependence on the Chinese market. They are also balanced by efforts to negotiate a range of free trade agreements, in particular with Japan and the United States, as a means of countering China's active economic diplomacy and entrenching these key countries economically in Southeast Asia.

Because of the relative lack of ambivalence about China and the clarity of Singapore's long-term vision, the future of Singapore's relationship with China has a greater level of certainty than any other Southeast Asian nation. As China becomes more powerful, Singaporean leaders will do everything they can to ensure a continued balance of power in the region, one in which China does not dominate. This effort will almost surely guarantee continued close diplomatic and security relations with the United States. However, in the absence of unprovoked Chinese aggression, Singapore will neither encourage nor support a "containment" or explicitly "anti-China" balancing coalition.

Australia

There are distinct cross pressures in Australian-Chinese relations. First, rapidly growing trade relations and the perception among Australian policymakers that China is key to Australia's future prosperity have been the drivers of bilateral relations. Second, few in Australia see rivalry or conflict with China as likely or inevitable. Australia wants to avoid being drawn into a regional rivalry with China, perhaps led by misguided U.S. policymaking. Third, Australian policymakers share a deep uncertainty mixed with a nagging concern about China's growing power and influence in Asian economic and security affairs. China's diplomatic activism in Asia and its military modernization are areas of growing focus among Australian strategists.

Canberra has improved and will continue to improve its bilateral relations with Beijing, with economic ties clearly leading the charge. As China looms larger in Australia's foreign policy, Canberra will continue to be sensitive to and will accommodate some of Beijing's interests, such as its policies on Taiwan and human rights. Australia's concerns about China's growing influence and behavior will persist as well, limiting to a degree the expansion of Chinese-Australian relations and enabling to a degree greater alliance cooperation related to Asia.

Under the Howard administration, Australia's concerns about China motivated a series of foreign and defense policies that expanded alliance cooperation and sought to ensure that the United States would remain highly influential in the Asia-Pacific. The new Labour Party government, led by Kevin Rudd, appears committed to continue a similar, but not identical, approach to China and Asia. Rudd has chosen to distinguish his foreign policy from that of his predecessor on global issues, such as Iraq policy, nuclear nonproliferation, and climate change, rather than on China policy. Kevin Rudd has made clear that, while China may be an increasingly important "partner" for Australia, the United States is a "strategic ally." He has noted that a strong alliance bolsters Australia's position in Asia and that the alliance contributes to broader regional stability.

To be sure, there are different schools of thought in the current Australia government about how to engage China effectively, which Chinese interests to accommodate, how closely to coordinate with the United States, and the implications of Australia's China policy for alliance relations. How these various debates will play out under the new domestic political context of a young Labour government remains an open question.

Implications for the United States

The United States remains well positioned to continue to achieve its core objectives in the Asia-Pacific region. In contrast to many analyses, this book concludes that the United States does not face a crisis in Asia, in which an ascendant China is gradually replacing U.S. influence. The six East Asian nations assessed in this book are simply not jumping on a Chinese bandwagon, and none desire such an outcome. Most of these nations are hedging their security bets regarding China's reemergence in East Asia. U.S. policy should reflect this reality. In fact, the rise of China has made the United States more relevant in many ways.

Moreover, the quasi-regional consensus favoring engaging and cooperating with China is largely driven by an economic logic: that doing so is both to benefit from China's growing economy and to keep China growing and stable. But this consensus has a tentative quality to it. Several East Asian nations have their own concerns about how China might use its growing power, such as reasserting its historical and domineering patterns of bilateral relations. Others fear an economically stagnating and socially volatile China that exports instability abroad. Thus, there is still abundant geopolitical space for the United States to grow its Asian security relationships in support of a regional security order marked by cooperation among several major powers but in which no single power dominates.

Moreover, it is early days in East Asia's responses to China's growing weight in regional affairs. The region is still coming to terms with China's expanding involvement in Asian political, social, economic, and security affairs. Our analysis indicates that China would face difficulties translating its growing economic links with East Asian nations into political influence over them. Therefore, given the historic centrality of the United States to Asian security affairs (at least in the last 50 years) and the U.S. role as a provider of critical public goods to the region, the United States has both the time and space necessary for responding effectively to the challenges regional reactions to China's rise pose.

It is not in U.S. interests to take a highly competitive approach to China's security alliances and partnerships in the region. U.S. policy needs to be sensitive to the changing constellations of equities of its East Asian allies and partners—none of which want to provoke China into becoming a strategic adversary. Also, none want the United

States to depart the region either; fear of abandonment is as strong or stronger a motivation as concern about becoming entrapped in a U.S. regional policy that confronts China.

The United States should pursue a finely calibrated policy that is tailored to meet the individual needs and national interests of its allies and security partners. Washington should pursue a differentiated strategy with the following general characteristics: greater involvement in and contribution to regional economic and security institutions, both rhetorically and substantially; appreciation of each nation's economic and national-security priorities and capabilities and security cooperation that accords with these interests; sensitivity to local views of the United States and China, at both the popular and elite levels; efforts to broaden security cooperation to increase the quality of U.S. defense assistance; and more burden sharing in defense and diplomatic cooperation. This represents a distinct challenge for the United States, especially in its dealings with its smaller allies, such as Thailand and the Philippines, which confront dynamic—and often quite volatile—political and economic environments. The United States has much to bring to these relationships, including trade and investment opportunities, extensive security cooperation, policy coordination in multilateral forums, and politically salient high-level bilateral interactions. It is incumbent on the United States to calibrate the right mix of policy tools to ensure that the "balance of influence" stays in America's favor as China becomes more relevant to U.S. allies and security partners in East Asia.

Acknowledgments

This book benefited enormously from the assistance of several individuals. All the authors are supremely indebted to the numerous officials and scholars from Australia, Japan, the Philippines, South Korea, Singapore, and Thailand who were willing to share their time and insights about their home nations during interviews for this project during 2005 and 2006. They necessarily must remain anonymous, but their contributions have been substantial. We are very grateful to Ralph Cossa, President of the Center for Strategic and International Studies Pacific Forum, and Greg Treverton, our RAND colleague, for reviewing and commenting on the book. Toy Reid provided research assistance for several chapters. Hilary Wentworth and Megan Katt provided extensive assistance in reading, editing, formatting, and organizing this document at various stages of its evolution. It could not have come together without Hilary's and Megan's attention to detail and endurance with such a long and detailed document.

Abbreviations

ACMECS	Ayeyawady–Chao Phraya–Mekong Economic Cooperation Strategy
ADMM	ASEAN Defense Ministers Meeting
ALP	Australian Labour Party
AMRAAM	Advanced Medium-Range Air-to-Air Missile
ANZUS	Australia, New Zealand, and United States Security Treaty
ASDF	Air Self-Defense Forces [Japan]
ASEAN	Association of Southeast Asian Nations
BCE	before the common era; in chronology, equivalent to BC
BIMSTEC	Bay of Bengal Initiative for Multisectoral Technical and Economic Cooperation
BRIC	Brazil, Russia, India, and China
CAFTA	China-ASEAN Free Trade Agreement
CCP	Chinese Communist Party
CE	common era (in chronology, equivalent to AD)
COMTRADE	United Nations Commodity Trade Statistics Database
CRF	Central Readiness Force [Japan]
DDH	destroyer helicopter
DFAT	Department of Foreign Affairs and Trade [Australia]
DPJ	Democratic Party of Japan
EAS	East Asia Summit
FDI	foreign direct investment
FTA	free trade agreement
GDP	gross domestic product
GMS	Greater Mekong Subregion
GSDF	Ground Self-Defense Forces [Japan]
IISS	International Institute for Strategic Studies
IMF	International Monetary Fund
JBIC	Japan Bank for International Cooperation
JCG	Japanese Coast Guard

JDA	Japan Defense Agency
KMT	Nationalist Party [Taiwan]
LCAC	landing craft, air cushioned
LDP	Liberal Democratic Party [Japan]
LNG	liquefied natural gas
LST	landing ship, tank
MDP	Midterm Defense Plan [Japan]
METI	Ministry of Economy Trade and Industry [Japan]
MND	Ministry of National Defense [Republic of Korea]
MOD	Ministry of Defense [Japan]
MOFA	Ministry of Foreign Affairs [Japan]
MOU	memorandum of understanding
MSDF	Maritime Self-Defense Forces [Japan]
NATO	North Atlantic Trade Organization
NDPG	National Defense Program Guidelines [Japan]
NGO	nongovernmental organization
NIDS	National Institute for Defense Studies [Japan]
NPT	Nuclear Nonproliferation Treaty
OECD	Organisation for Co-Operation and Development
OSC	Open Source Center
PAF	RAND Project AIR FORCE
PLA	People's Liberation Army [People's Republic of China]
PRC	People's Republic of China
RAAF	Royal Australian Air Force
SDF	Self-Defense Forces [Japan]
TRT	Thai Rak Thai [Thais Love Thailand]
TSD	Trilateral Security Dialogue
UN	United Nations
UNCTAD	UN Conference on Trade and Development

CHAPTER ONE

Introduction

This is not a book about China but one about East Asia's reactions to China, specifically those to China's growing role in Asian economic and security affairs. The proverbial rise of China has emerged as one of the most rapid and consequential developments in regional politics since the end of the Cold War. China is the big, new, but highly uncertain variable in Asia's interstate relations. In economic terms, China has emerged not only as a magnet for expanded bilateral interactions but also as a hub in a regional production chain that ties together economies throughout East Asia. In terms of regional diplomacy, China has expanded its influence on numerous regional security questions; at the same time, the Chinese military is rapidly on its way to possessing regional power-projection capabilities that could threaten regional military balances. Given these trends, this monograph addresses three major questions: How have U.S. allies and major security partners in East Asia responded to China? What forces are driving these reactions, and how are they likely to change? What are the implications for U.S. regional security interests and policies?

Documenting and assessing the responses to the rise of China from U.S. allies and security partners in East Asia are important for several reasons. First, China is already having an identifiable influence on the domestic affairs and foreign policies of countries throughout the Asia-Pacific region. China's influence there is likely to increase further, perhaps substantially. The nature of regional responses to these developments needs to be better understood.

Second, understanding the reactions of U.S. allies and security partners is critical to the United States' substantial and growing economic and security interests in East Asia. China's influence in Asia is growing at the very time that Asia is becoming more important to the United States and to much of the rest of the international community. The maintenance of the system of U.S. alliances in Asia is central to protecting and preserving these interests, as well as to the region's stability and prosperity more broadly. Understanding whether and how China's rise will alter the content or operation of U.S. alliances and security partnerships will help the United States maintain the robustness of its alliance network.

Third, limited research on Asian responses to China has been done. Although the media have reported extensively on this subject, their reports have been selective, highly anecdotal, and from only a few East Asian countries. The conclusions, supported by a limited data set, range from alarmist predictions about America's rapid marginalization in the region to more sanguine reports of an Asia asking for forceful American leadership against the rising Chinese tide. None of this reporting has been systematic and, thus, its conclusions have dubious applicability to other nations in Asia.[1] Academic and policy research on this subject is growing and of high quality, but none of it has focused on the responses of U.S. allies and security partners—the core of the region's *de facto* security architecture. Also, this research has often looked at functional issues and not conducted systematic and comparative country-specific analyses.[2] This book aims to fill these gaps in the existing literature.

Scope and Methodology

We addressed these issues using structured focused comparison. This methodology involves careful selection of a set of case studies (six, in our case) and structuring an investigation suitable for examining all the cases in the set in parallel.[3]

First, for our case studies, we selected six specific nations: Japan, South Korea, the Philippines, Thailand, Singapore, and Australia. We chose these six because the first five are formal U.S. allies (possessing mutual-defense treaties with the United States)

---

[1]   Joshua Kurlantzick, *Charm Offensive: How China's Soft Power Is Transforming the World*, New Haven: Yale University Press, 2007; Tyler Marshall, "Image Wars: China Versus the United States," *The National Interest*, September–October 2006, pp. 119–124; Jane Perlez, "China Is Romping with the Neighbors (U.S. Is Distracted)," *New York Times*, December 3, 2003; Jane Perlez, "Across Asia, Beijing's Star Is in Ascendance," *New York Times*, August 24, 2004; Jane Perlez, "Chinese Move to Eclipse U.S. Appeal in Southeast Asia," *New York Times*, November 18, 2004; Jane Perlez, "China's Role Emerges as Major Issue for Southeast Asia," *New York Times*, March 14, 2006; Jane Perlez, "U.S. Competes with China for Vietnam's Allegiance," *New York Times*, June 19, 2006; Jane Perlez, "China Competes with West in Aid to Its Neighbors," *New York Times*, September 18, 2006; Joshua Kurlantzick, "China's Charm Offensive in Southeast Asia," *Current History,* September 2006, pp. 270–276.

[2]   David C. Kang, *China Rising: Peace, Power, and Order in East Asia*, New York: Columbia University Press, 2007; David Shambaugh, ed., *Power Shift: China and Asia's New Dynamics*, Berkeley, Calif.: University of California Press, 2006; Robert G. Sutter, *China's Rise in Asia: Promises and Perils*, Boulder, Colo.: Rowman and Littlefield Publishers, 2005; Richard L. Armitage and Joseph S. Nye, *The U.S.–Japan Alliance: Getting Asia Right Through 2020*, Washington, D.C.: Center for Strategic and International Studies, 2007; Michael R. Chambers, "Rising China: The Search for Power and Plenty," in Ashley J. Tellis and Michael Wills, *Strategic Asia 2006–07: Trade, Interdependence and Security*, Seattle, Wash.: National Bureau of Asian Research, 2006, pp. 65–104; Denny Roy, "Southeast Asia and China: Balancing or Bandwagoning?" *Contemporary Southeast Asia*, Vol. 27, No. 2, August 2005; "Summaries of Seminar Presentations and Core Group Discussions," China in Asia Seminar Series, Washington, D.C.: American Enterprise Institute and National Defense University, 2006; Dick K. Nanto and Emma Chanlett-Avery, *The Rise of China and Its Effect on Taiwan, Japan and South Korea: U.S. Policy Choices*, Congressional Research Service, Washington, D.C.: Library of Congress, April 12, 2005.

[3]   Alexander L. George and Andrew Bennett, *Case Studies and Theory Development in the Social Sciences*, Boston, Mass.: MIT Press, 2005.

and the sixth, Singapore, is a major U.S. security partner.[4] These countries constitute the core of the U.S. alliance network in the region. Like all Asian nations, these are actively expanding their bilateral relationships with China and thus constitute a representative sample from which to evaluate the regional reactions to China most relevant for U.S. security interests. Moreover, the six nations encompass wide variations in national capabilities—from weak to strong governments, young to mature democracies, robust to fragile economies, strong historical ties to China to more-limited links. These nations also possess substantial variations in the breadth and depth of their interactions with China. For example, all the nations appear to have growing relations with China, but their trade and investment links are quite different. Collectively, variations like these allowed us to assess numerous possible drivers in these nations' responses to the rise of China and, indeed, may permit a degree of generalizability to other Asian countries that we have not addressed here.

Second, we analyzed the responses of these six nations using a uniform set of variables. The responses to China fell into four functional areas:

- domestic politics and public opinion
- economic affairs
- foreign policy and diplomacy
- defense policy.

These four categories capture the main areas in which these nations—arguably, any nation—face critical choices in responding to China.

These four categories, as conceptualized here, focus primarily on assessing the national responses in each substantive area. That said, each category also considers the national interests or *inputs* for that particular substantive area, both as they relate to China and as the relevant actors perceive them. Thus, these four categories encompass both how a state is interacting with China in a given category and whether and how these interactions (or related views of policymakers) have influenced national responses in the same functional area. The conclusions of each case study explore how interactions in one area have shaped responses in other arenas, the relative importance of each type of response in shaping overall views of China, and whether and how considerations in each area were integrated into a single coherent strategy (or, alternatively, were not).

This methodological approach facilitates conclusions about the areas in which the responses to China are most and least substantial among the six nations, as well

---

[4] United States–Republic of the Philippines Mutual Defense Treaty, 1952; Australia, New Zealand, and the United States Security Treaty, 1952; United States–Republic of Korea Mutual Defense Treaty, 1954; U.S. security commitments to Thailand are based on the 1954 Manila pact of the former Southeast Asia Treaty Organization (which dissolved in 1977) and the Thanat-Rusk communiqué of 1962; and U.S.–Japan Mutual Defense Treaty, 1960 (treaty dates based on entry into force).

as those that are most and least common. It answers such questions as the following: What changes are occurring across the region, and why? What national conditions in these countries enable or constrain certain reactions to China? Which trends in national responses to China are likely to continue in the future?

In addition, this approach allowed us to compare and contrast the responses *across* the six nations to draw broader conclusions that are not country specific. It addresses such questions as the following: Do differences in the structure of economic trade with China appear to influence responses to China? Is public opinion a major variable, and do shifts in public opinion influence China policy in select nations? Do the military capabilities of these states influence their outlook toward and reactions to China?

Organization

Chapter Two provides a critical context by analyzing China's economic interactions with the six nations. It helps us understand the unique patterns of regional trade and investment in East Asia and their relative significance for China's economic growth and development. The chapter thus looks at Asia from China's perspective, focusing on recent changes in economic interactions between China and six U.S. allies and security partners.

Chapters Three through Eight are the country-specific case studies. Each chapter begins with a section on national conditions that assesses the nation's domestic political and economic contexts as they relate to its responses to China. Each chapter then examines the nation's responses to China in the four functional areas, addressing several specific questions: How substantial have the responses to China been in each area, and why? What are the drivers for and mechanisms by which such changes have occurred? Have these responses been part of a China-directed effort to shape the nation's policies? Is there a relationship among the responses in the four functional areas? What types of responses are to be expected in the future, and can benchmarks of potential future reactions be identified?

Chapter Nine, the conclusion, looks across all six nations. It begins by highlighting the most common responses to China among the six case studies. It isolates some of the key differences among the six nations and examines the responses to China by functional category. The chapter ends by drawing several implications for U.S. regional security interests and U.S. Air Force equities in East Asia. These implications confront conventional thinking in certain respects, while highlighting important challenges facing U.S. diplomacy and military policy in the region.

CHAPTER TWO

China's Changing Economic Relations with Asia

China's rise in importance both in Asia and globally since the 1970s has been driven by the rapid growth in its economy and trade. Not surprisingly, the most intensive bilateral interactions the six nations we examine here have had with China have been economic. Although most of these countries have had long-standing economic relations with China, the rate of growth and the scale of these interactions over the past ten years have often been extraordinary. The role of China in the six economies now rivals that of the United States, heretofore the most important economic partner for most of these countries.

To elucidate these economic relationships, we describe here how China's economic rise is changing trade and investment patterns in Asia, focusing on China as an economic actor in aggregate terms. We assess changes in flows of goods, services, and investment within Asia over the past decade that have been directly or indirectly tied to China. This content is distinct from the economic analysis in each chapter because it focuses on Chinese economic behavior and its overall effects on the six nations covered here; the economic analysis in each case study evaluates bilateral economic relations and their influence on national economic well-being.

Although the six economies are similar in that China's role is now much more salient for each, the group is in other respects heterogeneous. Japan's is the second largest economy in the world. Korea, Singapore, and Australia are highly developed; Korea's and Australia's economies are large relative to those of most of the rest of the world, although both are much smaller than Japan's (or China's). In contrast, Thailand and the Philippines are still classified as developing countries; the Philippines is still relatively poor by global standards. In light of these great differences, the nature and scale of economic interactions with China vary greatly across these countries, although China now looms much larger in economic interactions than it did in the 1990s.

Trade Flows

China as a Key Export Market

Over the last decade China has become one of the top three export markets for all six nations, competing with the United States and Japan for pride of place in each.

According to Chinese customs data, exports from the six nations have risen more than fivefold, from $51 billion in 1996 to $278 billion in 2006.[1] According to the customs data from the six nations, China's share of their total exports rose from 5.1 percent in 1996 to 14.3 percent in 2006 (Figure 2.1).

Although growth has been very strong, some of this reported increase is due to the diversion to mainland Chinese ports of exports that had previously gone to China via Hong Kong. In most cases, exports to China through Hong Kong are reported as exports to Hong Kong. Because so much of what passes through Hong Kong is reexported to China, it is useful to look at combined exports to both Hong Kong and mainland China when evaluating changes in trade flows between China and the six nations. The combined total still grew rapidly between 1996 and 2006, from $95 billion to $317 billion, but the rate of increase was much slower than for exports just to

Figure 2.1
Exports to China, 1996 and 2006

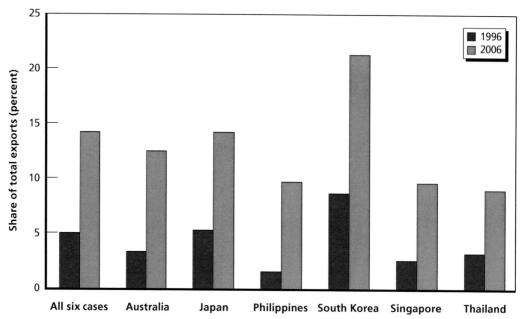

SOURCE: National Bureau of Statistics of China, *China Statistical Yearbook,* Beijing: China Statistics Press, 1996, 2006.
RAND *MG736-2.1*

---

[1]   Many of the figures in this chapter are based primarily on trade data that *China* reported to the United Nations (UN). In the country chapters, we use trade data reported *by the country* to the UN. Because trade flows through Hong Kong and Macao and because of discrepancies stemming from customs, insurance, freight, and other costs (which are often added to the value of imports), figures differ, sometimes substantially, depending on which trade partner is reporting. For example, trade flows that the Philippines reported to the UN, which we used in Chapter Five, also show substantial growth, but that growth is not as rapid as the figures from China suggest.

China; combined exports grew 3.3 times, not 5.4 times over this period. The share of total exports from these countries that went to mainland China and Hong Kong also rose but also at a slower pace, from 11.8 percent in 1996 to 20.5 percent in 2006. During this period, Hong Kong's share of the six nations' total exports dropped one-half a percentage point, from 6.7 percent in 1996 to 6.2 percent in 2006.

As a group, the six nations examined here continue to be the largest exporters to China in the world. Yet their *share* of world exports to China has actually fallen over the course of the decade, from 29.5 percent in 1996 to 25.5 percent in 2006, because other countries have increased their exports to China so rapidly. Japan's role, however, obscures trends in these exports because its own share of global exports to China plummeted between 1996 and 2006, from 15.8 to 10.7 percent. The others' shares of global exports to China have, in general, risen.

Driving the growth in exports from these countries have been China's thirst for raw materials; investment goods from Japan and South Korea; and intermediate goods, especially electrical, electronic, and computer parts and components. As shown in Figure 2.2, China's largest purchases from the six nations in both 1996 and 2006 were in electronics.[2] Chinese purchases of these products from the six nations rose from

Figure 2.2
Top Exports of the Six Case-Study Nations to China, 1996 and 2006

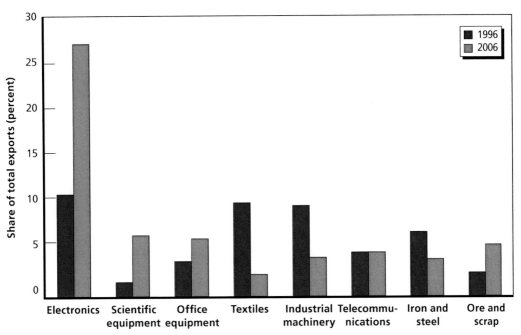

SOURCE: UN Statistics Division, UN Commodity Trade Statistics Database, 1996, 2006.
RAND MG736-2.2

[2] UN Standard International Trade Classification 77.

11 percent of total exports in 1996 to 27 percent in 2006, with Japan being the most important source in both years. The second largest export in 2006 was scientific equipment (such as meters and sensors), at 6.6 percent of total exports to China, up from 1.5 percent in 1996. This was followed by office equipment (6.1 percent in 2006, and 3.6 percent in 1996). Interestingly, exports of metal ores and scrap exceeded exports of iron and steel. In 1996, the reverse was true. The expansion of China's steel industry has increased the importance of its imports of iron ore from the six nations (especially Australia) and decreased its need to import steel from its two biggest suppliers, Japan and Korea.

Declining Importance to China

In aggregate, the six nations form one of China's biggest export markets, accounting for 19.4 percent of China's exports in 2006, slightly less than the shares of China's exports going to the United States and Europe, 21.0 and 21.9 percent, respectively (Figure 2.3). China's exports to the six nations grew rapidly between 1996 and 2006, more than quadrupling. Despite this rapid growth, the share of China's total exports going to these countries has fallen sharply, down from 30.5 percent in 1996.

The decline in the relative importance of these markets for China is primarily due to Japan. In 1996, Japan purchased 20.4 percent of China's exports, making it

Figure 2.3
China's Exports, by Country and Region, 1996 and 2006

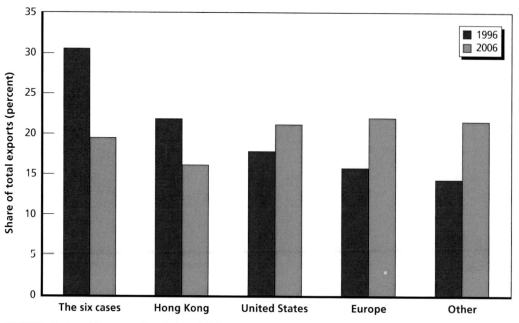

SOURCE: National Bureau of Statistics of China, 1996, 2006.
NOTE: The six cases are Australia, Japan, the Philippines, South Korea, Thailand, and Singapore.
RAND MG736-2.3

China's largest single export market. Even though China's exports to Japan quadrupled between 1996 and 2006, Japan's share of China's total exports had shrunk to only 9.5 percent by 2006, one-half the share of the United States or Europe.

Growth in economic output and consumption in Japan has been slow since the early 1990s. As a consequence, Chinese exports to Japan have increased less rapidly than to the rest of the world, including the other members of the six nations. Even though China has successfully penetrated Japanese markets for food, especially vegetables and seafood, Japan's high barriers to certain imports, such as rice, fruit, and meat, have stymied growth in China's exports of other food items. Japanese manufacturers have invested heavily in assembly plants in China, but the plants' products are for China's domestic market or global export markets, not for export to Japan. For example, in recent years, the automobile industry has been among the largest Japanese investors in China. But Japanese automobile companies have concentrated on making cars in China to sell to the Chinese, not to export them from China to sell in the Japanese domestic market or to supplant Japanese exports to the rest of the world.

South Korea is the second most important export market for China among the six nations. However, the share of all Chinese exports going to South Korea has fallen between 1996 and 2006, although not as sharply as for Japan, from 5.0 percent in 1996 to 4.6 percent in 2006. Despite better growth, the other four countries (Australia, the Philippines, Singapore, and Thailand) have increased their shares of China's exports, although only slightly, from 5.1 percent in 1996 to 5.4 percent in 2006.

China as an Assembly Hub for East Asian Electronics

The composition of China's exports to the region has changed dramatically from 1996 to 2006 (Figure 2.4). By a significant margin, exports of machinery and equipment now account for the greatest share of China's exports to the six nations and to the rest of the world. Most of this increase is due to a surge in exports of electronics, computers, and telecommunications equipment. These products are primarily manufactured by companies headquartered in Japan, South Korea, the United States, Europe, or Taiwan. These foreign companies have created an interlocking web of designers, manufacturers, suppliers, and assemblers that tie together the electronics industries in East Asia, creating what might be called an "East Asia Electronics, Inc."

The growing importance of electronics in Chinese exports to the six nations is shown in Figure 2.5. In 1996, consumer goods (such as clothing, textiles, footwear, and furniture) and raw materials or intermediate goods (iron and steel and petroleum products) dominated China's exports to the six nations. By 2006, clothing was still the most important export item at the two-digit trade classification level, but electronics (e.g., electrical equipment and electronics), office equipment (mostly computers), and telecommunications equipment had become the three next-most-important categories. Products like these play a different role in the recipient economies that import them from China than do such items as gasoline or clothing. The six nations in our study are

Figure 2.4
Composition of China's Exports to the Six Case-Study Nations and to the World,
1996 and 2006

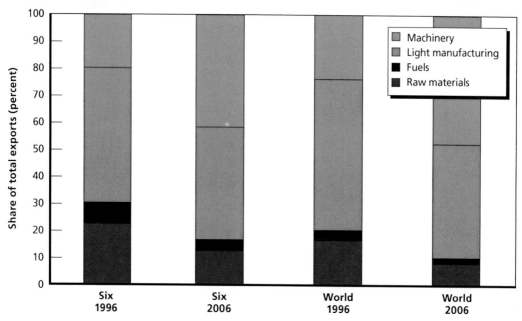

SOURCE: UN Statistics Division, 1996, 2006.
NOTE: The six cases are Australia, Japan, the Philippines, South Korea, Thailand, and Singapore.
RAND MG736-2.4

likely to import such goods as clothing or gasoline for local consumption. Much of the output of China's electronics industry, on the other hand, is shipped to the six nations for further processing and reexport, not final sale.

Foreign-owned exporters in China are not only important for integrating the East Asian economies into the electronics industry (Australia does not play a major role in trade in electronics); they also drive increased trade in other manufactured goods, from clothing to Christmas tree ornaments. In 2002, nine of China's top 20 exporting firms were foreign-owned, as were 87 of the top 200.[3] Many of these companies use China primarily as a location for assembling final products; the value China adds, although rising as a share of the total, is often confined to providing local labor. In 2004, foreign-owned companies accounted for 57 percent of total Chinese exports.

The role of foreign-owned firms and joint ventures in Chinese trade has been changing. Although these firms, especially those controlled by Taiwanese and overseas Chinese, remain key producers of Chinese exports of clothing, footwear, and other manufactures, much recent foreign investment has shifted toward serving the Chinese domestic market. For example, Japanese car companies have made very large invest-

---

[3] Hideo Ohashi, "China's Regional Trade and Investment Profile," in Shambaugh, 2006, pp. 81–82.

Figure 2.5
China's Top Exports to the Six Nations, 1996 and 2006

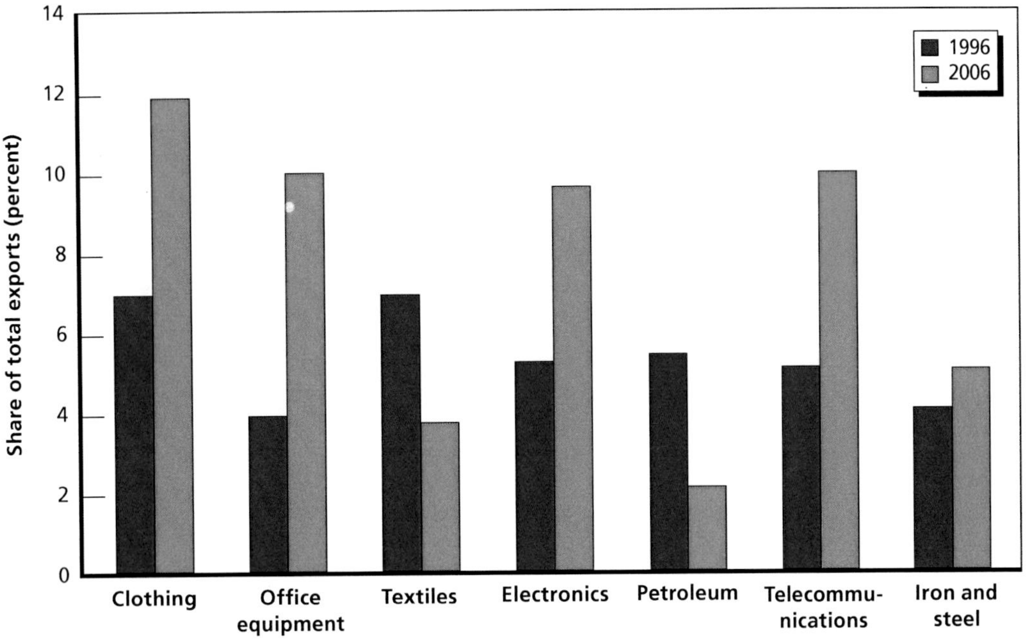

SOURCE: UN Statistics Division, 1996, 2006.

RAND *MG736-2.5*

ments in China. To date, these plants have focused on selling to the Chinese domestic market. They have had a larger effect on Chinese imports than on exports because a number of automotive components continue to be imported from Japan. Simultaneously, Chinese firms have shifted from acting as subcontractors to becoming global manufacturers and exporters in their own right. Both Japanese and South Korean companies are wary of transferring too much in the way of technology, management, and marketing know-how because of concerns that their joint venture partners will become serious competitors.

Trade in Services

China does not only export and import merchandise; its trade in services (tourism, insurance, transport, etc.) is also sizable. In addition, China earns interest on the foreign bonds that it purchases, including U.S. Treasury bonds. It also pays interest on loans and trade credits. Overseas Chinese transfer sizable sums to relatives.

In general, earnings from such flows—services, factor incomes (that is, earnings from and payments for investments and labor), and transfers—are far more important for the six nations than they are for China. China is primarily an exporter of goods:

In 2006, earnings from services, factor incomes, and transfers ran 18.0 percent of exports of goods. In contrast, these earnings run 37 percent of export earnings for the six nations on average (Figure 2.6). The sources of these incomes vary: For Thailand, most of these earnings are from tourism. In the Philippines, worker remittances are most important: Transfers, primarily remittances, run over 29 percent of the value of exports. Because these sources of income add much higher shares of value than do most exports, they are more important to the economies of the six nations than the figures suggest.

Hong Kong's role as an *entrepôt* partially explains the small role services play in China's foreign activities.[4] The value of services, transfers, and incomes from factors represent 49 percent of the value of Hong Kong's exports, substantially more than the average share of these items for the six nations. However, for Hong Kong, most of these earnings stem from transactions with China.

Figure 2.6
Services, Factor Incomes, and Transfers as a Share of Exports in China, Hong Kong, and the Six Nations, 2006

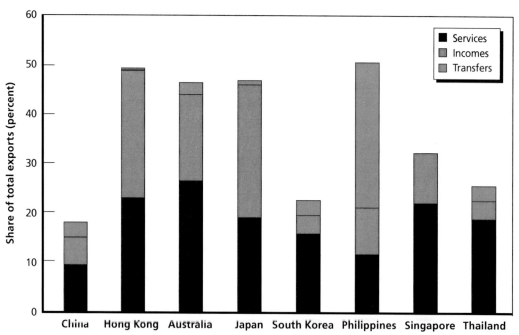

SOURCE: International Monetary Fund, International Financial Statistics, database, 2006.
RAND *MG736-2.6*

---

[4] An *entrepôt* (from the French for *warehouse*) is an international transshipment center through which goods move between their countries of origin and their final destinations. In certain circumstances, they eliminate the need to pay duties in intermediary countries while in transit.

Chinese Payments for Services, Factor Incomes, and Transfers

Services. China purchases more services than it sells. These purchases ran $101 billion in 2006, which was 13.4 percent of merchandise imports, compared to earnings of $92 billion, 9.5 percent of merchandise exports. China runs surpluses on factor incomes from the interest on its large foreign exchange reserves and on transfers primarily from gifts overseas Chinese send to their relatives in China.

Although information on trade in services by country is limited, the data available suggest that the six nations play an important role in China's service, factor income, and transfer transactions. However, for each nation, trade in services and earnings from factor incomes with China play very different roles and affect different groups.

China's largest service expenditure is for transportation (Figure 2.7). It spent $28 billion on transportation services in 2005, one-third of total expenditures on services. Of the six nations, South Korea and Japan are the most important suppliers of these services. In Japan, Kawasaki Kisen Kaisha, Ltd.; Mitsui O.S.K. Lines; and Nippon Yusen Kaisha, three of Japan's largest shipping companies, earn substantial revenues from trade with China. In South Korea, Hanjin Shipping and Hyundai Logistics have large operations with China. Besides the six nations, Hong Kong and Taiwan are also major providers of shipping services.

Tourism is the second most important expenditure item, constituting a little over one-quarter of total expenditures in 2005, at $22 billion. Most Chinese go to Hong

Figure 2.7
Chinese Expenditures on Services, Factor Incomes, and Transfers, 2005

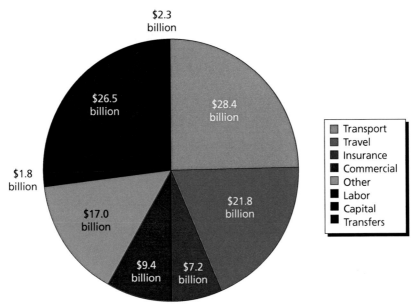

SOURCE: National Bureau of Statistics of China, 2005, Table 3-25:
Balance of Payments 2005.
RAND MG736-2.7

Kong or Macao, although Australia, Japan, the Philippines, and Thailand are attracting increasing numbers of tourists. However, Chinese tourists are still much less important to these destinations than those from other countries, especially because expenditures per Chinese tourist remain modest.

China also purchases substantial amounts of insurance, $7.2 billion in 2005, concentrated in shipping insurance and reinsurance. Only Japan plays much of a role in supplying this insurance.

Factor Incomes. China spends substantial sums for factor services (payments for capital and labor). Almost all these payments consist of dividends on investments in and interest on loans to China. Not surprisingly, China imports virtually no labor services because of its own massive supplies of labor. In 2006, expenditures on factor services ran $39 billion, equivalent to more than one-third of imports of services.

The three big Japanese banks (Bank of Tokyo-Mitsubishi UFJ, Mizuho Bank Ltd., and Sumitomo Mitsui Banking Corporation) have lent heavily to Chinese companies. Earnings from China provide a welcome addition to profits from other operations. Although operating on a smaller scale, banks in Australia and Singapore also profit from the Chinese market.

Transfers. Chinese transfers abroad have grown very rapidly over the past three years, from $811 million in 2002 to $2,378 million in 2006. Official aid from China has risen, but most of the transfers appear to be from Chinese citizens to relatives in other countries, such as students. Payments for transfers still account for a negligible share of total Chinese foreign currency expenditures: 0.3 percent.

Chinese Earnings from Services, Factor Incomes, and Transfers

China now runs a surplus on services, factors, and transfers. Earnings are substantial, $175 billion in 2006. Of these earnings, services account for a little over 50 percent, with factor incomes running a little less than one-third and transfers equal to less than one-fifth of the total.

Services. Tourism is the most important source of service incomes, accounting for two-fifths of the total. The six nations generate a substantial share of these earnings, probably about 50 percent (one-half of all foreign tourists to China come from these countries). Visitors from Japan constitute the largest cohort, accounting for about one-fifth of all foreign visitors to China, but South Korea is not far behind, with one-sixth of the total. The other countries send a total of 300,000 to 750,000 tourists to China each year, mostly ethnic Chinese. Visitors from these countries tend to spend less than their Japanese counterparts, in part because their incomes are lower and in part because they go to visit relatives rather than see the sights.

Transportation and commercial services, primarily in the form of payments to the contractors who run assembly operations, are the other two sectors that account for the bulk of China's service income. China Ocean Shipping Company and China Shipping Company are major contributors to transport earnings. Because the two companies serve Chinese exporters, their revenues are diversifying, reflecting Chinese export patterns. The Chinese shipping companies understand the importance of the six nations to their earnings; as a group, these countries constitute one of China's three largest export markets.

Factor Incomes. Since 1994, China has been piling up current account surpluses. The surpluses have been especially large since 2003, hitting $250 billion in 2006. As these surpluses have risen, so have Chinese financial assets abroad. As of 2006, China had $1,627 billion in foreign assets and $964 billion in foreign liabilities, leaving it with $662 billion more in foreign assets than in liabilities. This represents a large shift in the balance of China's factor incomes, from a deficit of $19 billion in 2001 to a surplus of $12 billion in 2006.

China's factor incomes derive primarily from interest and dividend payments and other earnings on capital. Although precise data on the composition of Chinese assets are not available, official reserves are heavily skewed toward dollar assets, especially U.S. Treasury securities. The six nations appear to play a much smaller role in these payments to China than does the United States.

Transfers. Despite the rapid rise in personal incomes in China in recent years, the country still receives a substantial influx of foreign transfer payments, $32 billion in 2006. In contrast to such countries as the Philippines, where transfer payments primarily consist of money sent back home from family members working abroad, the rapid growth in China in recent years suggests that these flows are really the repatriated earnings of Chinese entrepreneurs who had parked money abroad. Inflows have risen six times since the late 1990s, when they ran about $5 billion a year. The six nations do not play much of a role in transfer payments, although ethnic Chinese in the Philippines, Singapore, and Thailand do send money to family members in China.

Foreign Direct Investment: Competitors or Collaborators?

Patterns of Foreign Direct Investment into China

Along with many other countries, three of the six nations—Japan, South Korea, and Singapore—have been investing heavily in China (Figure 2.8). Aside from Hong Kong (which is technically part of China) and the Virgin Islands, Japan was the largest single source of foreign direct investment (FDI) in China in 2005, followed by South Korea. Flows of FDI from the six nations tripled from $4.4 billion in 1994 to $14.6 billion in 2005. These countries' share of the total FDI has also risen, from 13 percent in 1994 to 24 percent in 2005. In 2005, total FDI from the six nations dwarfed that of the United States ($3.1 billion) and Europe ($5.6 billion). However, inflows from the six nations are smaller than those from Hong Kong, which ran $17.9 billion in 2005, 30 percent of the total FDI into China. Much of this FDI, however, has made a round trip: Mainland Chinese firms in China pass investments through offshore accounts to hide funds

Figure 2.8
Inflows of FDI into China, 1994, 2000, and 2005

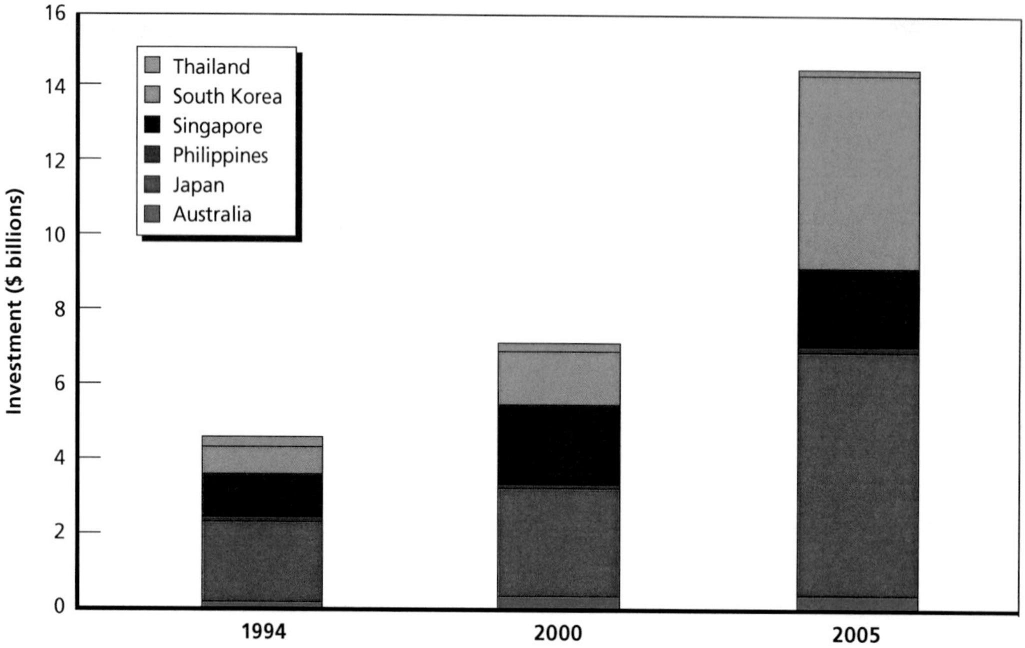

SOURCE: National Bureau of Statistics of China, 1994, 2000, 2005.
RAND MG736-2.8

from tax collectors and to take advantage of Chinese legal provisions that are friendlier to foreign investors than to domestic firms, such as those on transfers of capital and earnings abroad. These firms also use a host of other offshore accounts to launder earnings for reinvestment at home. Major offshore centers include Bermuda, the Cayman Islands, Mauritius, Samoa, and the Virgin Islands. Investment from these countries plus Hong Kong and Macao totaled $32 billion in 2005, more than 50 percent of the total FDI into China in that year. If FDI from these sources is deducted from total FDI, the six nations provided 50 percent of the FDI flowing into China in 2005.

As of 2005, the six nations' total cumulative investment in China was $114 billion, approximately one-fifth of the total cumulative FDI in China from 1994 to 2005. Within the group, Japan is the largest investor, accounting for two-fifths of the total, followed by South Korea and Singapore, each with about one-quarter of the six-nation total (Figure 2.9). These countries' share of the cumulative FDI in China has been rising, primarily because of South Korea's large increases over the last decade, which totaled 13 percent in 1994 and rose to almost 20 percent in 2005.

Data on the composition of FDI by country and sector are limited. Japan has invested heavily in electronics and motor vehicles; South Korea has focused more on electronics and clothing. Singapore has invested in a wide range of sectors, including industrial parks. Most of the small investments from the Philippines and Thailand

**Figure 2.9
Cumulative FDI in China from the Six Nations, 1994–2005**

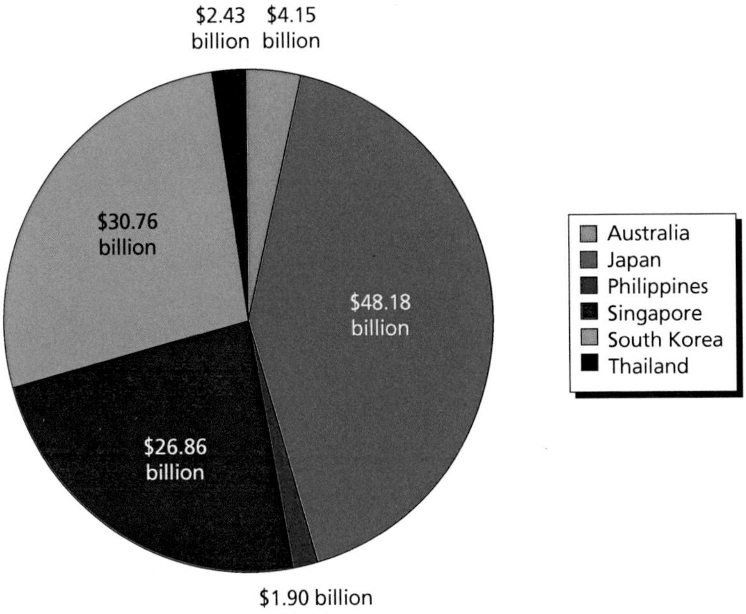

SOURCE: National Bureau of Statistics of China, 2005, Table 18-15: Actual Foreign Investment by Country or Region.
RAND *MG736-2.9*

have been undertaken by ethnic Chinese. These individuals concentrate in real estate or assembly operations for clothing, shoes, small household appliances, or other items for which labor is an important component of the total cost.

Chinese Investment in the Six Nations

Over the 1990s, China invested about $2 billion a year abroad, a small fraction of the more than $30 billion that flowed into China. However, starting in 2001, China began to invest appreciably more abroad, although the amounts fluctuated quite sharply. In 2000, China invested only $1 billion abroad, but invested $6.9 billion in 2001, and $2.85 billion in 2003, then rose sharply to $12.26 billion in 2005.[5] In 2006, China's outward FDI peaked at $21 billion. According to Chinese data, "more than 5,000 domestic Chinese investment entities had established nearly 10,000 overseas direct invested enterprises in 172 countries (regions) around the world."[6]

---

[5] Ministry of Commerce of the People's Republic of China, "2005 Statistical Bulletin of China's Outward Foreign Direct Investment," September 30, 2006.

[6] Ministry of Commerce of the People's Republic of China, "2006 Statistical Bulletin of China's Outward Foreign Direct Investment," September 30, 2007.

Some relatively small investments have gone to the six nations. According to Australian data, China invested less than $100 million in Australia between 1992 and 2003.[7] Chinese investment in Japan is similarly insignificant.[8] Chinese firms are venturing into the Philippines and Thailand, but cumulative flows are small even in these countries. In short, for these, China has yet to emerge as an important investor.

Most Chinese FDI has gone into purchasing American or European companies or subsidiaries with established brands that have become uncompetitive. Notable acquisitions include the Lenovo Group's purchase of IBM's personal computer business and the TCL Corporation's purchase of the Thomson Group's television-manufacturing business.[9] China has also been an active investor in oil fields and suppliers of raw materials. The large Chinese oil companies—China National Offshore Oil Company; China National Petroleum Company; and China Petrochemical Company and its listed subsidiary, Sinopec—have all been investing heavily in new fields abroad, making major investments in Kazakhstan, Russia, Sudan, and the North Sea.[10] But the six nations have yet to attract significant investments in the extraction of natural resources despite Australia's generous endowments.

Competition for FDI

China and the poorer among the six nations may be more competitors than partners for FDI. Figure 2.10 compares aggregate flows of FDI into the four groups shown.

The rise of FDI in China does not appear to have affected flows into the six nations as a group—or even for the subset that excludes Singapore and Australia, the two largest recipients of FDI. FDI has risen for these groupings almost as rapidly as it has for China.[11] However, the increase of FDI in China may have affected flows into the Philippines, Thailand, and the other three members of the Association of Southeast Asian Nations (ASEAN) noted above. For this group of countries, flows of FDI have yet to regain the peaks they had attained in the mid-1990s, peaks before the Asian financial crisis. As the recessions that followed that crisis are long over in all five countries, the less-than-rapid recovery of FDI may be traced partly to competition from China.[12]

---

[7] UN Conference on Trade and Development (UNCTAD), "Country Profile on Australia," FDI Database, 2005.

[8] UNCTAD, "Country Profile on Japan," FDI Database, 2005.

[9] TCL is China's largest television manufacturer.

[10] Pete Engardio, Dexter Roberts, and Catherine Belton, "Chinese Oil Giants Grow Up Fast," *Business Week* (online), March 31, 2003.

[11] The flows for Australia are net and reflect a very large acquisition in 2004 and a very large sale of an Australian-held asset abroad in 2005. These transactions greatly skew the trends shown in Figure 2.10.

[12] However, some observers argue that large FDI flows into China may have actually stimulated FDI into ASEAN countries. According to this view, foreign-owned producers (especially in the electronics industry) have chosen to expand their ASEAN operations in response to rapidly growing demand from Chinese computer and telecommunications equipment manufacturers and assemblers. See, for example, Lieu Ligang, Kevin Chow, and

Figure 2.10
FDI in China, the Six Nations, a Subset, and Five ASEAN Countries

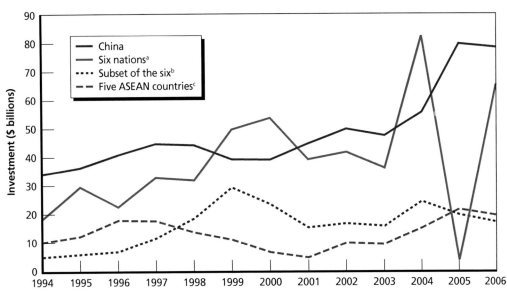

SOURCE: International Monetary Fund, 1994–2005.
[a] The six nations are Australia, Japan, the Philippines, South Korea, Thailand, and Singapore.
[b] The subset consists of Japan, the Philippines, South Korea, and Thailand.
[c] The ASEAN countries are Indonesia, Malaysia, the Philippines, Thailand, and Vietnam.
RAND *MG736-2.10*

Winners and Losers from Trade with China

By definition, *trade* implies interdependence: For every seller, there is a willing buyer. Although buyers and sellers always benefit directly from the transaction, trade also generates losers: domestic producers that have lost markets and the workers that they employed. Increased economic interaction also has indirect effects: Entrepreneurs may face increased competition for capital and must therefore pay higher interest rates, or consumers must now pay higher prices for goods and services because of the increased demand from foreign buyers. These winners and losers voice their preferences and complaints in the political arena, pressuring governments to adopt or change policies. Below, we identify the winners and losers among the six nations because of the increased economic interactions with China.

Winners
Exporters to China from the six nations have benefited both directly and indirectly from the growth in Chinese trade and the increases in Chinese demand for imports.

Unias Li, "Has China Crowded Out Foreign Direct Investment from Its Developing East Asian Neighbors?" *World Economy,* Vol. 15, No. 3, May–June 2007.

Such companies as Australia's Rio Tinto and BHP Billiton have benefited enormously from Chinese demand for Australian coal and ores. Australian exports of iron ore to China have exploded, rising 11 times between 1996 and 2006. The increase for these commodities has been so great that it has pushed up world market prices for Australian exports to other markets.

Although Japan and South Korea have had to pay higher prices to import coal, petroleum, and iron ore, they too have benefited from the boom in China because Japanese and South Korean producers of steel, petrochemicals, and other bulk commodities have increased exports to China. This increase has, in fact, given older Japanese plants in these industries a new lease on life.

As noted above, East Asian members of the six nations and China have become part of an integrated supply chain of electronics-manufacturing operations. The flows of electronic and computer components among China and the five Asian members of the six nations have become the most important exports and imports for these countries. Substantial employment growth in assembly operations in the Philippines and Thailand has benefited the local economies and contributed to the bottom lines of the owners of these facilities, often major Japanese and South Korean electronics firms.

However, the gross figures on exports of these products overstate their importance for each nation. In many instances, an operation in a given country performs only one in a series of steps in the manufacture of the product. Consequently, the value added is low. For example, if a plant that makes a certain component to be exported for assembly into another product closes, the closing directly affects only the workers at the factory and will not likely have severe repercussions for the nation's economy. Other products end up adding considerably more value because they involve many more operations. One example is processed food intended for export, which involves such local resources as farmers, manufacturers of related agricultural products, labor to harvest crops, processing plants and their staffs, and shipment facilities.

Because the owners of most companies engaged in electronics are foreigners, the political repercussions of attempting to use trade restrictions to penalize or reward other countries is more convoluted than if the owners were Chinese or local entrepreneurs. Using such measures would make it more difficult for the Chinese government to convince foreign owners of electronics plants to lobby their governments to change policies toward China.

Lower-cost imports from China have been as much a boon for consumers in the six nations as they have been for consumers around the world. It is striking how frequently interviews and press accounts from the poorest country in the six nations, the Philippines, cite the benefits of cheap goods from China for consumers. Because the poorest people tend to be farmers, not factory workers, and because manufacturing employment has risen in sectors other than clothing and cheaper consumer goods, the influx of cheap Chinese manufactures has not generated the backlash that it has in other countries. However, except for store owners, the constituency for maintaining cheap imports from China is fairly diffuse. It is not clear that the beneficiaries of cheap Chinese consumer goods would be able to translate economic interests into political influence.

Service providers also have gained from increased economic ties with China. Shipping companies in Japan, South Korea, and Singapore have expanded operations and profits on the back of trade with China. China has become an important market for major banks, especially the big money-center banks in Japan.

Losers

The major losers from Chinese exports are the companies and the workers who compete with the Chinese domestically or on foreign markets. In Japan, much of the political backlash from increased Chinese exports has been from companies that compete against imports from China. Some of the most vociferous complaints have come from farmers who face competition from imports of much cheaper Chinese vegetables, fruits, and mushrooms. Japanese farmers have been especially effective at maintaining barriers to Chinese imports. Australian firms dealing in electronics, textiles, and other industries in which China has been successful and in industries in which Chinese competition is less well known, such as machinery components and plastics, have launched a number of antidumping cases in Australia. In the Philippines, Chinese competition has wiped out an entire industry, the manufacture of Christmas tree ornaments. In every country, clothing manufacturers have lost out or shifted operations to China.

Net Assessment

The traditional analysis of forces for and against trade liberalization argues that the particular interests that suffer from more-open trade are politically more powerful than the broader public that benefits from cheaper imported goods. Initiatives to cut tariffs or other trade barriers frequently run aground on the opposition of powerful special interests.

We argue that national policies toward China stand this state of affairs on its head. The winners from Chinese trade tend to be very aware of the benefits they have accrued from the expanding Chinese market. Even on the import side, the consensus among retailers and consumers in countries as diverse as Australia and the Philippines is surprisingly strong on the benefits of lower-cost Chinese products. Losers, on the other hand, tend to be a more-diffuse and, therefore, politically less-powerful group. For the smaller countries, the most serious, keenly felt loss is for exports to third-country markets. In this case, the national government can do little to forestall loss of market share. Larger economies, such as Japan's, have maintained or erected barriers to imports from China. But in many instances, competing domestic products are so much more expensive than Chinese imports (as in the market for mushrooms in Japan) that domestic opposition to greater economic ties in China is muted.

In short, economic interactions between China and the six nations have expanded at a torrid pace since 1996; they have yet to show signs of slowing down. Most of this economic activity involves trade. In contrast to Chinese trade with the United States, many of the six nations run trade surpluses with China; large imbalances are relatively rare. Trade in services is also expanding, with the larger, wealthier economies of Australia, Japan, South Korea, and Singapore playing major roles. The smaller economies of Thailand and the Philippines are enjoying increased earnings from Chinese tourists. As trade has expanded, so has the importance of commercial and financial relations with China. Not surprisingly, all six governments are devoting more attention to their economic relations with China.

In some areas, the importance of trade with China is exaggerated. Trade in electronics, although booming, adds less value than do such products as food, which have higher domestic content. Moreover, much of the trade in electronics between China and the six nations involves trade among affiliates of foreign-owned firms, few of which are owned by Chinese entrepreneurs. The ability of the Chinese government to utilize these foreign employers to influence the governments in which their plants lie is probably fairly limited.

CHAPTER THREE

Japan

Among the United States' Asian allies, only Japan is a major power in its own right. At market exchange rates, its gross domestic product (GDP) is twice that of China. Japan's cutting-edge technology and its overseas development assistance budget, which is second only to that of the United States, make it a valued economic and political partner to states in and beyond Asia. Japan's military budget hovers just below 1 percent of its GDP, but that is enough to qualify it as one of the world's top three military spenders. To the extent that Japan's military capabilities might be described as sufficient rather than dominant, this restraint is a function of national choice, not of economic resources or physical constraints.

Japan's economic might and political and military power give it interests and options beyond those of the other nations examined in this volume. Japan's production chains stretch across Asia, giving it interests in the harmonization of regional economic and legal regulations and, consequently, in working with China and ASEAN to create an orderly environment in which to trade and invest. Japan's economic, political, and potential military capabilities also give it the resources to challenge China's rising influence and power, should it choose to pursue this course. The alliance with the United States provides Japan with a useful defense shield. But unlike the region's smaller states, Japan could also fashion itself into a more-independent power.

The rise of China has clearly stirred Japan's competitive impulses, but its posture toward China remains, like its larger sense of national purpose, characterized by considerable ambivalence. Japanese leaders are now more willing to cite China explicitly as a potential military threat, and the two nations have engaged in heated disputes over territorial boundaries, historical issues, and regional leadership. Japan has edged closer to the United States and strengthened ties with other regional partners, from India to Australia to Taiwan, and these moves are increasingly justified in reference to China. The government has loosened restrictions on the use of military force and is increasingly willing to use its warships and aircraft to patrol areas it disputes with China.

At the same time, however, Japan's economic planners remain convinced that the nation's economic well-being remains tied to continued trade and investment with China. In 2005, after several years of worsening relations with Beijing, a loose but broad alliance of Japanese business, political, and media actors strengthened calls for better ties. Leaders in Beijing, also alarmed at the deteriorating relationship, looked for an opportunity to improve it. That opportunity came when Prime Minister Koizumi Junichiro left office in September 2006. With support from both sides, Chinese-Japanese relations have improved significantly since then, although they are unlikely to return soon—if ever—to the optimism of the mid-1990s.

Both international and domestic factors have shaped Japan's changing posture toward China. For the first time, both China and Japan are unified internally, powerful in economic and military terms, and capable of influencing events beyond their borders. At the same time, the United States is pushing for Japan to assume larger regional and global roles. Domestically, the demise of the Socialist Party during the mid-1990s nudged the political center of domestic politics to the right. Fifteen years of sluggish economic growth have helped usher in the rise of nationalist sentiment. At the same time, a new breed of popular politicians has challenged the long-dominant bureaucracy for control of national policy, including foreign policy.

National Conditions

Since the mid-1990s, the Japanese system of government and policymaking has changed dramatically; these changes help explain the evolution of Japan's thinking on various foreign policy questions, including its response to the rise of China.[1]

For several decades prior to the 1990s, two patterns defined Japanese policymaking. The first was the strength of the bureaucracy relative to—in some areas, dominance over—political authorities in policymaking.[2] The second was the power of the economic ministries within the bureaucracy, their influence extending even into foreign and security policymaking. Foreign policymaking was characterized by caution, stability, and a privileged place for economic priorities. Japanese strategists often view security in both economic and military terms, and allies in one of these realms can be threats in another.[3] The commentator Okamoto Yukio observed that "the United States can be a military ally, but I do not think that it can be an ally in economic affairs."[4] China, on the other hand, was often regarded as an economic ally, even as it represented a latent military threat.

---

[1]   On the general changes affecting the Japanese system, see Jennifer Amyx and Peter Drysdale, eds., *Japanese Governance: Beyond Japan, Inc.*, New York: RoutledgeCurzon, 2003, and Shinoda Tomohito, *Kantei Gaiko: Seiji Ridashippu no Yukue* [*Kantei Foreign Policy: Political Leadership Direction*], Tokyo: Asahi Shimbunsha, 2004.

[2]   Career bureaucrats wrote most Diet legislation. Political appointees were sparse (two per ministry compared with 3,000 appointees in the U.S. system). They generally remained in office for less than one year. Jacob M. Schlesinger, *Shadow Shoguns,* Stanford, Calif.: Stanford University Press, 1997.

[3]   Eric Heginbotham and Richard J. Samuels, "Mercantile Realism and Japanese Foreign Policy," *International Security*, Vol. 22, No. 4, Spring 1998.

[4]   "Paradaimu wa kawatta no ka? [Paradigm Shift?]," *Gaiko Foramu*, January 2002, p. 36. The article is not found in the English-language version of the magazine from the same date.

Since the mid-1990s, Japan's governing system has evolved considerably. Political reforms adopted in 1994 made politics more transparent and competitive and encouraged politicians to appeal directly to the public.[5] Administrative reform and deregulation, meanwhile, have made it easier for politicians to assert themselves over the bureaucracy. The 1999 Cabinet Law specified the Cabinet Secretariat, directly under the prime minister, as "the highest and final organ for policy coordination." During his five years in office, Prime Minister Koizumi and his cabinet secretaries used the offices to short-circuit political and bureaucratic consultative processes and assert executive control over economic and foreign policy.[6]

These changes have important implications for Japanese foreign policy generally, as well as for its relationship with China specifically. They have allowed Japanese foreign policy to become more nimble and responsive. After September 11, 2001, the Japanese government was able to pass legislation for military assistance to the United States in 24 days—in stark contrast to the two years (1997–1999) required for new guidelines for Japanese-U.S. defense cooperation.[7] The rise of the politician has the potential to bring greater integration to a wider range of interests in foreign policy. Clearly, many politicians have a very different view of Japan's national interests than the one Japan's economic planners hold. At the same time, Japan's shifting polity provides new incentives for leaders to appeal to populist nationalist causes. The age in which economic considerations trump all in Japanese diplomacy is clearly over. What replaces it, however, may be a period of policy instability and flux—at least until a new foreign policy consensus is cemented.

Domestic Politics and Public Opinion

Within this evolving political system, domestic debates over the implications of China's rise loom large, more so than in the other countries addressed here. A broad range of officials and politicians, from both the LDP and Democratic Party of Japan (DPJ), have expressed concern over China's opaque military buildup; some have described China as a potential military threat. Nevertheless, many in both parties, including those concerned about China's growing military power, criticized Koizumi's China policies and what they viewed as his willingness to damage the relationship over symbolic or historical issues, especially Yasukuni. They have since sought to put Chinese-Japanese relations back on a stable footing.

---

[5]   Reforms included introducing single-member parliamentary districts and reforming campaign financing. Both reduced the importance of "gamesmanship" in elections and the power of factions within the Liberal Democratic Party (LDP).

[6]   See Shinoda, 2004, and Shinoda Tomohito, "Koizumi's Top-Down Leadership in the Anti-Terrorism Legislation: The Impact of Political Institutional Changes, *SAIS Review*, Vol. 23, No. 1, Winter–Spring 2003.

[7]   Shinoda, 2003, pp. 28–32. The legislation was passed on October 29, 2001.

The History Question and Yasukuni

Because mutual history was at the center of Japan's debate on China policy during Koizumi's tenure and remains important, discussion is warranted.

The Chinese government has long held that Tokyo has not been forthright in acknowledging the aggressive nature of Japan's war in China during the 1930s and 1940s or the scale of atrocities committed during it. Tokyo points to the apology Prime Minister Murayama Tomiichi made in 1995, one that the government has repeated several times since, and argues that China is merely using the question of war responsibility to marginalize Japan. Many Chinese, however, believe that frequent revisionist or otherwise inaccurate historical statements of high-level Japanese officials belie the sincerity of Japan's apologies. Developments during Koizumi's tenure as prime minister widened the gap in perceptions between the two sides.

Much of the conflict centered on the prime minister's visits to the Yasukuni Shrine, a Shinto shrine in Tokyo established in the late 19th century to memorialize Japan's war dead. The visits Japanese officials made to the shrine did not become an issue until 1978, when Class A war criminals—individuals who had been convicted of being responsible for Japan's entry into what became World War II—were added to the rolls.[8] Emperor Hirohito himself stopped visiting the shrine at that point, and his son, Emperor Akihito, has not worshiped there. Koizumi was not the first prime minister to have visited since 1978 but was the first to visit many times in what appeared to be an official capacity. Koizumi's visits came in conjunction with the completion of a large, glossy museum inside the Yasukuni Shrine glorifying the war and the approval of new textbooks that downplayed Japanese actions during World War II. The shrine's exhibits suggest that Japan's various wars of conquest were forced on the nation, primarily in response to Western imperialism, and give a special place of honor to the suicide pilots of Japan's *tokkotai* [special attack units] (known popularly in the United States as "Kamikaze").

The conflict over Yasukuni challenged Tokyo's and Beijing's ability to manage their problems during Koizumi's tenure. The Chinese refused to agree to summit meetings between 2001 and the end of Koizumi's administration, and although many high-level contacts continued, some meetings at the ministerial and vice-ministerial levels were affected. Both sides were spooked by the speed and degree to which their relationship cooled. The Chinese side agreed to resume summit meetings after Koizumi's departure, and Koizumi's successors have thus far refrained from visiting the shrine. The damage to public perceptions on both sides, however, has been harder to repair. On the Japanese side, many supported Koizumi's visit to Yasukuni—not in spite of

---

[8]   The 14 Class A criminals were added secretly, without prior public debate or notification by the shrine's priests. Class B and C war criminals (convicted of "war crimes" and "crimes against humanity") had been added previously. No war dead, whether war criminals or soldiers killed in action, are actually buried at the shrine. All are simply listed on its rolls of individuals honored there.

Chinese protests but because of them. On the Chinese side, suspicions about Japan's atonement for the war, as well as its future direction, deepened.

Although the Yasukuni issue remains one of the most divisive in Chinese-Japanese relations, it is not only an issue for China. Japan's own public opinion is also sharply divided.[9] At least six former Japanese prime ministers registered strong reservations about Koizumi's visits,[10] and the issue has strained relations with South Korea, which, by many standards, should be a natural ally. Japan's historical relationship with the United States has also been central to this debate. The new Yasukuni museum suggests that the United States forced Japan into war to boost the ailing U.S. economy. A broad segment of Japanese opinion, including high-profile mainstream figures, questions the legitimacy of the Tokyo War Crimes Trial. An open public discussion of these issues could be healthy, but given the intimidation of prominent individuals (such as Kato Koichi, as discussed below) who have argued against nationalist positions on historical questions, it is not clear whether the conditions are yet present.

In a narrow, short-term sense, the history issue divides Japan and China and may rebound to the benefit of the U.S.–Japanese alliance. In more-fundamental ways and over the long term, however, it is likely to prove a distraction at best and may, at worst, divide the United States and Japan and hinder Washington's pursuit of larger regional and even global objectives.[11] In July 2007, after then–Prime Minister Abe made ambiguous statements about Japanese responsibility for sexual slavery during World War II, the U.S. House of Representatives passed House Resolution 121, calling on the Japanese government to "acknowledge, apologize, and accept responsibility in a clear and unequivocal manner for its Imperial Armed Force's coercion of young women into sexual slavery."[12] Whatever the U.S. government's position on history and moral responsibility, continued disputes over history between Japan and its neighbors may create instabilities that complicate U.S. global diplomacy.

Since late 2006, both Beijing and Tokyo sought to mute the shrillest voices on historical issues. Nevertheless, given the gap in public perceptions on historical questions and the ability (and willingness) of nationalists on both sides to manipulate the issues, we are unlikely to have heard the last of these debates.

---

[9] In an August 2006 survey by the *Mainichi Shimbun*, 50 percent supported Koizumi's visit and 46 percent were opposed. "50 Percent of Japanese Support Koizumi's Visit to Yasukuni Shrine," *Mainichi Shimbun*, August 17, 2006.

[10] These included Hashimoto Ryutaro, Nakasone Yasuhiro, Kaifu Toshiki, Miyazawa Kiichi, Murayama Tomiichi, and Mori Yoshiro. Other prominent LDP critics included Fukuda Yasuo, Lower House Speaker Kono Yohei, and former chief cabinet secretary Nonaka Hiromu.

[11] In this, we agree with the conclusions outlined in Brad Glosserman et al., "Sino-Japan Rivalry: A CNA, IDA, NDU/INSS, and Pacific Forum CSIS Project Report," *Issues and Insights*, Vol. 7, No. 2, March 2007.

[12] U.S. House of Representatives, "Whereas the Government of Japan . . . ," H.R. 121, 110 Cong., 2nd Sess., July 30, 2007.

Popular Perceptions of China

History, together with other disputes and insecurities, has pushed public views of the "other" in Japan and China to historic lows, limiting room for maneuver (Figure 3.1). According to Cabinet Office public opinion surveys, favorable sentiments toward China plummeted from 48 to 32 percent between October 2003 and October 2005, while unfavorable sentiments rose from 48 to 63 percent.[13] The numbers improved slightly in the October 2006 survey but remain far below the levels seen in and before 2002. Chinese attitudes toward Japan have generally declined. Chinese Academy of Social Sciences surveys have found that the proportion of those who do not feel close to Japan rose from 43 to 54 percent between October 2002 and October 2004 and remained at 53 percent as of October 2006. The proportion of those who felt close to Japan remained unchanged at 6 percent between 2002 and 2004 but rose to 8 percent in 2006.[14]

In Japan, the decline in positive public sentiment toward China was accompanied by an increase in anti-China tracts. *An Introduction to China*, by Akiyama

Figure 3.1
Japanese Perceptions of China

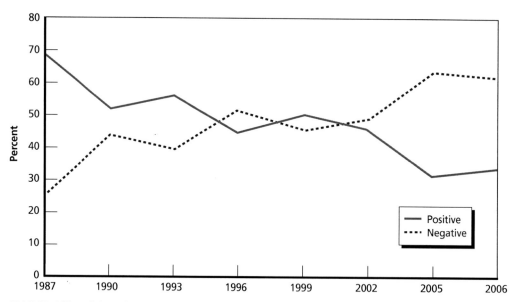

SOURCE: Office of the Cabinet Secretary (Japan), 1987–2006.
RAND MG736-3.1

---

[13] Office of the Cabinet Secretary, Japan, *Yoron Chosa* [*Public Opinion Surveys*], October 2003 and October 2005.

[14] "CASS Survey Says Chinese Residents Have Feelings of 'Not Being Close' to Japan," *Zhongguo Qingnian Bao*, November 24, 2004; Chinese Academy of Social Sciences, "Disanci Zhongri Yulun Diaocha (2006 Nian 9–10 Yue)" ["Third Chinese-Japanese Public Opinion Survey (September–October 2006)"], *Riben Xuekan*, December 2006.

Jyoji and Ko Bunyu, a runaway best seller, describes Chinese culture as being a "cannibal" and claims, without evidence, that 10 percent of China's GDP is accounted for by prostitution.[15] Anti-Chinese writings intersect with a larger "new nationalist" literature.[16] *Hating the Korea Wave*, a 275-page anti-Korean comic that claims Korea has contributed nothing of value to world civilization, sold even better than Ko's book on China.[17] As the relationship with China has stabilized since September 2006, the appetite for anti-China tracts has abated somewhat, and at least some of their authors have turned to other projects, including, in the case of Ko Bunyu, a book predicting Japanese-American conflict.

Evaluating the importance or influence of nationalist literature is difficult. From the beginning, there have been other voices in the debate. Japanese scholars continue to produce excellent and objective treatments of historical and contemporary subjects, even if they do not generate the sales of the more-sensationalist pundits. In February 2006, the chairman of the *Yomiuri Shimbun*, Japan's flagship conservative newspaper, switched positions and came out publicly against the Yasukuni Shrine.[18] Policymakers in various parts of the bureaucracy continued to pursue avenues for mutual gain with China and South Korea even as the relationship with China hit its nadir in late 2005–2006 and have been far freer to do so since that low point. As a result, the relationship between China and Japan has improved somewhat since 2006.

Although passions have cooled somewhat since mid-2006, journalists, scholars, and politicians who advocate more conciliation toward Beijing say that they have been intimidated. Some have been publicly accused of selling out Japanese interests.[19] Others have been threatened physically. On August 15, 2006, the anniversary of Japan's surrender, the home and office of Kato Koichi, a onetime LDP candidate for prime minister and critic of then–Prime Minister Koizumi's visits to Yasukuni, were torched.

---

[15] Akiyama Jyoji and Ko Bunyu, *Chugoku Nyumon* [*Introduction to China*], Asuka Shinsha, 2005; Norimitsu Onishi, "Ugly Images of Asian Rivals Become Best Sellers in Japan," *New York Times*, November 14, 2005.

[16] For an assessment of the intellectual origins and underpinnings of this literature, see John Nathan, *Japan Unbound: A Volatile Nation's Quest for Pride and Purpose*, Boston, Mass.: Houghton Mifflin Company, 2004.

[17] Yamano Sharin, *Kenkanryu* [*Hating the Korea Wave*], Tokyo: Shinyusha, September 2005; Onishi, 2005. Other bestselling works include books by Tojo Hideki's granddaughter, a glossy volume that purports to show that all photos of the Nanjing massacre are fakes, and a book that argues the Manchuria of the 1930s was not a Japanese colony.

[18] "Taidan: Yasukuni wo Kataru, Gaiko wo Kataru, Watanabe Tsuneo x Wakamiya Yoshibumi [Interview: Watanabe Tsuneo and Wakamiya Yoshibumi Discuss Yasukuni and Foreign Policy]," *Ronza*, February 2006. Watanabe claims his remarks are not a reversal, but his statements ran counter to the spirit of much of *Yomiuri's* past reporting on this issue.

[19] Interviews with politicians, reporters, and think-tank researchers, Tokyo, October–November 2005. Reporters from the liberal *Asahi Shimbun* have been favorite targets of printed attacks. See, for example, Yamagiwa Sumio, Asahi Shimbun *ga Chugoku wo Ogoraseru* [*The* Asahi Shimbun *Makes China Arrogant*], Tokyo: Nisshin Hodo, 2005.

The LDP's China Posture

Four identifiable schools of thought on China exist within the LDP: pacifist, mercantilist, nationalist, and realist. Although few politicians have views that fit neatly into a single one of these schools, they nevertheless provide a useful heuristic. They should also be seen against the LDP's decades-long history of operating more like Japan's legislative system than as a single party. The party's size and breadth, as well as its factional fragmentation, militated against unity on foreign policy. Since the mid-1990s, the pacifists and, to a lesser extent, the mercantilists have lost ground, while the nationalists and realists have gained it.

Pacifism has been one of the better-known fixtures of political thought in postwar Japan. Many of its proponents, like much of the Japanese public, have felt a sense of obligation to China dating from the war. This pacifist view meshed nicely with the views of mercantilists, who saw a strong relationship with China tying into Japan's national interests. The Chinese and Japanese economies were complementary, and the mercantilists saw cooperation between Asia's two biggest powers as a precondition for East Asian economic integration. The influence of those favoring a special relationship with China has, however, declined within the LDP and in the country at large. The generation with direct experience of World War II is passing from the scene. Mercantilist impulses remain strong, but the negative popular mood toward China discourages politicians from putting economic interests before political ones.

In contrast, the nationalists and realists have gained influence. Because both tend to favor greater assertiveness toward China and a stronger defense, their adherents are sometimes lumped together. Their priorities, however, differ significantly, and the implications for the United States are important.

Nationalists are largely concerned about reviving what they perceive as traditional (critics say "idealized") Japanese values. They favor not only revising the constitution to acknowledge the legality of Japan's military forces but also strengthening patriotic education and the power of the state. To the nationalists, Yasukuni is a critical symbolic issue. Former prime ministers Abe Shinzo and Aso Taro are representative of this thinking. Abe is the grandson of former Prime Minister Kishi Nobusuke, who at one time was arrested as a Class A war criminal, and advocates patriotic education. Prior to taking office, he argued that the prime minister has a duty to visit Yasukuni—although he himself refrained from visiting the shrine during his one-year tenure. Aso has suggested that the Emperor himself should visit Yasukuni, although, again, it remains to be seen whether even Aso will visit while prime minister.[20] Realists emphasize balance-of-power issues more than either mercantilists or nationalists do.[21]

---

[20] "Aso Shooting from the Lip: Minister's Sound Bites Boost Profile but Raise Hackles," *Yomiuri Shimbun*, February 20, 2006.

[21] The word *realism* is not meant to connote a more realistic view of the world, but rather a certain view of international politics: the belief that states dominate world politics and that they generally give a privileged place to

Many realists share the nationalists' sentiment for stronger Japanese defense and alliance with the United States but are less inclined to push aggressively for patriotic education or other symbolic causes. While finding it prudent to hedge against possible Chinese misbehavior, they believe it is in Japan's national interests not to antagonize China needlessly. Older-generation realists include former Prime Minister Nakasone Yasuhiro, who helped break the 1-percent limit on defense spending. The younger generation includes Kono Taro, who favors constitutional revision and championed the deployment of a U.S. nuclear-powered carrier to Japan. Both have argued against the prime minister visiting Yasukuni.

Former Prime Minister Koizumi's recent dominance of the party has complicated evaluation of the LDP's balance of power. Koizumi's support for Abe and Aso allowed the party's nationalists to punch above their weight. Discounting Koizumi and his political skills and patronage of the nationalist camp, the realist position may, in fact, represent a larger segment of LDP thinking than it may appear at first. Mercantilist sentiment, although diminished, continues to influence thinking within the LDP. By the end of Koizumi's tenure, considerable pressure had built for a course change on China and an end to the foreign policy instability that his policies had wrought. After his accession to prime minister, Abe initiated a policy shift on China: He struck a relatively balanced and careful posture, seeking to mend relations with China and Korea, even as he pushed other parts of the nationalist agenda. During his tenure as prime minister, Fukuda, a long-time advocate of stronger relations with China, sought to deepen economic cooperation with China and made progress toward resolving the dispute over oil and gas in the East China Sea. Despite a history of tough rhetoric on China issues before taking office, Aso appears set to visit China early during his administration and to continue rebuilding a more-stable and cooperative relationship.

The Opposition

The demise of the socialists in parliament and changes in DPJ rhetoric have led some to talk of political convergence on security and foreign policy issues. Certainly, the debate on security and foreign policy now takes place within a narrower band than it once did. The center in Japanese politics has shifted toward the right. The discussion of convergence, however, obscures two other truths. First, there is wide divergence *within* both parties, and second, the center of gravity within the two parties is different. All four of the intellectual traditions outlined above (pacifist, mercantilist, nationalist, and realist) are present in the DPJ, just as they are in the LDP. But while the rising groups in the LDP are nationalists and realists, with a rough balance between the two, the DPJ is divided more equally between realists and pacifists, with the former having made

---

military security. See Paul R. Viotti and Mark V. Kauppi, eds., *International Relations Theory: Realism Pluralism, Globalism, and Beyond,* New York: Macmillan, 1999.

the most rapid gains. This difference would have important and arguably nonintuitive implications for the U.S.–Japanese alliance if the DPJ ever gains power.

The implosion of the Japan Socialist Party during the mid-1990s eliminated, at one stroke, the largest single concentration of pacifists in Japanese politics. Along with defectors from the LDP, some of these individuals ultimately migrated to the DPJ, and the party has had strong ties with China since its founding in 1998. The big surprise (to those unacquainted with the records of individual party members) came after Maehara Seiji took control of the party in September 2005 and began making tough statements about security and China. In Beijing, Maehara took China to task for the opacity of its defense spending, military procurement, and activities. In a December 2005 speech in Washington, Maehara called China a "real" threat,[22] language that none of the LDP leadership had yet used in public. He also came out strongly in support of constitutional revision and, to a lesser extent, stronger military ties with the United States.

But Maehara is clearly a realist, not a nationalist, and he shares more in common with Kono Taro than Abe Shinzo. He repeatedly condemned Koizumi's visits to Yasukuni and the resulting damage to Japan's relationship with China even as he urged the Chinese to improve transparency. Seeking to avoid a split with former Japan Socialist Party members in the DPJ, Ozawa Ichiro, who has led the DPJ since April 2006, has vowed to stick closer to party consensus than Maehara has. In practical terms, this means less-outspoken advocacy of strong defense and the U.S. alliance. But Ozawa, like Maehara, has long embraced many realist positions. During the first Gulf War, he pushed for the dispatch of Japanese troops and subsequently coined the term *normal nation* as he pushed for Japan to abandon its attachment to pacifism.

The other two positions, mercantilist and nationalist, are also present in the DPJ but are less prominent than in the LDP. To highlight the implications for the alliance, the nationalist position embraced by many in the LDP may yield benefits for the U.S.–Japanese alliance in the short term but may, in the longer term, prove to be a less stable and predictable basis for alliance than the realist position significant elements of both parties embrace—an idea that may run counter to much of the conventional wisdom in Washington.

Economic Responses

Japan's economic relations with China have deepened dramatically in recent years and continue to provide incentives for both governments to manage their problems. China (including Hong Kong) is now Japan's largest trade partner, and the value of Japan's annual investment in China is now approaching that of its investment in the United States. Some economic agencies in Tokyo are beginning to highlight the risks of over-exposure in China. But Japanese businessmen continue to be drawn to China by the

---

[22] "Maehara Stands Firm on China Warning," *The Daily Yomiuri*, December 15, 2005.

potential scale of the Chinese market and its value as a production base. Although some Japanese have won and some have lost in the nation's economic intercourse with China, the following factors tend to mitigate potential trade frictions:

- The two economies are complementary.
- Japan has an overall trade surplus with China.
- Japan's strategic approach to trade emphasizes competition against high-value-added producers (generally competitors from the United States; Europe; and, more recently, South Korea).
- Japan's large firms enjoy more-privileged access to policymakers than the smaller producers.

Trade with China

Over the last decade, Japanese trade with China has expanded far more rapidly than its trade with the rest of the world. Between 1996 and 2006, Japanese trade with China grew by 239 percent, while its overall global trade grew by only 61 percent (or 45 percent, if trade with China is excluded from the equation). Trade with the United States grew by only 12 percent over the same period. In 1996, Japan did less than one-third as much trade with China as it did with the United States; as of 2006, the trade levels were roughly equal. In 2006, trade with China comprised 17 percent of Japan's global trade, including 14 percent of its exports and 21 percent of its imports (Figures 3.2 and 3.3).

All the above figures for trade with China are of course higher if Japanese trade with Hong Kong is added into the balance. In most international accounting, figures for Hong Kong, Macau, and the mainland are maintained separately, yet much if not most of Japan's trade with (and especially exports to) Hong Kong are intermediary goods bound for factories in the mainland. Japan's trade with China—including Hong Kong—is already 20 percent of its global trade and 15 percent larger than its trade with the United States.

Unlike Japan's trade with the United States, its trade balance with China is relatively balanced. In 2006, Japan had a deficit of $26 billion with the mainland (with imports 28 percent larger than exports). If trade with Hong Kong is also included, however, Japan enjoyed a surplus of $9 billion with China (with imports 9 percent lower than exports). In contrast to this relatively balanced trade with China, Japan ran a surplus of $80 billion with the United States, with exports to it exceeding imports by 115 percent. Between 1996 and 2006, Japanese exports to the United States rose by 31 percent, while its imports from the United States actually *declined* by 13 percent.

Looking at the composition of Chinese-Japanese trade, some 19 percent of imports from China were in the category of clothing and footwear, and seafood made up an additional 5 percent (Figures 3.4 and 3.5). But many of Japan's imports from China consist of manufactured goods, including office machines (12 percent), electrical and

Figure 3.2
Japanese Imports, by Country of Origin, Selected Years

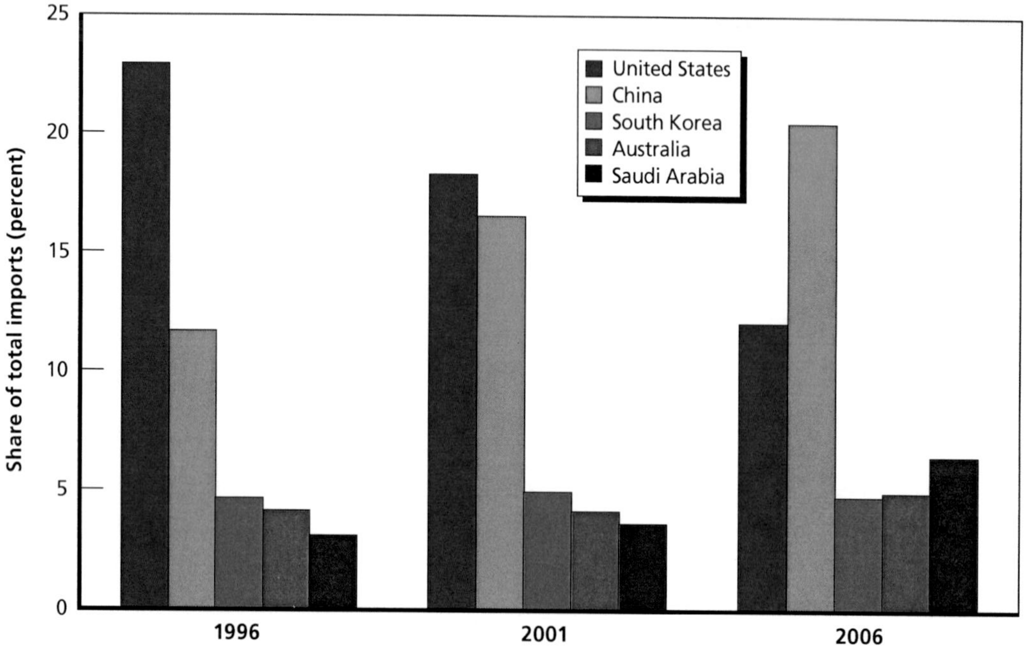

SOURCE: UN Statistics Division, 1996, 2001, 2006.
RAND *MG736-3.2*

electronic equipment (11 percent), and telecommunications equipment (7 percent). The latter exports come largely in the form of *reimports*—products or components produced in China in factories owned or controlled by Japanese firms. Many of Japan's exports to China, including electronic equipment (20 percent of the total) and industrial machinery (15 percent) are tied to Japanese investment in China, although Japan also exports substantial volumes of intermediate goods (e.g., iron, steel, and chemicals) to China. The relationship largely, although not entirely, is defined by Japan's use of China as a production base for its export industries—with many of its exports to China destined, ultimately, for markets in the United States and elsewhere (and held in U.S. trade figures, therefore, against China's trade balance with the United States, rather than Japan's).

Foreign Direct Investment Flows

Figures for FDI tend to vary from year to year more than trade figures do, but the general trajectory for Japanese investment in China has clearly been rapidly upward, both in absolute numbers and as a share of Japan's total outward FDI (Figure 3.6).[23] At the

---

[23] All the statistics in this paragraph are from Japan External Trade Organization, which referenced Ministry of Finance balance of payment statistics.

Figure 3.3
Japanese Exports, by Country of Destination, Selected Years

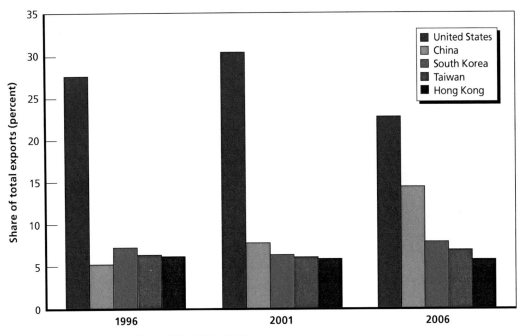

SOURCE: UN Statistics Division, 1996, 2001, 2006.
RAND *MG736-3.3*

Figure 3.4
Composition of Japan's Imports from China, 2006

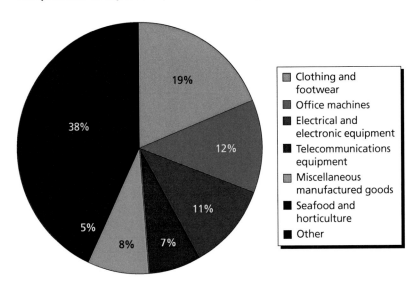

SOURCE: UN Statistics Division, 2006.
RAND *MG736-3.4*

Figure 3.5
Composition of Japan's Exports to China, 2006

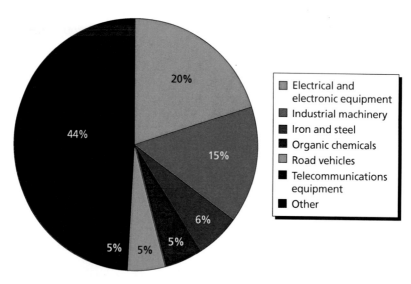

SOURCE: UN Statistics Division, 2006.
RAND *MG736-3.5*

Figure 3.6
Japanese FDI in China and the United States

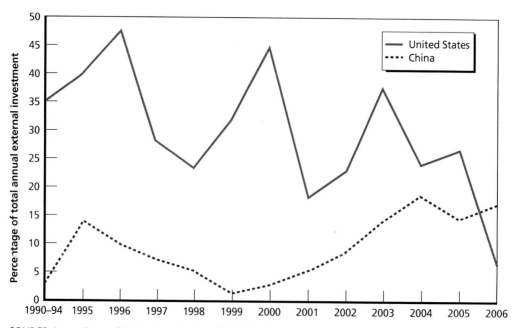

SOURCE: Japan External Trade Organization (JETRO), 1994–2006.
NOTE: Figures for 2006 are for January to June only and are tentative estimates.
RAND *MG736-3.6*

end of 1996, the total accumulated stock of Japanese FDI in China represented only 3 percent of its total overseas stock. By the end of 2005, that figure had risen to 6 percent. Between 2003 and 2005, China was the second largest destination for Japanese FDI, behind only the United States, and it accounted for 15 percent of Japan's total FDI outflow (or 31 percent of its investment in non–Organisation for Co-Operation and Development [OECD] states). During the first half of 2006, investment in China rose to nearly 17 percent of Japan's total outflow and outstripped investment in the United States (although the amount was lower than investments in the United Kingdom and the Netherlands during the period).

Foreign investments in Japan have always been small relative to the size of the economy, and the total stock of foreign investment in Japan by the end of 2005 equaled only 26 percent of Japan's stock of investment outside the country. Of this, OECD states accounted for the lion's share of investment in Japan—more than 85 percent—and China accounted for only around 0.1 percent.

The Economic Ministries' Position

Most of the government's reports on international trade and investment continue to highlight the complementarity of the Japanese and Chinese economies. In 2005, however, a subtle but noticeable subtext appeared in government reports: China has great promise as both a market and a production base, but business should hedge its bets against overexposure. The first chapter of the Ministry of Economy Trade and Industry's (METI's) "White Paper on International Economy and Trade 2005" set the stage with an extended discussion of the danger of overheating in China.[24]

Both METI's white paper and reports by the Japan Bank for International Cooperation (JBIC) promote greater attention to the other countries among "the BRICs" (a nickname for Brazil, Russia, India, and China as a group).[25] Officials from the Japan External Trade Organization have promoted a "China-Plus-One strategy."[26] Japanese companies with heavy investments in China should, according to this strategy, balance their portfolios with investments in at least one other location. These documents give particular emphasis to Southeast Asian states, which served as Japan's primary production bases during the 1980s. The Japanese government has announced plans

---

[24] Ministry of Economy, Trade, and Industry (Japan), "White Paper on International Economy and Trade 2005," Tokyo, July 2005.

[25] JBIC, *Wagakuni Seizogyo no Kaigai Jigyo Tenkai ni Kan Suru Chosa Hokoku* [Survey Report on Our Nation's Manufacturing Industries' Development Overseas], Tokyo, November 2005. For the original concept of "the BRICs" as a dominant force, see Dominic Wilson and Roopa Purushothaman, *Dreaming with the BRICs: The Path to 2050*, New York: Goldman Sachs Group Inc., Global Economics Paper No. 99, October 1, 2003.

[26] See, for example, speeches by Japan External Trade Organization Chairman and CEO, Watanabe Osamu. Watanabe Osamu, "Chugoku Purasu 1 to Chiiki Keizai [China Plus One and the Regional Economy]," October 27, 2004; and Watanabe Osamu, "Higashi Ajia Bijinesu Keizaiken wo Misueta Chugoku Bijinesu Tenbo [Developing China Business with Eyes on the East Asian Business Economic Zone]," September 21, 2005.

to redouble its overseas development assistance to and other financing efforts for the ASEAN states to facilitate new investment, particularly by small and medium-sized Japanese firms.[27]

This shift in the government's message is significant but should not be overstated. The discussion of economic risks is not entirely targeted at China. METI's 2005 white paper devotes equal space to the dangers of America's twin deficits and to overheating in China. Warnings about vulnerability in China focus primarily on overheating and cyclical (and arguably temporary) threats to profitability. The 2006 white paper highlights similar themes and observes that, between 2003 and 2005 (the most recent year assessed), Japanese corporations' return on investment in the ASEAN Four (Thailand, Philippines, Indonesia, and Malaysia) was higher than its return on investment in China—a change from the five preceding years, when return on investment in China was higher.[28] Nevertheless, the government's economic agencies still hail the benefits of economic engagement with China. The foundations of the economic relationship rest on proximity; culture; and, especially, complementarity. Japanese bureaucrats and businessmen believe they have an understanding of Chinese culture and have invested in the personal and political relations to operate effectively there.

The idea of complementarity lies at the heart of Japanese thinking on economic security and competitiveness.[29] METI and other economic agencies rate trade and other economic interactions between Japan and most Southeast Asian states, and China, as highly complementary. Several Asian states have moved rapidly up the economic ladder and have increased the sophistication of the goods they produce. South Korea and Taiwan are already tough competitors in several sectors, including electronics, shipbuilding, automobiles, and information technology, and there are pockets of excellence elsewhere. But Japan's economic planners believe coordination and the planned division of labor can extend the natural life of the region's complementarity. To a degree, Japanese firms have achieved this by establishing integrated production chains across the region. In the eyes of Japan's economic planners, then, Asia in general, and China and Southeast Asia in particular, remain critical to Japan's competitive position globally.

Improvements in Chinese quality control and technological sophistication have helped foster greater trade and investment. But Japanese economic planners argue that these improvements enhance, rather than detract from, China's value as a complementary economy. METI argues that most Chinese high-end development has been

---

[27] "Japan to Set Up Aid and Trade Plan for ASEAN Amid China Rift," *Agence France Presse*, May 30, 2005; and comments by Watanabe Osamu, "Economic Integration of East Asia and Japan's Future," speech delivered at the Foreign Press Center, Tokyo, March 10, 2004.

[28] METI, "Tsusho Hyakusho [White Paper]," Tokyo, 2006.

[29] See, for example, work on China by Nomura Research Institute's C. H. Kwan. C. H. Kwan, *Kyozon Kyoei no Nicchu Keizai* [*Coexistence and Coprosperity of the Japanese and Chinese Economies*], Tokyo: Toyo Keizai Shinposha, 2005.

among parts suppliers, increasing China's value as a production base and trade part-ner.[30] Its 2005 white paper on international trade devotes a chapter to the merits of Japan's *triangular trade*: critical components, manufactured in Japan, are married with components made in Southeast Asia, assembled into final products in China, and reex-ported to the United States and Europe.[31]

There are some questions about the accuracy of METI's depiction. Japanese sunset industries face intense competition from China.[32] But with the recent revival of Japa-nese manufacturing, industrial hollowing-out—a topic once hotly debated—has fallen out of currency.

Japanese Businesses Embrace China

However one assesses the change in the government's message, business enthusiasm for China has dimmed only slightly and continues to be higher than it is for any other region or country.[33] Anti-Japanese protests rocked Beijing and at least a dozen other Chinese cities in April 2005. These disturbances, however, had little effect on Japanese business attitudes toward China. According to JBIC's survey, 96 percent of compa-nies that presently do business there said the protests would not change their future plans. Indeed, the course of the April disturbances confirmed their assessment that they could successfully hedge against risks in China by maintaining close relations with local officials. A number of Japanese companies were hit with labor strikes. Local police were, however, successful in identifying ringleaders and subsequently managing the situation, according to one Japanese executive. Overall, labor unrest in China is less significant than in Indonesia and India, where Japanese factories have faced prolonged battles over wages and conditions.[34]

Perhaps as a result of the attention on the BRICs, the JBIC survey does show some increase in the interest Japanese businesses have in Brazil, Russia, and India. Never-theless, almost five times more companies indicated that they had plans for expansion in China than in the other three BRICs combined. According to Chinese govern-ment figures, Japanese investment rose 20 percent in 2005.[35] Most corporate leaders are willing in principle to look elsewhere, but see few alternatives that are as attractive as China. Interest in Vietnam is significant, and investment there is growing, but the

---

[30] METI, "East Asia as the Hub of a MegaCompetition Era," white paper, 2001, p. 32.

[31] METI, 2005.

[32] *Sunset industries* are no longer globally competitive and hence have a short future.

[33] Interviews with business leaders, mostly from leading high-tech or manufacturing companies, October–November 2005.

[34] In India, Toyota workers struck for two months in 2002 and again in January 2006, while Honda lost $57 mil-lion from labor disturbances in 2005. "Toyota Shuts India Plant After Strike by Workers," Reuters, January 8, 2006.

[35] "China-Japan Economic Ties Glow Amid Political Chill," *Los Angeles Times*, April 17, 2006.

potential scale is modest. India has the scale, but many Japanese businessmen regard its culture as "non-Asian," with some suggesting it is more alien than European or American cultures.

Of course, some industries lose in trade with China. A boom in Chinese agricultural products led Tokyo to impose temporary safeguard tariffs on Chinese vegetables in 2001. China retaliated with tariffs on Japanese cars, mobile phones, and air conditioners. The dispute, however, was settled relatively quickly, and nothing similar has arisen since.[36] Japan's consistent trade surpluses with China mitigate negative voices. Japan's most important trade federations (the Keidanren [The Federation of Economic Organizations] and the Keizai Doyukai [Japan Association of Corporate Executives]) represent the nation's larger, more-advanced firms, which overwhelmingly favor strong ties with China.

Japanese business, particularly big business, represents the most powerful lobby for maintaining and deepening political ties with China. During the 1990s, the Keidanren and Keizai Doyukai published periodic strategy papers on Japan's economic relations with China—and on the larger question of political and popular relations.[37] During most of Koizumi's tenure, the business community remained relatively quiet. Business may have felt that, given Koizumi's famous resistance to external pressure, public pressure on him would backfire. There may also have been an element of fear: Some of those who did speak out were threatened by right-wing groups.[38] But business leaders again became more outspoken in urging the government to improve relations as Koizumi entered his last year in office, and they have since strongly supported improvements in the China relationship.[39]

Diplomatic and Foreign Policy Responses

Japan's diplomacy in Asia reflects an intensified sense of rivalry with China. It is embracing the United States more closely; has reached out to form or strengthen strategic relations with India, Taiwan, and Australia; and has sought to buttress its position

---

[36] Lim Hua Sing, "Settlement of Japan-China Trade Dispute Vital," *Asahi Shimbun*, August 31, 2001.

[37] See, for example, Nippon Keidanren [Japan Federation of Economic Organizations], "Japan-China Relations in the 21st Century," February 20, 2001, and Keizai Doyukai, *Heiwa to Han'ei no Nijuyi Seiji wo Mezashite [Aiming Toward a Peaceful and Prosperous Twenty-First Century]*, Tokyo, April 25, 2001.

[38] After the Chairman of Fuji Xerox, Kobayashi Yotaro, urged Koizumi not to visit Yasukuni in September 2004, he found Molotov cocktails on his doorstep. "Molotov Cocktails Found Outside Home of Fuji Xerox Chairman," *Mainichi Shimbun*, January 11, 2005.

[39] At a meeting in October 2005, the chairmen of Keidanren and the Keizai Doyukai and other top executives appealed for improved relations with China. Participants in a similar July meeting did not, due to "an air of resignation." "Business Leaders Wary of Negative Fallout from Yasukuni Visit," Japan Economic Newswire, October 17, 2005.

in Southeast Asia. At the same time, however, Tokyo is struggling to find a message, or set of values, to underpin its regional diplomacy in Asia as a means of expanding its influence. The historical question has damaged its relations with South Korea as much as it has with China; Japan has arguably damaged its leadership position in Southeast Asia and has even ruffled feathers in the United States. Japanese thinking on China itself is torn between competitive impulses and the belief that cooperation is essential to East Asian integration, long seen as essential to Japan's global position.

Tighter Embrace of the United States

Japan's clearest and most significant response to China's rise has been a tighter embrace of the United States. The rise of China has been the most important driver of Japan's new affinity for the alliance, but other motivations have also been important, including uncertainties surrounding North Korea's direction and nuclear intentions; fear that, with the end of the Cold War, U.S. attention to Asia may wane; and the politically expedient view that the best way to cultivate Japan's own diplomatic and military capabilities without inviting a domestic or international backlash is by framing its activities in the context of the U.S. alliance.

In the face of divided public opinion on defense issues and seeking to avoid damaging Japan's economic relations with China, Japanese leaders have generally justified closer relations with the United States on these other (non-China) grounds. In particular, they have highlighted changes in the international structure. Since the end of the Cold War, they assert, U.S. interest in unilaterally providing security to the region has diminished, and Japan must do more to prevent its American partner from leaving the region. The specific foreign threats justifying the need for an external security guarantor are often left ambiguous, and until recently, only North Korea was identified by name.

But while North Korea was once the only specified threat, leaving Japan free to hedge against China without alienating it, many Japanese leaders have long identified China as a greater long-term concern in their private discussions with each other and with American interlocutors. More recently, Japanese officials have begun publicly specifying China's regional activism and its robust military modernization as the basis for Japan's alliance with the United States. (For more specifics on Japanese public statements about the rise of Chinese military power, see "Defense Policy Responses," below.)

The embrace of the United States has been evident in a variety of areas, such as Japan's speedy endorsement of American military operations in both Afghanistan and Iraq and its decision to assist militarily in visible—if largely symbolic—ways. This embrace is also seen closer to home, for example, in Japan's decision to conduct joint development and deployment of missile defense and in Tokyo's cooperation with Washington's plans to restructure its Asian forces. The increased colocation of U.S. and Japanese forces, as well as the U.S. deployment to Japan of more-significant command elements (particularly I Corps ground forces, with responsibility for contingencies in Asia), signals a new willingness to be openly identified with U.S. power.

One important caveat about Japan's alliance posture is that its true motives may be mixed. Some Japanese elites may be using the alliance to achieve more-robust military posture, one that can, in the long run, be more independent of the United States.[40] Because the alliance provides politically palatable cover for Japanese military development, these individuals may support the alliance for tactical reasons. One example of this is when the Self-Defense Forces (SDF) asked the United States to request Japan to dispatch Aegis cruisers as part of Japan's force mix in the Indian Ocean. A variation on this theme was the suggestion Sugawa Kiyoshi, a senior foreign policy advisor for the DPJ, made that a more-robust military posture would allow Japan to pursue integration with its Asian neighbors with less U.S. interference.[41]

Strategic Relations with India, Taiwan, and Australia

While Japanese diplomacy remains largely focused on reinforcing the nation's relationship with America, Japan has also sought to build strategic ties with India, Taiwan, and Australia. These budding ties are not justified explicitly with reference to China. But in emphasizing the shared democratic values that serve as their glue, Japanese leaders highlight their difference with China.

Tokyo's nascent willingness to play the great power game and seek new strategic options is most visible in its rapidly evolving relationship with New Delhi. Although left unsaid, this relationship can best be understood in the context of Japan's unease with China. Tokyo's early efforts to improve ties with New Delhi can also be seen partly as a response to Washington's diplomacy with India and a desire not to be left behind. Whatever the impetus, Japan's diplomacy with India is remarkable given Japan's traditional nuclear allergy and India's May 1998 nuclear tests. Immediately following the tests, Japan suspended new aid to India and was one of its most outspoken critics in the subsequent G-7 meetings. Tokyo's proactive courting of New Delhi is also remarkable in that the flag, in this case, has preceded trade and investment: Despite government urging, Japanese business evinces little enthusiasm for India.

The strategic relationship between the two powers began to emerge in January 2000 when Indian Minister of Defense George Fernandes and Japan Defense Agency (JDA) chief Kawara Tsutomu initiated an annual dialogue on security and defense. In August 2000, Mori Yoshiro became the first Japanese prime minister in ten years to visit New Delhi. He and Indian Prime Minister Atal Behari Vajpayee announced a Japanese-Indian global partnership. In 2003 Japanese Foreign Minister Kawaguchi Yoriko, visiting New Delhi, declared that aid would be restored to pre-1998 levels,

---

[40] See J. Patrick Boyd and Richard J. Samuels, *Nine Lives? The Politics of Constitutional Reform in Japan*, Policy Studies 19, Washington, D.C.: East-West Center, 2005.

[41] Sugawa Kiyoshi, "Time to Pop the Cork: Three Scenarios to Redefine Japanese Use of Force," working paper, Washington, D.C.: Brookings Institution, Center for Northeast Asian Policy Studies, June 2000.

effectively signaling an end to sanctions imposed after the nuclear tests. Tokyo's diplomatic and military relationship with India has since developed rapidly. In June 2003, JDA chief Ishiba Shigeru met Fernandes and agreed to expand the exchange of military students and warships. In 2004, Japan, India, Brazil, and Germany agreed to support one another's bids for permanent seats on the UN Security Council.

A watershed was reached in April 2005, when Prime Minister Koizumi visited New Delhi and signed the "Eightfold Initiative for Strengthening Japan-India Global Partnership." The provisions included measures for deeper security cooperation. The coast guards of both states should "work together on a sustained basis" and conduct "joint exercises against piracy." Strictly military cooperation was more limited but would include exchanges and "friendship visits," especially by maritime forces. The Indian strategic relationship with Japan is likely to deepen.[42] Given New Delhi's strategic partnership with China, however, it is unclear to what extent Japan's partnership with India will become an effective counterweight to China.

Japan and Taiwan have also gravitated toward each other over the last several years. Officially, Tokyo endorses the One-China policy, and Japanese officials are loath to speak openly about anything resembling state-to-state relations, but diplomatic and security ties are nonetheless developing.[43] In January 2003, Tokyo dispatched its first *de facto* military attaché, retired Ground Self-Defense Forces (GSDF) General Nagano Yoichi, to Taipei. In 2004, Japanese Diet members formed a committee on Taiwanese security. And in August 2006, the Taiwanese army's commander in chief, General Hu Chen-pu, visited Tokyo to observe live-fire exercises.[44] Perhaps of greatest concern to Beijing, Tokyo hinted for the first time in early 2005 that it might support U.S. military operations in the event of a conflict with China over Taiwan—although Western reporting on this subject exaggerated the extent and clarity of the statement. In February 2005, senior officials of the United States and Japan both specified, in the "two-plus-two" statement, that it is a common alliance interest to encourage "the peaceful resolution of issues concerning the Taiwan Strait."[45] Although this did not represent a Japanese commitment to defend Taiwan (or even necessarily to support U.S. operations), Taiwan President Chen Shui-bian has sold his own interpretation: "Japan has a requirement and an obligation to come to the defense of Taiwan," he declared.[46]

---

[42] Koizumi Junichiro, Prime Minister of Japan, and Manmohan Singh, Prime Minister of the Republic of India, "Japan-India Partnership in a New Asian Era: Strategic Orientation of Japan-India Global Partnership," New Delhi, April 29, 2005.

[43] Anthony Faiola, "Japan-Taiwan Ties Blossom as Regional Rivalry Grows: Tokyo, Wary of China, Tilts Toward Taipei," *Washington Post*, March 24, 2006.

[44] "Japan Dismisses Chinese Protest over Taiwan General's Visit," BBC, August 28, 2006.

[45] U.S.–Japan Security Consultative Committee, Joint Statement, February 19, 2005. According to some accounts of the meeting, it was the Japanese side that pushed for the inclusion of explicit language on Taiwan.

[46] Faiola, 2006.

The relationship between Taipei and Tokyo intersects with historical and political issues; it could change significantly depending on which party holds power in Taipei. Some independence-oriented Taiwanese have celebrated the island's colonial status under the Japanese empire. In April 2005, the leader of the Taiwan Solidarity Union visited the Yasukuni Shrine to pay "respects to about 28,000 Taiwanese soldiers enshrined there."[47] President Chun Shui-bian's Democratic Progressive Party, while subtler, has also highlighted the history between Japan and Taiwan. The Nationalist Party (KMT), seeking better ties with the mainland and having fought the Japanese during World War II, is critical of the stance of the Democratic Progressive Party and the Taiwan Solidarity Union. Having won the presidency, Ma Ying-jeou and his KMT are likely to promote strong—but less "special" relations—with Japan.

Given India's uncertain position vis-à-vis China and the political variables in the relationship between Japan and Taiwan, Japan's budding strategic relationship with Australia might prove to be the most stable and meaningful in the long run. A trilateral security dialogue began between the United States, Australia, and Japan in 2002 and now serves as an important channel for high-level consultation on regional security affairs among Canberra, Tokyo, and Washington. The dialogue was elevated to the ministerial level in spring 2006. Japan and Australia share common strategic interests and complementary military capabilities (with Japan enjoying advantages in some areas of technology, but Australia possessing greater operational experience, particularly in distant areas). During an August 2006 visit to Tokyo, Australian Foreign Minister Alexander Downer declared that Australia-Japan security ties were undergoing "a complete transformation" and proposed a "bilateral security agreement."[48] In March 2007, the two sides signed a declaration on security cooperation, a broadly framed agreement that commits both sides to intensify personnel exchanges; joint exercises and training; and coordination on law enforcement, peace operations, and regional capacity building.[49]

The apparent culmination of Koizumi, Abe, and Aso's efforts to cultivate Asia-Pacific allies came in August and September 2007. In August, Prime Minister Abe visited New Delhi and, in an address to Indian parliament, appealed for quadrilateral security partnership between Japan, India, the United States, and Australia.[50] In September, two Japanese destroyers joined warships from India, the United States, Australia, and Singapore for the Malabar '07 naval exercises, hosted by India in the Bay of Bengal. By early 2008, however, it was clear that there was little enthusiasm

---

[47] "Taiwan Opposition Leader to Visit Japan War Shrine Amid Criticism," Agence France Presse, April 4, 2005.

[48] "Security Pact to Deepen Japan Ties," *Weekend Australian*, August 12, 2006.

[49] See text of Abe Shinzo, Prime Minister of Japan, and John Howard, Prime Minister of Australia, "Japan-Australia Joint Declaration on Security Cooperation," March 13, 2007.

[50] "Abe for 'Arc of Freedom' in Asia-Pacific," *Hindustan Times*, August 22, 2007.

for a formal or institutionalized quadrilateral arrangement, particularly one aimed at China.

Reengaging Southeast Asia

In Southeast Asia, Japan was consistently outmaneuvered by China between 2000 and 2003, but Tokyo has again begun to play to its strengths and the two are now competing on a more equal basis. China's advantage in regional diplomacy has rested on a relatively open trading system and imaginative economic diplomacy. In November 2002, China and ASEAN announced a free trade agreement (FTA). This agreement includes *early harvest* protocols, which require lifting tariffs on some agricultural goods, of particular interest to China's Southeast Asian partners, at an early stage. Japan was left scrambling for an effective response, hastily announcing a series of regional initiatives that Tokyo was subsequently unable to develop.

While China has clearly made gains in Southeast Asia, Japan is nevertheless finding its competitive footing. Errors Beijing made have helped. In 2004, Chinese leaders overplayed their hand in regional discussions over what the shape of the East Asia Summit (EAS)—then seen as a possible successor forum for the ASEAN Plus Three—should be. China, with support from Malaysia and to a lesser extent Thailand, pushed for an exclusive approach, with membership limited to ASEAN Plus Three states. Japan, with support from Singapore and Indonesia, pushed for a more-inclusive membership. Ultimately, a more-inclusive compromise allowed Australia, New Zealand, and India to participate, provided they signed the ASEAN Treaty of Amity and Cooperation.[51]

More important, Japan has also turned to its strengths: bilateral economic diplomacy supported by aid. In May 2005, Japan concluded a bilateral FTA with Malaysia, its second such agreement after reaching one with Singapore in 2002. Tokyo is currently negotiating FTAs with the Philippines, Thailand, and Indonesia and is redeploying its overseas development assistance budget from China to Southeast Asia to buttress its diplomacy. In December 2005, Japan announced a new fund that would increase Japanese aid to the less-developed states of East Asia, such as Cambodia, Laos, Burma, and Vietnam. The government also committed itself to help small- and medium-sized Japanese businesses invest in the states with which Japan is currently pursuing FTAs. Indonesia has received particular attention.[52]

Democracy, History, and Asian Leadership

Japan is reaching out to form new political-military relationships more actively than at any time since World War II. Historically, it has promoted itself as a non-Western alternative to U.S. leadership in Asia. Increasingly, it rests its claim to regional leadership on

---

[51] Martin Walker, "Asia's New Map Lacks U.S.," United Press International, December 8, 2005.

[52] "Japan to Set Up . . . ," 2005.

and differentiates itself from China through its status as one of Asia's longest standing and most powerful democracies. The presence of less than fully democratic regimes in East Asia, including Singapore, Malaysia, and Brunei, complicates the use of this message, as does Japan's continuing support for nondemocratic regimes in Burma and Pakistan. More problematic in the long run, however, may be Japan's ambivalent attitude toward its own imperial past.

Issues related to Japan's history have had different effects in different parts of Asia. Southeast Asian governments take no official position on Japan's treatment of history, except insofar as it has impinged on efforts toward regional integration. Nevertheless, many Southeast Asian diplomats and other elites (particularly those of Singapore, Malaysia, and Indonesia) privately express concern about both Japan's direction and the perceived lack of American engagement. The history issue—and the tensions between a realist-based approach to foreign policy and a more-emotional, nationalist one—has its largest effect on Tokyo's problematic relationship with Seoul. As an independent midsize power, South Korea is a natural security partner for Japan. Were South Korea a hostile state, its proximity, technology, and animosity would make it Japan's biggest headache.

Japan has made efforts to strengthen strategic ties with South Korea. In April 1999, the United States, Japan, and South Korea initiated the Trilateral Coordination and Oversight Group to coordinate policy toward North Korea and to promote cooperation more generally. Tokyo and Seoul interact in the ASEAN Plus Three forum, as well as in side meetings of foreign and economic ministers of the "plus-three" grouping (with China). Despite common interests and some progress toward stronger ties, leaders in both countries have exploited differences over history for political ends. Contested sovereignty of the Takeshima Islands (Dokdo Islands to Koreans) fuses historical and territorial issues. Japanese claims to the islands are largely based on their acquisition in 1910, when Korea was colonized. The Japanese Education Ministry's encouragement of writers to assert Japanese claims more clearly and increasing Japanese surveillance of the islands have excited Korean passions. President Roh did little to calm the situation. In March 2005, he declared that Korea could no longer tolerate Japanese attempts to "revive regional hegemony" and urged South Koreans to prepare for a "hard diplomatic war."[53] In April 2006, Korea mobilized 20 armed vessels to block a Japanese Coast Guard survey of the area and has since conducted related maneuvers in response to Japanese "provocation."

Bilateral Relations with China

What of Japan's relations with China itself? Between 2001 and 2006, tensions between Tokyo and Beijing rose sharply, and diplomacy suffered accordingly. Many on both sides, however, believe that, despite the differences between the two nations, it is in

---

[53] Erich Marquardt, "The Price of Japanese Nationalism," *Asia Times Online*, April 14, 2005.

their interests to maintain a stable working relationship. Some still hope for meaningful partnership. After Abe's accession as prime minister, both sides worked to stabilize diplomatic relations, and relations have begun to improve further under Prime Minister Fukuda. The relationship remains fragile, however, and without sustained political support over the long term, will likely continue to be characterized by wide swings and punctuated by intense crises.

A variety of structural and proximate causes have driven Japan and China apart. Both see themselves as natural leaders in Asia and, at a minimum, are wary about the other taking a dominant role. As described above, Tokyo has been perplexed by a relative loss of influence to Beijing in Southeast Asia, which Japan has long considered its economic and, to a lesser extent, strategic backyard. After April 2005, with tensions rising over historical and other issues, Beijing campaigned against Tokyo's bid for a permanent seat on the UN Security Council, working with African states to derail Japan's efforts. Chinese leaders suggested that they would support India's effort to gain a seat—but only if India did not tie its inclusion to Japan's. Japan, for its part, has excluded China, at least under its present government, from its vision of an "arc of freedom and prosperity" in Asia. It has also sought to limit Chinese entry into multilateral forums, such as the Inter-American Development Bank.[54]

In addition to general leadership issues, a variety of more-specific disputes divide the two. Japan and China compete for oil and gas contracts, most pointedly in Russia. They are engaged in territorial conflicts, including contested sovereignty over the Senkaku Islands (the Diaoyu Islands to the Chinese) and parts of the East China Sea, as well as over Japan's claim to an exclusive economic zone around Okinotori. China is deeply suspicious of Japanese historical revisionism, a suspicion that, from Beijing's perspective, takes on added significance in light of growing Japanese military capabilities (discussed below, under "Defense Policy Responses"). From the Japanese perspective, several military-related incidents, such as a submarine incursion into its territorial waters in November 2004, combined with rapidly rising Chinese defense budgets, raise similar concerns about China's intentions and future trajectory as a rising power.

Of particular concern, at least from a military standpoint, was the possibility of an unintended clash in the East China Sea—an area that continues to remain under dispute. The conflict revolves around exclusive economic zone boundaries and the rights to exploit mineral resources.[55] China raised the stakes in August 2003 by establishing drilling platforms. Although the Chinese facilities are on the Chinese side of the "median line" Japan has drawn, they may draw from deposits that cross the line. Both sides have dispatched surveillance ships and aircraft to the area with increasing

---

[54] "China Bid to Join Inter-American Devt Bank Exposes Divisions—Report," AFX–Asia, April 11, 2005.

[55] On legal issues related to the East China Sea dispute and the history of negotiations, see Selig S. Harrison, ed., *Seabed Petroleum in Northeast Asia: Conflict or Cooperation?* working paper, Washington, D.C.: Woodrow Wilson International Center for Scholars, 2005.

frequency. Elements from both sides have crossed the median line (which, even if it had been mutually agreed to, would not delineate sovereign territory). With no agreement on how to handle incidents at sea, the possibility of an unintended clash and local escalation cannot be ruled out.[56]

These various rivalries, suspicions, and disputes led to an acute rise in bilateral tensions between 2001 and 2006, and these issues all remain points of friction today. In 2001, the Chinese suspended summit meetings with Japan in response to Koizumi's visit to Yasukuni; by 2005, channels of communication had narrowed significantly with the cancellation of several ministerial-level meetings.[57] This limited the ability of Japan and China to manage their differences and contain crises at a time when their differences were as numerous and contentious as they have ever been.

Even at the lowest point in this relationship, a variety of channels remained open. These have since been widened and thickened as Tokyo and Beijing have sought to halt the diplomatic downward spiral. The Ministry of Foreign Affairs (MOFA) and the JDA continued to hold regular meetings of the Japan-China Security Dialogue with their Chinese counterparts throughout this period. As of January 2007, MOFA's Vice Minister Yachi Shotaro had conducted seven rounds of less-formal (and by most accounts, more-meaningful) talks with his Chinese counterpart, Executive Vice Foreign Minister Dai Bingguo, under the rubric of the Japan-China Comprehensive Policy Dialogue—now called the Japan-China Strategic Dialogue.[58] Since 2001, multilateral meetings, especially meetings with China and South Korea on the sidelines of ASEAN Plus Three, have supplemented this bilateral diplomacy and were particularly important when bilateral summits were on hold.

The diplomatic relationship has taken a turn for the better since Abe succeeded Koizumi in September 2006. In contrast to Koizumi, who relied largely on his own political instincts and a small circle of close colleagues for policy advice, Abe proved more open to advice and opinion from a wider range of sources. Partly as a consequence, he came to office determined to improve relations with China, even as he pursued other, largely nationalist, objectives. His first overseas destination as prime minister was Beijing. There, in October 2007, he and Chinese President Hu Jintao

---

[56] The prospect of a clash will rise only if Japan acts on threats to establish its own drilling platforms, which would, unlike Chinese rigs, be located in contested territory. The government authorized Teikoku Oil Company to begin exploratory drilling, but the company is hesitant to do so without security assurances. There are increasing calls in the media and Diet for such assurances. See, for example, Yumi Wijers-Hasegawa, "Time for Japan to Shut Up and Drill: Energy Expert," *The Japan Times*, April 11, 2006.

[57] See, for example, "China Cancels Meetings with Japan, S. Korea in Shrine Row," Agence France Presse, December 9, 2005; "Chinese, South Korean Leaders Blame Japan for Cancelled Trilateral Summit," BBC, December 12, 2005; and "China Puts Off Japan, China, S. Korea Ministerial Telecom Meeting," Kyodo World News Service, December 21, 2005.

[58] The Comprehensive Policy Dialogue is seen as more effective because it involves only one ministry and fewer participants, has no fixed agenda, and is off the record. Meetings were held in May 2005, June 2005, October 2005, February 2006, May 2006, September 2006, and January 2007.

described the Chinese-Japanese relationship as "strategic and complementary."[59] In April 2007, Chinese Prime Minister Wen Jiabao reciprocated Abe's visit and delivered a well-received speech to the Japanese Diet.[60] With the economy encountering renewed difficulties and the LDP challenged on domestic policy, prime ministers Fukuda and Aso have continued to support stabilizing and improving relations with China.

The political and, especially, the bureaucratic establishments have backed the moves of Koizumi's successors to improve the relationship. Many high-profile figures in the LDP and in the DPJ believe that Japan has both direct economic interests and broader regional interests in a working partnership with China. Many in METI and the Ministry of Finance, as well as in some parts of MOFA, share this view. Business also supports efforts to smooth relations with China. These groups do not advance a utopian vision in which rivalry would be suppressed for the greater good and do not suggest that Japan should not continue to hedge its position. They do, however, press an essentially realist calculus that rivalry should be managed in the national interest.[61]

Both the Chinese and Japanese sides are now committed to improving the relationship, and much diplomatic activity can be expected. But the fundamental issues at stake are knotty; members of the general public in both countries are not, at present, particularly inclined toward compromise; and there are numerous political uncertainties. On the Japanese side, Koizumi demonstrated that under some circumstances, it is possible to generate political capital with tough positions on China issues.

Defense Policy Responses

As the Chinese-Japanese relationship worsened during the first decade of the 21st century, Japanese officials became increasingly willing to cite their concerns about Chinese military modernization publicly in official statements and planning documents. The JDA, which was upgraded to the status of the Ministry of Defense (MOD) in January 2007, plays a prominent role in Japan's tighter embrace of the United States, and parts of Japan's new defense thinking and activity appear to revolve around China. Currently, however, there is little public or parliamentary support for increasing defense spending to counter China, and Japanese military budgets have declined since 1999. The MOD has compensated for budgetary constraints by reallocating existing resources to tasks

---

[59] The Chinese had long been interested in cementing "strategic" relations with Japan, but Tokyo had resisted the label.

[60] The speech, simultaneously broadcast in Japan and China, was vetted extensively beforehand by Chinese experts on Japan. While it did not shy away from historical questions entirely, it focused clearly on building stronger ties for the future. Wen's speech was also a major departure from one Jiang Zemin delivered in 1998, which greatly emphasized historical issues and lambasted Japanese positions.

[61] See, for example, Kohara Masahiro, *Higashi Ajia Kyodotai* [*The East Asian Community*], Tokyo: Nihon Keizai Shimbunsha, 2005. Kohara is a MOFA official.

most relevant to Japan's current strategic situation, including, among other things, possible conflicts with China.

Military Planning and Guidance

Since the end of the Cold War, Japanese officials have generally specified North Korea as the primary threat, carefully framing discussions of China more ambiguously.[62] By the mid-2000s, however, such niceties largely disappeared. In early December 2005, Maehara Seiji, the leader of the DPJ, suggested to an American audience that China is a "real threat."[63] Asked about Maehara's comments, then–Foreign Minister Aso Taro agreed, reiterating Maehara's concerns over China's large increase in defense spending, calling it a "considerable threat."[64] In January 2006, JDA Director General Nukaga Fukushiro cited China in addition to North Korea in drawing a contrast with Europe, which, he said, currently does not confront any traditional security threats.[65]

This willingness to discuss China openly as a potential threat is also manifest in military planning documents. The 2005 *National Defense Program Guidelines* (NDPG) is more explicit than past documents in identifying China as a security concern.[66] *The East Asian Strategic Review 2006*, published by the JDA's National Institute for Defense Studies (NIDS), devotes significantly greater space to the challenges China poses than in previous years. Without labeling China a threat, the 2006 report nevertheless devotes four of seven paragraphs in its overview of "destabilizing factors in East Asia" to China, its military modernization, its relations with Taiwan, and its attitude toward Japan.[67] The 2007 version of the NIDS report leads with a chapter on "China's Cooperative Strategy toward East Asia—Aiming at Seizing the Regional Leadership." The report's message is mixed but generally cautious about how Japan should respond to China's rise: "Japan should encourage China's constructive efforts for East Asian cooperation, while keeping close watch over China's attempt to assume dominant leadership in the region."[68]

---

[62] Former JDA Director Ishiba Shigeru barely mentioned China in his book, *National Defense*, focusing instead on Korea and hypothetical threats. Ishiba Shigeru, *Kokubou* [*National Defense*], Tokyo: Shinchousha, 2005.

[63] Maehara Seiji, "Make Them Trigger Revitalization of Party," remarks, *Mainichi Shimbun*, December 14, 2005, tr., Foreign Broadcast Information Service, FBIS-JPP20051214026004, December 14, 2005.

[64] See Aso Taro, Foreign Minister, statement at press conference, Ministry of Foreign Affairs, Japan, December 22, 2005.

[65] See Nukaga Fukushiro, "Japan's Defence Policy and International Peace Cooperation Activities," speech delivered to the Royal United Service Institute for Defence and Security Studies, London, January 11, 2006.

[66] The 2005 NDPG states that China "continues to modernize its nuclear forces and missile capabilities, as well as its naval and air forces. China is also expanding its area of operation at sea. We will have to remain attentive to its future actions." Japanese Government, Ministry of Defense, *National Defense Program Guidelines FY 2005*, December 10, 2004, pp. 2–3.

[67] NIDS, *East Asian Strategic Review 2006*, March 2006.

[68] NIDS, *East Asian Strategic Review 2007*, April 2007.

New Missions, Old Budgets

The SDF is being asked to assume a variety of new roles and missions. Some have little to do with China. The 2005 NDPG specifies that military forces serve a variety of purposes, "including the prevention of conflict and the [sic] reconstruction assistance." Japan continues to maintain a naval presence in the Indian Ocean and to refuel U.S. warships in the region. But some of the SDF's new tasks appear directly aimed at China-related contingencies. Tasks outlined in the 2005 NDPG include responding to attacks by ballistic missiles, guerrillas, and special operations forces; repelling an invasion of Japan's offshore islands; and conducting patrols and surveillance in the sea and airspace surrounding Japan.

Whatever the drivers, all these new missions require resources. Yet Japanese defense planning continues against a backdrop of stagnating budgets (Table 3.1). In constant yen terms, the defense budget for 2007 was lower than it was in 1996. Even adjusting for chronic deflation, the budget remained slightly lower in 2007 than it was in 2000. Military budgets have also slipped as a percentage of GDP. In the long term, it is not unreasonable to expect budgets to recover. In the short and medium terms, however, Japan's national debt, which is now 150 percent of its GDP, is a powerful impediment to increasing expenditures. (The U.S. national debt amounts to around 66 percent of its GDP.) And there is little support among the general public or in the Diet for increasing defense spending.[69]

Facing severe budget constraints, the JDA and SDF have shifted resources to focus on new priorities. They have not, however, shifted the allocation of resources to Japan's three services. Given its historical role in preparing guerilla defenses against a possible Soviet invasion, the army has traditionally garnered more resources than its sister services. As of 2005, the army's budget, at 38 percent of the total defense budget, remained substantially larger than the navy's (23 percent) or the air force's (23 percent)—and virtually unchanged from its share in 2000.[70] Despite the Ministry of Finance's calls for the military to cut army manpower, the army was able to secure an increase in its full-time manpower under the 2005 NDPG, even as it reduced the number of reservists.[71] Reorganization, then, takes place against a backdrop of both budgetary constraints and bureaucratic politics.

Within these limits, the adjustments to Japanese military resource allocations have been substantial. As early as the mid-1990s, Tokyo began gradually shifting its mili-

---

[69] Among the general public, a 2006 cabinet office survey indicates 65.7 percent think the SDF should be maintained at "around the same strength," while only 16.5 percent believe it should be increased and 8.3 percent believe it should be reduced. Cabinet Office, Government of Japan, "Jieitai, Boei Mondai ni kan Suru Yoron Chosa [Public Opinion Survey on Self-Defense Force and Defense Issues]," 2006. For the Diet, see Cabinet Office, Government of Japan, "Survey of Lower House Members," *Aera*, August 5, 2004.

[70] JDA, 2005, p. 121. JDA, *Boei Hyakusho Heisei 12 Nenpan [Defense of Japan 2000]*, August 28, 2000, p. 107. In 2000, 22 percent of the budget went to the navy, with the others receiving the same as in 2005.

[71] JDA, *Nihon no Boei Heisei 15 Nenpan [Defense of Japan 2003]*, Tokyo, 2003, p. 106.

Table 3.1
Japanese Defense Expenditures

Year	Expenditures (¥, billions)		Percentage of GDP
	Nominal (current)	Real (2000)	
2000	4,921	4,921	0.98
2001	4,938	4,974	0.95
2002	4,939	5,021	0.95
2003	4,926	5,021	0.98
2004	4,876	4,970	0.97
2005	4,830	4,939	0.94
2006	4,790	4,888	0.93
2007	4,781	4,894	0.92

SOURCE: Defense expenditures from JDA, *Nihon no Boei Heisei 19 Nenpan* [*Defense of Japan 2007*], 2007.

NOTE: Japanese consumer price index used for inflation adjustment from OECD. Adjusted 2007 expenditure is an estimate.

tary center of gravity from Hokkaido and northern Honshu, where it faced the threat of Soviet invasion during the Cold War, southward, where assets could be deployed against Chinese threats. It also reduced the force structure, while improving mobility. Under the 1995 National Defense Program Outline (as the NDPGs were designated before 2005), the number of divisions in the GSDF was reduced from 13 to nine. The four divisions eliminated were converted into smaller, more-mobile brigades, raising the number of independent brigades from two to six. Under the 2005–2009 Midterm Defense Plan (MDP, the JDA's five-year defense plan), an additional division and two combined brigades, with one infantry regiment each, are to be converted into three full brigades, with two or more regiments each.

Divisions have been downsized primarily in northern and eastern areas, while divisions deployed in western and southern areas have been left largely intact. Some new units have also been formed in or moved to positions farther south. In 2002, the 700-strong Western Army Infantry Regiment charged with amphibious operations was formed in Nagasaki Prefecture, Kyushu. The conversion of the Western Army's 1st Combined Brigade based in Naha, Okinawa, into a regular brigade will double its maneuver elements and add at least 850 personnel. The Defense Agency has decided to replace the Air Self-Defense Forces (ASDF) F-4 squadron on Okinawa with a squadron of F-15s, substantially improving Japan's ability to operate over its southernmost territories.[72] And JDA officials are discussing deploying GSDF elements on Miyako Island and opening an airstrip on Shimoji Island for fighter use.[73] Both islands are located about halfway between Okinawa and Taiwan.

The 2005–2009 Mid-Term Defense Program established the Central Readiness Force (CRF). The CRF brings many of Japan's mobile and special units under a single command reporting directly to the Defense Chief. CRF units include Japan's Helicopter Brigade, Airborne Brigade, Special Operations Group (established 2004), and Chemical Defense Unit. CRF Headquarters may also include a rapid reaction regiment. The force will head overseas deployments and provide support for mobile operations in any of Japan's five regional armies. It would, then, play an important role in any operations against a hypothetical Chinese seizure of the Senkaku Islands.

Air and sea capabilities, including power-projection capabilities, are also improving, even as the number of units shrinks. Between 1998 and 2003, the Maritime Self-Defense Forces (MSDF) commissioned three 14,700-ton (loaded) Osumi-class ships, designated as landing ships. Four times as large as any previous Japanese landing ship, the Osumi can accommodate two large hovercraft. With a flush deck and an island offset to starboard, the Osumi resembles a small aircraft carrier, although its elevator is too small to accommodate aircraft. Under the next MDP (2010–2014), two new large helicopter carriers are to be built, in this case designated as a *destroyer, helicopter* but resembling small aircraft carriers even more closely than the Osumi. At 20,000 tons fully loaded, the new ships will have the elevators and deck length to handle AV-8s or even some versions of the F-35 Joint Strike Fighter and could carry as many as 11 aircraft.[74] Overall, the surface fleet will shrink by three ships under the 2005–2009 MDP, but the average size of each will grow. Building plans also include two improved 7,700-ton Aegis-equipped Kongo-class destroyers, bringing the Aegis fleet to six.

The ASDF is also increasing both its lift capacity and combat capabilities; however, because of unit cost inflation in the F-2 support fighter program, equipment inventories will suffer even more than those of the MSDF. The MDP calls for the acquisition of eight new-design transport aircraft, which will be designed with three times the lift capacity and three times the range of existing C-1 transport aircraft, currently the largest in the Japanese inventory. The ASDF will also acquire its first aerial refueling aircraft. Despite its costs and shortcomings, the F-2 provides a significant

---

72 "Defense Agency to Upgrade Fighter Jets at Naha Base," *The Daily Yomiuri*, March 4, 2005. The transfer is to take place in 2008, although funds are earmarked for base improvements starting 2006.

73 "Ground Unit in Okinawa to Be Beefed Up to Defend Islands," *Kyodo News Service*, September 20, 2004; James Brooke, "Japanese Island Tries to Evade Flight Path," *New York Times*, September 20, 2004.

74 On the Osumi and new DDH, see Jane's, "Procurement, Japan," January 27, 2006; Jane's, "Navy, Japan," April 12, 2005; "Japan's New Defense Posture: Towards Power Projection," *IISS Strategic Comments*, Vol. 10, Issue 8, October 2004; GlobalSecurity.org, "LST Osumi Class," November 14, 2006; GlobalSecurity.org, "DDH '13,500-ton' Ton Class," August 29, 2006.

new capability for Japan: the ability to launch Joint Direct-Attack Munitions and other precision ground-strike weapons.

Contingency plans for operations against China have been generated for the first time, and the SDF's training has been adjusted accordingly. In November 2004, the JDA compiled plans for counteroffensive operations in the event China seized the disputed Senkaku Islands east of Taiwan. These plans call for dispatching 55,000 members of the GSDF, as well as warplanes, destroyers, and submarines. During the first phases, MSDF and ASDF reconnaissance assets would provide intelligence, while civilian ships would be pressed into service to help GSDF units establish logistics and communications bases on nearby islands. Two fleets from the Chugoku region and Kyushu Island would be dispatched to gain control of nearby waters. Finally, units of the Western Army Infantry Regiment (Nagasaki), designated as Japan's amphibious assault force, would retake the captured islands.[75]

As early as 2001, the SDF began lifting military units to islands in the Ryukyu chain as part of disaster relief exercises. Starting with small-scale movements, some of these have come to resemble rehearsals for the plan outlined above. In September 2004, for example, the SDF simulated a response to a magnitude 7 earthquake near Ishigaki Island. F-4 fighter aircraft provided "an aerial platform from which SDF officers could view images of the area."[76] Forward communications bases were established on two nearby islands. Privately owned ships were drafted to provide logistical support. Helicopters, flying off the LST Osumi, landed a platoon of GSDF troops on a landing zone 5 km from the mock disaster site on Ishigaki. One GSDF officer confessed of the exercise, "Even if there is a [military] threat, we can't afford to come out and say we're holding drills for that. So we call it 'disaster prevention.'"[77]

Explicit combat training has also become more realistic and focused. In January 2006, 150 soldiers from the Western Army Infantry Regiment received three weeks of intensive training in amphibious reconnaissance and assault training from U.S. Marine Corps instructors at Camp Pendleton, California.[78] While their numbers were few, these individuals may be expected to serve as trainers within their own units back in Nagasaki. In February 2006, a Yamasaki exercise, a biannual joint Japanese-U.S. army command post exercise, focused for the first time on a counteroffensive scenario against enemy forces occupying one or more small southwestern islands. This exercise, too, rehearsed the general plan for counteroffensive action established in December

---

[75] "Japan Prepares Defence Plan for Islands Disputed with China," Asia Africa Intelligence Wire, BBC Monitoring International Reports, January 16, 2005.

[76] "Protecting Japan—Part IV: Meeting New Threats to the Realm," *Yomiuri Shimbun*, September 18, 2004.

[77] On these exercises, see "Protecting Japan—Part IV . . . ," 2004.

[78] Tony Perry and Bruce Wallace, "Japanese Troops Shore Up Skills," *Los Angeles Times*, January 13, 2006.

2004 and included civilian officials charged with evacuating civilians.[79] In June 2007, eight Japanese F-2s deployed to Guam and conducted the aircraft's first-ever live-fire bomb runs. It was only the third time that any ASDF aircraft had conducted bombing runs in the organization's 60-year history.[80]

Strengthening the Coast Guard

The Japanese Coast Guard (JCG) would play a role in a China-related contingency, and its budget, in contrast to the SDF's, is increasing. As an ostensibly nonmilitary force, the JCG's activities are more politically palatable than the MSDF's, particularly in forward areas. JCG vessels pursued a North Korean surveillance ship into China's exclusive economic zone and sank it in December 2001. Unlike China, which maintains no armed coast guard vessels over 1,000 tons, the JCG is an oceangoing force. Counting only armed, oceangoing ships, Japan's coast guard has 145,000 tons, or around 65 percent as much tonnage as China's entire naval surface fleet. These JCG vessels are, needless to say, armed with guns, rather than missiles, and lack other features of modern warships. More problematic, many were constructed in the 1970s and suffer from mechanical problems.

In December 2005, however, the Japanese government, announcing a major modernization plan, moved to address this issue. The coast guard's annual equipment budget for 2006–2025 was increased by 233 percent from its 2005 level (rising from $130 million to $436 million annually).[81] The funds will pay for 21 new boats and seven new jets, as well as the replacement of six older boats and four aircraft. A coast guard spokesman defended the request with explicit reference to China: "We demanded this increase in size because of mounting concerns in the East China Sea area, especially the area near the disputed gas field."[82]

Conclusions and Implications

Drawing on the data and analysis presented above, we conclude this chapter by reviewing Japan's political, economic, diplomatic, and military responses to the rise of China, focusing not on responses within each issue area but how consistent the responses are across these issues. We then outline the key domestic and international variables likely

---

[79] "*Tosho Boei Nado Sotei–Nichibei Shikisho Enshu Hajimaru* [*Envisioning Small Island Defense: U.S.–Japanese Command Post Exercise Begins*]," *Kyodo Tsushin*, January 27, 2006; "Nichibei Shikisho Enshu Hajimaru–Hajime no Tosho Boei Sotei [Japanese–U.S. Command Post Exercise Begins: The First to Envision Small Island Defense]," *Sankei Shimbun*, January 27, 2006.

[80] Ashleigh Bryant, "F-2 Makes Live Bomb Debut During Exercise," Air Force Link, June 15, 2007.

[81] "Patrol Ships, Planes to Be Stationed in East China Sea; Japan Coast Guard to Spend 350 Billion Yen to Upgrade Equipment," *Sankei Shimbun*, December 2, 2005.

[82] "Japan Plans to Boost Patrols of Gas Field Disputed with China," AFX News Ltd., December 2, 2005.

to shape the future outcome of Japan's China policy and list indicators that might suggest movement toward either a more-concerted effort to achieve a security balance or make an accommodation with China.

Policy Integration

Has Japan produced, or is it developing, a well-integrated policy response to China's rise? Clearly, Japan has reacted to the rise of China, in some cases dramatically, but the evidence on coherence is more mixed. A number of new integrative mechanisms are available to Japanese leaders that should, and in some cases have, helped in this regard. But thus far, countervailing (i.e., disintegrative) forces have proven at least as strong. Different parts of the Japanese bureaucracy, in short, perceive and react to China's rise very differently, often working at cross-purposes.

Differences can be seen most prominently in the economic and military components of Japanese policy. The reaction of economic bureaucrats has been based on the view that China's rise is primarily an opportunity, while security elites have considered it a potential threat. As a general statement, this pattern is not remarkable and is, for example, typical of the difference between the way U.S. economists and defense planners view China. In the Japanese case, however, the degree of difference is exacerbated by the existence of a powerful economic bureaucracy, which has historically embraced state-centered conceptions of trade and economic development.

In principle, and to some extent in fact, new integrative mechanisms are improving the coherence of Japanese policy toward China.[83] The 1999 Cabinet Law established policy offices in the Cabinet Secretariat to coordinate the efforts of the various ministries.[84] (In the past, ministries had generally coordinated among themselves, with little political oversight or intervention.) In the area of China policy, the secretariat's office on East China Sea issues, a new organization, focuses primarily on boundary and energy disputes with Beijing. METI's Agency for Natural Resources and Energy supplies data on energy issues; MOFA coordinates diplomatic efforts; and JDA provides satellite imagery on Chinese activities. The East China Sea office is an example of successful institutional innovation, but with only eight such offices to handle everything from economic restructuring to social security reform, the limitations of this mechanism are also evident.

Prime Ministers Koizumi and Abe have also sought to elevate the role of the military security apparatus and integrate it better into the foreign policymaking process, affording it greater influence over foreign (as opposed to strictly military) policy. Koizumi sponsored legislation, effective April 2006, that strengthened the chairman of the joint chiefs of staff, expanded his staff, and gave him direct access to the chief of

---

[83] Except where otherwise noted, the information from this section is derived primarily from interviews with METI, MOFA, and JDA officials, October–November 2005.

[84] Shinoda, 2004.

the defense agency (eliminating JDA civil servants as a strict civilian filter). The JDA moved into a larger and newer building in 2000 in preparation for its elevation from an agency to a ministry. The new MOD is no longer restricted to administrative activities, and its NDPG now touches on larger security and foreign policy issues (changes that date back to the planning for the 2005 NDPG and that therefore long predate the transition from JDA to MOD). During his tenure as prime minister, Abe made the creation of an American-style national security council a top priority, one that may be downgraded under Prime Minister Fukuda but is unlikely to disappear completely from the LDP's agenda.

Efforts have also been made to improve coordination within ministries. Within MOFA, as in most other ministries, policymaking has traditionally been characterized by extreme stovepiping. China policy was dominated by the China school—China specialists within the East Asia and Oceania bureaus—with little input from other geographic or functional areas. Several incidents in which MOFA personnel were perceived to have failed to defend Japan's interests in the face of Chinese challenges brought pressure for change. The China school's influence was downgraded by drawing on other parts of the East Asia Bureau for bureau leadership. And in 2005, the vice minister established regular strategy sessions for bureau directors to meet and hammer out China strategy. (It is indicative of the bureaucracy's continuing power, however, that no appointed officials are present at these meetings.)

In principle, political and administrative reform should produce more consistent positions on China. The effects to date, however, have been more mixed. Clearly, the strengthening of Japan's security apparatus and the attitude of Japan's political leadership have shifted the center of Japanese policy on China issues. But except in certain specific areas (such as East China Sea policy), these changes have not improved the integration of Tokyo's policy toward Beijing. It has proven easier to build up the military security establishment, however gradually, than to change the culture or preferences of the nation's powerful economic bureaucracy. Japan's economic and military policies toward China, then, have been pursued on two tracks that seldom intersect, with the economic ministries seeking to establish closer partnership with China and other actors (both political and bureaucratic) seeking greater distance.

Politically, Prime Minister Koizumi's visits to Yasukuni and the debate between nationalists and others focused attention for several years on emotional and symbolic issues rather than on relatively practical aspects. This often left the bureaucracy with little clear guidance on China issues. In the diplomatic arena, MOFA has played an increasingly deft hand in balancing Japan's various interests. With both economic and security specialists, it has, for example, spearheaded Japan's efforts to strengthen comprehensive strategic relations with nations from Australia to India. But at the same time, no agency has been as strongly buffeted by the political crosswinds on China policy (or foreign policy more generally). During Koizumi's tenure, MOFA was forced to spend much of its time reacting to and seeking to explain the prime minister's visits to Yasukuni. Since then, it has had to change gears quickly and embrace the new strategic relationship with China.

Domestic and International Variables

The preceding discussion of policy integration has focused largely on the domestic determinants of Japan's reaction to China. Here, then, we will summarize the domestic variables that will affect Japan's future posture only briefly and focus on international ones.

Domestically, the continued evolution of the political and administrative system will have a significant effect on Japan's positions on China and, all things being equal, will work to increase the coherence of Japanese policy. Political leadership on China policy will, of course, also be critical. Leaders as politically adept as Koizumi (whether or not one agrees with his policies) are rare, and weaker leadership might provide even-more-mixed signals on China policy. Beyond the *strength* of leadership, political priorities and preferences will shape the coherence of Japanese foreign policy. Specifically, political leadership (whether strong or weak) will determine whether the current debate over patriotism signals a modest corrective to Japan's post–World War II pacifist exceptionalism or a more-fundamental and divisive struggle over national values—one that could undermine Japan's ability to play a regional and global leadership role.

Apart from these domestic variables, Japan's posture toward China policy will also hinge on a number of international variables, including the nature of Japan's relationship with the United States, Beijing's attitude, and regional developments (not least of which will be the future of North Korea and its nuclear program).

The state of the U.S.–Japanese alliance is probably the most important of these variables. Tokyo's security posture is evolving and will almost certainly continue to do so regardless of what the United States does. A healthy alliance, one that includes collocation and close cooperation between U.S. and Japanese military forces, will, however, work to improve Japanese capabilities (particularly the human elements) more quickly and effectively than would otherwise be possible and, at the same time, will minimize pressures for the development of the military capabilities (especially nuclear capabilities) that would most alarm neighbors.

At the same time, the U.S. position will influence the debate, one way or the other, over historical and nationalist issues in Japan. A Japan that is allied with the United States is, on balance, less likely to move toward virulent nationalism. That said, complete U.S. silence on these issues may encourage Japanese leaders to view history as a local, Northeast Asian concern. A truly healthy relationship, then, will include dialogue on historical issues but will still reassure Japan of the ultimate security guarantee. In July 2007, Abe's government warned the United States of "lasting and harmful effects" to the U.S.–Japanese relationship if the U.S. House resolution on comfort women were passed, but the real effect was on the ability of Abe's nationalist camp to claim that this historical issue was a "China problem."[85] (Interestingly, with Japan and China having called a truce on historical issues and South Korea's position unchanged, many Japanese policymakers now see history as a "Korean problem.")

Beijing's attitude and position will be critical. Abe's succession to prime minister gave both Beijing and Tokyo an opportunity to reset their bilateral relationship, especially in the last year and following Hu Jintao's visit to Tokyo. Both have shown every desire to capitalize on that opportunity. Even before Abe took office, Beijing emphasized the future prime minister's strengths (from China's perspective) and largely ignored his record of nationalist statements. But many aspects of China's position remain unclear. Would Beijing overlook private visits to Yasukuni, should a future prime minister go? Will Beijing work with Tokyo on issues related to regional integration? Again, the early indications on most of these issues are positive, but only time will provide definitive answers.

Finally, regional developments, including events on the Korean peninsula, could cut different ways—and specific outcomes may depend more on the will of Beijing and Tokyo to cooperate or compete than on developments in third countries. Beijing's and Tokyo's priorities on the Korean peninsula (as with those of all other actors) diverge in several areas, and the two have butted heads over Korea policy in the past (such as when China objected to a toughly worded draft U.N. Security Council resolution that Japan introduced in July 2006). More recently, however, Tokyo and Beijing have emphasized their common interests in denuclearization on the Korean peninsula, with Prime Minister Abe and Chinese President Hu Jintao seizing on the North Korean issue as an area in which they can rebuild cooperative relations.[86]

Indicators of Change

In addition to the variables that are likely to influence Japan's posture toward China, we also considered indicators of actual change. Against today's baseline, what developments—viewed a year or two or five from now—would indicate movement toward either closer collaboration with China or a more-distant relationship, characterized by hedging or even active balancing, in the diplomatic, economic, and military arenas? Many of these are not entirely or even primarily dictated by a larger China policy but may nevertheless influence the future path of Japan's policy toward China:

- Diplomatic indicators of balancing against China would include the following:
  - expanded aid for India or Southeast Asian states and further discussion of expanded strategic relationships with them

---

[85] Blaine Harden, "Japan Warns U.S. House Against Resolution on WWII Sex Slaves," *Washington Post*, July 18, 2007.

[86] "Abe Off to Impressive Start," *Japan Times*, October 16, 2006.

- diplomatic support for Taiwan's international efforts, such as its bid to gain representation in the World Health Organization
- resolution of historical or boundary disputes with South Korea with no corresponding efforts or success with China.
- Diplomatic indicators of increased cooperation would include the following:
  - mutually acceptable accommodation on Yasukuni visits and broader historical issues
  - joint development or a profit-sharing arrangement for oil or gas deposits in contested areas of the East China Sea or straddling the exclusive economic zone boundary
  - reinvigoration of ASEAN Plus Three summitry and cooperation along the sidelines of ASEAN Plus Three and/or the EAS.
- Economic indicators of balancing against China would include one of the following:
  - a change in business sentiment away from the view of China as an economic opportunity toward a view of China as an economic threat
  - a shift in new investment away from China, early indications of which might be observed in the JBIC survey
  - changes in the thinking of the government's economic agencies, which currently promote China as an important investment destination.
- Positive economic indicators would include one of the following:
  - business renewing efforts to weigh in positively on China policy (by, for example, publishing reports on political relations)
  - conclusion of state-to-state trade or investment agreements with China or trilateral ones that also include South Korea.
- Military indicators of balancing against China would include one of the following:
  - a rise in the defense budget as a percentage of GDP, particularly if justified as a response to China or "destabilizing influences in the region"
  - increased scope of military cooperation with the United States
  - more-detailed planning or rehearsals for China-related contingencies
  - efforts to match or counter new Chinese military capabilities
  - early acquisition of systems useful for power projection
  - expanded coast guard and military exchanges or cooperation with Taiwan, India, Australia, or other regional actors.

- Military indicators of a more-cooperative relationship would include one of the following:
  - confidence-building measures (e.g., on incidents at sea) with China
  - increased military-to-military engagement with China.

CHAPTER FOUR

South Korea

Few countries have gone through the kind of rapid transformation that South Korea has over the past few decades. Within the lifespan of anyone over 50 today, the country has risen from war and destitution (with a per capita GDP of $67 in 1953) to become the world's 11th largest economy (with a per capita income of $18,481 in 2006). In the last few years alone, South Korea has become the world's most wired country, with 70 percent of its households having broadband access to the Internet.[1] Today, South Koreans are watching television on their cell phones, are introducing a superfast wireless Internet service that enables them to remain online wherever they go, and are on the verge of mass producing networked robots for use both inside and outside the home.[2] In short, South Korea is aggressively targeting the future. Using futuristic technologies that are still years away in the United States, it is openly striving to become one of the world's leading high-technology nations.

At the same time, however, South Korea remains weighed down by the past. Fundamental unresolved ideological and historical issues have spawned acute political polarization, which is reinforced by generational change and geographical divides.[3] The intensity of the polarization reflects a continuing struggle between the country's "competing nationalisms."[4] In this environment, a new reformist leadership has come

---

[1] Compare this with 45 percent of Japanese and 33 percent of American households. Anthony Faiola, "When Escape Seems Just a Mouse-Click Away," *Washington Post*, May 27, 2006.

[2] Norimitsu Onishi, "In a Wired South Korea, Robots Will Feel Right at Home," *The New York Times*, April 2, 2006. South Koreans are even building a new "ubiquitous city" (New Songdo) in Inchon—which will become South Korea's first free economic zone when completed in 2010 and will serve as a center of free trade and international business—where all major systems share information through computers embedded in houses, streets, and office buildings. See Kim Hyun-cheol, "Inchon Rises as New Far East Hub," *The Korea Times*, March 31, 2006; Ryan Block, "New Songdo, the South Korean 'Ubiquitous City' of the Future," *Engadget*, October 5, 2005.

[3] For background, see Sung-Joo Han, *The Failure of Democracy in South Korea*, University of California Press, 1974. For a critical assessment of the current situation, see Hahm Chaibong, "The Two South Koreas: A House Divided," *The Washington Quarterly*, Summer 2005.

[4] Rooted in the origins of modern Korean nationalism in the early 20th century and intensified by the 1910–1945 Japanese occupation and the national division at the end of World War II, this struggle pits conservatives and moderate nationalists who emphasize freedom, a market economy, economic growth, and an independent

to power (the self-styled people's participatory government) that has made righting perceived historical wrongs part of its domestic political agenda. One result is an uneasy fit between the leadership's ideological predispositions and the socioeconomic reality of South Korea today. Another is frequent policy ambiguity and vacillation. A third is periodic tension between the leadership's policy aspirations and its willingness to bear the consequences of related policy choices.[5]

All this adds up to a complex situation. South Korea is a complicated, sophisticated, and rapidly changing country. Few simplistic statements capture what is going on today. Many of the variables affecting its policy responses, moreover, cut more than one way. Any analysis must try to capture the complexity of the current situation without avoiding judgments about its character and future direction.

This chapter assesses South Korea's response to the rise of China from this perspective. The chapter first describes several broad trends that influence the national situation in South Korea today and shape the context within which South Korean responses to China are fashioned. It then examines these responses in detail, focusing on the political, economic, foreign policy, and military variables that appear most influential in determining South Korea's responses. We conclude with an assessment of the forces driving South Korea's response to China today and the likely future of South Korean–Chinese relations, the state of South Korea's security relationship with the United States and its likely future, and potential tests of will that could signal potential South Korean movement toward or away from the United States. The mixed picture emerging from the analysis suggests that U.S. policy must be at least as complex and sophisticated as the situation inside South Korea itself, with U.S. policymakers demonstrating understanding of and sensitivity toward the inherent internal tensions—and occasional contradictions—without losing sight of long-term U.S. interests.

---

state against liberals and radical nationalists who are focused on Korean "peoplehood," unification, more "equitable" distribution of wealth, and broader social transformation. For more details, see Norman D. Levin and Yong-Sup Han, *Sunshine in Korea: The South Korean Debate over Policies Toward North Korea*, Santa Monica, Calif.: RAND Corporation, MR-1555-CAPP, 2002.

[5] This is reflected, for example, in the government's emphasis on the principle of self-reliance and its reluctance to fund its defense buildup sufficiently to meet what it terms its "self-sufficiency" objectives. South Korea's effort to delay the withdrawal of U.S. troops from Korea is another reflection, as is its attempt to slow down the transfer of military responsibilities from the United States to the Republic of Korea (South Korea). These tensions affected U.S.–South Korean talks on the transfer of operational control of South Korean forces to South Korea—a high priority of the Roh administration since its inception—with South Korea pushing for a considerably later target date (2012) for the transfer than the one the United States sought (2009). See Park Song-wu, "Korea Can Take Wartime Control Now," *The Korea Times*, August 9, 2006; Jack Kim, "Seoul Says Wartime Command Shift Won't Harm U.S. Ties," *Washington Post*, August 9, 2006.

National Conditions

Four broad trends help set the background for, and influence the nature of, South Korea's response to the rise of China. One is the ending of the era of rapid growth. In contrast to its average annual growth rate of 8 percent between 1963 and 1996, the nation's GDP grew at an average of only 4.6 percent between 2001 and 2007. While this rate of growth itself represents an impressive recovery from the financial crisis of 1997–1998, it is far from the kind of economic performance most South Koreans had grown used to over the preceding decades.

The end of the rapid-growth era has had two important effects relevant to South Korea's response to China. First, it has increased South Korean interest in finding new sources of growth to serve as the economy's future engine. The dramatic growth of the Chinese economy makes it an attractive candidate over the short to middle term, yet simultaneously compels South Korean companies to produce higher quality, higher value products to compete with their Chinese counterparts over the longer term. Second, the end of the rapid-growth era has shifted South Korean economic policy priorities away from the protection of indigenous industries toward creating new jobs and keeping unemployment low. This has induced South Korea to lower barriers to foreign trade and seek as many FTAs as possible and, at the same time, to seek to attract investment, regardless of its origin.

A second broad trend is the ongoing shift in the inter-Korean conventional balance of power in South Korea's favor. This shift accelerated because of the collapse of the Soviet Union, which, among other things, set off a decade-long free fall in the North Korean economy. As the economic gap widened dramatically between the two Koreas, annual South Korean military spending far outpaced what North Korea could afford.[6] By 2005, South Korea's defense budget of over $20 billion was larger than the entire North Korean economy, while its spending on force improvement plans alone (over $7.4 billion) was larger than the entire North Korean defense budget.

Along with significantly improved South Korean military capabilities, this trend dramatically altered the South Korean public's views of North Korea. Instead of seeing North Korea as a menacing competitor on the verge of sudden attack, South Koreans have come to see it as a hapless sibling on the verge of implosion. To be sure, most South Koreans continue to recognize the real dangers emanating from North Korea. But the recognition of continuing danger does not equate to concern about an imminent, or even likely, threat. Indeed, most polls show that a large majority of South Koreans have little fear of a North Korean attack. This finding reflects the widespread view that the North, despite its nuclear weapons programs, is simply no longer able to

---

[6]   Between 1990 and 2003, for example, South Korea's defense spending rose from less than $10 billion to nearly $17 billion, or well over three times the roughly $5 billion annual expenditure estimated for North Korea.

initiate and sustain a large-scale conflict.[7] The dismantlement of the Soviet empire and China's preoccupation with its domestic development have reinforced the reduction in the perception of a threat and have stimulated increasingly relaxed South Korean views of the regional security environment. They have also fostered a sense among the South Korean policy elite of greater "space" in which South Korea can pursue its own policy objectives.

A third trend relates to engagement with North Korea. South Korean efforts to establish some form of peaceful coexistence date at least to the administration of Roh Tae-woo (1988–1992), which actively sought to expand inter-Korean exchanges as a means for creating a joint national community in which both Koreas could live peacefully and prosper.[8] But it was only a decade later (1998–2003) that engagement reached its apogee under the Kim Dae-jung government's "sunshine policy." During this period, North-South political dialogue, economic cooperation, cultural and humanitarian exchanges, and even military-to-military discussions established a host of new precedents, stimulated in particular by the historic June 2000 summit meeting between Kim Dae-jung and paramount North Korean leader Kim Jong-il.

Engagement with North Korea has had profound effects in South Korea across the board. It is an important part of the background for South Korea's response to the rise of China in certain key respects. Kim Dae-jung's government has actively stimulated and encouraged this engagement, and South Koreans now see the North less as an enemy seeking their subjugation than as a brother needing South Korea's assistance. Second, engagement has shifted the fundamental goal of South Korea's policy toward North Korea. Instead of seeking the short-term overthrow or absorption of the North, the official goal has become preventing the instabilities and costs likely to be associated with a precipitate North Korean collapse and fostering gradual, long-term inter-Korean reconciliation. Finally, engagement has opened up conceptual possibilities for broader tension reduction and regional cooperation in Northeast Asia. In this environment, replacing the temporary armistice arrangements on the Korean peninsula with a permanent peace regime, if the nuclear issue is resolved, and positioning Korea as an important hub of regional interactions have risen to the top of South Korea's policy agenda. Given China's unique relationship with North Korea, its heavy responsibilities for keeping North Korea afloat, and its own interests and roles in maintaining regional

---

[7] For a comprehensive analysis of South Korean public attitudes on issues related to the United States, see Eric V. Larson and Norman D. Levin, Seonhae Baik, and Bogdan Savych, *Ambivalent Allies? A Study of South Korean Attitudes Toward the U.S.*, Santa Monica, Calif.: RAND Corporation, TR-141-SRF, 2004. Also see Derek J. Mitchell, *Strategy and Sentiment: South Korean Views of the United States and the U.S.–ROK Alliance*, Washington, D.C.: Center for Strategic and International Studies, 2004.

[8] The December 1991 North-South "Basic Agreement," which renounced the use of force and established an intricate web of committees to implement an array of measures promoting inter-Korean cooperation, was the crowning achievement. For a description of the origins and evolution of South Korea's engagement policies, see Levin and Han, 2002.

stability, these effects have contributed to elevating China's perceived importance to the range of core South Korean interests.

The fourth broad background trend influencing the nature of South Korea's response to the rise of China has to do with the country's ongoing process of democratization. The extent and speed of this process are almost staggering: Within less than a decade, South Koreans have returned the military to the barracks; institutionalized the peaceful transfer of power between ruling and opposition parties; and fostered the growth of an extensive, vibrant, and increasingly influential civil society. Not surprisingly perhaps, the process has stimulated—or at least enabled—a significant transition in South Korean politics. This transition first became noticeable with the election of Kim Dae-jung in 1997—the first time a leader of South Korea's political opposition was ever elected president. But it was conspicuously furthered in 2002 by the election of Roh Moo-hyun—a human rights lawyer born to a poor farming family in southeastern South Korea who never went to college, had a career defending striking workers and political dissidents, and participated actively in the June 1987 "Democratic Struggle" against former South Korean President Chun Doo-hwan. The outcome represents a decided move away from historic patterns, with the traditional political opposition to South Korea's conservative rule becoming ensconced as its new Establishment.

An important product of this transition is a shift in the ruling elite's social and ideological center of gravity as new leaders from all parts of South Korean society having considerably more liberal (or progressive, in Korean terminology) ideas about national policy than their predecessors come to the fore. Reinforcing this shift is a broader generational change in South Korean politics, with young voters who have no personal memory of the Korean War or emotional bond with the United States now becoming a significant force in South Korean elections. These trends have strengthened long-standing South Korean aspirations for greater policy autonomy and have increased support for a more-activist set of foreign policies. They have also stimulated considerable flux in South Korean politics, with South Korean leaders now having to appeal to the electorate differently than their predecessors did.

Together with continuing Korean antipathy toward Japan and renewed difficulties in South Korean–Japanese relations, these trends have given China a certain attractiveness that it largely lacked in South Korea's traditional political setting.[9]

As this general setting might suggest, the context in which South Korean policies are set has changed considerably over that of much of the post–Korean War period. The overall effect of this change has been to subject South Korean policies to a new range of competing demands and cross pressures. The next section describes how South

---

[9] Attitudes toward Japan certainly influence South Korean foreign and security policies, as described later in this chapter (see "Defense Policy Responses"). But too much should not be made of South Korea's "enduring enmity" with Japan. Over time, Korean attitudes have fluctuated significantly, as have the nature and quality of South Korean–Japanese relations.

Korea is responding to the rise of China and the political, economic, foreign policy, and military variables affecting its response.

Domestic Politics and Public Opinion

Domestic Politics

In terms of domestic politics, the most basic point to make about South Korea's response is that China's growing role in and influence on Asian affairs do not loom anywhere near as large in Seoul as they do in Washington. Indeed, for a visitor coming from the United States, where so much attention is focused on the rise of China, it is a bit of a shock to see how low the salience of this issue is in South Korea. As in most democracies, most South Koreans focus on *domestic* issues—such as jobs, private school reform, labor strife, corruption, and a host of other concerns close to the home or pocketbook. Among *foreign policy* issues on the public's mind, China ranks far behind inter-Korean relations, the Six-Party Talks on North Korea's nuclear activities, South Korean–Japanese relations, and U.S.–South Korean relations. China's importance in domestic political terms is currently increasing, but it is still probably safe to say that the *United States* is more of an issue in South Korea than China is.

Neither has China's rise been particularly controversial. Most South Koreans consider China important to their own prosperity. Some, expecting China to emerge as the dominant country in the region over the next decade, see the country becoming their closest bilateral partner. Even less-idealistic South Koreans believe that their nation benefits from China's economic growth and interest in stability on the Korean peninsula and value good relations between the two nations. This includes many South Korean conservatives, with some seeing China in commercial terms and others seeing China as a potential counterweight to Japan.

Generally positive public attitudes toward China have reinforced the relative lack of political contention. For example, South Koreans have long seen China (unlike Japan—or, for that matter, the United States) as the foreign country that most respects them. Until recently, South Koreans have ranked China highly, as a country they value as a long-term partner.[10] To be sure, a range of views exists among the political parties and interest groups on China, and there is criticism of various South Korean policies toward China—particularly the government's handling of the issue of North Korean refugees in China. But fundamentally, China has not been a highly politicized or even partisan issue. It has been neither sufficiently high on the policy agenda nor sufficiently contentious to give people much to fight about. Indeed, outside of very small groups

---

[10] See, for example, Norman D. Levin and Yong-Sup Han, *The Shape of Korea's Future: South Korean Attitudes Toward Unification and Long-Term Security Issues*, Santa Monica, Calif.: RAND Corporation, MR-1092-CAPP, 1999.

on the far ends of the political spectrum, it is hard to identify a genuinely "pro-China" or "anti-China" constituency in South Korean politics.

Notwithstanding this generally relaxed situation, it is striking how much the domestic political atmosphere has soured in the last couple of years toward China. One element of the souring started with a historical dispute over whether the Koreas or China has the rightful claim to the ancient kingdom of Koguryo, which included most of the modern Koreas and a very large section of modern northeast China. Koreans consider Koguryo to be one of their three ancient kingdoms and are accordingly proud of the fact. The dispute emerged when the Chinese Foreign Ministry deleted references to Koguryo from the Korean history section of its Web site in spring 2004 and approached crisis proportions later that fall, when China's state-controlled media called the kingdom a subordinate state under the jurisdiction of Chinese dynasties.[11] This set off large public rallies and a storm of China-bashing in South Korea. Many South Koreans interpreted China's actions as an attempt either to lay claim to Korean territory after reunification or to position itself as the arbiter of the character of a unified Korea. The dispute revealed a level of suspicion of China in South Korea that few commentators had previously noted.[12]

But an even bigger issue is the dramatic expansion of Chinese economic activity in North Korea. China has been a mainstay for North Korea, keeping it afloat for well over a decade by providing food and, especially, energy. Its economic involvement in the North has, however, skyrocketed recently. From 2003 to 2006, Chinese investment in North Korea increased from a mere $1 million to nearly $100 million. China's economic activities during this period expanded to include not only trading in food and energy—which are more than one-half of North Korea's total exports and imports today—but also investing in manufacturing, developing fisheries, and acquiring long-term rights to North Korean mines and ports.[13] This investment, moreover, is spread throughout the country, whereas South Korean investment in North Korea has been limited to two small special economic zones.

The scope and pace of China's economic penetration have stimulated new concerns among South Koreans that China will turn North Korea into a Chinese satel-

---

[11] Standard Korean history texts see Koguryo as one of the three kingdoms of ancient Korea (the other two being Paekchae and Shilla). At its peak, the Koguryo kingdom (37 BCE–668 CE) extended from the northern part of the Korean peninsula to the greater part of what is now Manchuria. For more on the history of this issue, see Park Doo-bok, "History of Goguryeo Calls for Fact-Based Approach," *Korea Focus*, January–February 2004; "Koreas Jointly Counter Chinese Moves to Lay Claims to Ancient Koguryo Kingdom," Yonhap News Agency, February 22, 2004; and Seo Hyun-jin, "Nationalism Fuels Asian History Row," *The Korea Herald*, September 8, 2004.

[12] Bruce Klingner, "China Shock for South Korea," *Asia Times* (online), September 11, 2004.

[13] See, for example, Michael Rank, "Minerals, Railways Draw China to North Korea," *Asia Times*, November 18, 2005; Andrei Lankov, "China Raises Its Stake in North Korea," *Asia Times*, December 17, 2005; and Sekai Nippo, "Korea in Crisis: Is N. Korea Becoming a Chinese Colony?" February 11, 2006.

lite.[14] Although some officials and nongovernmental observers see this penetration as linked more to Chinese efforts to develop its three "rust-belt" provinces of Northeast China than to Chinese designs on North Korea per se, there is a visceral and growing fear among the South Korean public that—were North Korea to collapse—the result might not be Korean reunification but Chinese control of North Korea.

This reaction is certainly rooted in Korean nationalism. It is intensified, however, by the prevalent view that China is exploiting North Korea's needs to bring it under de facto Chinese control. Worse, many South Koreans believe China is doing this at a time when South Korea itself is constrained from fully competing by the unresolved nuclear issue. Whatever his or her political inclinations, no South Korean wants to see North Korea become more integrated economically with Beijing than with Seoul. This concern has set off new debate in South Korea over China's political intentions and appropriate South Korean policy responses. One component is increased support for the view that South Korea needs to hedge against China's regional activism and prevent North Korean economic dependence on China.

Important differences over other issues, some of which are also tinged with nationalist overtones, have reinforced the recent downturn in the mood in South Korea toward China. Perhaps the major difference has to do with China's handling of North Koreans seeking refuge in China. As a general policy, China does not regard these North Koreans as refugees warranting humanitarian transfer to South Korea (or some third country) but as economic migrants or criminals requiring repatriation to North Korea (where they face an uncertain, but certainly unpleasant, fate). In the past couple of years, such treatment has generated bad press in South Korea and negative sentiments toward China among the South Korean public. The effects these have had on South Korean domestic politics have further increased recently because of two developments: the growing prominence of South Korean human rights activists and other nongovernmental organizations (NGOs), which are pushing the South Korean government to take a harder line on the refugee issue, and the sharp decline in Roh Moo-hyun's public popularity and growing lame-duck status, which muffle the voice of those inclined to counter such criticisms.

Incipient Chinese meddling in South Korean politics has reinforced such differences. An apparent Chinese effort to constrain South Korean support for the U.S. goal of strategic flexibility, for example, was poorly received in South Korea.[15] The inter-

---

[14] Anna Fifield, "Beijing's Rising Influence in Pyongyang Raises Fears in Seoul," *Financial Times*, February 3, 2006. For early warnings, see Scott Snyder, "All Eyes on Beijing: Raising the Stakes," *Comparative Connections*, January–March 2005, and Nam Sung Wook, "North Korea Invites China into the Inner Room of Its Economy," *Korea Focus*, May–June 2005.

[15] China's ambassador to South Korea, Ning Fukui, publicly warned South Korea to restrict the role of U.S. troops based in South Korea to its defense and not to allow them to be used in any conflict involving "a third country." Choe Sang-Hun, "Shift GIs in Korea to Taiwan? Never, China Envoy Says," *International Herald Tribune*, March 22, 2006.

vention brought to mind China's earlier heavy-handed efforts to prevent South Korea from allowing Taiwanese flag carriers to resume flights to Seoul (which were suspended when South Korea and China established diplomatic relations). It also reminded South Koreans of other incidents—such as the rough treatment Chinese agents gave South Korean opposition party lawmakers in January 2005 when they tried to hold a press conference in Beijing on the North Korean refugee issue—that highlight the differences between the two countries' political systems. Growing concern at both the official and public levels over South Korea's increasing economic dependence on China has bolstered the effects of such differences and has stimulated latent South Korean wariness—rooted in the long history of Chinese invasions of Korea—over the implications of China's rise for South Korea.

Other recent trends in South Korean politics bolster the sense of changing elite and popular sentiments toward China. The following are among the most significant:

- The formation of new centrist forces in South Korean politics, symbolized in particular by the emergence of the new right (and, to a lesser extent, the new left) and new conservative NGOs. These groups generally share the policy orientations of their respective predecessors. But they are tired of South Korea's political parties' ideological strife and rigidly dogmatic policy positioning and are looking for pragmatic, practical responses to the challenges Korea faces.[16] The relatively nonideological orientation of these forces—and, in the case of the new right, their strong emphasis on global interdependence and human rights—strengthens those in South Korea calling for greater balance in South Korean policies toward China.

- A split among the progressives themselves between the progressive realists and the purists. The former group, widely said to include President Roh himself, has learned much during its time in power and has come to regard strong relations with the United States as the essential foundation for its policies. The latter group, generally described as consisting of a small number of individuals who are focused on achieving greater South Korean independence and view China as a potential counterweight to the United States, has demonstrated neither the same learning nor balance. The ascendance of the former, bolstered in part by North Korea's

---

[16] For early journalistic accounts of these new forces, see Yu Jae-dong and Min Dong-yong, "New Right Movement Finds Supporters," *Dong-A Ilbo*, November 22, 2004; Kim So Young, "New Conservative Groups Band Against Roh, Uri Party," *The Korea Herald*, November 30, 2004; and Min Seong-jae, "The 'New Right': How New Is It?" *JoongAng Daily*, March 14, 2005. For more-recent accounts, see Ser Myo-ja and Bae Young-dae, "'New Right' Group Launched," *JoongAng Daily*, November 8, 2005; Lee Chi-dong, "Would-Be Moderates Roll Up Sleeves to Tackle Ideological Conflict," Yonhap News Agency, November 29, 2005; Jung Sung-ki, "New Ideological Groups to Gain Momentum," *The Korea Times*, January 8, 2006a; Chun Su-jin and Bae Young-dae, "Postwar History Gets Makeover from a 'New Right' Perspective," *JoongAng Daily*, February 4, 2006; and Jin-hyun Kim, "Finding a New Center or a Zigzag? Elections and FTA Negotiations with the U.S.," *PacNet Newsletter*, No. 9A, March 10, 2006. See also the "New Right" Web site (in Japanese).

recalcitrance on the nuclear issue, is fostering greater South Korean pragmatism on a range of issues, including those related to China.

- The rise of a new "new generation," consisting of those in their 20s. By all accounts, this newest generation is an entirely different breed from its predecessors (the so-called *386 generation*).[17] Self-confident, comfortable in their skins, and heavily internationalized as a result of their access to and familiarity with information technologies, the emergence of this much-less-ideological generation is contributing to hopes for decreased political polarization and the development of a more-pragmatic South Korean polity.

Popular Views and Public Opinion

These developments have begun to affect the general mood toward China. They have also begun to affect public attitudes themselves. Polls now show China lagging behind the United States in perceived importance to South Korea and value as a future partner. A November 2005 poll by the *Dong-A Ilbo*, for example, showed that nearly twice as many South Koreans think the South Korean government should see the United States as the most important country for South Korea's diplomatic relations (55.2 percent) as see China in that role (28.6 percent).[18] Other polls show that South Koreans overwhelmingly see the United States rather than China as the country most helpful to South Korea (82 to 6 percent, respectively) and as South Korea's preferred foreign partner (79 percent among opinion leaders and 53 percent among the public at large for the United States, versus 13 and 24 percent, respectively, for China). The sense of a significant decline in public attitudes toward China is further bolstered by a 2005 poll that the Gallup organization conducted for the U.S. Department of State. This poll, one of many periodic surveys widely considered to be the most authoritative sampling of South Korean public opinion, found that favorable opinions of China had fallen from the 70-percent level a couple of years earlier to 53 percent in November 2005, while South Koreans who identified the United States as their key security partner "over the next decade" (62 percent) vastly outnumbered those who so identified China (12 percent).[19] As if to add an exclamation point, another South Korean poll in 2006 showed that a robust 38 percent of South Koreans identified China as the biggest threat to South Korea "ten years from now," with Japan following at 24 percent,

---

[17] Working backward, the "386 generation" denotes South Koreans who were born in the 1960s, attended college in the 1980s, and were in their 30s when the term was coined in the 1990s. Many of this generation were active in the movement for democracy that ultimately ended South Korea's military rule.

[18] The Maureen and Mike Mansfield Foundation, tr., "November 2005 *Dong-A Ilbo* Opinion Poll on the Roh Administration's Performance and Potential Presidential Candidates," Mansfield Asian Opinion Poll Database, November 5, 2005.

[19] U.S. Department of State, Office of Research, Bureau of Intelligence and Research, "INR Poll: Asian Views of China," Opinion Analysis, Washington, D.C., November 9, 2005.

North Korea ranking third at 21 percent, and the United States coming in at less than 15 percent.[20]

Taken together, these developments have begun to alter China's image in South Korea and increase public doubts about China's long-term intentions. They have also heightened the perceived need for balance in South Korean policies toward China, especially among younger government officials (in their 40s and 50s) at the director-general level. One by-product is increased awareness of the importance of, and support for, the U.S.–South Korean relationship.[21] Polls now show that a large majority of South Koreans believes the United States should be the priority among South Korea's bilateral relationships (85.1 percent, as opposed to 11.9 percent for inter-Korean relations and 2.0 percent for South Korean–Chinese relations); opposes either partial (13.9 percent) or complete (59.4 percent) withdrawal of U.S. troops from Korea (as opposed to the 23.8 percent favoring the eventual withdrawal of all U.S. troops except a "minimum level of presence" and the 1.0 percent wanting a complete withdrawal); and wants either to maintain the status quo or to further strengthen the U.S.–South Korean relationship (11.9 percent and 54.5 percent, respectively), rather than "be more independent and diversify its alliance relations" (28.7 percent).[22]

Economic Responses

On the economic side, the explosive growth of mutual trade and investment over the past decade has raised China's importance to number one for South Korea in several key areas. China is now South Korea's largest export market, for example. Exports to China in 2006 reached $69.5 billion, accounting for 21.3 percent of South Korea's total exports (Figure 4.1). This is a striking contrast with the situation as recently as 1996: South Korea's exports to China then amounted to just 8.8 percent of total exports. In dollar terms, South Korea's exports to China rose more than six times between 1996 and 2006, more than twice as fast as the total export growth.

The makeup of South Korea's exports to China has shifted from intermediate goods for light manufacturing to electronics and chemicals. In 1996, the largest Korean export to China was the textiles used in China's burgeoning clothing industry. Plastics, iron and steel, and petroleum products ranked second, fourth, and fifth. By 2006, textiles had been supplanted by electronics, office equipment, and telecommunications

---

[20] This poll by the state-funded Korea Institute for Defense Analyses was widely reported in South Korea. For a Western account, see "South Koreans See China as Threat Later, Not North—Poll," Reuters, March 20, 2006.

[21] For a good summary of public opinion polls documenting this recent trend, see Lee Nae-Young, "South Korea and the U.S.–ROK Alliance—Public Opinion About ROK–U.S. Relations," in Korea Economic Institute, *Challenges Posed by the DPRK for the Alliance and the Region*, Washington, D.C., 2006.

[22] The Maureen and Mike Mansfield Foundation, tr., "*Monthly JoongAng* Survey Research on US-Korea Alliance," June 30–July 8, 2005.

Figure 4.1
South Korea's Major Export Markets, Selected Years

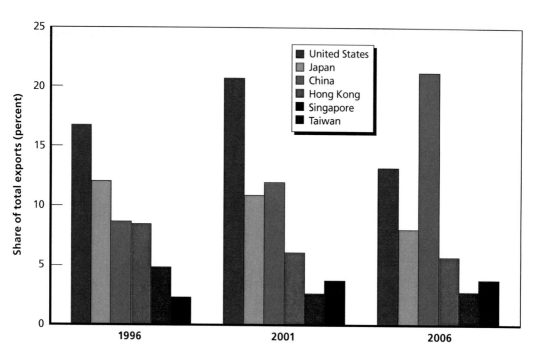

SOURCE: UN Statistics Division, 1996, 2001, 2006.
RAND *MG736-4.1*

equipment (Figure 4.2). South Korean manufacturers were shipping components to Chinese plants for assembly of household electronics, computers, and mobile phones. This recent trade pattern reflects a complementary division of labor among industries resulting from the continuing gap between technology and human capital. The general complementarity has made China a magnet for Korean investment and an engine for South Korea's own growth.

Imports from China have also grown rapidly (Figure 4.3). China has become South Korea's second largest source of imports, supplanting the United States. China now accounts for 15.7 percent of South Korea's imports, compared to just 5.7 percent in 1996. As with exports, imports have shifted from light manufactures and intermediate goods to electronics and telecommunications equipment, part of the two-way exchange of components and finished products that takes place between subsidiaries of the large South Korean conglomerates in China and South Korea and their suppliers. The flows are very large: Imports of electronics, office equipment, and telecommunications equipment now account for over one-third of South Korea's imports from China. These shifts in imports illustrate how the trade structure is becoming dominated on both sides by intermediate goods (such as parts for electronic equipment, motor vehicles, and electric machinery), particularly those for high-technology industries, such as telecommunications and electronic equipment.

Figure 4.2
Composition of South Korean Exports to China, 2006

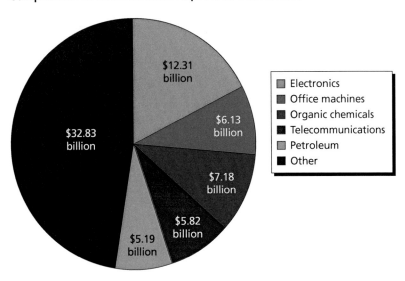

SOURCE: UN Statistics Division, 2006.
RAND *MG736-4.2*

Figure 4.3
Composition of South Korean Imports from China, 2006

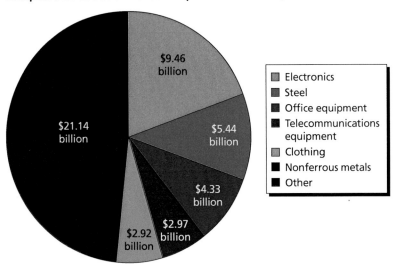

SOURCE: UN Statistics Division, 2006.
RAND *MG736-4.3*

China has also become the largest destination for South Korea's FDI. As Figure 4.4 shows, South Korea's annual direct investment in China has increased sharply in the last several years, far surpassing its annual investment in the United States. With this sharp increase, South Korea's cumulative FDI in China reached an estimated

Figure 4.4
South Korea's Annual FDI in the United States and China, 1995–2005

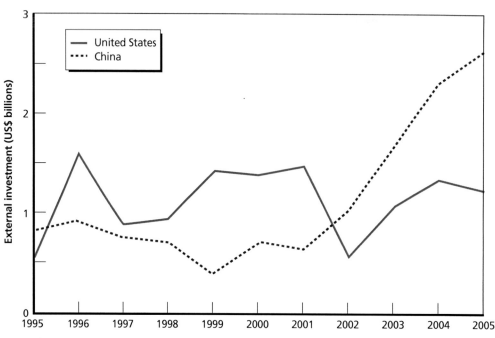

SOURCE: The Export-Import Bank of Korea, 1995–2005.
RAND MG736-4.4

$14.3 billion by the end of March 2006. As indicated in Figure 4.5, this is only slightly less than South Korea's cumulative FDI in the United States ($15.5 billion) and is 24 percent of South Korea's cumulative FDI globally.

The relative ease South Korean firms have had entering the Chinese market and the technological and human resource gap between the two countries have stimulated explosive growth in South Korean trade and investment. Another stimulant has been business conditions inside South Korea itself that created something of a push toward China. South Korean businessmen, especially in the large conglomerates (*chaebol*), have long complained about rigid government regulations over the business sector. Many of them cite the prolabor policies and increases in property, real estate transaction, and other taxes that the Roh Moo-hyun government has imposed as factors contributing to their interest in China. Some describe China almost as an escape from the oppressive climate in South Korea.[23]

China itself is much less a factor when it comes to Chinese investment in South Korea. By the end of 2005, cumulative U.S. investment reached nearly $35 billion,

---

[23] One businessman put it even more starkly in an interview, saying that South Korean businessmen would like to stay in South Korea, but given the high government taxes, high labor costs, intense labor strife, and general attitude of the government toward business, this was, for many of them, "simply not an alternative."

Figure 4.5
South Korea's Cumulative FDI, by Destination, 2006

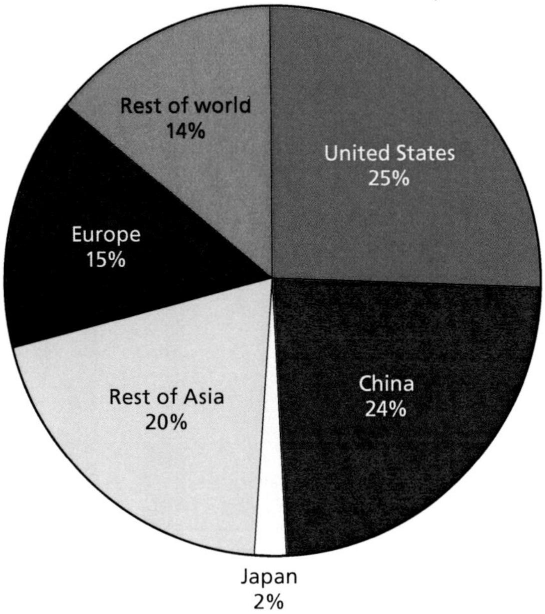

SOURCE: The Export-Import Bank of Korea, 2006.
RAND *MG736-4.5*

30 percent of the cumulative FDI in South Korea between 1962 and 2005. Japan ranks second, at $17.4 billion (15 percent). China's cumulative investment, in contrast, is tiny: $1.8 billion, a mere 2 percent of the total cumulative FDI in South Korea. Although China's annual investment in South Korea has increased in the past few years, as shown in Figure 4.6, the scale remains quite small relative to that of the United States and Japan. Moreover, China's investment in South Korea is highly concentrated, with more than 80 percent going toward transportation equipment, chemicals, and a few other manufacturing industries. In contrast, U.S. investment in South Korea is much more diversified and is oriented toward South Korea's service industries.

Fading Optimism and Growing Concerns

Despite these beneficial economic relations, the earlier South Korean exuberance for China's economic growth is waning, even in business circles. To some extent, this is a result of the realization that China poses a growing challenge to South Korean competitiveness in both Chinese and world markets. South Korean businessmen vary in their estimates of how long their competitive advantage will remain in China's market. But most see the Chinese as steadily—and in some cases rapidly—bridging the gap between the two sides in technology and human capital on which the current comple-

Figure 4.6
FDI from the United States, Japan, and China, 1995–2005

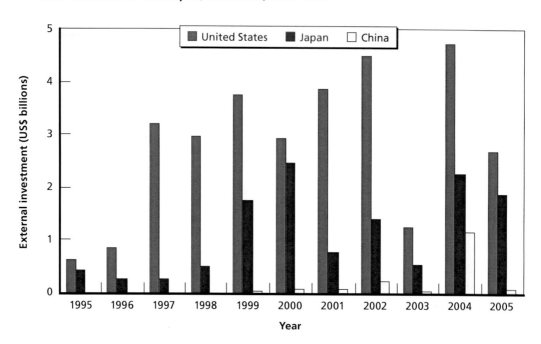

SOURCE: South Korea, Ministry of Commerce, Industry, and Environment, 1995–2005.
RAND *MG736-4.6*

mentary intraindustry division of labor rests. Even South Korean businessmen who have been successful in China stress that their countrymen do not have much time.

Although South Korea has generally maintained its position in world markets despite China's rapid expansion, the composition of China's exports now is quite similar to South Korea's. As a result, South Korea's shares of the world export market frequently move in the opposite direction of China's in regional and product markets. South Korea's decreasing market shares, moreover, are not limited to traditional labor-intensive industries, such as footwear, textiles, and clothing, but are spreading to high-technology industries, such as electronic parts and semiconductors. Hardly a day goes by without some South Korean official, scholar, or commentator warning about China's increasing threat to South Korea's competitiveness and urging its people to either increase investment in research and development and human resource training, add more value to existing products, or find other ways to climb the technology ladder rapidly.[24]

Other economic factors undoubtedly also contribute to the fading of the "China boom" in South Korea today. The high failure rate of South Korean companies in

---

[24] See, for a recent example, Kim Sung-jin, "Finance Minister Warns Against China Threat," *The Korea Times*, March 21, 2006.

China, for example, has begun to sober many small- and medium-sized enterprises and spur a search for new strategies to compete in China's market. Increased awareness of the speed with which China is ascending the learning curve has made executives more cautious about long-term projections, as has growing unease about China's internal conditions. The diminished exuberance for China may also, in part, be a natural result of economic interactions that are nearing a saturation point, as the recent slowdown in the growth rate of South Korean investments suggests.

Two other trends reinforce this decreased optimism. One is what economists describe as *job losses* (the media and public characterize it more colorfully, as a *hollowing out*) of South Korea's economy as South Korean companies shift their manufacturing bases to China. With roughly 85 percent of South Korea's investments in China directed either to manufacturing products for eventual export or to exploiting China's cheap labor, the effect on South Korean jobs could be significant. This is particularly true in the context of additional overseas production by South Korean companies and increasing labor productivity inside South Korea itself.

The other trend is a growing awareness at both the official and public levels of South Korea's potential vulnerability to Chinese economic and other pressures. Seoul's new interest in an FTA with Washington—something in which South Korean leaders had long shown little interest because they were concerned that politically important domestic constituencies would react adversely—is one manifestation. Another is increasing government emphasis on diversification and the need for companies to explore potential new markets in India, Thailand, Vietnam, and other parts of Asia. Both evince growing concern that South Korea is becoming too dependent on China and that it needs to protect itself through a relationship with large economies outside of China's sphere of influence.

To be sure, China will remain a focus of South Korean energies as long as the Chinese economy keeps growing. But the previous excitement about China is being replaced by careful, and more sober, assessments. This is particularly true for small- and medium-sized enterprises, whose capabilities and operating strategies are generally much more limited than those of the large South Korean conglomerates. These enterprises are challenged not only by China but by the information technology revolution and by globalization more broadly.[25] But even the *chaebol* are seriously assessing the long-term challenge of China.

South Korea's short-term strategy for dealing with China's economic rise is to seek a division of labor that effectively cedes labor-intensive areas to China and concentrates South Korean energies on services, higher technology intermediate goods, and research and development. The dominant view—especially in the large South

---

[25] A more-careful differentiation would distinguish among the small- and medium-sized enterprises themselves, with some doing well in China (such as those who subcontract for the large *chaebol* and some who are highly specialized) and most of the others being in trouble. But the broad distinction still is useful.

Korean enterprises—is that China's ongoing growth and the continuing technological gap between China and South Korea will keep this strategy viable for the next decade or so. But there is a wide consensus in South Korea that, for the long term, it must rapidly climb the technology ladder. The aim is to move to higher-end manufacturing and knowledge-intensive service industries, while restructuring domestic industries. At the same time, the country is seeking to balance its growing dependence on the Chinese market through increased diversification.

Perhaps ironically, this consensus highlights the continued importance of South Korea's economic ties with the United States. The United States not only leads the world in terms of market size, investment opportunities, and technological capabilities but is also the source of many of South Korea's high-value technologies. More directly, the United States leads in knowledge-intensive services that are both underdeveloped in South Korea and critical to its long-term productivity growth.[26] In this sense, South Korea's commitment to an FTA with the United States can accurately be seen as the result of two important trends: growing South Korean fears of excessive dependence on China and awareness of the importance of the United States to South Korea's own long-term economic competitiveness. The decision to pursue an FTA with the United States itself constitutes, at least in part, an important response to the rise of China.

Assessing Winners and Losers

In general, as mentioned above, the large *chaebol* have done very well in China, as have many of the small- and medium-sized enterprises that either subcontract for the *chaebol* or provide highly specialized products and services. Many other small- and medium-sized enterprises have been adversely affected. More specifically, South Korean export industries involved in ships and other transportation equipment, petroleum products, and specialized machinery have had considerable success. Those involved in traditional labor-intensive industries (such as textiles, clothing, and footwear), low-technology industries, and some subsectors of electronic, telecommunication, and other high-technology industries (such as semiconductors and electronic parts and components) have suffered from competition from China. Some of these industries (such as footwear) are being phased out of the world export market.

This process is not without political effect. Declining industries in South Korea, as in other democracies, seek protection against foreign competition. In particular, the sharp decline in labor-intensive industries has increased the salience of the issue of jobs in an economy that is growing much more slowly than it has in the past. Any government must demonstrate sensitivity on this issue. More broadly, the tough competition

---

[26] These are among the points the United States itself is making to help increase public support in South Korea for the FTA. See, for example, Alexander Vershbow, U.S. Ambassador to the Republic of Korea, "U.S.–Korea Free Trade Agreement: A Path to Sustainable Growth," speech, Seoul: Institute for Global Economics, February 14, 2006, and Wendy Cutler, U.S. Trade Representative, "United States–Korea Free Trade Agreement: A Win-Win Proposition," speech, Seoul: American Chamber of Commerce, March 7, 2006.

probably reinforces South Korea's generally insular political culture and strengthens opposition by particular civic and other interest groups to additional FTAs and foreign pressures for further opening the South Korean market.

In policy terms, however, the importance of specific winners and losers appears limited. For one thing, as noted above, the awareness of China's importance to South Korea, particularly in terms of the South Korean economy, is broadly shared. Most South Koreans see expanded economic ties with China as essential to both South Korea's current performance and future prospects; even many of the losers accept the need to avoid riling the bilateral relationship.

Similarly, most South Koreans recognize the need in today's global economy for labor-intensive and low-technology industries to seek new business in higher-technology areas. The government's drumbeat on the need for South Korean firms to increase their emphasis on developing human resources and technology and the nearly universal South Korean aspiration to become one of the world's leading high-tech nations reinforce this general recognition. In this environment, it is easier to mobilize mass demonstrations against the import of U.S. movies than to generate significant political support in South Korea for firms thrown out of business and workers thrown out of work because of Chinese competition.[27]

Among the winners, the key actors are the large, conservative conglomerates, most of which have a *global* view of their interests and approach China as one component of a global strategy. Moreover, as perhaps the major interest group in South Korea outside the military with strong interests in maintaining close ties with the United States, few members want to see good relations with China come at the expense of South Korea's relationship with the United States.

The major reason for the limited importance of specific winners and losers in policy terms, however, is more practical: Roh Moo-hyun's reformist, "people's participatory government" does not appear to listen much to either group. This is in part a product of the government's philosophical and policy shift away from economic growth toward political reform and economic redistribution, a shift that has reinforced the Roh administration's innate suspicions of the business community and precipitated a significant decline in the latter's traditional political standing and influence. It is also a product of the administration's prolabor orientation, which increases strains and suspicions on both sides of the government-business relationship. Although the government has tried at times to open communication channels with the business sector, the results have been meager. Certainly, few South Korean businessmen see themselves as having significant political influence. When asked about their access to and influence on the government today, most respond with something between a laugh and a snort.

---

27 The relative lack of pressure from labor groups is particularly striking, given their concern with a "hollowing out" of the South Korean economy and position as a key component of President Roh's constituency. As their support for development of the Kaesong Industrial Zone in North Korea suggests, however, the lack of visible protest over the outsourcing of South Korean jobs is not limited to the case of China.

Diplomatic and Foreign Policy Responses

South Korea's foreign policy and diplomacy have no overarching framework today. As the variety of phrases South Korean leaders use to describe their foreign policy and diplomatic objectives may suggest ("peace and prosperity policy," "hub of Northeast Asia," "cooperative self-reliance," "balancing role," "middle-power role," etc.), they are groping for a vision or policy framework to characterize South Korea's foreign policy. Thus far, however, they have had difficulty communicating any clear sense of direction. This has given South Korean policies a somewhat ambiguous quality, with the government seeming to swing or vacillate between alternative dispositions.

Having said that, the underlying *thrust* of South Korean foreign policy is toward achieving two long-standing aspirations. The first is to break out of its perceived position as a junior partner to the United States and to greatly improve its ability to protect its *own* sovereign interests.[28] The second is to carve out a regional and broader global role that reflects South Korea's demonstrable political, military, and diplomatic success. The central aim is to become more of an actor—rather than simply being acted upon—that can play a useful role building bridges in Asia and beyond.

This underlying thrust appears to be predicated on three main assumptions: that the post–Cold War world and the emerging rivalry between China and Japan provide both a degree of policy space for South Korea and a potentially useful role to play, that South Korea's own successful transformation gives it the capabilities that make it an attractive candidate for that role, and that playing such a role is not only the way to fulfill South Korea's desire to become more of a regional and international actor but also the key to peace on the Korean peninsula. Implicit in South Korean aspirations is a long-term vision of Korea as something of a model nation-state, a unified, democratic country that constitutes a threat to no one and plays a useful role helping others get along.

Most Koreans intuitively understand the importance of China for achieving this vision. This understanding has underpinned the expansion of South Korean–Chinese interactions since diplomatic relations were formally established in 1992. The substantive content of these interactions has focused overwhelmingly on two issues: promoting South Korean–Chinese economic cooperation and dealing with North Korea. This growth, however, has helped foster a broader atmosphere of cordiality and awareness of mutual interest.

Summit diplomacy has strengthened this awareness. The presidents of both countries have traveled to each other's capitals on official visits several times over the

---

[28] This aspiration, which was present as far back as the Park Chung-Hee era (the 1960s and 1970s), was a notable feature of the Roh Tae-woo "Nordpolitik" policies (the late 1980s through the early 1990s). It became particularly pronounced under the government of Kim Young-Sam as a result of strongly negative South Korean reactions to U.S. policies during the 1994–1996 nuclear crisis with North Korea. For details, see Larson and Levin, 2004.

past decade. Building on the rhetorical agreement reached between Chinese President Jiang Zemin and South Korean President Kim Dae-jung in 1998 to establish a cooperative partnership, Premier Zhu Rongji and President Kim agreed two years later to upgrade relations by pursuing comprehensive cooperatives ties. These focused heavily on expanding economic cooperation (four of the eight cooperative activities identified, for example, involved expanded trade or investment efforts). But they also called for continued high-level political exchanges, as well as mutual visits of warships. During President Roh's visit to China in July 2003, both countries agreed to continue to develop a comprehensive cooperative partnership, signing specific agreements to strengthen economic cooperation in 17 core sectors, including information technologies, automobiles, and steel.

In the course of this diplomacy, China has officially backed South Korea's engagement policy toward North Korea, while Seoul has publicly endorsed Beijing's One-China policy and supported China's entry into the World Trade Organization. During the era of Japanese Prime Minister Koizumi (2001–2006), Seoul's interest in good relations with Beijing was reinforced by growing concerns about domestic political trends in Japan, Japanese efforts to secure permanent membership on the UN Security Council, and heightened tensions with Japan over disputed territories.

The value South Korean leaders place on good relations is reflected in the efforts they have made to prevent periodic disputes on particular issues (such as Koguryo and incidents of contamination in imported food products) from damaging the bilateral relationship. South Korean officials work assiduously with China to dampen such disputes when they arise or flare up, simultaneously urging South Koreans to avoid reactions that might harm larger interests.[29] The importance South Korea places on good relations is also reflected in the January 2006 agreement to establish a regular exchange mechanism between China's National People's Congress and South Korea's National Assembly. Intended to enhance bilateral ties, this represents the first time the South Korean legislature has signed such a cooperation agreement with a foreign parliament.

Notwithstanding South Korea's perceived interest in harmonious bilateral relations, it is important to note that the South Korean–Chinese relationship today is neither robust nor multidimensional. On the diplomatic side, China hardly registers on the South Korean policy agenda beyond issues dealing with North Korea. A formal Foreign Ministry listing of South Korea's key diplomatic tasks, for example, includes eight separate sets of efforts, starting with the "peaceful resolution of the North Korean nuclear issue" (task 1) and "efforts to build a comprehensive and dynamic South Korean–U.S. alliance" (task 2) and ending with "diplomatic contribution to the creation of new job opportunities" (task 8). But expanding relations with China

---

[29] This contrasts with how the Roh administration generally responds to issues in South Korean–Japanese relations, often showing the opposite tendency.

is not specifically included.[30] The limited depth of South Korean–Chinese diplomatic relations is reflected even in how they deal with Japanese issues. Although both sides have tended to make similar statements on sensitive issues (such as Yasukuni Shrine visits and history textbooks), there is little evidence to date of formal South Korean–Chinese efforts to produce a coordinated response to Japanese actions of mutual concern. Indeed, their divergent responses to Prime Minister Abe's election as Japanese prime minister suggest the opposite: China turned down the heat and used Abe's election as an opportunity to improve Chinese-Japanese relations, but South Korea continued to play the Japan card and allowed Seoul's ties with Tokyo to fester.

In addition, South Korean leaders have no clear guidelines, doctrines, or policy statements directing the development of South Korean–Chinese diplomatic relations. Their absence hinders the setting of concrete policy goals. More to the point, little energy is going into expanding the relationship. As noted above, China is not high on South Korea's policy agenda, in part because it is not a major domestic political issue. At the same time, long-standing irritants—such as China's handling of North Korean refugees and refusal to discuss confidence-building measures for potential scenarios involving North Korea, even informally—continue to constrain major improvements in South Korean–Chinese relations. Perhaps less directly, so too does China's vague support for Korean unification—a lack of clarity noted (if not widely discussed) by many in the South Korean foreign policy establishment.

In this context, such issues as Koguryo, North Korean refugees, and China's ham-handed statements regarding U.S. strategic flexibility not only constitute diplomatic problems for South Korea but also revive latent South Korean wariness about China and help undermine advocates of expanded South Korean–Chinese ties. Indeed, the single biggest way China is currently registering in South Korea has to do with its recent economic penetration of North Korea. As noted above, this development has been influential in part because of the nearly universal South Korean concern that China will turn the North into a Chinese satellite. But it also is because of the way this issue stirs up public sensitivities about Chinese challenges to Korean sovereignty.

In a nutshell, South Korea's diplomatic response to the rise of China reflects efforts to benefit from China's rapid economic growth, and to leverage Beijing's rise to advance other important South Korean policy interests—most of which relate to North Korea. However, the general salience of the China issue in South Korea today is low.

---

[30] The Web site of the Ministry of Foreign Affairs and Trade makes only two brief references to China. The first, under task 6 (on the "development of a future-oriented global diplomacy"), states that "Korea will further develop its comprehensive cooperative partnership with China and secure China's cooperation in resolving the North Korean nuclear issue and promoting reforms in North Korea." The second, under task 4 (described as "laying the diplomatic groundwork for the development of a Northeast Asian economic hub") is more indirect, stating that cooperation between South Korea, China, and Japan is "vital" and that South Korea will participate in the trilateral committee between the respective foreign ministers to regularize consultations and help promote regional cooperation among the three nations.

South Koreans are not investing much energy in the bilateral relationship, and grow-ing uncertainties about China and its long-term intentions constrain major advances in South Korean–Chinese ties. The souring of the public mood toward China in recent months is palpably dampening South Korean enthusiasm for expanded South Korean–Chinese relations.

For these reasons, the development of South Korean–Chinese diplomatic ties should not be overstated. Bilateral interactions are certainly growing, with cooperation developing when the interests of the two sides clearly converge. But the diplomatic rela-tionship remains thin and, thus far, of limited substance apart from the North Korea issue. Meanwhile, concerns are growing in South Korea about how China might affect South Korea's ability to achieve core national objectives.

The main area in which China does have significant influence is in the Six-Party Talks. South Koreans have high hopes for China's efforts toward a peaceful resolution of the North Korean nuclear issue, and there is broad agreement between the two, at least on tactical approaches.[31] South Koreans are looking to China more broadly to help prevent a sudden North Korean collapse and encourage internal reform and external opening in North Korea. These goals loom large in South Korea and should not be understated. Among other things (as discussed below), they contribute to South Korean sensitivity about appearing to be against China or appearing to collude with the United States in "containing" China.

Defense Policy Responses

Defense Policy

The starting point for assessing South Korea's military policy is a general perception that the nation's security environment is relatively benign, a view that many current government officials outside the Ministry of National Defense (MND) and the public at large share. Even North Korea's July 2006 missile tests did not significantly alter this general perception.[32] To be sure, the government takes North Korea's nuclear programs very seriously—as do most South Koreans in the wake of the nuclear test—and is com-mitted to their dismantling. At the same time, however, there is a tendency in both official and public circles to regard the nuclear issue as being well on its way toward resolution; by fall 2007, attention had shifted to establishing a "peace regime" on the Korean peninsula. The public perception of China has been particularly relaxed, with most South Koreans expecting the exigencies of China's internal situation to keep it

---

[31] Potentially, China could also wield important influence over negotiations toward a "peace regime" for the Korean peninsula, should such a process get started.

[32] Press reports characterize the public reaction in South Korea to the missile tests, particularly among the younger generation, as indifference, with little concern manifested over a North Korean threat. For example, see Kim Sue-young, "South Koreans Insensible to Missile Tests," *The Korea Times*, July 9, 2006.

focused on its own domestic development long into the future. Indeed, if the public has any widespread *military* concerns related to China, it is probably that the United States might drag South Korea into a war against its wishes.

South Korean military planners, of course, are not quite as sanguine about North Korea. Traditionally, this has been virtually their singular focus, the main objective being to identify the capabilities required to counter—in conjunction with the United States—a potential North Korean invasion. South Korean military planners remain concerned about the continuing array of conventional power that North Korea has forward deployed close to the Demilitarized Zone and about North Korea's determined pursuit of weapons of mass destruction. They also are concerned about North Korea's missile-development efforts and destabilizing transfers of weapon systems and related goods and technologies. South Korean Defense Minister Kim Jang-soo effectively conveyed the strength of these concerns in a press conference with U.S. Secretary of Defense Robert Gates in November 2007. "Although it is true that North Korea has begun the process of disabling its nuclear program," he said,

> we cannot say that the threat from North Korea has reduced tangibly or discernibly. We don't have any intelligence to indicate that sort of conclusion . . . . What is certain is that North Korea is continuing to pursue the acquisition of asymmetrical weapons. So therefore, we cannot conclude that the threat from North Korea has been reduced.[33]

These concerns continue to influence South Korean defense plans and military procurement programs.

Over the last two decades, however, as North Korea's economy has imploded and as the Cold War structure of world politics collapsed, the thrust in South Korean long-range defense planning has shifted perceptibly away from these threats toward two broader concerns: rapid global advances in military technologies and the need to develop more self-reliant defense capabilities for the period after Korea's unification.

This thrust has been reflected in South Korean force improvement programs since at least the mid-1990s, which have placed a high priority on procuring advanced command, control, communications, computers, and intelligence systems; early warning and long-range strike capabilities; a blue-water navy; and naval air-defense capabilities.[34] Documents accidentally posted on the Web site of South Korea's weapon procurement office suggest that South Korea's strategic weapon plans for the middle term (15 years) include developing nuclear-powered submarines, long-range fighters, and

---

[33] Robert M. Gates, U.S. Secretary of Defense, and Kim Jang-soo, Republic of Korea Minister of National Defense, transcript of joint press conference, Seoul, November 7, 2007.

[34] For a useful summary, see Jane's, "South Korea at a Glance, Jane's Sentinel Security Assessment—China and Northeast Asia," January 13, 2006a.

unmanned aerial surveillance vehicles.[35] These plans are intended less to counter anticipated North Korean aggression than to develop an elite force capable of waging high-
tech warfare more broadly in the 21st century.

This thrust is also reflected in MND's recent military transformation plan.[36] This
sweeping plan calls for radical changes in the structure of South Korea's military forces
by the year 2020—including a dramatic 57-percent reduction in the number of army
divisions (from 47 to 20) and a 27 percent cutback in the number of military personnel (from 681,000 to 500,000, with the army alone reduced by nearly one-third, from
548,000 to 371,000). The goal is to improve the forces' qualitative capabilities while
reducing their size and the number of weapon systems.

Defense Reform 2020 addresses the need for structural reform in the South Korean
military occasioned by South Korea's declining birth rate and other environmental
changes. It also addresses the broader global trend toward military transformation in
response to developments in information and other technologies. In laying out the
components of South Korea's transformation, moreover, it provides a useful guide to
South Korean intentions for the near future. What the reform plan does not provide
is a detailed assessment of the projected military capabilities of North Korea (which
continues to maintain a standing military in excess of 1 million men) or of other neighboring powers. Neither is there any explicit linkage between the transformation plan
and the long-term security challenges of potential adversaries.[37]

In this context, it is not surprising that many knowledgeable observers both inside
and outside South Korea describe its force improvement programs as not being driven
by any specific perceived threat. South Korean force development plans, they insist,
are based on general notions of what is currently required for a middle-ranking power
or on a desire to avoid being sandwiched in an arms race between China and Japan,
although interest in developing South Korea's industrial technology also plays a role.
The major goal is to develop the kinds of capabilities (such as strategically placed naval
bases, advanced fighter planes, Aegis-equipped destroyers, and state-of-the-art submarines) necessary for South Korea to be taken seriously as a regional actor.[38]

This general characterization of South Korean defense planning is apt for the
China factor as well. MND planners certainly see China as an emerging power and are

---

[35] Jin Dae-woong, "Junior Officials Blamed for Secrets Leak," *The Korea Herald*, January 12, 2006.

[36] Republic of Korea, MND, *Defense Reform 2020*, Eng. undated.

[37] For a preliminary attempt to make such a linkage, see Bruce W. Bennett, *A Brief Analysis of the Republic of
Korea's Defense Reform Plan*, Santa Monica, Calif.: RAND Corporation, OP-165-OSD, 2006. For other useful
commentaries, see Hong Kyu-dok, "The Strategic Linkage Between the Republic of Korea's Defense Reform
2020 and Changing Security Environment," *Korea Focus*, April 2006; Han Yong-sup, "Analyzing South Korea's
Defense Reform 2020," *The Korean Journal of Defense Analysis*, Spring 2006.

[38] See, for example, Open Source Center, *OSC Analysis 08 June: ROKAF Upgrade, Modernization Continues
Despite Challenges*, June 8, 2007; Jin Dae-woong, "South Korea Eyes High-Tech Navy," *The Korea Herald*, June
4, 2007; Jung Sung-ki, "'Peace Island' in Dilemma Over Naval Base," *The Korea Times*, July 17, 2006b.

aware of its improving military capabilities. Indeed, with the possible exception of the-ater missile capabilities (the importance of which appears to be little appreciated), the MND is generally aware of most important military trends. But it is not particularly worried about China. Visions of a standing Korean military force of some 400,000 to 500,000 troops after unification (Defense 2020) suggest that China's emergence may not be completely missing from MND's long-term thinking.[39] South Korea's long-term defense buildup plan, however, offers little evidence of a perceived need to develop the capabilities required for a war with China—much of which would be fought on land and, most likely, over North Korea.

Accordingly, few observers see China as a driving force today behind South Korea's long-term defense buildup. Indeed, during off-the-record conversations in South Korea in 2006, individuals involved in or knowledgeable about South Korean defense plan-ning insist that China is a negligible factor and that there has been little internal debate over the implications of China's rise for South Korea. In part this is because of the absence of any major South Korean military issues with China. In part it is because the South Korean military sees China's near-term role in North Korea as positive and generally considers China's broader regional and global role as an issue for the United States. And in part it is because of the larger political climate in Seoul, which makes it difficult to address the military implications of China's long-term rise for South Korea (just as it is virtually impossible to address what a nuclear North Korea would mean for South Koreans).[40] China thus does not drive South Korea's force development. If any country is widely said to influence South Korea's long-term defense calculations, it is Japan, not China.[41]

China's influence on South Korean security cooperation with the United States is more significant. This is reflected first and foremost in conspicuous South Korean sensitivity toward perceived Chinese interests. Few suggestions for new or expanded security cooperation are made without eliciting a "what will China think" or "how will China respond" reaction from South Korea. As South Korea's refusal to partici-pate in U.S.–led theater ballistic missile efforts indicates, this sensitivity manifests itself in a marked reluctance, and occasional unwillingness, to engage in certain kinds of security activities. Some of this relates to fears that South Korea will lose control over matters related to its sovereign interests, as shown by its lack of enthusiasm for develop-ing a new joint U.S.–South Korean war plan for dealing with potential instability in North Korea. In particular, concerns have been both strong and visceral among senior

---

[39] Republic of Korea, MND, undated.

[40] A bureaucratic shift in the last few years giving much greater authority over South Korean defense policy to the National Security Council and, to a lesser extent, parts of the Ministry of Foreign Affairs has reinforced this climate. With MND becoming more of an executor of policy than a decisionmaker, political (i.e., Blue House) control over South Korean defense planning has been tightened significantly.

[41] OSC, 2007; Jin D., 2007; Jung, 2006b; and Richard Halloran, "S. Korea Looks to the Open Seas for Regional Military Strength," *Taipei Times*, July 3, 2007.

South Korean leaders that the United States could take unilateral actions without prior South Korean approval that adversely affect South Korean interests—especially toward North Korea but regarding China and Taiwan as well. But the potential Chinese reaction to any such operations is also important. Such sensitivity exacerbates the difficulty of the United States and South Korea reaching a common viewpoint on such issues as Taiwan in bilateral discussions over the future of the alliance.

Having said that, China's negative influence on South Korea's security cooperation with the United States to date ought not be exaggerated. On most of the big issues critical to the United States—September 11, Iraq, U.S. strategic flexibility, the consolidation and restructuring of U.S. military forces in South Korea, etc.—South Korea has gone along with the United States, even at the risk of incurring some Chinese displeasure (not to mention criticism from President Roh's domestic political base). How South Korea will respond to future potential contingencies will depend heavily on context, as well as on the state of U.S.–South Korean relations. At the same time, South Korean military leaders' views are influenced not merely by their sense of external threat but also by their awareness of South Korean military shortcomings and vulnerabilities. MND's foot-dragging over everything from the withdrawal of U.S. troops to the handover of wartime operational control to South Korea is symptomatic of this. However benign the general view of China may be and however much South Koreans may aspire in their hearts to becoming fully independent someday, the South Korean military is neither prepared nor willing to disengage from security cooperation with the United States.

In view of this reality, South Korean leaders came up with the convoluted term "cooperative self-reliant national defense" to describe their current policy. As one South Korean scholar pointedly put it, this term "means cooperation with the United States, not cooperative security with its neighbors."[42] Except for a handful of people on the fringe of the political spectrum, moreover, few South Koreans in or out of the military identify China as a serious strategic alternative to the United States. Greater pragmatism in the political leadership and broader awareness of the importance of the United States to South Korean interests constrain radical departures in South Korean policies toward China.

Military Relations with China

South Korea and China have undertaken three categories of military-to-military interactions:

- high-level exchanges; thus far, South Korea has made three visits to China, and China has made one to South Korea

---

[42] Taik-young Hamm, "The Self-Reliant National Defense of South Korea and the Future of the U.S.–ROK Alliance," Nautilus Institute for Security and Sustainable Development Northeast Asia Peace and Security Project, Policy Forum Online 06-49A, June 20, 2006.

- periodic working-level and information exchanges
- exchanges of military research institute students, athletes, and other personnel.

The South Koreans would like to see these exchanges become more balanced and frequent, as well as more substantive. Their primary interest today is in discussing a possible bilateral agreement on maritime security. They would also like to pursue maritime search and rescue exercises, exchanges toward an air-defense identification zone, and discussions about confidence-building measures for potential North Korean scenarios. South Korea's main purpose in pursuing these kinds of activities is both to educate the People's Liberation Army (PLA) about South Korean perceptions on important issues and to address practical problems between the two militaries.

At present, bilateral military relations might best be described as both thin and one sided. They are very formal at the high-level exchange level and—as the apparent lack of South Korean insight into the August 2005 Chinese-Russian military exercises showed—not very forthcoming when it comes to intelligence exchange.[43] They do not include significant arms sales, joint military exercises, or other common features of mature bilateral military relationships, although both sides agreed in April 2007 to stage their first joint naval rescue drill and set up hotlines between their respective naval and air forces by the end of the year.[44] In general, military interactions have focused more on improving the general atmosphere in South Korean–Chinese political relations than on addressing concrete security problems and improving prospects for peace.

Conclusions and Implications

Drawing on the previous analysis, this section provides an overall assessment of the forces driving South Korea's response to China today and the likely future of South Korean–Chinese relations. It also assesses the current state of South Korea's security relationship with the United States and the likely future of that relationship in the context of projected South Korean relations with China. The section concludes with some potential tests of will that could signal potential South Korean movement toward or away from the United States.

---

[43] South Korea, for example, reportedly received no information about the joint China-Russia military exercise, despite the exercise's apparent focus on a potential emergency on the Korean peninsula and despite the strong interest South Korea had expressed. Kim Kwi-ku'n, "Military Keeps Watchful Eye on How China-Russia Joint Exercise Proceeds—'No Information on Military Exercise Provided to South Korea,'" Yonhap News Agency, August 17, 2005.

[44] "S. Korea, China to Stage Joint Naval Training," Yonhap News Agency, April 24, 2007.

Driving Forces and Likely Futures

The two main variables affecting South Korea's response to China are China's effects on South Korean economic prospects and the perceived implications of China's rise for other South Korean strategic objectives. South Korea's goal of peaceful reconciliation, and ultimately unification, with North Korea is at the top of these strategic objectives, although protecting the South's sovereign prerogatives and assuming international roles commensurate with its status are also high priorities. Lesser, but still important, variables affecting South Korea's response are its threat perceptions, attitudes toward China, China's peninsular and regional roles, and perceptions of the United States and state of U.S.–South Korean relations.

Although the terms *main* and *lesser* suggest general, if notional, weighting of the variables affecting South Korean policy today, it is important to stress that most South Koreans do not believe that they have to choose among these variables. So far, at least, they see China's rise as an opportunity to advance South Korean economic *and* strategic interests, with caveats on the evident growing caution and realism about China.

The simplest answer to the question of what is driving South Korea's response to China is thus a generally benign view of China and the perceived benefits of good South Korean–Chinese relations. Given these perceived benefits, there is considerable sensitivity toward China in South Korea today and reluctance either to challenge major Chinese interests or to ruffle Chinese sensitivities needlessly. At the same time, however, there are forces holding the relationship back, if not driving it in the opposite direction. These include uncertainties about China's prospects and long-term intentions, especially in North Korea; awareness of potential South Korean vulnerability to Chinese economic or other pressures; continuing irritants in the bilateral relationship; a widely shared awareness of the importance of the United States; and a continuing gap between South Korean aspirations and capabilities.

These cross pressures suggest that South Korea will continue to try to expand ties with China, with the economic side of the relationship remaining dominant as long as Chinese growth continues. South Korea is likely to emphasize solving actual problems between the two countries, such as the need for a maritime security agreement, but still likely to try to use the relationship to discuss confidence-building measures and other steps that could help improve prospects for peace on the peninsula. Because of geography alone, sensitivity toward Chinese interests will remain a characteristic of South Korean policies.

The irritants in and constraints on the relationship, however, will likely continue as well. If or as China continues to ensconce itself in North Korea, issues pertaining to the North could come to have as many negatives as positives for South Korean–Chinese relations. Even short of this, a new strategic alignment between South Korea and China is not likely in the absence of some major external event. South Korea will seek to maintain good relations with China on the basis of—rather than instead of—continued close allied relations with the United States. A North Korean refusal to verifiably dismantle its nuclear programs and a clear Chinese unwillingness or inability to bring the North to resolve the nuclear issue peacefully would reinforce this inclination.

Having said that, a number of issues could precipitate more-radical movement in South Korean policies, including the following:

- *North Korea's nuclear activities:* Although almost all South Koreans are opposed to these activities and want them to stop, they also want this to happen peacefully. Fears that unilateral U.S. actions on this issue will trample on South Korean sovereign prerogatives and endanger critical South Korean interests are widespread— and they are reliably reported to be particularly intense among South Korea's top leaders. U.S. moves toward a policy that actively seeks regime change in Pyongyang or that uses military force without South Korea's prior agreement could well spur South Korean efforts to develop a more-strategic relationship with China.
- *Inter-Korean relations:* Strong differences exist in South Korea concerning the government's policies toward North Korea, but most South Koreans agree on the need for some form of engagement. The widely shared goal is to encourage peaceful change in the North and to foster long-term inter-Korean reconciliation. If South Koreans perceive that the United States is an obstacle to reconciliation or if the United States mishandles instability in the North, Seoul could decide to reexamine its strategic options.
- *Japan:* The recent expansion of U.S.–Japanese security cooperation has inadvertently stimulated the long-standing (if largely unfounded) view among South Koreans that the United States favors Japan over South Korea. Although the logic of this expansion is generally understood, many South Koreans feel the United States is insufficiently respectful of their sensitivities toward potential Japanese military assertiveness. In the event of a crisis in South Korean–Japanese relations, South Korean resentment could provide an opening for increased Chinese influence.
- *The United States:* Although the explicit and often expressed U.S. desire for a strong and enduring U.S.–South Korean alliance is clear, widespread frustration in the United States with South Korea over differences in the respective policies toward North Korea and other matters is fueling a tendency in the United States to dismiss or devalue the importance of the alliance. A U.S. failure to ratify the FTA would be seen in this light and, while not directly related to the U.S.–South Korean security relationship, could precipitate more-significant movement toward China. In short, how the United States values its relationship with South Korea will have a critical influence on future South Korean strategic calculations. How South Korea responds to the challenges of the new era, in turn, will critically influence U.S. valuations.

The Strength of U.S.–South Korean Security Relations

The U.S.–South Korean relationship today remains something of a paradox.[45] On the one hand, both governments insist that government-to-government relations are actually very good, and each is working hard, with considerable success, to address a range of bilateral problems pragmatically. On the other hand, the atmosphere is not good outside these channels, in part because of sharply divergent perceptions of North Korea, in part because of fundamental policy differences that cannot be wished away, and in part because of the accumulating frustration the sides have with one another's statements or actions.

The good news is that, despite this general atmosphere, such concerns about the United States currently have little prominence in South Korea, particularly compared to the early part of the 2000s. This is to some extent because the United States has made efforts to scale back its military presence and avoid inflammatory issues and because of its broader (and largely unheralded) responsiveness on the FTA, operational control, and other matters. But other things have contributed as well. South Korea is playing a larger role on the North Korean nuclear issue, for example, and feels less excluded than it has previously. Greater South Korean realism about China has also contributed, as has the splits within both the conservative and progressive groups and the rise of new schools of thought seeking less-ideological approaches to the challenges South Korea faces.

South Korea's long-term vision of itself as a model nation-state playing a useful role in helping others get along reinforces this trend. This vision suggests, of course, that South Korea itself must get along with everyone—a need that current South Korean attitudes toward and relations with Japan challenges. But this vision does *not* suggest neutrality. Indeed, there is growing agreement among South Koreans that the nation can play such a role *only* if it maintains strong ties with the United States. Without such ties, many South Koreans fear, the Korean peninsula will revert to its history as a focal point for competition among the great powers. One manifestation of this view is the virtual disappearance from South Korean political discourse of talk about playing a balancing role in the region. Another is the effort of the former Roh government in the mid-2000s to differentiate its desire for greater self-reliance from its pursuit of genuine independence and also to differentiate its pursuit of this self-reliance from its increased willingness to publicly stress the long-term importance of the U.S.–South Korean relationship.[46]

---

[45] For a previous assessment elaborating on this view, see Norman D. Levin, *Do the Ties Still Bind? The U.S.–ROK Security Relationship After 9/11*, Santa Monica, Calif.: RAND Corporation, MG-115-AF/KF, 2004.

[46] For a conspicuous example of the latter, see Lee Tae-sik, Ambassador of the Republic of Korea to the United States, "The Korea–U.S. Alliance—A Partnership for the Future," speech delivered at the St. Regis Hotel, Washington, D.C., February 7, 2006.

The currently low ranking of the United States on South Korea's policymaking priority scale, however, cannot be taken for granted. The nuclear challenge, the operational control issue, continuing U.S. military consolidation, FTA ratification, and many other matters will invariably keep the United States in the news. More fundamentally, South Korea has grown up and will almost surely continue to seek to adjust the U.S.–South Korean relationship accordingly. By its nature, this process will involve challenges that should not be underestimated.

The most likely projection for U.S.–South Korean security relations, therefore, would describe them as neither fish nor fowl. On the one hand, those who expected a return to the good old days after the December 2007 presidential election have been disappointed. South Koreans are serious about the need for change and are unlikely to be content simply continuing to act as a junior partner to the United States. On the other hand, those who expected South Korea to jettison its alliance with the United States and move toward either true independence or a new strategic alliance with China have also been disappointed. The odds that anyone significantly further to the left than President Roh can win the election is very low, and the likelihood of a really radical regime coming to power and evicting the United States is even more remote. Moreover, aside from the continuing strong public support for the security alliance in South Korea, the growing South Korean tendency to see relations with the United States not so much as a hedge against China but as a prerequisite for the achievement of other important South Korean policy objectives suggests continued support for the security relationship.

This mixed picture suggests that, barring unexpected developments, South Korea will stick with the United States, including—as with Iraq—at critical decision points that test the alliance. But China's rise will continue to challenge U.S. efforts to expand U.S.–South Korean security cooperation. South Korean agreement to U.S. military operations outside Korea will be particularly difficult to obtain, although this will depend heavily on the context. The key to the future of the relationship will be reconfiguration of the alliance correctly. This means, first and foremost, successfully implementing the operational control decision.

Potential Tests of Will

In a relationship as mature and complex as that between the United States and South Korea, testing goes on naturally and essentially all the time. In this sense, it is probably unnecessary to devise artificial tests of will to get a sense of potential South Korean reactions. Moreover, other than a Taiwanese contingency, relationship tests are more likely to be related to North Korea or to the bilateral U.S.–South Korean relationship itself rather than to relations with China.

Having said that, a few possible tests that have a Chinese component either have already been proposed elsewhere or are easily identifiable. At the low end of the scale, one test might be to see whether South Korea is willing to participate in peacekeeping exercises that have nothing to do with China but that are held near China. Moving up the scale, another might be to use the future alliance planning process to see whether South Korea will agree to common views on the major regional challenges. Moving up again, and in the context of reduced South Korean–Japanese tensions, could be renewed testing of South Korea's willingness to participate in expanded trilateral activities with the United States and Japan. At the high end might be a test that encourages South Korea to limit China's role and influence in potential peace regime negotiations on the peninsula. Such tests have the added virtue of advancing important U.S. interests, were South Korea to respond positively. In a close and successful alliance relationship, however, they would probably not be thought of as tests of will but more as initiatives to advance common interests.

CHAPTER FIVE

The Philippines

The Philippines is the United States' oldest treaty ally in Asia. The country hosted major U.S. naval and air bases until 1992 and is an important U.S. partner in the global war on terrorism. In addition to the defense relationship, the Philippines has deep and long-standing political, economic, and social ties with the United States. The close U.S.–Philippine relationship, the country's role as a founding member of ASEAN, and its front-line status in the South China Sea dispute make its response to the rise of China a particularly interesting and important issue.

A key determinant of the Philippines' response to the rise of China is the nature of the state, specifically its relative internal instability. The Philippines has a democratic political system, and the U.S. security umbrella protects it from outside attack. Yet the country suffers from chronic political instability, which is manifested in periodic military rebellions and extralegal "people power" movements against incumbent governments. Domestic political instability and military weakness inhibit the country's ability to play a more-active role internationally or to protect its equities in the South China Sea vis-à-vis other claimants, including China. These weaknesses, combined with the prospect of China-oriented economic growth, have produced a policy of general accommodation toward China—an orientation that is likely to continue. At the same time, this has not corresponded with a reduction in U.S. influence with the Philippines because ties have continued to grow between the two nations since the early 2000s.

As with other ASEAN states, economic considerations play an important role in the Philippines' response to the rise of China. During the 1980s and 1990s, economic growth rates here lagged considerably behind those of other ASEAN partners. However, since 1998, Philippine economic growth has accelerated, and economic performance has improved. Because of the importance of remittances from Filipino workers overseas—a characteristic of the Philippine economy that sets it apart from other countries in this volume—the Philippine economy is less dependent on trade with China. Nevertheless, Philippine elites regard the China market as an important engine of economic growth.

China is not currently at the forefront of the Philippines' security concerns. Major internal security threats, including the Communist and Moro insurgencies, Islamist terrorist groups, and criminal networks, are the focus of the Philippines' national security and defense policymaking. Foreign and security policy issues—including the rise of China—do not rank high on the order of priorities of the informed Philippine public. As former National Security Advisor General Jose Almonte noted, there is an absence of real interest in foreign policy unless the interests of certain social groups are directly involved.[1]

Manila's political, economic, and military weaknesses give it few options for protecting its territorial claims in the South China Sea. Philippine military expenditures were 0.77 percent of GDP in 2006.[2] The military budget is largely absorbed by personnel costs, operations, and maintenance of basic equipment, leaving very little to maintain or modernize its deteriorating air and naval capabilities. As a result, the Philippines lacks the ability to defend areas beyond the main islands of the Philippine archipelago. The country's alliance with the United States provides it with a security shield, but the alliance does not extend to Manila's offshore claims. Therefore, in responding to China's rise, Manila has chosen to pursue a policy of leveraging its international relationships by seeking to regionalize the South China Sea dispute through ASEAN and by developing closer defense cooperation with the United States.

At the same time, like other Southeast Asian governments, the Philippines is pursuing close economic engagement with China. With the South China Sea dispute currently quiescent, China is regarded primarily as a benign power and a promising economic partner. China (including Hong Kong) is now almost tied with the United States as the Philippines' largest export market. This is not to say that some Filipino elites—especially in the military—are unaware that China could adopt more-threatening regional policies in the future. The direction of these trends suggests that, barring a major shock to the regional status quo, economic and political ties between the Philippines and China will continue to expand—as will its ties with the United States.

National Conditions

The Philippines' public is relatively inattentive to the external environment and its nation's foreign affairs. This is likely due to perennial domestic political instability: Since the fall of the authoritarian regime of Ferdinand Marcos in 1986 (with the exception of the presidency of Fidel Ramos from 1992 to 1998), the Philippines has lurched from one political crisis to another. One president, Joseph Estrada, was driven out by "people's power" in 2001, and his successor and current incumbent, President Gloria

---

[1]   Interview with General Jose Almonte, Manila, November 29, 2005.

[2]   International Institute for Strategic Studies (IISS), *The Military Balance,* London, 2007, p. 369.

Macapagal-Arroyo, was under political siege from 2005 to 2006 due to allegations of voting fraud during the May 2004 presidential election.[3] In May 2007, during legislative and local elections, President Arroyo's coalition won the majorities in the house of representatives, among governors, and city mayors, adding a modicum of stability to domestic politics. But, as of this writing, the government also faces numerous internal challenges, including an internal terrorist insurgency, incessant political battles among rival parties, population growth, and the need to alleviate poverty, among others. The implications of these challenges for foreign and security policymaking are that, with political leaders focused on short-term political maneuvering, it is difficult for the country's leadership to pay sustained attention to foreign and security policy issues or strategies to foster long-term economic growth. The Philippines also has a very substantial and influential ethnic Chinese community that plays a role in Philippine-Chinese relations, discussed in more detail under "Domestic Politics and Public Opinion," below.

The Philippine political system is and has always been personality driven. There are no institutionalized political parties. Philippine parties are essentially pyramids of patron-client relationships stretching from *barangays* (the lowest government unit) all the way to the national government in Manila that exist to satisfy particular demands and not to implement a nationwide program. National party leaders—senators and representatives—are usually members of influential provincial families linked together in shifting coalitions. Politics is characterized by competition among local elites for access to government patronage. Since none of the parties have an effective way to enforce party discipline, politicians switch capriciously back and forth among parties.[4] Because, at the base of the electoral system, the power and status of families are at stake, all means are availed of to achieve victory, including violence.[5]

Foreign policy falls largely within the sphere of the executive, but the constitution gives some important roles to the legislature, such as treaty ratification. When the president is weak, political opponents can seize the initiative on important foreign policy issues. For instance, despite President Corazon Aquino's support, the Philippine Senate defeated the new treaty on U.S. bases in the Philippines that Aquino's government had negotiated with the United States in 1991. Similarly, the president and his or

---

[3] The scandal broke when the opposition released recordings of what were said to be Elections Commissioner Virgilio Garcillano and Arroyo discussing plans to fix the results of the elections. The allegations were that Arroyo ordered Garcillano to rig the election results to give Arroyo a 1-million-vote victory over her opponent, the late Fernando Poe, Jr.

[4] Ronald E. Dolan, ed., *Philippines: A Country Study*, Washington, D.C.: Library of Congress, Federal Research Division, 1991; Joel Rocamora, "Philippine Political Parties, Electoral System and Political Reform," *Philippines International Review*, Vol. 1, No. 1, Spring 1998; John L. Linantud, "The 2004 Philippine Elections," *Contemporary Southeast Asia*, Vol. 27, No. 1, April 2005.

[5] The police reported the killing of 64 people during the 1998 elections and of 132 people in the 2001 midterm elections. The death count in 2004 was 117, including 29 candidates. Amnesty International, "Philippines: Human Rights Need to Be Respected as Election Campaign Intensifies," London, May 6, 2004.

her economic team set economic policy but need to accommodate established interests, which include foreign investors, landed and financial interests, and groups that provide crucial political support.[6] Two institutions, the Ministry of Finance and the Central Bank, are key players in economic policy.

Domestic Politics and Public Opinion

Filipinos were deeply suspicious of Chinese intentions because of Chinese activities in the South China Sea in the mid-1990s. Perceptions have shifted in favor of China in recent years. A poll of 33 nations completed in January 2006 by GlobeScan and the Program on International Policy Attitudes for the BBC World Service shows that 54 percent of Filipino respondents had a favorable view of China—a lower percentage than registered favorable views of the United States (85 percent) or Japan (79 percent). The 54-percent favorable view of China was a decline from the 70-percent favorable rate noted in 2005. (The decline in favorable ratings of China from 2005 to 2006 appears to have been consistent throughout Asia.) The poll also showed comfort with China's growing economic influence. Sixty-three percent of Filipino respondents thought it would be positive if China were to become "significantly more powerful economically than it is today." Asked how they would feel if "China becomes significantly more powerful militarily than it is today," the Filipino respondents were divided: 45 percent favorable, and 46 percent negative.[7]

A 2005 U.S. Department of State Bureau of Intelligence and Research poll compared Philippine views of the future influence of China, the United States, and Japan in Southeast Asia. The poll showed that, by a wide margin, Filipinos chose the United States (62 percent) as the most influential in the region until the end of this decade (2006–2010). China (14 percent) and Japan (12 percent) trail in second and third places. Sixty-two percent said that the United States will be the Philippines' closest future economic partner, followed by Japan (13 percent) and China (10 percent). By a somewhat smaller margin than other Asian publics, 42 percent of Filipinos expected China's economic power to increase (34 percent expect no change) and thought China's growth will have a mostly positive effect on the Philippine economy (49 to 25 percent negative; 15 percent see no effect). When asked which country will be the Philippines' closest security partner in five to ten years, Filipinos once again overwhelmingly named the United States (72 percent).

---

[6] Emmanuel S. de Dios, "Philippine Economic Growth: Can It Last?" in David G. Timberman, ed., *The Philippines: New Directions in Domestic Policy and Foreign Relations*, New York: The Asia Society, 1998.

[7] World Public Opinion, "World Opinion on China More Positive than on US, But Slipping," Washington, D.C., April 17, 2006, describes a poll by the Program on International Policy Attitudes conducted for the BBC World Service between December 2004 and January 2005.

Filipinos still carry some residual sense of a threat from China. Asked what nation or group threatens Philippine national security, 9 percent named China, after Iraq (16 percent) and the Abu Sayyaf Group (15 percent).[8] However, in a choice between two visions of China, a small majority (56 percent) said it is "a peaceful country that is more interested in economic growth than in military adventures." Thirty-five percent chose the alternative view of China as "an expansionist power that is building up its military to enforce its claims to sovereignty in the South China Sea."[9]

In the Philippine political environment, foreign policy issues take a back seat to local politics (with the exceptions of the U.S. defense relationship with the Philippines, which is always controversial in some sectors of Philippine public opinion, and matters relating to Filipinos overseas). China has rarely emerged as an issue in Philippine politics. There do not appear to be substantial differences among the Philippine political parties on China policy. All see the benefits of engagement, although some may be more wary than others about China's long-term intentions.

The ruling Lakas-Christian Muslim Democrats have cultivated good relations with the Chinese Communist Party (CCP), and the Chinese have scored some significant successes in their outreach to Philippine and other Asian political parties. Lakas-Christian Muslim Democrat president Jose de Venecia, Liberal Party leader Rodolfo C. Bacani, and Nationalist People's Coalition leader Alfredo G. Maranon are all government supporters; opposition leader Edgardo Angara attended the Third International Conference of Asian Political Parties in Beijing in September 2004 and met with senior Chinese government and CCP leaders (and voiced the obligatory support for the One-China policy). CCP officials reciprocated with a visit to Manila for meetings with Philippine congressional leaders in 2004.[10]

Philippine policy toward China—as in other areas of public policy—is determined by the president and his or her closest advisors. President Ramos relied on Jose Almonte, Director-General of National Security and National Security Adviser; Foreign Minister Roberto Romulo and his successor, Domingo Siazon; and Under Secretary of Foreign Affairs Rodolfo Severino. Estrada relied on Executive Secretary Ronaldo Zamora and a small coterie of businessmen and power brokers,[11] and Arroyo relied on her National Security Adviser Norberto Gonzalez, who also serves as Director-General

---

[8] A higher view of the China threat than in Thailand (1 percent), Malaysia (1 percent), or Indonesia (2 percent).

[9] U.S. Department of State, Bureau of Intelligence and Research, 2005. According to the same survey, positive images of China predominate in Malaysia and Indonesia. Among urban Malaysians, 91 percent have a favorable opinion of China; among urban Indonesians, fewer than one in ten have negative images of China.

[10] "Top Legislator Appreciates Philippines' One-China Policy," *People's Daily* (online), September 4, 2004; "CPC to Conduct Various Exchanges, Cooperation with Philippine Parties, says Wu Guanzheng," 3rd International Conference of Asian Political Parties, Xinhua News Agency, September 4, 2004; "Senior Chinese Leader Meets Philippine Congress Leaders," *People's Daily* (online), October 20, 2004.

[11] Antonio Lopez and Sangwon Suh, "The Troubleshooters," *Asiaweek*, March 19, 1999.

of the National Intelligence Coordinating Agency.[12] As noted above, key constituencies, such as the foreign affairs bureaucracy and Filipino-Chinese businessmen and others involved in business with China, also influence policy toward China.

At the institutional level, the function of some government agencies is to think strategically about Philippine public policy. These include, in the security area, the National Security Council and the Department of Defense. Some influential think tanks also exist to analyze foreign and security issues, such as the Institute for Strategic and Development Studies, headed by Carolina Hernandez; the Ramos Peace and Development Foundation, chaired by former President Fidel Ramos; and the National Defense College of the Philippines.

Economic Responses

In the course of one decade, China has vaulted from the Philippines's 12th largest export market to its third largest (Figure 5.1). If exports to Hong Kong are added

Figure 5.1
Philippine Exports, by Country of Destination, Selected Years

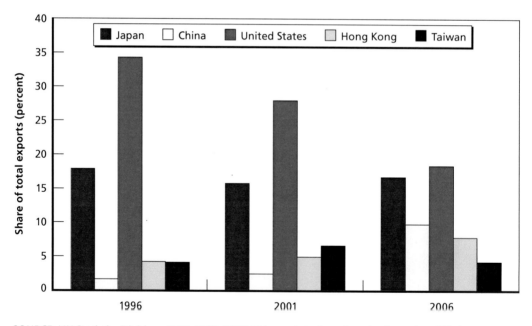

SOURCE: UN Statistics Division, 1996, 2001, 2006; Taiwan data from Bangko Sentral ng Pilipinas, "Philippines: Balance of Payments," statistical database, 2006.
RAND MG736-5.1

---

[12] Malou Mangahas, "Despite Hard Times, GMA Hires Pricey Foreign Consultants for Charter Change," Philippine Center for Investigative Journalism, September 13, 2005.

to those to mainland China, China rivals the United States as the Philippines' most important trade partner. Growth in Philippine exports to China has been truly phenomenal: They have jumped from $328 million in 1996 to $4.6 billion in 2006, up 14 times. Including Hong Kong in the equation somewhat dampens growth: Combined exports rose seven times over the decade, from $1.2 billion to $8.3 billion in 2006.

Most of the growth in exports to China consisted of intermediate, rather than final, products. As shown in Figure 5.2, electronics, primarily components, accounted for over three-fifths of all Philippine exports to China. Most of these exports were shipped to China for final assembly, from which the computers, television sets, and other products made from them were either exported to the rest of the world or sold to Chinese buyers.

Almost all Philippine exports of electronics originate from foreign-owned plants, primarily Japanese. They are shipped to plants in China owned by the same company for final assembly. Matsushita (which owns the Panasonic brand), Fujitsu, Hitachi, Sanyo, Mitsubishi, and NEC are among Japanese electronics firms that have major operations in the Philippines.[13] Taiwanese and South Korean companies have also invested in

Figure 5.2
Composition of Philippine Exports to China, 2006

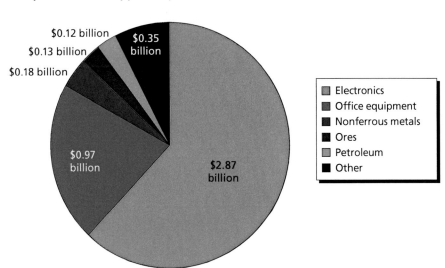

SOURCE: Authors' calculations based on UN Statistics Division, 2006.
RAND MG736-5.2

---

[13] Marianne V. Go, "JPEPA: More Japanese Investments, Trade Opportunities Seen," *The Philippine Star*, February 24, 2005.

electronics plants in the Philippines. South Korean firms have invested $770 million in the Philippines, of which $555 million is in manufacturing. Of that, $324 million, or 60 percent, has been invested in electronics plants. The decline in Philippine exports to Taiwan since 2001 reflects the relocation of Taiwanese plants from Taiwan to the mainland. Ironically, despite the growth in Philippine exports to China, none of the major electronics plants in the Philippines are owned by mainland Chinese companies. Companies in which Filipinos own a majority interest are also notable by their absence. Thus, the political influence factory owners have over Philippine policy toward China is indirect because the first allegiance of the owners of these companies is to their own governments, not to the governments of either China or the Philippines.

Philippine imports from China have also grown rapidly, but less so than have exports. Imports increased five times between 1996 and 2006, while exports rose 14 times. As with Philippine exports, the largest commodity groups, as a share of total imports, were electronic components, parts for office equipment, and telecommunications equipment, 37, 12, and 9 percent, respectively (Figure 5.3). These imports consist largely of components that will become subassemblies and final products in Philippine plants, the counterparts to Philippine exports of these products to China. Although metals and refined-oil products loom large in both Philippine imports from and exports to China (compared, for instance, to consumer goods), the remaining Philippine imports from China are much more diversified than its exports, including a variety of intermediate goods and commodities, such as chemicals, fertilizers, foods, and machinery. Surprisingly, China is just beginning to become a supplier of consumer goods to Philippine retailers. Imports of clothing, appliances, and consumer durables are only just taking off.[14]

In contrast to U.S. trade with China, China has reduced, not added to, the Philippine trade deficit. As exports of electronic components have risen, Philippine trade with China has moved into surplus. In 2006, this surplus ran $758 million; trade with the rest of the world was in deficit to the tune of $6.7 billion. This has not always been the case. The Philippine trade balance with China was deeply in deficit throughout the second half of the 1990s.

Winners and Losers from Trade with China

Winners. The main Philippine winners from trade with China have been employees in the burgeoning electronics, office equipment, and telecommunications industries, as well as the other major exporting industries.[15] Although manufacturing employment has grown slowly over the past decade, up just 12.6 percent between 1997 and 2006,

---

[14] In 2006, imports of iron and steel and of refined oil products from China ranked three and six, respectively. Clothing accounted for less than $20 million of the $3,869 million in total imports from China, or 0.5 percent. Imports of footwear and furniture accounted for similar amounts. (UN Statistics Division, 2006.)

[15] The discussion of trade and investment in this section is based largely on interviews with Filipino business leaders and academics, Manila, November–December 2005.

Figure 5.3
Composition of Philippine Imports from China, 2006

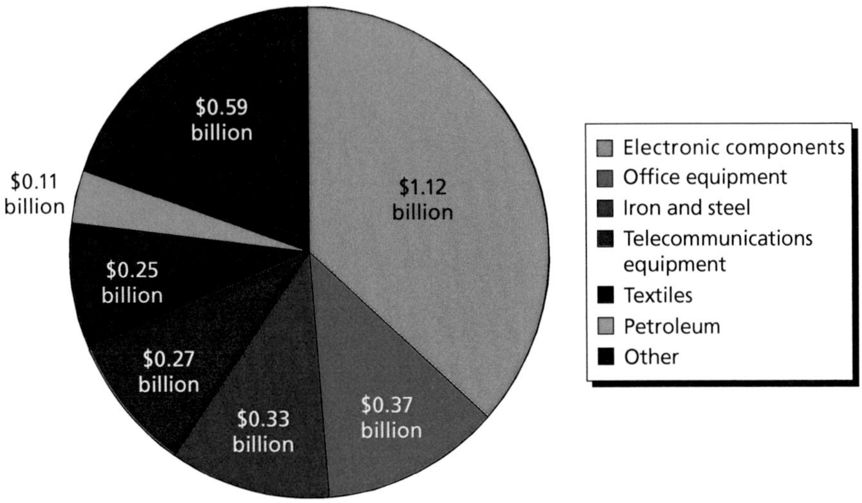

SOURCE: Authors' calculations based on UN Statistics Division, 2006.
RAND *MG736-5.3*

employment in the electronics industries has boomed, while that in other sectors, such as textiles, has fallen. Outside electronics, employees of mining and food-processing companies have also benefited from the China trade.

The Philippines is exporting large amounts of tropical fruits to China and has the dominant market share in bananas. Increases in exports of agricultural products to China have contributed to higher incomes and sustained employment in this sector. However, China's importance here should not be exaggerated. Agriculture is the largest employer in the Philippines, accounting for almost one-third of total employment. Agricultural exports to China were $67 million in 2006, small compared to total exports of $2.6 billion in agricultural products and foodstuffs or to the size of the agricultural sector in the Philippine economy.[16]

Retailers are also benefiting from the China trade. Mall operators and department stores, such as the large mall retail operator Robinson's, import cheap products from China for sale in the Philippines. They also invest in shopping malls in China. These large merchants (known as *taipans*) are ethnic Chinese for the most part, although some, such as the large mall operator Ayala, are not.

Losers. The major Philippine losers from trade involving China are companies and workers that were engaged in exporting products to the rest of the world in sectors in which China has a major comparative advantage. Figure 5.4 shows Philippine

---

[16] The agricultural sector accounted for 14.8 percent of 2005's estimated GDP of $90.3 billion. Central Intelligence Agency, "Philippines," *The World Factbook*, 2006.

global exports of clothing, textiles, and shoes over the last decade. As can be seen, shoe exports have been devastated, while exporters of clothing and textiles have just held their own. The Philippines used to be a major global producer of denims and children's wear, but Chinese competition has wiped these sectors out. The biggest exporters produce middle-range wear (Gap, Ralph Lauren, Polo, Liz Claiborne, Levi's, Tommy Hilfiger), largely for the U.S. market, not high fashion. They, too, are under pressure from Chinese competitors. Some Filipinos complain that China now dominates the global export market for Christmas decorations—in which the Philippines (a heavily Catholic country) used to have a major share—even though the Chinese workers do not understand the symbolism of such goods.

Until recently, Philippine imports of consumer goods from China were limited: Most consumer goods were imported from other countries or produced domestically. Over the course of 2005 and 2006, the Philippines reportedly experienced a surge in imports of cheaper Chinese products—garments, appliances, and household items. These products are sold not only in malls and department stores but also in street-side kiosks and open-air markets, in which the bulk of the population buys cheaper goods. Even Chinese vegetable growers have made some inroads into the Philippine market, because China's labor costs are low, its farms are productive, and it has good processing and exporting facilities.

Figure 5.4
Total Philippine Exports of Clothing, Textiles, and Shoes, 1995–2006

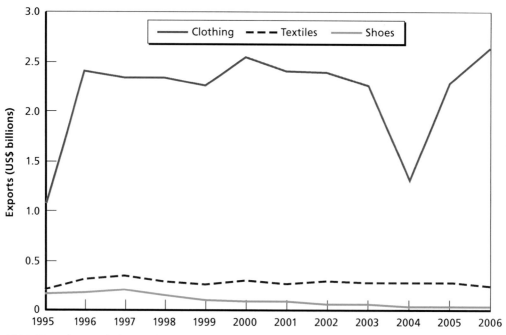

SOURCE: Authors' calculations based on UN Statistics Division, 1995–2006.
RAND MG736-5.4

Thus, the political forces that benefit from or are hurt by Chinese trade are diffuse. The owners of most of the electronic plants that have been the most dynamic source of exports to China are foreign companies—Japanese, Taiwanese, and South Korean. Their interest in and ability to affect Philippine politics, especially with respect to China policy, is limited. Industries that have been hurt by competitive pressures from China have made their concerns heard: The Philippines was the last ASEAN country to sign the ASEAN-China FTA and has kept a long exclusion list.[17] On the other hand, trade with China is expanding, and importers, retailers, and consumers are benefiting from low-cost Chinese goods.

Trade in Services

The Philippines' largest single export after electronics is labor. In 2006, remittances from Filipinos working overseas ran $12.5 billion, equal to one-quarter of the nation's merchandise exports.[18] An additional $2.8 billion comes directly into the country in the form of compensation for work performed abroad but paid in country. Remittances have been rising rapidly, more than tripling since 1996; 2006 levels were equivalent to about 10 percent of GDP. In terms of incomes, remittances are even more important than exports of electronics because every single remittance dollar goes into a Filipino pocket; the wages and profits (value added) earned from electronics exports probably run on the order of $2.5 billion, one-fifth of the value of remittances.

Because China has plenty of its own workers, it is not a major source of remittances. Only 9,000 Filipinos worked in China in 2004, out of 1,063,000 Filipinos working abroad (over one-third of the total number of Filipinos were in manufacturing). Key countries for the Philippines in terms of remittances are the United States (over 50 percent), Saudi Arabia (10 percent), and the remainder in other Gulf countries.

Tourism is important for the Philippine economy but less so than in other ASEAN states, such as Thailand or Singapore. The hotel and restaurant industry employs 866,000 Filipinos, almost as many people as work abroad. The estimated value that tourism, domestic and foreign, added to the Philippines' GDP was 13 percent in 1998, the latest year for which information is available.[19] After declining between 1999 and 2003, earnings from foreign tourism have been on the upswing, running $3.5 billion in 2006, equivalent to 3 percent of GDP. Tourism is the largest component of service income on the Philippines balance of payments; earnings from exports of all services

---

[17] Interview with Dr. Aileen Baviera, Dean of the Asian Center at the University of the Philippines, Manila, November 2005.

[18] Bangko Sentral ng Pilipinas, 2006.

[19] Romulo A. Virola, Marriel M. Remulla, Lea H. Amoro, and Milagros Y. Say, "Measuring the Contribution of Tourism to the Economy: The Philippine Tourism Satellite Account," paper prepared for the 8th National Convention on Statistics, Manila, October 1–2, 2001, Appendix Table 5, "Estimated Value Added of Tourism Industries in the Philippines, 1994 and 1998."

(shipping, telecommunications, tourism, etc.) were equivalent to 5.5 percent of GDP in 2006.

Tourism from China has been growing rapidly. Chinese tourists are now the second largest contingent in the Philippines, after South Koreans, for whom the Philippines is an increasingly popular honeymoon destination.

Foreign Direct Investment

Filipinos have not been major investors in China from Beijing's perspective. Nonetheless, China has been an attractive destination for Filipino investors. According to Chinese data, the Philippines invested $189 million in China in 2005, 0.3 percent of total flows into China in that year.[20] However, net Philippine FDI outflows in 2005 ran the exact same amount, $189 million in 2005.[21] Thus, China was a major recipient of Philippine direct investment abroad. (Given that these data came from different sources, we cannot draw the inference that *all* Philippine outward investment went to China in 2005.)

For its part, China has not been a major investor in the Philippines. The Chinese have made no major equity investments in large Philippine corporations, although Chinese companies have shown interest in mining, particularly copper and tin, following a key 2005 Supreme Court decision that opens up opportunities for foreigners to hold equity stakes in the mining sector. The largest proposed Chinese investment in the Philippines is the Northern Luzon railroad, a $480 million project supported by the Chinese government. The proposed project is regarded as more of a political than an economic investment. It has been stalled because the Philippine Senate, which is controlled by parties hostile to the Arroyo government, is reviewing the deal.

China and the Philippines may be more competitors than partners in FDI. Average Chinese flows of FDI into the Philippines have fallen in this decade compared to the second half of the 1990s. Flows into China have continued to rise. Although political turmoil in the Philippines and concerns about economic policymaking may be the main causes of the decline in FDI, the attraction of China may have contributed to the fall as well.

Many members of the Philippine business community and political elite believe that expanding trade with China will provide substantial market opportunities, particularly in electronics, tropical fruit and other agricultural products, and tourism. However, they are also concerned about China as a competitive threat, considering previous experience in shoes, textiles, and Christmas ornaments. Moreover, a number of Filipinos worry about the competitiveness of the Philippines in sectors requiring

---

[20] The Philippines does not appear to publish statistics on FDI received from or sent to China. We searched the Web sites of the National Statistics Office of the Republic of the Philippines and the Central Bank of the Philippines without finding any data.

[21] This figure is taken from official Philippines balance of payments data on the Bangko Sentral ng Pilipinas Web site.

higher skill levels. Because these sectors tend to pay better wages, competition with China over these industries is a concern.[22] It is unlikely that Philippine manufacturers will be competitive in the Chinese consumer market, although Philippine businesses may be able to fill specialized niches. In contrast, the Chinese are formidable competitors in the domestic Philippine market for manufactured products.

Role of the Ethnic Chinese Business Community

As in other ASEAN countries, the ethnic Chinese community in the Philippines plays a much larger role in the economy than its share of the population might suggest. Although ethnic Chinese constitute between 1 and 2 percent of the population, they control an estimated 60 percent of corporate wealth (and these percentages are even higher in Indonesia, Malaysia, and Thailand).[23] As elsewhere, the commercial success of the Chinese community has engendered jealousy and some animosity among other Filipinos, coloring Filipino views of the Chinese and China.

The Philippines' ethnic Chinese community largely originated in Fujian province. Many also have business relationships in Taiwan. Despite the opening of economic relations in the 1970s, during the Marcos administration, Filipino-Chinese businessmen did not make significant investments in China until 1984 and 1985 because of the lack of clear rules on the protection and security of foreign investments and because the Chinese limited FDI to the special economic and export processing zones, whose operation was unfamiliar to Filipino-Chinese businessmen. After China liberalized the regulations on foreign capital participation in property development in 1991, Filipino FDI in China increased significantly.

Currently, the Filipino-Chinese business community is becoming increasingly oriented toward China. Filipino-Chinese capital has gone largely into established industries, such as breweries, cigarettes, malls, resorts, and manufacturing of household appliances and rubber shoes. Except for San Miguel beer, Philippine businesses that have invested in China have not brought Philippine brands to the country.[24] Among the ethnic Chinese tycoons most closely involved in business with China are Alfonso Yuchengco, the recently retired chairman of the Yuchengco Group of Companies and former ambassador to China and Japan; Lucio Tan, a tobacco (Fortune Tobacco Corporation) and brewery (Asia Brewery) magnate who has invested in breweries across in China; the Gokongwei family (JG Summit Holdings Inc.), which has invested in manufacturing of processed food in Guangzhou; "mall king" Henry Sy, whose SM Group has entered the China market with a mall in Xiamen and is opening two more

---

[22] Discussion with Dr. Evelyn Goh, Institute for Defence and Strategic Studies, Singapore, December 7, 2005.

[23] Amy Chua, interview with Harry Kreisler, Conversations with History series, Institute of International Studies, University of California at Berkeley, posted February 2, 2004.

[24] Benito Lim, "The Political Economy of Philippines-China Relations," Philippine APEC Study Center Network, Discussion Paper 99-16, 1999, pp. 23–24.

malls on the mainland;[25] and Eduardo "Danding" Cojuangco, Jr., chairman of the San Miguel Brewing Company, a major investor in China with breweries in Baoding, North China, and Guangdong.

The record of Philippine investment in China has been mixed. There have been some successes but also disappointments. Tan sold his Shanghai brewery because of large losses. San Miguel closed down one of its two breweries in Guangdong province, which failed to make a profit in 2005. A number of businesses owned by Filipino-Chinese flour millers have closed. The problems Filipino businessmen in China have experienced are similar to those investors from other countries have reported. The Chinese banking system is underdeveloped, and Beijing tightly controls the financial sector, especially foreign exchange.[26] Nevertheless, some Filipino investors are taking the long view, that it might take 10 to 20 years to build a strong presence in China but that manufacturing their products in China is more cost-effective than in the Philippines and would enable them to access the domestic Chinese market.[27]

Influential Filipino-Chinese businessmen are increasingly involved in business deals in China and can be an important force for closer Chinese-Philippine relations. According to one Filipino academic, however, Chinese officials do not know how to deal with overseas ethnic Chinese communities. For instance, when President Hu Jintao visited the Philippines in June 2005, he did not meet with the local ethnic Chinese business community, which felt snubbed as a result.[28]

Diplomatic and Foreign Policy Responses

Bilateral Relations with China

Chinese-Philippine diplomatic relations have improved significantly over the last decade. During the 1990s, relations between the Philippines and China were tense and largely dominated by the territorial dispute over the Spratly Islands in the South China Sea. Since the turn of the 21st century, however, Chinese-Philippine relations have moved beyond the South China Sea dispute into a more-productive stage of cooperative economic and political relations. At least three factors account for the improvement in Chinese-Philippine relations: China's policy of reassurance on the South China Sea, China's charm offensive toward the Philippines, and growing economic ties.[29]

---

[25] Michael Schuman, "Families Under Fire," *TimeAsia*, February 16, 2004.

[26] For information on Singapore, see Chapter Seven.

[27] Elena R. Torrijos, "Doing Business in China," *Newsbreak*, May 27, 2002.

[28] Interview with Dr. Renato Cruz de Castro, Manila, November 29, 2005.

[29] Ian Storey, "China and the Philippines: Moving Beyond the South China Sea Dispute," *China Brief*, Vol. 6, No. 17, August 16, 2006a.

The tacit decision by both sides at the end of the 1990s to lower the profile of the South China Sea dispute allowed Chinese-Philippine relations to develop. President Joseph Estrada paid a state visit to China in May 2000, during which both sides agreed to promote peace and stability in the South China Sea and the peaceful settlement of disputes in accordance with international law. The two governments also agreed on a framework for Chinese-Philippine relations in the 21st century covering science and technology, culture, agriculture, and business relations.[30] During the visit, Estrada expressed the view that "China does not pose a threat to the Philippines."[31]

Estrada's successor, Arroyo, has used cooperative diplomacy as the cornerstone of her policy toward China. Arroyo visited China as vice president in March 2000; after her installation as president, she paid a state visit to China in October 2001. During Arroyo's visit, the two countries signed five agreements, covering law enforcement and counterterrorism cooperation, expansion of diplomatic representation, and economic development cooperation.[32]

The tempo of high-level Chinese-Philippine exchanges and consultations accelerated between 2002 and 2006. The secretaries of Agriculture, Tourism, Foreign Affairs, and Interior and the speaker of the House of Representatives visited China in 2003, the Secretary of Defense in 2004, and the foreign secretary and the chief justice in 2005. President Arroyo made a state visit in September 2004 with a high-powered delegation of Filipino business leaders. The president paid official visits to China in October 2006, in connection with what she heralded as a golden age in Chinese-Philippine relations, and again in October 2007.[33] High-level Chinese visits to the Philippines included Secretary-General of the State Council Wang Zhongyu, Defense Minister Chi Haotian, and National People's Congress Chairman Li Peng in 2002; National People's Congress Chairman (and second-ranking CCP member) Wu Bangguo in 2003; President Hu Jintao in 2005; and Premier Wen Jiabao in early 2007 to attend the 10th ASEAN-China Summit and the broader EAS meeting.

During Hu's 2005 visit, China agreed to invest $1.1 billion in the Philippines, including $850 million in a nickel-mining project in Mindanao, and to provide a $542 million concessional loan for the upgrade of the North Luzon Railway. The two sides also set a target of $30 billion in bilateral trade by 2010.[34] Consultative mechanisms were established or continued, including foreign ministry and consular consulta-

---

[30] People's Republic of China and the Government of the Republic of the Philippines, "Joint Statement on the Framework of Bilateral Cooperation in the Twenty-First Century," May 16, 2000.

[31] "Estrada Says China Does Not Pose a Threat to the Philippines," *Asian Political News*, May 22, 2000.

[32] Gloria Macapagal-Arroyo, "Arrival Statement by President Gloria Macapagal-Arroyo," October 31, 2001.

[33] "Philippine Leader Heralds 'Golden Age' with China Ahead of Visit," *Asia Pacific News*, October 27, 2006.

[34] Storey, 2006a.

tions, the Joint Committee on Agriculture, the Joint Trade Committee, and the Joint Committee for Fisheries.[35]

China has been expanding cultural exchanges with the Philippines through the 1979 Cultural Cooperation Agreement and its implementing protocols, which cover exchanges in music, performing arts, education, research, and other areas. Filipino-Chinese businessmen have bankrolled some of these cultural exchanges. For instance, business tycoon and former Philippine Ambassador to China Yuchengco sponsored a conference at De la Salle University in Manila on China's peaceful rise.

China has been particularly interested in expanding educational exchanges with Philippine universities, especially those having a relationship with the United States. China has asked the American-founded De la Salle University in Manila to reestablish its Chinese Studies Program and to establish a satellite campus in China, with a curriculum focused on English, commerce, and engineering. For the Chinese, English appears to be the drawing card for Philippine academic institutions. The English spoken in the Philippines is derived from American English, and China finds it more cost-effective to establish academic relationships with U.S.–influenced universities in Asia than with U.S. universities themselves.[36]

At the China-ASEAN Commemorative Summit marking the 15th anniversary of the establishment of the China-ASEAN Dialogue in Naning, China (Guangxi) in October 2006, President Arroyo emphasized the benefits for Southeast Asia of the China-ASEAN economic relationship. Arroyo stated that the ASEAN region represents a market of over 500 million people for Chinese exports, and ASEAN is also a supplier of resources. In turn, she said that, by trading with China, ASEAN countries can reduce "our dependence for our exports on Western markets, such as the United States and Europe."[37] In the past, Arroyo had not expressed interest in using China to reduce dependence on Western markets; thus, it is not clear that her statement represents a departure in Philippine policy. Most likely, it was meant to ingratiate herself with the Chinese and perhaps to get more attention from Washington.

Philippine-ASEAN Interactions

An important component of the Philippines' response to China's growing role in Asian affairs has been its efforts to regionalize the South China Sea territorial dispute in the context of ASEAN. Manila hoped that ASEAN's involvement would constrain Beijing's freedom of action by presenting China with a united front and raising the political costs to China of an overly aggressive stance on the South China Sea.

The Philippine strategy of involving ASEAN in its territorial dispute with China produced some limited results at first, when Manila convinced ASEAN, as a group, to

---

[35] Embassy of the Philippines, "Philippine-China Relations," Beijing, 2005.

[36] Interview with Dr. Renato Cruz de Castro, Manila, November 29, 2005.

[37] "China Opportunity, Not Threat, for Southeast Asia: Arroyo," Agence France Presse, October 31, 2006.

raise the issue with Beijing at the ASEAN-China Senior Officials' Meeting in Hang-zhou in August 1995. However, ASEAN's intervention did not deter the Chinese from expanding their presence on Mischief Reef.[38] Despite the agreement the Philippines and China reached in August 1995 for both to resolve the dispute in accordance with the principles of international law, pursue confidence-building measures, and refrain from using force, PLA Navy vessels were sighted near Mischief Reef again in 1997. In 1998, the Chinese began upgrading the structures on the reef—which it claimed were fishing shelters—into multistory buildings on concrete platforms, large enough to serve as landing pads for helicopters and to be manned by Chinese military personnel.[39]

After 1999, a more-consistent Chinese policy of reassurance effectively reduced tensions with the Philippines. As part of a broader regional strategy to address growing security concerns about China among Southeast Asian nations, China agreed to adopt and implement a number of confidence-building mechanisms and agreements, which facilitated the normalization of Chinese-Philippine relations.[40] These steps included China's signing of the Declaration on the Conduct of Parties in the South China Sea (2002);[41] China's accession to ASEAN's Treaty of Amity and Cooperation (2003), which commits China to the principles of nonaggression and noninterference in the ASEAN Charter; and conclusion of the Tripartite Agreement for Joint Marine Seismic Undertaking in the South China Sea (2005), leading to joint exploration of energy resources in the disputed areas. Although no party renounced its territorial claim, the tripartite agreement was presented as a major step toward maintaining peace and stability in the area.[42]

The bottom line is that the Chinese policy of reassurance has largely defused the South China Sea dispute as a source of overt tension in Chinese-Philippine relations for the time being, but the South China Sea issue has not dropped completely out of sight. There is pending legislation in the Philippine Congress regarding the nation's obligation under the UN Law of the Seas Convention to delineate baselines to establish an exclusive economic zone—an issue that has a direct bearing on the South China Sea dispute and could be seen as an indicator of Philippine policy toward China. Manila also sees the issue, however, in the context of ASEAN and China rather than between the Philippines and other claimants, including China. So far the perception is that the

---

[38] Ang Cheng Guan, "The South China Sea Dispute Revisited," working paper, Singapore: Institute of Defence and Strategic Studies, Nanyang Technological University, August 1999, p. 13.

[39] Ian Storey, "Creeping Assertiveness: China, the Philippines, and the South China Sea Dispute," *Contemporary Southeast Asia,* Vol. 21, No. 1, April 1999.

[40] Zhang Yunling and Tang Shiping, "China's Regional Strategy," in Shambaugh, ed., 2006.

[41] ASEAN, Declaration on the Conduct of Parties in the South China Sea, 2002. The declaration is not a code of conduct. It is a political statement that includes language committing the parties to negotiate a code of conduct but lacks monitoring or verification mechanisms.

[42] Ronald N. Montaperto, "China Shows Its Sensitivity to SE Asia," *Asia Times,* April 27, 2005.

South China Sea issue is being managed but that it could become more unpredictable if oil were to be found in the area.[43]

The nation's role in the negotiations leading to the EAS and the East Asian Community constitute another barometer of Filipino views of China. On two key issues, the Philippines (with Singapore and Indonesia) found itself opposing China. Manila supported the inclusion of India, Australia, and New Zealand in the EAS and opposed Beijing's proposal to divide EAS into two blocs—a core group (ASEAN Plus Three), which would have made China the dominant player,[44] and the peripheral states, which included India, Australia, and New Zealand. Manila also voted with the rest of ASEAN to turn down Beijing's offer to host the second summit. As a result, the EAS will be held annually in conjunction with the ASEAN Summit, which is held in Southeast Asian countries only. The 2006 Summit, therefore, was held not in Beijing but in Cebu, the Philippines, in January 2007.[45]

Relations with the United States

Another dimension of the Philippine response to China's rise is its closer defense and security cooperation with the United States. In October 2003, the United States designated the Philippines a "major non–North Atlantic Treaty Organization (NATO)" ally; as such, Manila is a major U.S. partner in the global war on terrorism. For the Philippines, security cooperation with the United States is a critical source of military training, equipment, and related assistance to address its severe internal security challenges from Islamic insurgents. Also, by restoring the defense relationship with the United States, Manila hoped to reestablish some level of deterrence vis-à-vis China.[46]

Naturally, there is more to U.S.–Philippine bilateral relations than the growing defense relationship. The United States and the Philippines have a long and complicated relationship that dates back to the U.S. role as a colonial power from 1898 until 1945 and as the principal patron and ally of the Philippines after its independence. Although this relationship is not free of ambivalence, the Philippines, as much as any other Southeast Asian state, supports a continued U.S. presence in the region as a stabilizing force.

---

[43] Interview with Dr. Aileen Baviera, Dean, Asian Center, University of the Philippines, Manila, November 30, 2005. Some Filipinos talk with concern about China's unquenchable thirst for energy.

[44] This is because Japan on its own cannot balance China's influence, and South Korea is China's de facto ally in the ASEAN Plus Three forum. Robyn Lim, "East Asia Summit: China Checkmated," Alexandria, Va.: International Assessment and Strategy Center, January 8, 2006.

[45] The meeting had originally been scheduled for December 2006 but had been delayed by a typhoon alert.

[46] Manila has long been disappointed with the United States' refusal of support during the Mischief Reef incident. The U.S. position was that the U.S. security guarantee in the U.S.–Philippines Mutual Defense Treaty does not extend beyond the metropolitan territory of the Philippines and, therefore, does not extend to the Philippines' offshore claims in the South China Sea (Roy, 2005, p. 314). The treaty, however, does extend to Philippine military forces operating in the area.

Social ties between the Philippines and the United States are very strong. The Filipino-American community is the second largest community of Asian origin in the United States (after Chinese-Americans). An estimated 4 million Filipino-Americans, most of whom are U.S. citizens or dual citizens, live in the United States, and over 250,000 U.S. citizens live in the Philippines.[47] Integration of the U.S. and Philippine economies has lagged, however. Although discussions about a U.S.–Philippine FTA began in 2004, negotiations have not yet begun.

Taiwan Policy

Because of Taiwan's importance as a commercial partner and historical ties to influential sectors of Philippine society, Philippine policy toward the island can be considered an indicator of the nation's approach to China. Even after the Philippines recognized China in 1975, Taiwan retained significant economic and political influence in the Philippines.[48] Over the last decade, however, as Manila has pursued a policy of closer engagement with China, Taiwan's influence has declined relative to that of China. The official Philippine position is that Taiwan is part of China, but the Philippines reserved the right to maintain economic and trade links with Taiwan. As with other ASEAN states, the Philippines adheres to the One-China policy, and like some other ASEAN states, it has avoided taking sides in cross–Taiwan Strait disputes; for instance, Manila was officially silent on China's 2005 Anti-Secession Law.[49]

Taiwan remains an important commercial partner of the Philippines. It maintains a representative office in the Philippines and retains the support of a sector of the Philippine political and economic elite. Military and intelligence exchanges with Taiwan continue, although at a low profile. Philippine military personnel visiting Taiwan do not wear their uniforms and neither do Taiwanese military personnel visiting the Philippines. Taiwan holds annual ministerial-level trade meetings with the Philippines (as well as with Singapore, Malaysia, Indonesia, and Vietnam).[50]

Filipinos are one of the largest groups of migrant workers in Taiwan. Some are employed in companies as technicians, some in hospitals and clinics, some as musicians in entertainment centers, others in construction projects, still others as domestic helpers, and the majority in manufacturing companies. In June 2000, a Philippine

---

[47] These data were drawn from U.S. Department of State, Bureau of East Asian and Pacific Affairs, "Background Note: Philippines," October 2007.

[48] During the Corazon Aquino administration, pro-Taiwan members of the Filipino-Chinese Chamber of Commerce led a campaign that resulted in the introduction of bills in the Philippine Senate that proposed recognizing Taiwan as a separate state and granting diplomatic status to Taiwanese representatives.

[49] "China–Southeast Asia: Limited Regional Enthusiasm for Anti-Secession Law," Open Source Center, SEP20050318000098, March 18, 2005.

[50] Government Information Office, *Taiwan 2005 Yearbook: Foreign Relations*, Taipei, Taiwan, 2005.

Presidential Fact Finding Commission visited Taiwan and held hearings in Taipei on the work conditions of expatriate Filipino workers.[51]

Defense Policy Responses

In contrast to the situation in the 1990s, when Philippine security concerns centered on the South China Sea, current Philippine military planning and modernization plans are not driven by considerations relating to China's regional activism or its accelerating military modernization. Philippine defense policy has been intensely focused on internal security threats, and this will likely continue for some years. Philippine defense procurement and planning could eventually have a China dimension after 2010, but until then, the Philippines will rely on diplomatic means and, ultimately, on its alliance with the United States for the defense of its territory against external threats. The evolution of the Philippines' defense posture toward China is the result of three factors: (1) the easing of tensions in the South China Sea, (2) the Philippines' weak and eroding air and naval power-projection capabilities, and (3) the military's focus on combating internal threats.

Philippine defense planning focuses principally on internal security. Little energy and few resources are devoted to military procurement or planning for external threats, Chinese or otherwise. The defense relationship with the United States remains the keystone of Philippine security, but it is viewed largely in the context of counterterrorism, counterinsurgency, and military rationalization. Interaction between the Philippine and Chinese military establishments has also increased, but to no evident strategic end.

The Philippines defines the main threats to the security of the country, in order of importance, as the Communist Party of the Philippines New People's Army, the terrorist-criminal Abu Sayyaf Group, the Moro secessionist groups that the government calls the "Misurai Breakaway Group" (i.e., forces loyal to former Moro National Liberation Front Chairman Nur Misuari), and the Moro Islamic Liberation Front (which is currently engaged in a peace process with the government). To the extent the government recognizes external threats, it defines them in terms of transnational threats (drug smuggling, piracy, etc.).

Consistent with this threat assessment, the Arroyo government decommissioned the F-5 fighter air wing that formerly constituted the Philippines' only air defense capability. This action suggests that decisions about force structure do not reflect concerns about China. Philippine defense officials say that the cost of maintaining the aging F-5s was too high and that only one of the aircraft was operable when the decision to

---

[51] Hsu-Su-Fen, "A Short Report on the Migrant Fishworkers in Taiwan," Hong Kong: Asian Human Rights Commission—Asian Charter, November 9, 2001.

close down the fighter wing was made.[52] Some Philippine defense intellectuals have criticized the decision to decommission the F-5s.[53]

The Philippine military also lacks a maritime patrol and reconnaissance capability. The air force used to have F-27s that were used as maritime patrol aircraft. Attrition (only one is currently operational) and the loss of sensors have eroded that capability. The Air Force uses OV-10s as maritime patrol aircraft and S2-11 trainers for the fighter-attack role. The Philippine military recognizes the need to rebuild its air force's maritime patrol aircraft capability. The current defense procurement priority list includes three maritime patrol aircraft with sensors and communications capabilities.[54] In 2007, the armed forces reported the completion of the service-life extension program for the OV-10 Bronco close-support aircraft and acquisition of one Fokker F-27-500 transport aircraft.[55]

Aside from the maritime patrol aircraft, air force procurement priorities are largely related to the counterinsurgency mission. These include additional C-130 heavy transport aircraft (the requirement is for nine, with two currently in the inventory) and 120 utility helicopters (preferably U.S. Blackhawks) for mobility, attack helicopters, and trainer aircraft (decommissioned U.S. Navy Trojans being of interest). In early 2007, the United States turned over 10 UH-1H Huey helicopters, refurbished through the U.S. Foreign Military Financing program at $1.1 million per helicopter.[56]

After 2010, assuming a reduction in the internal threat, the Philippine armed forces foresees a shift to the external defense mission.[57] What is interesting about the post-2010 military modernization plan is that this anticipated shift suggests that—despite official assertions that there are no external threats—China remains a factor in Philippine strategic thinking and defense planning.

Philippine officials and defense analysts are well aware that the lack of an air defense capability creates a security gap. Defense officials say that this is a studied strategic risk that the country is willing to accept while resolving its internal conflicts. According to a senior Philippine official, the key to this assessment is the situation in the South China Sea. Because of concerns about potential risks in this area, the Philip-

---

[52] Interview with Lt. Gen. Reyes, Commander, Philippine Air Force, Villamor AFB, Pasay City, December 2005. According to the Philippines Department of Defense, the decision resulted in savings of P563.4 million (slightly over US$10 million) in maintenance costs per year. Interview with Under Secretary of Defense Antonio Santos, Camp Aguinaldo, Quezon City, November 2005.

[53] Interview with Dr. Aileen Baviera, Dean, Asian Center, University of the Philippines, Manila, November 2005.

[54] At the end of 2005, the Ministry of Defense was planning to acquire one aircraft a year. The platform has not yet been chosen, but the aircraft should be able to stay aloft for 8 hours at 200 knots/hour. Interview with Lt. Gen. Reyes, Commander, Philippine Air Force, Villamor Air Force Base, Pasay City, December 2005.

[55] Raymund Quilop, "Philippines Lists Equipment Priorities," *Jane's Defence Weekly*, April 11, 2007.

[56] "Radios, Helicopters for the Philippines," *Defense Industry Daily*, June 12, 2007.

[57] "Radios . . . ," 2007.

pines is engaged in dialogue and in strengthening security engagement with strategic partners.[58]

Rebuilding of U.S.–Philippine Military Ties

The key defense relationship for the Philippines is with the United States. Although, as noted earlier, the U.S.–Philippines Mutual Defense Treaty does not extend to the Philippine claims in the South China Sea, Philippine leaders believe that the defense relationship with the United States provides indirect deterrence vis-à-vis China. The Mischief Reef incident in 1995 led directly to a Philippine decision to rebuild its defense relationship with the United States, which had deteriorated after the withdrawal of the U.S. military from the Philippines in 1992.[59] The highlights of the rapprochement between the United States and the Philippines were the 1998 U.S.–Philippine Visiting Forces Agreement, which permitted the resumption of U.S.–Philippine combined military exercises, and the 2002 Mutual Logistics Support Agreement, which provided for reciprocal logistic support. On the Philippine side, there was the hope (not yet realized) that the restoration of defense ties would lead to the resumption of U.S. assistance to rebuild Philippine air and naval capabilities.

After September 11, 2001, the main Philippine rationale for U.S.–Philippine defense cooperation shifted to counterterrorism. President Arroyo saw the global war on terrorism as an opportunity to engage the United States in the government's military campaign against the Abu Sayyaf Group. Manila allowed U.S. overflights of Philippine airspace and use of airfields as transit points in support of Operation Enduring Freedom in Afghanistan. The United States, in turn, provided antiterrorism training and advice and deployed military personnel to train the Philippine army in counterterrorism operations on Mindanao.[60] U.S. security assistance to the Philippines increased to levels not seen since the withdrawal of the U.S. bases in 1992, from $2 million in foreign military financing in fiscal year 2002 to a sustained level of $19.0 million or more in subsequent years, in addition to transfers of significant amounts in excess defense articles.

The Philippines' proximity to the Taiwan Strait makes it potentially highly valuable for conducting U.S. military operations in the event of an armed confrontation between the United States and China over Taiwan. As a 2001 RAND Corporation report noted, while Manila is 650 nmi from the centerline of the Taiwan Strait, an air base in northern Luzon would be some 450 nmi away (a little closer to the Taiwan Strait than Kadena Airbase on Okinawa), and Batan Island in the Philippines is even

---

[58] Interviews with Philippine defense officials and analysts, Manila, December 2005.

[59] Although the basing agreement was terminated, the mutual defense treaty between the United States and the Philippines remained in force.

[60] Article XVIII, Section 25 of the Philippine Constitution prohibits the stationing of foreign military bases, troops, or facilities except under a treaty. Visits, exercises, or training missions by U.S. forces are considered to be legal under the constitutional prohibition.

closer, at 300 nmi.[61] As with other Southeast Asian states, a key factor in the Philippine response to a Taiwan contingency would be the circumstances that might have triggered a Chinese attack on Taiwan. If the immediate cause of the conflict is perceived as having been provoked by Taiwan, such as a Taiwanese declaration of independence, the Philippines, like most ASEAN countries, might be reluctant to become involved. If the attack is not perceived as having been provoked by Taiwan, however, the use of Chinese military force might revive fears of an aggressive China and might make the Philippines more amenable to cooperating with the United States in such a military conflict against China, including rallying public opinion around the venture.

Defense Cooperation with Other Countries

While the Philippines' most important defense relationship is with the United States, Manila also has cooperative defense relations with other countries within the Asia-Pacific region. After the United States, Australia is the second-largest provider of military training to the Philippine armed forces. In 1995, Australia and the Philippines signed a memorandum of understanding (MOU) to permit the countries to access each others' defense facilities, exchange defense information, and conduct cooperative activities in science and technology. During Australian Prime Minister Howard's visit to the Philippines in July 2003, the countries signed MOUs on cooperation to combat international terrorism and on combating transnational crime. Australia pledged a three-year A$5 million in counterterrorism assistance to the Philippines; in October 2004, Australian counterterrorism assistance was doubled to A$10 million per year for five years. The Philippines will also benefit from elements of the A$92.6 million Regional Counter Terrorism Package announced in the 2006–2007 budget. In August 2005, Australia and the Philippines agreed to establish interagency counterterrorism consultations among their senior officials to further enhance security cooperation.[62]

The Philippines has bilateral defense and intelligence exchanges with other Southeast Asian countries, but these are neither driven by nor directed at China. The closest ASEAN has come to developing a defense mechanism is the ASEAN Defense Ministers Meeting (ADMM), held in Kuala Lumpur in May 2006. The purpose of the meeting was to expand ASEAN's security focus beyond the ASEAN Regional Forum, the main mechanism for discussion of security issues among ASEAN members and partners. The ADMM has a mandate to establish an agenda and set up a senior officials' meeting to support ADMM activities; aside from holding the inaugural meeting in 2006 and issuing a joint statement, the group has done little of substance to date.

---

[61] Zalmay Khalilzad, David T. Orletsky, Jonathan D. Pollack, Kevin L. Pollpeter, Angel Rabasa, David A. Shlapak, Abram N. Shulsky, and Ashley J. Tellis, *The United States and Asia: Toward a New U.S. Strategy and Force Posture*, Santa Monica, Calif.: RAND Corporation, MR-1315-AF, 2001, p. 72.

[62] Australian Government, Department of Foreign Affairs and Trade (DFAT), "People's Republic of China," country brief, Canberra, December 2007b.

Military Exchanges with China

The Chinese and the Philippines have been expanding their military exchanges, driven in part by China's initiative. This program of military engagement includes exchanges of senior and working-level officials, including annual meetings at the minister-of-defense level; ship visits; and a small amount of military assistance to the Philippines. All these are common elements of China's military diplomacy. At the Hu-Arroyo summit in September 2004, the two sides agreed to initiate regular high-level talks on defense cooperation, increase military exchange visits, and swap intelligence on transnational threats. The first Philippines-China Defense and Security Dialogue was held in Manila on May 23, 2005. The Philippine delegation was headed by Under Secretary of Defense for Policy Antonio Santos, and the Chinese delegation by General Xiong Guangkai, Deputy Chief of Staff of the PLA. China proposed to hold combined naval exercises, but the Philippines declined. In October 2006, an older Chinese destroyer (*Luhu*-class) and replenishment ship (*Fuqing*-class) made a rare port visit to the Philippines.

Chinese military assistance to the Philippines is modest, especially in relation to U.S. assistance. Following the signing of a defense cooperation agreement in 2004, China offered the Philippines $1.2 million in military assistance to procure engineering equipment and offered five slots for Philippine officers to attend training courses in China. The military equipment, consisting of six bulldozers and six earth graders, was delivered in December 2005.[63] The second round of the dialogue took place in October 2006 in Beijing. The Chinese delegation was headed by General Zhang Qinsheng, Assistant Chief of the PLA General Staff, and the Philippine delegation by Undersecretary of Defense Antonio Santos.[64] Chinese Defense Minister Cao Gangchuan visited the Philippines in September 2007 (on the eve of Cao's retirement from the PLA) and met with Philippine Defense Secretary Gilbert Teodoro, Jr., President Arroyo, and other senior officials to discuss new ways to enhance bilateral military cooperation.[65]

Conclusions and Implications

Key Findings

The main factor affecting the Philippine response to China is the country's fundamental and myriad weaknesses. Chronic political instability, debilitating domestic insurgencies, and deteriorating military capabilities have left the Philippines unable

---

[63] Beting Laygo Dolor, "China Gives Military Aid to Philippines," *Philippine News*, March 14, 2005; Storey, "China and the Philippines," pp. 6–9.

[64] "China, the Philippines Hold . . . ," *People's Daily* (online), October 10, 2006.

[65] Noel Tarrazona, "US, China Vie for Philippine Military Influence," *Asia Times* (online), September 20, 2007.

to ensure peace and order even within the main islands, let alone defend its offshore territorial and natural resource claims vis-à-vis China. These weaknesses have spurred Philippine efforts to reestablish close defense ties with the United States to cope with the country's severe internal security challenges. Given its inability to rely completely on the United States to protect its territorial claims in the South China Sea, however, this weakness has inclined the Philippines toward some accommodation with China and has induced efforts to leverage its membership in ASEAN to regionalize the South China Sea issue.

A significant reduction in external threat perceptions reinforces this general orientation. The decrease in China's activism in the South China Sea since the end of the 1990s coupled with Beijing's confidence-building efforts and broader charm offensive in the last several years have helped diminish both bilateral tensions and domestic Filipino suspicions about China's regional intentions. This is perhaps the area of greatest change over the past decade and is reflected in notably more-favorable Filipino public attitudes toward China today.

Increasingly, China has come to be seen not as a major security threat but as a relatively benign power—at least for now. This is reflected in current Philippine military modernization plans, which do not appear to be driven by considerations relating to China (or any external threats, for that matter). Although public opinion polls continue to suggest a lingering wariness about China's long-term intentions, the generally relaxed view Filipinos have of their external security environment today and preoccupation with their internal situation reinforce the government's basic response to the rise of China.

A final major contributing factor is the draw of the Chinese economy. The Philippine economy depends less on trade with China than do the economies of many other Asian states. As with other Asian economies, however, China has become an increasingly important market for Philippine exports, with the burgeoning trade relationship becoming a growing source of the Philippines' own economic growth. The broad consensus in the Philippines over China's importance as an economic partner bolsters support for a policy of engagement and for efforts to strengthen bilateral ties.

While these are the major forces driving the Philippines' response to China, it is important to stress that the forces are not driving Philippine policy anywhere in particular. China is not a contentious issue in Philippine politics. The leadership is heavily focused on internal political, economic, and security challenges. And the public is relatively inattentive to China or, for that matter, most other foreign policy issues. Philippine-Chinese tensions have certainly decreased in recent years, and the tone of the relationship has become more productive. One result has been a significant increase in high-level consultations, confidence-building efforts, and sociocultural exchanges. But contentious issues, such as the South China Sea dispute and offshore resources, have been shelved rather than resolved. At the same time, the Philippines' economic stake in China—as measured by the level of FDI, for example—remains small both absolutely and relative to those of other major Asian countries, and the view of China as an important future economic partner is mixed with an incipient sense of China as a potential competitive threat. In this environment, there is little evidence of a Philippine strategy for harnessing relations with China for even economic, let alone strategic, purposes.

Moreover, while seeking to expand engagement with China, the Philippines has also moved to increase security cooperation with the United States. The principal impetus for this expansion is the war on terrorism, rather than China per se, with terrorist groups posing a threat to both Philippine and U.S. interests. But expanded security cooperation also reestablishes at least a degree of deterrence vis-à-vis China and strengthens the Philippines' ability to counter potential Chinese pressures. Strong historical, economic, and cultural ties between the Philippines and the United States reinforce these shared security interests and contribute to making the United States the overwhelmingly preferred security partner for most Filipinos.

Future Responses and the Implications for the United States

The analysis in this chapter suggests that, absent major new tensions over the South China Sea or other priority issues, the basic Philippine response to China is not likely to undergo dramatic change in the near future. On the one hand, all the major political actors agree on the value of moderate and gradual engagement with China, with a broad consensus, in particular, on the benefits of expanded economic interactions. Growing economic ties will help ground a relationship heavily constrained in the past by mutual suspicions and conflicting national interests. As with other countries in this volume, bilateral economic relations provide a core logic for sustaining stable political relations with China. Such relations will also increase Philippine incentives to accommodate China's interests on issues not directly affecting the Philippines' national security interests—particularly if the growth in economic ties is accompanied by such things as an agreement on an enforceable code of conduct on the South China Sea and successful joint exploration of energy resources in disputed areas.

On the other hand, the Philippines' weakness and vulnerability will continue to place the United States at the center of Philippine foreign and security policies. The continued preoccupation of Filipino policymakers with the exigencies of their internal situation will reinforce this inclination—as will latent public wariness over China's long-term intentions—and thus inhibit major Philippine policy departures toward China. Renewed Chinese assertiveness over contested territories, economic zone resources, or other priority issues could break the current Filipino consensus on engagement with China and increase support for a policy oriented more toward deterrence and overt defense cooperation with the United States.

What this suggests is continuation of a two-pronged approach. The Philippines will pursue closer engagement with China and, at the same time, reinvigorate its military alliance with the United States.

We drew three implications from this analysis for the United States. First, the principal challenge will not be the Philippines' external orientation but its internal weakness. This weakness prevents the Philippines from protecting its key security interests with long-term strategic planning and limits the scope of its defense cooperation with the United States. Furthermore, such weaknesses foster, or at least reinforce, some accommodation toward Beijing. As the oldest Asian treaty ally of the United States and an important current partner in the global war on terrorism, the key policy question is not so much whether the Philippines will have the *will* for meaningful security cooperation with the United States as whether it will have the *capability*.

Second, efforts to strengthen the bilateral relationship will have benefits beyond the relationship itself. As a founding member of ASEAN and front-line state in key East Asian disputes and as a democratic state with its own domestic Islamic insurgency, the Philippines can help advance important U.S. strategic interests in East Asia. Designating the Philippines as a major non-NATO ally, expanding on-the-ground security cooperation, and taking other steps to bolster the alliance will not only help strengthen the Philippine government's ability to deal with its internal security challenges. These actions will also help strengthen the nation's self-confidence and ability to resist external predation and help it conclude a negotiated settlement of the Moro insurgency, broadening the nation's horizons and increasing political support for enhanced contributions to regional security.

Third, the Philippine response to increased tensions over Taiwan or other issues directly affecting Chinese security interests will be heavily influenced by the particular context in which such tensions arise, as well as by the status of Philippine-Chinese and Philippine-U.S. relations. How the other states of ASEAN respond will also have major influence. At this point, the most that can probably be said is that the Philippines, like other states in Asia, will try to avoid having to make a choice between China and the United States—and that success in addressing the first two implications above will increase the chances of eliciting supportive Philippine responses on the third. Yet, as long as the United States remains so central to Philippine foreign and defense policy, Manila's material incentives and political proclivities to assist Washington in maintaining Asia-Pacific stability remain strong.

CHAPTER SIX

Thailand

Thailand has a distinguished history of bending with the wind when it comes to regional politics. The nation maintained its status as the only Asian state to preserve its essential sovereignty during the 19th century by balancing competing colonial powers against one another. During World War II, it allied with Japan and reconquered territories lost to the British in Malaysia and Burma and to the French in Indochina. However, enough of its senior leaders joined the anti-Japanese Free Thai resistance that Thailand was not treated as an enemy combatant by the allies after the war.[1] In today's world of nonexclusive strategic partnerships, Bangkok's efforts to remain close to both China and the United States are less extraordinary but nevertheless notable.

Thailand's 1997 constitution led to a more-decisive political system, one with fewer but more stable political parties and a greatly empowered prime minister. From February 2001 until he was ousted by the military in September 2006, Prime Minister Thaksin Shinawatra leveraged the new constitution to maximize his authority. He came to office talking about diversifying Thailand's strategic relationships and made no secret of his plans to strengthen relations with China. Thaksin did, in fact, nudge Thai foreign policy in that direction, inviting criticism from some quarters that he was jeopardizing Thailand's alliance with the United States. After September 11, 2001, however, Thaksin delivered strong support for the global war on terrorism, prompting a different critique: that he was risking Thai interests unnecessarily in a conflict not in Thailand's interests. It appears, then, that rather than moving Thailand decisively toward partnership with China and away from the United States, Thaksin pursued a bolder, less bureaucratically encumbered and arguably riskier version of Thailand's omnidirectional foreign policy.

While Thai foreign policy has always moved in one direction, several long-term trends suggest that relations with China have become more important to leaders in Bangkok, and barring a change in China's growth or behavior, the situation is unlikely to change in the near future. China's importance as a trade partner has grown. Between 1996 and 2006, Thai trade with China grew by 568 percent, several times faster than

---

[1] On Thailand's alignment with Japan and its swing toward alignment with the Allies during the closing stages of the war, see David K. Wyatt, *Thailand: A Short History*, New Haven: Yale University Press, 1982, pp. 252–263.

Thailand's trade with the rest of the world. Thai investment in China is picking up again, after retrenchments following the 1997 financial crisis, and Chinese companies are now beginning to invest in Thailand. With the Thai military's budgetary prospects improving after ten years of stagnation, it is again acquiring military hardware from China and from major Western suppliers. Internationally, combined engagement with and support for Burma from Thailand, India, and China has mitigated perhaps the single largest irritant in relations between Bangkok and Beijing.

While Thailand may move toward China, the magnitude of the shift does have limits. Thai leaders are committed to a balanced posture vis-à-vis China and the United States by dint of national disposition and interest. Bangkok is also working to develop options with other countries. Economically, it has moved to strengthen ties with India, Australia, New Zealand, and Japan. Politically and militarily, it cooperates with India, Singapore, Malaysia, and Indonesia, as well as with the United States and China. China's international behavior, especially in East Asia, will be one of the largest variables in how Thai attitudes toward the rise of China evolve. Events in Burma, the success or failure of FTA negotiations with the United States, and the future shape of Thai politics are important variables, albeit less widely appreciated ones.

Although the bulk of the research for this chapter was conducted prior to the September 2006 military coup, democratic rule has since been restored. The views of the new government are similar to those of the Thaksin administration, so there is little reason to believe that the coup fundamentally altered the expected patterns in foreign and defense policymaking described in this chapter.

National Conditions

Thailand's China policy in the last decade has developed in the context of a rapidly evolving Thai polity. Thailand made the transition from military to civilian, democratic rule during the 1980s. The 1997 constitution accelerated the trend toward more-democratic, more-transparent rule and strengthened the prime minister. The switch from multiseat districts to single-member districts weakened third parties and improved the prospects for single-party rule. New rules prohibited purchasing candidates from other parties on the eve of elections. New provisions required cabinet members to resign their seats in parliament, eliminating their ability to undermine the prime minister by resigning and joining the opposition.

Structural reforms empowered political leaders, particularly the prime minister, and made them less encumbered by procedural constraints and bureaucratic power. The victory by Thaksin's Thai Rak Thai [Thais Love Thailand] (TRT) Party in 2001 gave it a dominant position in parliament. In February 2005, it became the first one-party government in Thai history.[2] Thaksin campaigned against the bureaucracy and portrayed himself as a "CEO prime minister." He relied on a coterie of personal advisors, rather than the cabinet, and his achievements were impressive.[3] On the foreign policy front alone, he completed a remarkable eight FTAs and launched a number of regional initiatives during his tenure.[4]

As in Japan, political reform strengthened leading parties and the prime minister, but the politicians who gained in Thailand were far different from the professional politicians in Japan, who have benefited from their nation's political reforms.[5] In Thailand, politics remained a game dominated by business, with a smattering of bureaucrats and lawyers. During the 1980s and early 1990s, provincial businessmen proved adept at mobilizing votes and were disproportionately represented in parliament. The 1997 financial crisis motivated businessmen from companies with international, as opposed to provincial, reach to enter the fray. Politics moved from being a province of the rich to one of the superrich. Many of these businessmen, rich and superrich, are of Chinese descent.

Given their economic outlooks and interests, neither Thai politicians nor their generals are likely to change course on China along the lines of Japan's more-confrontational approach to China. Thaksin, who was the CEO of Thailand's largest telecom giant (the Shin Corporation), is ethnic Chinese. He took full advantage of the prime minister's new executive power to improve relations with China. The 2008 return to a democratically elected civilian government raises new questions about the precise orientation of Thailand's evolving China policy; the strong links between the new government and Thaksin suggest but do not determine a return to Thaksin's approach. If a professional class of politicians ever does emerge to replace the businessmen turned politicians, a wider range of interests and variables will affect Thailand's thinking on the rise of China. But it should be borne in mind that businessmen have dominated Thai politics under every constitution that has permitted relatively free and fair elections (and some that have not).

---

[2] The February 2005 election was also the first time a prime minister had been reelected since democracy was restored in 1988.

[3] Foreign diplomats in Bangkok say that they often seek those close to Thaksin personally, rather than members of government, when they want to understand or influence policy. See also Pasuk Phongpaichit and Chris Baker, *Thaksin: The Business of Politics in Thailand*, Bangkok: Silkworm Books, 2005, p. 102.

[4] Thaksin's preparation and follow-through have also not always matched his flair for creating new bodies or securing the adoption of new laws. ("Veteran Diplomat Asada Slams Thaksin's Foreign Policy in New Book," *The Nation* [Bangkok], August 17, 2004.)

[5] For more on Japanese reforms, see Chapter Three.

Domestic Politics and Public Opinion

Foreign policy has not been a driving political issue in domestic politics, except insofar as it affects economic welfare or other domestic concerns. The conflict in southern Thailand, the drug problem, economic recovery (from the financial crisis of 1997), and Thaksin and his military successors are the leading political issues. Although each has a foreign policy dimension, none is primarily a foreign policy issue. Coup leaders did not attempt to justify their actions on foreign policy grounds, and the policies they have pursued have not, for the most part, been appreciably different (except to the extent that U.S. sanctions have closed off certain possibilities). While China is not central to any of these issues, with the possible exception of economic recovery, each shapes Thailand's China policy. Taken as a whole, they push Bangkok closer to both Beijing and Washington simultaneously—and reinforce Thailand's proclivity for the middle position.

Thaksin elevated economic interests to the center of Thailand's foreign policy agenda, and that priority, in general terms, was reflected in moves to cement closer relations with China. At the heart of Thaksin's economic diplomacy was the idea of developing Thailand as a hub, tying subregions of Asia together, both physically (through infrastructure) and institutionally (through cross-cutting FTAs). As Pansak Vinyaratn, Chief Policy Advisor to the Prime Minister, explained, "A small open economy situated in a neutral zone, Thailand is in an ideal position to play a catalytic role in strengthening economic cooperation among Asian nations."[6]

While distancing themselves rhetorically, Thailand's military rulers largely followed Thaksin's lead in giving economic interests a privileged place in Thai foreign policy, and this does not appear to have changed now that civilian rule has been restored. Thai political parties make little effort to differentiate themselves on policy, especially foreign policy. Party policy platforms, to the extent they are published, are so vague and philosophical that they offer little sense of actual policy direction.

Typical in this regard is the posture adopted by the Democrat Party, the largest opposition party prior to the coup. During the 2001 election, which brought Thaksin into office, this party showed some interest in strengthening ties with Europe, while Thaksin made his desire for a more Asian-oriented foreign policy and closer ties with China known.[7] The opposition subsequently accused Thaksin of an excessive focus on economic issues, abandoning Bangkok's traditional emphasis on ASEAN, and leaning too far toward China. But apart from very occasional statements on these topics, the Democrat Party was largely silent on foreign policy. Moreover, in most of Thaksin's initiatives, precursors could be found in the policies of his rivals. Indeed, in many ways,

---

[6] Pansak Vinyaratn, *Facing the Challenge: Economic Policy and Strategy,* Hong Kong: CLSA Books, August 2004.

[7] "Foreign Policy Set to Take Center Stage in Election," *The Nation* (Bangkok), October 17, 2000.

the TRT inherited the Democrat Party's foreign policy agenda but molded it to its own purposes and pushed it with greater vigor.

Hence, regardless of whether the Democrat Party or the People's Power Party (the name given to the TRT when it was reconstituted after being banned by coup leaders) dominates in Thai politics, the general direction of foreign policy—and the place of China in it—is unlikely to change dramatically.

A Pro-China Tilt?

Thaksin's critics accused him of attempting to strengthen Thailand's strategic relations with China even further than his emphasis on economic interests would require. Some of the more-prominent evidence they offered for a pro-China tilt included Thaksin's frequent visits to China, his eagerness to sign a joint strategic-cooperation agreement (which he has since referred to as a strategic partnership), the signing of a bilateral FTA with China to supplement the China-ASEAN FTA, and his support for resuming arms purchases from China. In September 2003, Don Pathan of *The Nation* quoted a "TRT party insider" as saying that the government's relationship with China had become "one of allegiance, rather than just riding on the back of the People's Republic's rise."[8]

At least some critics focused on Thaksin's Chinese ethnicity. The columnist Chang Noi (a pseudonym) suggested that Thaksin had opened the government to Chinese influence. Hill people petitioning for Thai nationality, he wrote, could speak "Thai much better than, ummmm, several Cabinet ministers."[9] Thaksin is a fourth-generation Thai whose great grandfather, a member of the Chinese Hakka minority, emigrated from Guangdong in the 1860s. Having received his master's and doctoral degrees in the United States, his knowledge of the English language and the United States is almost certainly greater than his knowledge of contemporary China or the Chinese language. He employed his ethnic status in cultivating Thailand's relations with Beijing, but ethnicity is probably more of a political issue, in this case, than a major factor influencing Thai policy.[10]

---

[8] Don Pathan, "Is the World Getting an Accurate Image of Thailand?" *The Nation* (Bangkok), February 10, 2003. See also Kavi Chongkittavorn, "Relations with Asian Giants Hampered by Lack of Realism," *The Nation* (Bangkok), May 8, 2006b.

[9] Chang Noi, "Reimagining the Thai Nation," *The Nation* (Bangkok), August 19, 2002. "Chang Noi" is a pseudonym.

[10] On a visit to his ancestral home in Guangdong, he declared

> When the Chinese people see a Thai leader and so many entrepreneurs come to China to pay homage to the place where their ancestors may have once lived, they will understand that the Thais and Chinese are from one family, and they are relatives.

"Thai PM Concludes China Tour," Xinhua News Agency, July 3, 2005. Two hundred Thai businessmen accompanied him on the trip.

Indeed, Thaksin's departure from the scene, has, if anything, opened the door to an even closer—and more sustainable—Thai relationship with Beijing. His removal has depersonalized the relationship and eliminated ethnicity and business as political issues in it.[11] Both the economic relationship and political-military relationship between Bangkok and Beijing have grown closer under military government.

Party Differences

It is not clear how different the Democrat Party's approach to China is from Thaksin's approach. Economic aspects of statecraft have historically played a major role in that party's foreign policy. Chuan Leekpai's Democrat government employed the metaphor of Thailand as a hub before Thaksin did. Thaksin concluded a strategic cooperation agreement with China in 2001, but Chuan paved the way by signing what he referred to as a "21st-century cooperation program" with Beijing in 1999. Thaksin pushed through a bilateral FTA with China, but its significance paled in comparison to the much more-comprehensive coverage of the China-ASEAN FTA (CAFTA), which Chuan's government helped negotiate. While Thaksin's Chinese roots raised eyebrows, in part because he retained business interests on the mainland, three of the last four prime ministers before Thaksin were also ethnic Chinese.[12]

This is not to say the two parties, their China policies, or their compositions are indistinguishable. Thaksin clearly emphasized bilateral diplomacy more than his predecessors; to the extent he pursued multilateral approaches, he was far more inclined to pursue these outside the ASEAN context. Moreover, one cannot be sure what course the Democrat Party's current leader, Abhisit Vejjajiva, would take on China. He has been largely quiet on the issue, and while he might take a course similar to that of his Democrat Party predecessors, there is also no reason to believe he will slavishly follow precedent.

More predictable and important may be differences in style. The Democrat Party is an old liberal (in the classical sense) party. It is, in many ways, part of the larger elite establishment. Its members have deep ties to the bureaucracy; possess old money (relative to many in the TRT); and tend, by temperament and interest, to be more cautious in how they approach foreign policy.[13] During his 2001 election campaign, Thaksin, who made the bulk of his money during Thailand's 1990s "go-go" business days, attacked the bureaucracy for its cautious and unimaginative approach to everything from economics to foreign policy. Even when there were Democrat Party–sponsored precursors to most of his foreign policy initiatives, Thaksin took these initia-

---

[11] "Post-Coup Thailand in the Eyes of the U.S. and China," *The Nation* (Bangkok), February 12, 2007.

[12] Chinese candidates for parliament are confident enough of Thailand's multiculturalism that they increasingly use their Chinese names. Patrick Jory, "Multiculturalism in Thailand? Cultural and Regional Resurgence in a Diverse Kingdom," *Harvard Asia Pacific Review*, Winter 2000.

[13] Interviews with Thai scholars and politicians, Bangkok, May 15–23, 2006.

tives beyond the Democrat Party's comfort zone. So, he pursued foreign policy goals more aggressively, even if the relative importance accorded China and the United States has not shifted decisively.

There are other important political actors in Thailand. One of these is Beijing, which has made assiduous efforts to court the support of other key players in Thailand. One target has been the royal family, which remains a political force. Members of the royal family have made nearly 50 visits to China over the last 30 years and have been received there with great pomp and ceremony.[14] Crown Princess Maha Chakri Sirindorn, who speaks Chinese and is a tireless promoter of cultural exchange, has made 23 of these trips.[15] Beijing has also wooed the media. In January 2006, Thailand's *The Nation* began including the *China Business Weekly*, originally published by the *China Daily*, as an insert in its Monday newspapers. Beijing has also courted the Thai military.

A November 2005 survey sponsored by the U.S. Department of State's Bureau of Intelligence and Research found that more Thais had a favorable view of China (83 percent) than they did of the United States (73 percent).[16] A survey by Japan's *Yomiuri Shimbun* found that more than 80 percent of Thais had a favorable image of China.[17] And the Department of State survey shows that more than twice as many Thais believed China would be Thailand's most important economic partner five to ten years later than believed the United States would be (43 versus 21 percent, respectively).

Media images of China are generally favorable. Much of the positive sentiment may simply derive from an understanding of growing Chinese wealth; prosperity; and, in a personal and economic sense, increasing freedom. Although the image of the United States is also favorable, anger at the United States for its role in urging strict conditions on International Monetary Fund (IMF) loans during the 1997–1998 financial crisis lingers even today. China, for its part, earned a measure of goodwill during the crisis. Its aid was more modest but came without strings attached. More recently, however, U.S. popularity received a significant boost after its visible and extensive response to the December 2004 tsunami.

Despite the generally favorable view of China, far more Thais continued to see the United States as the country's "most important security partner" over the following five to ten years than saw China in that role (49 versus 17 percent) in the November 2005 Department of State survey.[18] Unfortunately, for all the survey's value, no follow-up questions were asked. Hence, it is not clear whether the United States was regarded as a

---

[14] Kavi Chongkittavorn, "Strategic Value of Thai-Chinese Relations," *The Nation* (Bangkok), January 9, 2006a.

[15] "Thai Princess Calls for More Exchanges Between Chinese, Thai Students" Xinhua News Agency, April 4, 2006.

[16] U.S. Department of State, Bureau of Intelligence and Research, 2005.

[17] "Japan Gets Good Marks in Poll," *Daily Yomiuri*, September 5, 2006.

[18] U.S. Department of State, Bureau of Intelligence and Research, 2005.

better security partner because it was more trusted or because the respondents believed it would remain the world's preeminent military power.

Economic Responses

Thailand competes with China for FDI, and its economy is less complementary with China's than are those of South Korea or Japan. Yet, Thai elites regard China as more of an economic opportunity than a threat. Thailand's economy is highly trade dependent, and its trade with China has grown significantly faster than its overall trade. A large ethnic Chinese business community, including the leaders of most of Thailand's largest business groups, has positioned Thailand well to capitalize on China's rise and represents a strong, if diffuse, lobby for strong ties with China.

Chinese-Thai Trade

The Thai economy is unusually export dependent, with exports accounting for almost 60 percent of Thailand's GDP of $206.3 billion in 2006.[19] Although roughly 60 percent of Thailand's labor force is employed in agriculture (rice is the country's most important crop), much of the country's strong economic growth in the decade prior to the 1997 Asian financial crisis was in the manufacturing sector. Thailand's economy has grown since the sharp dip of 1997–1999 but has not returned to the boom levels of the early and mid-1990s.

Growth in bilateral trade with China has been dramatic (Figures 6.1 and 6.2). In 1996, China was Thailand's eighth largest trade partner. As of 2006, it had become Thailand's third-largest trade partner, after Japan and the United States. Trade with China, at $25 billion (10 percent of Thailand's total trade) in 2006, still lagged significantly behind that of Japan, at $42 billion (16 percent of its world total). But while trade with Japan grew by just 42 percent between 1996 and 2006, and trade with the United States expanded by 48 percent (to $28 billion), trade with China grew by 568 percent. When Hong Kong trade figures are combined with those of China (Hong Kong is counted separately from China in most trade statistics), "Greater China" becomes Thailand's second largest trade partner in 2006, behind only Japan.

Thailand's trade with China is relatively balanced. In 2006, it exported $12 billion worth of goods to China, while importing $14 billion. If trade with Hong Kong is included, its exports to China ($19 billion) significantly exceeded imports from it ($15 billion). As shown in Figure 6.3, Thailand's main imports from China in 2006 consisted of office machines and electronic and telecommunication equipment, for a combined 44 percent of total imports from China. Other major import categories are

---

[19] Except where otherwise noted, all trade data in this subsection are from the UN Commodity Trade Statistics (COMTRADE) database (UN Statistics Division, various years).

Figure 6.1
Thai Imports, by Country of Origin, Selected Years

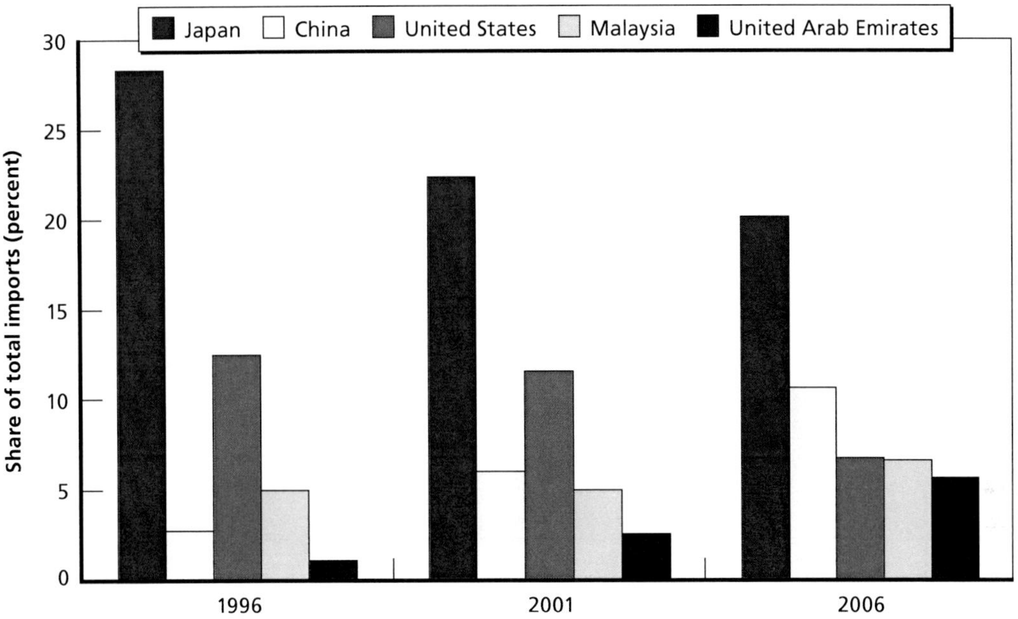

SOURCE: UN Statistics Division, 1996, 2001, 2006.
RAND *MG736-6.1*

iron and steel (9 percent) and industrial machinery (6 percent). Among Thai exports to China, office machines and electronic equipment are, again, the largest categories, for 33 percent of the total (Figure 6.4). However, primary goods account for a greater percentage of Thailand's exports to China than they do of its imports from China. These include crude rubber (12 percent), primary plastics (8 percent), petroleum (8 percent), and organic chemicals (10 percent).

Thailand and China in Regional Production Chains

Chinese-Thai trade cannot be adequately assessed in purely bilateral terms. Foreign investment and Thailand's role as a production base for major multinational firms, particularly Japanese firms, define key patterns in its trading relations—including those with China. Investment flows tend to vary widely from year to year, but incoming FDI amounted to $8.8 billion in 2006.[20] According to statistics from the Thai Board of Investment, Japan accounted for 43 percent of all investments (by value) approved in 2006 and 28 percent of those approved in the first nine months of 2007. The United

---

[20] Runckel and Associates, Inc., "Table of Comparison: Asian Countries' Foreign Direct Investment: Asian Development Outlook 2007," 2007.

Figure 6.2
Thai Exports, by Country of Destination, Selected Years

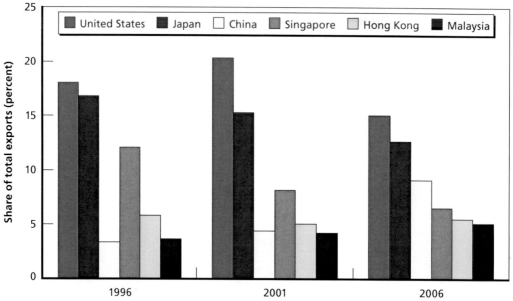

SOURCE: UN Statistics Division, 1996, 2001, 2006.
RAND *MG736-6.2*

Figure 6.3
Composition of Thailand's Imports from China, 2006

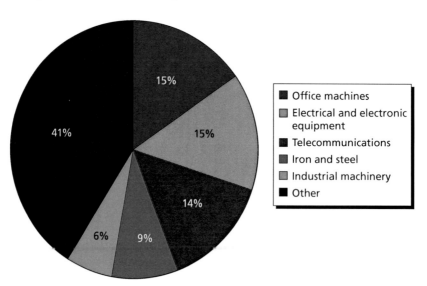

SOURCE: UN Statistics Division, 2006.
RAND *MG736-6.3*

Figure 6.4
Composition of Thailand's Exports to China, 2006

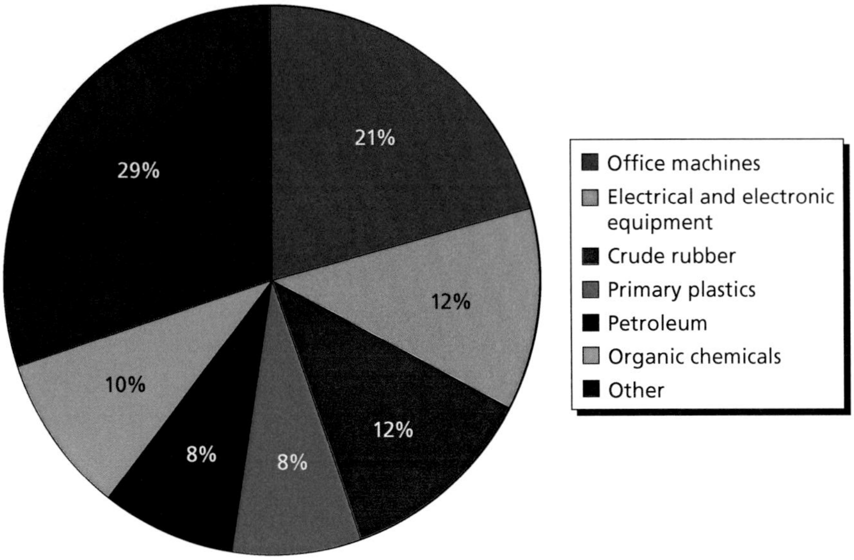

SOURCE: UN Statistics Division, 2006.
RAND *MG736-6.4*

States had the second largest share, with 27 percent and 19 percent, respectively.[21] Thailand is the world's 14th-largest producer of automobiles, mostly for export, with Toyota and Isuzu accounting for some 65 percent of the total. Electronic components (including computers) accounted for 15.8 percent of Thailand's worldwide exports in 2004, of which fully 80 percent were built by foreign firms.[22]

Investments by Japanese and Western multinationals shape trade patterns between Thailand and China. Neither China nor Thailand is particularly well known for globally competitive electronics and machinery industries (at least not indigenously owned industries), yet they conduct a high percentage of their trade in these sectors. About one-half of Thailand's computer hardware exports are hard disk drives, and Thailand accounts for one-half the world's production of these drives. The semiconductors inside Thai-manufactured drives come largely from Japanese or other companies in China (or elsewhere), while the finished drives are then sent back to China or other locations for incorporation into finished computer systems.[23]

This is not to say that all Chinese-Thai trade is externally driven or unimportant. Agricultural trade with China is important for Thailand's countryside, albeit with

---

[21] Thailand Board of Investment, Foreign Investment Web page, 2008.

[22] Royal Danish Ministry of Foreign Affairs, Danish Trade Council, "Sector Overview: The Electronics Industry in Thailand," Copenhagen, July 9, 2005.

[23] Royal Danish Ministry of Foreign Affairs, Danish Trade Council, 2005.

winners and losers from such trade. The countries' respective natural resources help drive different comparative advantages. Thailand imports iron and steel from China and exports plastics and petroleum. Even in the manufacturing sectors, not all trade with China is controlled by third-country firms. Indigenous Chinese and Thai firms collaborate in the motorcycle, telecommunications, and automotive sectors. China is Thailand's fourth-largest destination for outward foreign investment, and that investment is likely to grow with the recent completion of a four-lane highway from Thailand through Laos to Xishuanbanna in Yunnan Province. China is also beginning to invest in Thailand.

But the impressive trade numbers today, particularly in high-tech areas, should be viewed in the context of the dominant position of largely Japanese multinationals in Thailand, a reality that may change—but only gradually. Japan's cumulative investment in Thailand is 45 times larger than Thai investment in China, which, in turn, is significantly larger than Chinese investment in Thailand.

Thailand's Chinese Business Groups

The ethnic Chinese business community in Thailand has long accounted for the preponderance of Thai investment moving to China, as well as much of the trade with China. As many observers have noted, the ethnic Chinese community has largely been absorbed into Thai society and has intermarried with ethnic Thais in an effort to form local connections. But Thai conglomerates remain largely family-run businesses, and many heads of the *gongsi* (Chinese companies) have not lost their ability to work in a Chinese environment.

Thailand's largest conglomerate, the CP Group, is headed by a second-generation Thai, Dhanin Chearavanont. Dhanin's father came to Thailand from Guangdong Province in 1921 and established companies centered on agribusiness. Typical of many second- and even third-generation ethnic Chinese Thais, Dhanin was born in Bangkok but was sent to Guangdong for secondary school and Hong Kong for college. He speaks fluent Cantonese.[24] For a time during the 1980s, the CP Group was the largest single foreign investor in China—from any country. It supplied feed grain and owned a wide variety of manufacturing companies, including several motorcycle assembly plants.

The CP Group was hit particularly hard by the 1997 financial crisis and divested itself of much of its manufacturing in China. It has, however, largely recovered and is once again rapidly increasing its presence in China. Production in its streamlined motorcycle facilities has increased from 300,000 units annually in 1990 to 1 million units today with plans for future growth. It has also expanded into retail. Starting

---

[24] *Tai no Kajin Zaibatsu 57 Ke [57 Great (Ethnic) Chinese Thai Business Families]*, Tokyo: NNA, September 2005; Nikkei Net Interactive, The Future of Asia 2002, Bio/CV of Dhanin Chearavanont, Chairman & CEO, Charoen Pokphand Group (Thailand), 2002.

with one Lotus Superstore in 1997, CP now has 75 outlets in China competing with France's Carrefour and the U.S.'s Wal-Mart.[25]

Ethnic Chinese families either dominate or are well represented in all areas of Thai economic life. Thailand's richest five individuals are of Chinese extraction, as are most of its top 40 wealthiest individuals.[26] Ethnic Chinese families own and manage the largest Thai (that is, not foreign owned) firms in agribusiness (CP Group), textiles (Saha Union), rice export (Soon Hua Seng, or SHS, Group), steel (Sahaviriya Steel Industries), commercial banking (Bangkok Bank), construction (Italian-Thai Group), plastics (SITHAI), automotives (Siam Motors), home building (Land and House Plc), and several other sectors.[27] In several sectors, ethnic Chinese families also own the number two and three firms. Many are deeply involved in politics and government, and although their minority status makes it difficult for them to organize publicly, their direct involvement in or ties to government make them a force for improved relations with China.[28]

Interlocking FTAs and Thailand as Hub

The Thai government strongly supported the ASEAN FTA in 1992. Chuan's Democrat Party government backed FTA linkages of ASEAN with several outside states and groups, including China, Japan, South Korea, and the Closer Economic Relations group of Australia and New Zealand. It was not until Thaksin became prime minister, however, that strictly bilateral FTAs became a central focus of Thai foreign policy. (For a full list of Thailand's FTAs, see Table 6.1.)

In November 2002, China and ASEAN signed the CAFTA agreement, which covers some 7,000 items and phases in tariff reductions between 2004 and 2010. In June 2003, Bangkok signed a bilateral "early harvest" agreement with Beijing accelerating tariff reductions on 188 items, all fruits and vegetables. The original CAFTA agreement had been under negotiation since 1999—before Thaksin's tenure began— and was relatively uncontroversial. As a bilateral Thaksin initiative, however, the early harvest agreement with China, despite its relatively limited scope, attracted criticism. Senator Kraisak Choonhavan, then chairman of Thailand's Senate Foreign Affairs

---

[25] Figures on motorcycle production and outlets from interview with CP Group senior management, May 23, 2006.

[26] Assessing wealth, which is often spread among family members, is difficult, as is determining ethnicity. This statement is based on combining data from Justin Doebele, Chaniga Vorasarun, and Cristina Von Zeppelin, "Thailand's Top 40," Forbes.com, July 24, 2006.

[27] *Tai no . . .* , 2005. Some of the firms listed may have dropped in rank since the research for this source was conducted.

[28] The deputy chief of Thaksin's TRT Party, for example, is Prayudh Mahagitsiri, whose family owns "Thailand's only manufacturer and distributor of premium stainless steel." Doebele, Vorasarun, and Von Zeppelin, 2006.

Table 6.1
Thailand's Free Trade Agreements

Partner	Signing Date	Effective Date
ASEAN	January 1992	January 1993
ASEAN and China	November 2002	January 2004
Bahrain	December 2002	December 2002
China	June 2003	October 2003
India	October 2003	September 2004
BIMSTEC	February 2004	July 2006
Australia	July 2004	January 2005
New Zealand	April 2005	July 2005
Peru	November 2005	June 2006
Japan	April 2007	To be determined

SOURCES: Derived by author from multiple sources.

NOTES: Negotiations with the United States have been suspended but could resume if the political situation changes.

This list includes countries with which Thailand has signed framework agreements, as well as those with which it has full FTAs. Signing dates are for first agreements (usually framework agreements). Effective dates are for first tariff reductions (under initial or subsequent agreements), not date of full implementation.

Committee, called the deal "a huge mistake" and said Thai producers of fruits and vegetables could not compete with Chinese imports.[29]

The evidence about the effects on Thailand's economy, however, is mixed, and the issue has gained only limited political traction. The trade balance with China has deteriorated since the agreement was reached, but Thailand's trade balance with most partners has worsened. The recovery of the baht from its lows in 1997–1998 has been the most important driver, and the effects of this recovery on Thailand's trade balance predate the early harvest agreement with China. (The baht has appreciated 18 percent since mid-2001.) The agreement has clearly hurt Thai onion, garlic, and apple producers, but even in the agricultural sector, others, especially lychee growers, have gained. As Pramon Sutivong, the chairman of the U.S.–Thai Chamber of Commerce, has observed, trade liberalization frees up labor, produces specialization in areas of comparative advantage, and encourages economic reform—whether or not imports increase relative to exports in any particular case.

Politically, farmers, one of Thaksin's primary bases of support, were compensated for whatever losses they may have suffered from the FTA. Interviews with Bangkok

---

[29] Larry Jagan, "Farmers Devastated by Free Trade Deal with China," Inter Press Service, February 7, 2006.

elites, from journalists and academics to bureaucrats and politicians reveal another, subtler, concern: Trade liberalization with China is a net plus for Thailand, but the deal was hasty, with insufficient preparation. Thailand, they say, has not been able to capitalize on it the way it should have or to compensate likely losers. This critique, it should be noted, was widely applied to several of Thaksin's FTAs and is not limited to the discussion of China.[30]

Similar dynamics played out in Thailand's FTA negotiations with Japan. The agreement with Japan, signed by prime ministers Surayud Chulanont and Abe Shinzo in April 2007, has displaced the Chinan FTA as the focus of economic debate and criticism. Steel producers and small and medium-sized enterprises argue that the agreement will leave them defenseless against higher-tech Japanese competition, while both Japanese and Thai NGOs fear that provisions on toxic waste will make Thailand a dumping ground for Japan's industrial pollution. The agreement is, however, likely to significantly increase trade with and investment from Japan.

Thailand's FTA with Australia, which covers 5,500 items on the Thai side and even more on the Australian, ranks aside those with Japan and China in importance. As far as its effects on such sensitive industrial sectors as telecommunications, the agreement may have more-immediate—and bigger—consequences than the multilateral CAFTA.[31] Thailand's FTA with New Zealand, finalized in April 2005, also covers a comprehensive range of goods. Thailand has also signed a number of basic FTAs (or early harvest agreements) with other partners. The most important of these, for both political and economic reasons, are Thailand's agreements with the Bay of Bengal Initiative for Multisectoral Technical and Economic Cooperation (BIMSTEC) and India. Thailand is negotiating an FTA with the United States.

Thailand's numerous other FTAs are notable for several reasons. First, they demonstrate that Thailand is, in fact, taking measures to establish itself as a trading crossroads—as its economic planners have asserted—and is not putting all its eggs in the China basket. Second, most (including the agreement with China) carry negative externalities but are nevertheless seen in a generally positive light. Finally, by placing Thailand at the center of a web of agreements, these FTAs provide additional incentives for Chinese (and other) companies to invest in Thailand, and deepen bilateral relationships.

Chinese Investment in Thailand

FDI now increasingly flows from China into Thailand, although still in relatively small quantities that are miniscule compared to Japanese and U.S. investments. Thailand is the fifth-largest destination for Chinese investment. According to Thai statistics, Chinese investment for the first nine months of 2007 was more than double that of the

---

[30] Interviews in Bangkok, May 2006.

[31] Sakulrat Montreevat, "Prospect of Thailand's Bilateral Trade Pacts," *Viewpoints*, December 10, 2003.

same period in 2006, although (at $134 million) it remained a meager 2 percent of total Japanese investment.[32] In some cases, Chinese investments exploit unique local assets. Manufacturers of traditional Chinese medicines, for example, are already capitalizing on local herbs and other indigenously available ingredients. Other manufacturers may be interested in Thai labor skills—or, recently, even in their price. Increasingly, however, Chinese investors are looking to Thailand to capitalize on its network of FTAs.

Shifting production to Thailand enables Chinese companies to hedge against a variety of risks. A "made in Thailand" stamp may discourage nations that already have strong trade frictions with China (including the United States) from taking antidumping actions. Such a stamp may also allow the producers to hedge against Chinese currency revaluation or third-country pressures for voluntary restrictions on imports. These same motivations (together with wage differentials) propelled Japan to pursue the same strategy on a much more massive scale in China, Thailand, and across the rest of East Asia. The vice president of the Thai-China Business Council, Vikrom Kronsat, also serves as Chairman of the Amata Foundation, Thailand's largest industrial estate developer, and has recently created two Chinese industrial parks, each capable of hosting around 40 medium-sized facilities. He is currently lobbying the government for better terms for Chinese (and other) investors.[33]

Several large Chinese investment deals are already in progress. The Shanghai Automobile Industry Corporation, which has teamed up with General Motors and Volkswagen to become China's largest automobile manufacturer, has signed a deal with the Yontrakit Group and a subsidiary of the CP Group to produce automobiles for the Southeast Asian market. The Chinese National Offshore Oil Corporation has signed an MOU with the Petroleum Authority of Thailand, Thailand's largest energy company, to develop oil and natural gas in Thailand. The Chinese corporation has also formed a partnership with the Petroleum Authority of Thailand Exploration and Production to explore for natural gas in Burma, Iran, Cambodia, and Oman. The Chinese hydroelectric company Sino Hydro Corporation, meanwhile, has also agreed with Electricity Generating Authority of Thailand to develop a 7,000-MW hydroelectric power plant in Burma.[34]

Most Thai businessmen doing business with China are realistic (or experienced) enough to see the problems and difficulties of that business. Vikrom, the head of the Thai-China Business Council, blames Chinese customs regulations for the inability, thus far, of Thai fruit growers to capitalize on the early harvest agreement and believes

---

[32] Thailand Board of Investment, 2008.

[33] "Amata, PTT and EGAT Trying to Lure Chinese Firms Here," Global News Wire, September 30, 2005. Also, interview with Vikrom Kromadit, May 16, 2006.

[34] "Joint Venture of Thai and Chinese Companies to Make Automobiles in Thailand," Global News Wire, December 26, 2005.

the government needs to attack this and other regulatory issues aggressively.[35] Others say that payment for goods delivered tends to be a major problem and that economic intercourse with China can be more problematic than it is with several Southeast Asian states.[36] But while Thai businessmen have a clear understanding of the challenges involved in business with China, they nevertheless see economic intercourse with China as a great opportunity.

Diplomatic and Foreign Policy Responses

Thailand's China-related diplomacy is, broadly speaking, consistent with its historical tradition of maintaining a middle position between great powers while retaining maximum flexibility. During Thaksin's first two years in office, parts of the foreign policy and media elite criticized him for leaning too far toward China. Thailand's subsequent strong diplomatic and military support for the United States in the global war on terrorism sparked even stronger criticism from the other direction. In addition to looking toward China and the United States, many of Thaksin's efforts focused on diplomacy with other nations—in some cases with significant implications for Thailand's relations with China. International reaction to the coup in September 2006 constrained the foreign policy of the military-backed government of Surayud Chulanont. The subsequent suspension of U.S. military assistance opened new opportunities for Beijing, which the Chinese leadership skillfully exploited. It is, however, unclear how long-lived China's gains will prove, now that democratic rule has been restored

Bilateral Relations with China and the United States

In 2005, Thailand and China celebrated 30 years of diplomatic relations. Thailand's 1975 reestablishment of diplomatic relations with China came well before China normalized relations with Indonesia (1990), Singapore (1990), or Vietnam (1991). Although China's relations with Thailand were far from close during most of the 1970s, they became de facto allies after the Vietnamese invasion of Cambodia in 1979. China stopped funding and supplying Thailand's communist insurgency and instead became one of the Thai government's key military and political partners.

Rising trade with China and the arms relationship kept Bangkok's relations with Beijing stable and generally positive during the 1990s, even after Vietnam withdrew from Cambodia. Thailand was not a claimant in the Spratly Islands dispute and heightened conflict over the South China Sea did not, therefore, color its perceptions of Beijing as much as those of other Southeast Asian capitals. China's assistance during

---

[35] Interview, May 2006. See also Benjaprut Akkarasriprapai, "Free-Trade Deal with China Leaves Growers at a Loss," *The Nation* (Bangkok), February 12, 2004.

[36] Interview, May 23, 2006.

the 1997 financial crisis—modest though the aid was—was much appreciated in Thailand, particularly given the few strings attached. In February 1999, Chuan Likphai's government signed an action plan for a 21st-century cooperation program with China.[37] Despite closer ties with China, however, there was no discussion of a fundamental reordering of Thailand's diplomatic or strategic direction before 2001.

During Prime Minister Thaksin's first two years in office, however, a more-dramatic shift occurred. Prior to Thaksin's first trip to Moscow, he announced an intention to diversify sources of military equipment and "weigh other strategic options."[38] His rhetoric on China was sometimes effusive.[39] He raised eyebrows in Washington by suggesting to Chinese President Jiang Zemin that Thailand could act as mediator between the United States and China in the wake of the EP-3 incident.[40] During his August 2001 visit to Beijing, Thaksin signed a joint strategic-cooperation agreement with China. Several of Thaksin's multilateral initiatives also included important roles for China.

In several areas of great concern to Beijing, moreover, the Thai government practices self-restraint, accommodating Chinese interests. It has, for example, kept a tight lid on Falun Gong activists, particularly during high-level Chinese visits.[41] Bangkok supported Beijing's approach to the EAS during the debate over membership issues. Even accommodating Beijing's tacit desires, however, can bring negative press (albeit first and foremost in the English-language media). Beijing has not demanded that Bangkok adjust much in the way of policy, a point that Thai diplomats and politicians acknowledge and appreciate. And Thai foreign policy elites suggest that if Beijing moved from subtle suggestions to direct demands or pressure, relations with China would likely suffer.

Even as Bangkok built on its strategic relationship with Beijing during the first years of the new century, however, it also demonstrated a willingness to reinforce ties with Washington. Despite the urging of several members of parliament for a circumspect response to September 11, Thaksin dispatched troops to assist with the recon-

---

[37] "Sino-Thai Joint Communiqué," Xinhua News Agency, April 30, 1999.

[38] "Two Years of Thaksin: All the PM's Men," *The Nation* (Bangkok), February 10, 2003.

[39] "Thai Prime Minister Interviewed on Eve of China Visit," Xinhua News Agency, August 26, 2001.

[40] "Thaksin Willing to Mediate to Repair Sino-U.S. Relations," *South China Morning Post*, May 11, 2001. On April 1, 2001, a U.S. Navy EP-3 surveillance aircraft clipped wings with one of the Chinese F-8 jet fighters sent to intercept it 70 miles off China's Hainan Island. China contended that the United States had violated its airspace and did not precisely rush to repair and return the U.S. aircraft after it made an emergency landing at a Chinese airfield. Eric Donelley, "The United States–China EP-3 Incident: Legality and Realpolitik," *Journal of Conflict & Security Law*, Vol. 9, No. 1, 2004.

[41] Ian Storey, "A Hiatus in the Sino-Thai 'Special Relationship,'" *China Brief*, The Jamestown Foundation, Vol. 6, No. 19, September 20, 2006b, p. 5.

struction phase of the U.S. occupations of both Afghanistan and Iraq.[42] Cooperation in the East Asian theatre of the global war on terrorism was equally solid, highlighted by the 2003 arrest of Riduan Isamuddin (better known as Hambali, the most prominent al Qaeda leader in Asia) on Thai territory. Criticism of Thaksin's lean toward China during the early years of his first term may have influenced the prime minister's return to a more-balanced position. Whatever the cause, Thailand proved a strong enough ally after September 11 for the United States to name it a major non-NATO U.S. ally in October 2003. (Security cooperation between the United States and Thailand is extensive and is discussed under "Security Cooperation with the United States," below.)

A few caveats about Thailand's balancing act vis-à-vis China and the United States are in order. First, Thailand's justifications for strengthening the alliance with the United States refer overwhelmingly to cooperation in the global war on terrorism—not great-power politics or a potential threat from China. Second, under Thaksin's administration, Bangkok often showed at least a symbolic preference for Beijing over Washington. The Thai Ministry of Foreign Affairs drafted action plans with both Beijing and Washington, but the Beijing plan was rolled out first. Third, Thai officials are virtually unanimous that Thai security policy is internally focused, first on the war against insurgents in the south and second on the war on drugs. Finally, to the extent that Thailand does look at external security, its attention is largely centered on its immediate neighbors: Burma, Malaysia, Cambodia, Laos, Singapore, and Vietnam.

Improving Relations with Burma, India, and China

In addition to its closer cooperation with both Beijing and Washington, Bangkok has, in recent years, invigorated diplomacy with several other Asian governments. Foremost among these is Singapore, which has historically enjoyed a strong and well-rounded partnership with Thailand. This relationship could become important in the Chinese-Thai equation if, for example, China's interactions with Southeast Asia were to turn hostile. But there is no indication that this consideration has motivated Thailand's closer strategic relations with Singapore or that it has significantly affected Bangkok's relationship with Beijing.

More immediately relevant to Thailand's position vis-à-vis China has been its active engagement of Burma.[43] Until 2001, Thai-Burmese relations were highly contentious. They had recently engaged in border clashes, shows of force, diplomatic

---

[42] "MPs Urge PM: 'Be Cautious,'" *The Nation* (Bangkok), September 18, 2001. For more on the background of the U.S.–Thai military relationship, see Emma Chanlett-Avery, "Thailand: Background and U.S. Relations," Washington, D.C.: Congressional Research Service, January 13, 2005.

[43] While there is also no direct evidence that China provided the motivation in this case, one side effect was to mitigate Burma as a source of tension between China and Thailand.

démarches, and the employment of proxy forces against one another. Differences over Burma were among the biggest irritants in Chinese-Thai relations. China was and is Burma's biggest patron, supplying the weapons Burma used against Thailand. Chinese and Burmese supported the Wa State Army, which fought for Burma against ethnic Shan rebels, whom Thailand allegedly supported for years, but which also financed its operations by smuggling drugs into Thailand.[44] More generally, Bangkok was concerned about Beijing's near monopoly of influence in Burma.

Thailand had made some efforts to engage Burma before Thaksin. In 1992, Thailand supported the creation of the Greater Mekong Subregion (GMS), a developmental effort including Thailand, Cambodia, Laos, Vietnam, China (with special status for Yunnan), and Burma.[45] In 1996, Thailand initiated what is now known as BIMSTEC to promote economic cooperation between Thailand and the South Asian nations around the Bay of Bengal.[46] Despite the intensified interactions, however, the negative aspects of Thailand's relationship with Burma frequently outweighed the positive.

Thaksin came to power in 2001 with the idea of pursuing what he called forward engagement with Burma. Some of his initiatives, such as the so-called Bangkok Process, a multilateral effort to engage Burma without threatening sanctions, came to naught—primarily because Rangoon balked. But Thaksin's government greatly intensified economic interactions with and support for Burma. In 2003, Thaksin created yet another multilateral organization designed to hasten development in Burma and Indochina—the Ayeyawady–Chao Phraya–Mekong Economic Cooperation Strategy (ACMECS).[47] The group held its first summit in Rangoon in November 2003.

Under Thaksin, Thailand also redoubled efforts to fund projects sponsored by both new and existing organizations. In 2003, Bangkok agreed to help build a deep seaport at Dawei in southern Burma, together with a road link between Dawei and Kachanaburi, Thailand. Thailand, India, and Burma also agreed on a separate highway project running between Maesoot (Thailand), Bagan (Burma), and Moreh (India).[48] Thailand signed an MOU for survey concessions in two Burmese petroleum fields, an agreement on natural gas from the Yengtagun field, and a deal for the Petroleum Authority of Thailand to build infrastructure related to natural gas exploitation.[49]

---

[44] Kulachada Chaipipat, "China and the Delicate Task," *The Nation* (Bangkok), May 21, 2001.

[45] In a separate Mekong initiative, Thailand, China, Burma, and Laos agreed to push for a commercial navigation pact along the river in 1999. "Sino-Thai Joint . . . ," 1999.

[46] Although BIMSTEC did not originally include Burma, the country became a member in 1997.

[47] The group originally included Cambodia, Laos, Burma, and Thailand. Vietnam joined later.

[48] "Myanmar, Thailand to Build Deep Seaport," Xinhua News Agency, January 12, 2004.

[49] "Thailand Signs Four Agreements in Move Towards Becoming Regional Energy Center," Global News Wire, November 13, 2003.

Thailand also sponsored several Burmese industrial zones for Thai investors producing for the Chinese and Indian markets.[50]

The military-backed government of Surayud Chulanont has continued Thaksin's engagement policies. In large measure, Burma's position in the Thai economy may account for the Thai government's reluctance to change course. Between 2001 and the end of 2006, Burma moved from being the fourth-largest destination of external Thai investment to second place, accounting for 13 percent of Thailand's total.[51] Thailand now buys $1.2 billion worth of natural gas a year from Burma.[52] Whatever the motivation, Surayud traveled to Burma to meet with leaders there shortly after taking office and discussed loan forgiveness for Burma, as well as trade and investment issues.[53] In late 2006, the Thai government worked to keep Burma issues off the UN agenda.[54] And after protests broke out in Rangoon, Thai police and soldiers arrested scores of Burmese demonstrators appealing for international action on the Thai side of the border and repatriated them back to Burma.[55]

Thailand's engagement with Burma has had important effects on regional geopolitics and on Bangkok's international position. Engagement with Burma has largely neutralized the most open and direct source of conflict with China. It has not resolved problems related to the Wa or Shan inside Burma's eastern border or the spillover from these problems into western Thailand. But it has provided a new strategy for addressing the insurgency in Burma and its attendant consequences. Thai and Indian engagement of Burma has mitigated, if not eliminated, the concerns about excessive Chinese influence there. The negative effects of Thailand's forward-engagement strategy, at least in a geopolitical sense, are primarily found in increased friction with the West, particularly the United States, over how to deal with Burmese authoritarianism.

Multilateralism and Regional Politics

The ASEAN states have long used multilateralism to magnify their own importance, keep the larger powers engaged, and minimize the probability that Southeast Asian

---

[50] "Three Thai-Involved Myanmar Industrial Zone Projects to Start Sooner," Xinhua News Agency, June 3, 2004.

[51] Bank of Thailand, International Investment Position Team, Data Management Department, "Thailand's International Investment Position at the End of December 2006," 2007, Table 6: Equity Capital and Reinvested Earnings in Abroad Classified by Country, 2007.

[52] Michael Backman, "Burmese Junta Not in the Least Put Out by Western Sanctions," *The Age* (Melbourne), April 13, 2007.

[53] "Thailand Mulls Loan Repayment Extension After Burma Visit," BBC Monitoring Asia Pacific, November 26, 2006.

[54] Kavi Chongkittavorn, "Burma: Thai Diplomacy's Biggest Travesty," *The Nation* (Bangkok), December 4, 2006c.

[55] Geoffrey York, "The Junta's Enablers: Thailand, India, China," *The Globe and Mail* (Toronto), October 6, 2007.

states will be drawn into competing camps. As the discussion above of BIMSTEC, GMS, and ACMECS suggests, multilateralism remains an important tool of Bangkok's diplomacy. Many outside observers regard these organizations as powerless or superfluous, but Thailand's foreign policy community takes them seriously. Thai critics level a different charge: The new organizations detract from Bangkok's long-standing emphasis on ASEAN and Thailand's traditional leadership role in it. And, they say, Thaksin's emphasis on these non-ASEAN organizations reflected a desire to play the great-power game.

There is some truth to these contentions. Thaksin argued that his government's multilateral initiatives were designed to achieve goals that ASEAN endorses. GMS and ACMECS focus largely on the development of Indochina, which ASEAN agrees is essential for unifying the new and old states of ASEAN. But at the same time, these are subregional groups that either place Thailand clearly at the center (in the case of ACMECS) or join Thailand with a collection of weak ASEAN states and major outside powers, India in the case of BIMSTEC and China in the case of the GMS. Efforts to make the Thai baht the standard currency for intercourse with Burma, Cambodia, and Laos have done little to discourage the perception that Bangkok's ambitions grew under Thaksin.[56]

There is no better indication of these ambitions than the creation of the Asian Cooperation Dialogue. The intent was to be the first truly pan-Asian grouping that would include states from the Middle East, South Asia, Central Asia, and East Asia.[57] This dialogue preceded the Shanghai Cooperation Organization and was the first regional forum to seat China, Russia, and Iran at the same table. With Thaksin's backing, Russia joined the ostensibly Asian grouping in April 2005.[58] Thaksin used the group to promote regional energy initiatives and his idea of an Asian bond fund. The forum has survived Thaksin's ouster, with 30 nations represented at the meeting held in Seoul in June 2007.

Thaksin's multilateral initiatives were aimed at securing Thai national interests. But by promoting alternative groupings to ASEAN, including ones that encompass Chinese membership, these initiatives weaken the coherence of ASEAN as a potential counterweight to China and accommodate Chinese power. Although the initiatives break with Thailand's emphasis during the 1990s on ASEAN-centered diplomacy, they are consistent with Thailand's tradition of asserting itself as a middle power. While their future remains uncertain in the wake of Thaksin's departure, their demise is far from a foregone conclusion.

---

[56] "Regional Role Possible for Baht," *The Nation* (Bangkok), January 26, 2004; "Thailand to Offer Baht Denominated Loans to Neighboring Countries," Global News Wire, November 12, 2003.

[57] Amit Baruah, "Thais 'Vague' About ACD Process," *The Hindu*, June 17, 2002.

[58] The United States is considered a "dialogue partner."

Defense Policy Responses

The Thai military is streamlining and modernizing its forces, with military budgets having recovered from sharp declines after the 1997–1998 financial crisis. Modernization could help Thailand resist pressure or military action were China to become a threat, but there is no evidence that Thai military policy is motivated by this consideration. Thailand has long enjoyed close military ties with China that have deepened further since 2000. Bangkok's military links with Washington, however, have always been broader and deeper than those with Beijing. Even as Bangkok deepened its military relations with Beijing under Thaksin, it was intensifying its already extensive Thai military ties with Washington. The fallout from the 2006 coup d'état has most heavily affected security-related aspects of its relationship with Washington, but even during this period, both sides demonstrated a desire to maintain and, in the long run, improve military-to-military ties. Bilateral military relations have resumed now that democratic rule has been restored. Finally, Bangkok has also increased its military interactions with India and other ASEAN states, most noticeably with Singapore but also with Indonesia and Malaysia.

Force Modernization Plans

During the late 1980s and 1990s, Thailand began adjusting the focus of its force structure away from guerrilla warfare and serving social and economic functions toward external defense. In 1987, Chavalit Yoongchai, a strong advocate of conventional defense, became supreme commander and thereafter pushed this agenda from a variety of top positions for 15 years.[59] Chavalit called for reductions in army manpower, a switch from conscription to volunteer service, and a shift in the emphasis in the army's force structure from infantry toward mechanized forces.[60] The number of armored and mechanized divisions increased from three in 1989 to eight by 2006.[61]

Chavalit and his successors have placed considerable emphasis on air and, especially, maritime defense. In 1993, the government adopted three new defense-planning documents, all emphasizing the importance of naval power, and the navy's commander

---

[59] He first served as an advisor to the prime minister from 1979 to 1986, as supreme commander from 1987 to 1990, as defense minister from 1995 to 1997, prime minister from 1996 to 1997, and as defense minister and deputy prime minister from 2001 through October 2002.

[60] The transformation is incomplete: Manpower levels remain higher today than in 1987, though much of the force is now volunteer. The force structure maintains vestiges of its internal focus, including four "economic development" divisions.

[61] These include three armored, three mechanized, and two cavalry divisions, plus one independent cavalry regiment. Jane's, "Army, Thailand: Jane's Sentinel Security Assessment—Southeast Asia," *Jane's Sentinel Country Risk Assessments,* January 7, 2008c.

announced that the force was moving from a "brown water to a blue water" role.[62] The navy's force structure grew dramatically. In 1989, the navy had a total of seven principal warships (counting ships over 1,000 tons); today it has 20. Between 1987 and 1990, it signed contracts for three new corvettes from Italy, six frigates from China, and an aircraft carrier from Spain. In 1994, it signed a lease for two *Knox*-class frigates from the United States. The Royal Thai Air Force also expanded and modernized its inventory. Between 1988 and 1996, it took delivery of 36 F-16A/Bs to supplement its aging F-5s. In 1997, it agreed to purchase F-18s, but the deal was canceled after the onset of the financial crisis.

The 1997 financial crisis derailed plans for further military modernization, but these are only now getting back on track (Table 6.2). The defense budget declined 25 percent between 1996 and 1998, and the collapse in the baht decreased the military's overseas buying power significantly more. Even as the economy has slowly recovered, defense budgets were held constant to free funds for economic-related projects. Defense spending fell from 2.4 percent of GDP in 1996 to 1.7 percent in 1998 to 1.1 percent by 2005–2006. The decline in Thailand's military budgets as a percentage of GDP appeared to have halted by 2006 and, with the military in charge, reversed

Table 6.2
Thailand's Defense Budget

Year	Baht (billions)	US$ (billions)	Percentage of GDP
1996	109.0	4.3	2.4
1997	102.0	3.2	2.1
1998	81.0	2.0	1.7
1999	77.4	2.1	1.5
2000	77.3	2.0	1.6
2001	77.2	1.7	1.5
2002	78.6	1.8	1.5
2003	79.9	1.9	1.4
2004	78.5	1.9	1.2
2005	81.2	2.0	1.1
2006	86.0	2.3	1.1
2007	115.0	3.4	1.3

SOURCE: IISS, 1996–2007.
NOTE: All figures are current, not inflation adjusted.

---

[62] Panitan Wattanayagorn, "Thailand: The Elite's Shifting Conceptions of Security," in Muthiah Alagappa, ed., *Asian Security Practice*, Stanford: Stanford University Press, 1998, pp. 438–439; Rodney Tasker, "Silent Service: Navy Reaps Rewards of Steering Clear of Politics," *Far Eastern Economic Review*, October 21, 1993.

in 2007. Military spending rose some 34 percent in 2007, to 1.3 percent of GDP, although it remains to be seen whether the military's budgetary gains will survive the nation's return to democratic rule.

Although the military remains constrained by limited budgets, its 2005–2013 annual procurement budget received a 3 billion baht bump (to 20 billion baht), and all three services have once again begun shopping for new equipment—albeit on a limited scale.[63] The navy has recently procured several large patrol vessels and is considering buying at least two frigates from Britain.[64] In early 2008, the air force decided to spend $600 million to purchase six Swedish-made fourth-generation Gripen fighter jets and airborne early-warning aircraft. Some reports indicate that the Thai air force may buy up to 40 Gripens in total.[65] The army, for its part, is seeking to replace much of its stock of armored vehicles and is interested in purchasing 33 Sikorsky Black Hawk helicopters to improve mobility.[66]

Threat Perceptions and China

As in many Asian countries, public discussion of potential threats and how they are connected to the evolution of force structure is very limited. In Thailand's case, three factors exacerbate the poverty of this discussion: a history of military government and military secrecy; the dominance of the military services in determining how budgets are spent (if not their size); and Thailand's omnidirectional strategic culture, which places a premium on maintaining maximum flexibility and therefore discourages identifying potential competitors. There is, however, some discussion of security issues (and occasionally threats) in Thailand's vigorous free press and in security planning documents. These generally identify missions and occasionally conceptual threats, although they seldom identify the associated countries.

The question can, then, be asked: Do Thailand's modernization programs indicate a widespread sense that China is a potential threat? Four claims can be made. First, the new conventional missions justify capabilities that would be more useful in China-related contingencies than the guerrilla-oriented force structure that preceded it would be. Thailand's first (and as yet only) Defense White Paper, for example, highlights defense of the sea lanes of communication as one of the navy's primary missions.[67] Second, most military officers are, on balance, more sympathetic to the United

---

[63] J. M. Jamaluddin, "Thailand's Force Modernization Efforts," *Asian Defence Journal*, November 2005.

[64] Jane's, "Frigates, Thailand," Jane's Fighting Ships, May 2, 2006c.

[65] Richard A. Bitzinger and Curie Maharani, "Arms, Money, and Security: Southeast Asia's Growing Importance as an Arms Market," RSIS Commentaries, Singapore: S. Rajaratnam School of International Studies, Nanyang Technological University, April 8, 2008.

[66] Jamaluddin, 2005.

[67] Ministry of Defense, "The Defense of Thailand," Bangkok: Thailand Ministry of Defense, 1996.

States and cautious of China than are the civilian elites.[68] The military has enjoyed a partnership with the PLA since 1979, but before then, it was engaged in a bitter, decade-long war with Chinese-backed rebels. Third, even among the public, generally positive feelings toward China do not translate into a belief that Beijing is or should replace Washington as Bangkok's primary security partner.[69]

Fourth, and arguably most important, none of these observations imply that Thai strategists view China as a potential threat, much less an imminent one. Thailand has border disputes with Burma and Cambodia. During the 1990s, it disputed overlapping exclusive economic zones with Malaysia, Vietnam, Cambodia, and Burma. But it is one of the only nations in the region *without* overlapping territorial claims with China. Hence, the Royal Thai Navy's declarations during the 1990s that a stronger navy was needed to protect Thailand's interests in the resolution of exclusive economic zone boundary disputes may have been aimed at any of several neighboring states but not at China.[70] While Chinese military modernization generates some limited attention in the media, new procurements the neighbors make, Malaysia and Burma in particular, often receive more notice.[71] Military officers may, as a body, be somewhat more circumspect about China than other elites, but military opinion is divided, and most cannot imagine taking sides between the United States and China.[72]

Strategic Relations and Military Diplomacy with China

Thailand's military relationship with China dates back to 1979, when the two began cooperating against the commonly perceived threat from Soviet-backed Vietnamese forces. The strategic relationship was originally (and to a lesser extent remains) relatively narrow, focused primarily on Chinese arms exports to Thailand. Thailand was a major client for Chinese-built weapons, from tanks to artillery and, later, naval warships.[73] After a long respite following the financial crisis, arms deals are again being

---

[68] The assessment of elite views is derived from discussions with Thai civilian politicians and bureaucrats, Thai military leaders, and American and other foreign officials with long experience in Bangkok.

[69] U.S. Department of State, Bureau of Intelligence and Research, 2005.

[70] "Admiral Calls for Adjustment of Combat Forces," Bangkok Army Television, November 2, 1993, tr. Foreign Broadcast Information Service, FBIS-EAS-1993-1102, November 2, 1993; "Navy Chief on Modernization, PRC Technology," *The Nation* (Bangkok), December 26, 1993.

[71] This equivalent of "keeping up with the Joneses" is generally as widely discussed as defense of sea lines of communication. In 1999, the Royal Thai Navy's commander said, "We will monitor weapon buildup by every country and try to achieve a balance with it." In 2002, there was much hand wringing about how to respond to Malaysia's purchase of four French submarines. Quotation from "Navy Chief on Budget Cut, Foreign Threat," *Bangkok Post*, January 2, 1999.

[72] In response to the question about what Thailand would do in a Chinese-U.S. conflict, most officers assert that a core element of Thailand's strategy is to avoid putting itself in situations that would force it to choose sides.

[73] On Chinese efforts to woo Thai military officials, see "China Goes All Out to Woo Southeast Asia," *The Korea Herald*, August 6, 2001.

consummated. In 2002, Bangkok signed a contract for two 1,400-ton (fully loaded) offshore patrol vessels from shipyards in Shanghai that have since been delivered.[74] In 2004, Thailand agreed to purchase tanks from China, using lychees as currency, but the deal was subsequently cancelled.[75]

Historically, calculations about purchasing Chinese equipment have rested on two considerations. The first was price: When Thailand needed large numbers of armored vehicles to defend its borders against a possible Vietnamese invasion launched from Cambodia, the low prices and good terms China offered were an irresistible attraction. Chinese weapons were also appealing because they supplied the low end of a high-low mix in the Thai military's force structure. The second was the opportunity for bribes and kickbacks, not unheard of in deals with Western companies but more readily available in China.[76] Weighed against the benefits was poor quality. Few of the 550 armored vehicles purchased from China during the 1980s and 1990s are still operational.

Two parts of this equation may be changing. First, as civilian oversight becomes stronger, graft may become less important in determining procurement decisions—although this will happen only slowly. Offsetting this may be improvements in the quality of Chinese equipment.[77] Chinese corvettes and frigates are approaching Western standards, and Chinese armored vehicles are becoming more competitive. China has finished field testing a tank, designated the Type 96T (based on the Type 85II), specifically for the Thai market, and in 2005, the two nations agreed on the sale of 97 armored personnel carriers.[78]

Senior Thai and Chinese military officials have long enjoyed frequent contact, and the military relationship is beginning to broaden beyond the arms trade. Thailand and China initiated an annual defense security consultation between their defense ministries in 2002.[79] In December 2005, the Thai navy and the PLA navy held their first joint exercise (focused on search and rescue). And on the sidelines of the ASEAN foreign ministers meeting in Vientiane in 2005, China proposed a joint maritime regional exercise with Thailand and other states.[80]

On the heels of the U.S. suspension of military assistance in September 2006, Army Commander in Chief (and coup leader) Sonthi Boonvaratglin visited Beijing. He

---

[74] Jane's, "Corvettes, Thailand," *Jane's Fighting Ships*, December 6, 2007.

[75] James Murphy, "Chickens Could Fuel Thai Modernization Plans," *Jane's Defence Weekly*, December 7, 2005.

[76] Interviews, April 4, 2006, and May 15–23, 2006. See also Chang Noi, "The Board, the Management, and the Lollipops," *The Nation* (Bangkok), February 20, 2001.

[77] See Evan S. Medeiros, Roger Cliff, Keith Crane, and James C. Mulvenon, *A New Direction for China's Defense Industry*, Santa Monica, Calif.: RAND Corporation, MG-334-AF, 2005.

[78] Yihong Chang and Robert Karniol, "China Tempts Thailand with Modified MBT," *Jane's Defence Weekly*, February 15, 2006.

[79] State Council Information Office, *China's National Defense: 2004*, Beijing, December 2004.

[80] Jagan, 2006.

was well rewarded for his efforts, receiving a package that is said to include $49 million worth of military aid and training.[81] The suspension of U.S. assistance has also produced—or at least hastened—a qualitative shift in the Chinese-Thai military relationship. In July 2007, Thailand dispatched 30 special forces soldiers, including a lieutenant general, to Guangzhou for two weeks of combined exercises with their Chinese counterparts. In addition to being a milestone for Chinese-Thai military cooperation, the exercises were heralded in China as the first combined—as opposed to joint—training its forces had conducted with a foreign power.[82]

Security Cooperation with the United States

Thailand's military relationship with the United States is deeper and goes back further than its military relations and security ties with China. Bangkok contributed military units to the U.S. efforts in the Korean War, the Vietnam War, and the 1991 Persian Gulf War and was a leading member of the anti-communist Southeast Asian Treaty Organization between 1954 and 1977. In time for the launch of Operation Enduring Freedom, the Thai government authorized the U.S. military to use the U-Tapao naval airbase and Sattahib naval base for logistical support. After the fall of Kabul, Thailand dispatched 130 engineers, medics, and special forces troops to participate in reconstruction. Although it did not endorse the U.S. invasion of Iraq, Bangkok sent 450 engineers and medics to that country to help with road building and medical care after the occupation.[83]

Thailand has also cooperated closely in the Asian component of the global war on terrorism. The most conspicuous support was the August 2003 arrest of Jamaah Islamiah leader (and al Qaeda affiliate) Hambali and the capture of several other top leaders suspected of plotting attacks on embassies and soft targets.[84] The United States has reciprocated. Its October 2003 declaration of Thailand as a major non-NATO U.S. ally enabled the nation to purchase new types of U.S. military hardware and gave it easier access to the requisite credit guarantees. The United States and Thailand have also cooperated on other ad hoc security issues. Within two days of the Southeast Asian earthquake and tsunami of December 2004, military officials in Bangkok and Washington announced the dispatch of a U.S. forward command element to the U-Tapao base to serve as a hub and command center for U.S. relief operations throughout Southeast Asia.[85]

---

[81] "Post-Coup . . . ," 2007.

[82] Lin Li, "China, Thailand Stage Combined Training of Special Troops," GOV.cn, July 16, 2007.

[83] The Iraq dispatch was unpopular, and the troops were withdrawn in September 2004.

[84] For more on U.S.–Thai military relationship, see Chanlett-Avery, 2005.

[85] U.S. Department of Defense, "U.S. Military Support to Tsunami Relief Efforts," news release, No. 1325-04, December 28, 2004.

The United States has long maintained a significant military training relationship with Thailand, one that encompasses long-term individual training in the United States and over 40 joint training exercises a year. The annual Cobra Gold exercise, held in Thailand, is America's biggest annual joint exercise in Asia.[86] Many joint exercises are multilateral, placing Thailand near the center of a growing web of U.S. military arrangements in Asia.[87] Tens of thousands of individual Thai soldiers have been trained in the United States under the International Military Education and Training program.[88] The impression of U.S. military efficiency gained through these experiences, and the personal relationships formed, incline Thai military officers to value the U.S. alliance.

The consequences of the temporary U.S. suspension of most military cooperation after the 2006 coup were limited. During the suspension, both the Thai and U.S. militaries worked to maintain channels of communication and key aspects of their cooperative relationship. Both sides, for example, worked to ensure U.S. participation in the 2007 Cobra Gold exercises, which the United States treated as a multilateral exercise to facilitate its participation. Once the new, democratically elected, Thai government was sworn in in early 2008, Washington began the process of resuming normal military relations, including restoring arms sales and the International Military Education and Training program.

Some, but by no means all, Thai elites say privately that uncertainty about China's future intentions is one motivation for developing closer relations with the United States. But concerns about China are not the only, or even necessarily the most important, interest in the alliance. Securing support for the development of Thailand's defense force is at least as important and is tied to a variety of internal and external contingencies and to national prestige. To the extent military cooperation with Washington represents part of a Thai hedging strategy, Bangkok has no desire to make this motivation evident, much less explicit. Indeed, Thailand has invited Chinese observers to the Gold Cobra exercises, and some informed observers suggest it would welcome full Chinese participation.

Cultivating New Security Partners

In addition to strengthening military ties with both the United States and China, Thailand has also sought to develop strategic relationships with several other regional partners.

Thailand's security ties with India have deepened significantly since the early 2000s. As early as 1995, Thai naval elements began participating in India's annual

---

[86] Chanlett-Avery, 2005, p. 8.

[87] The 2005 Cobra Gold exercise included elements from the Philippines, Mongolia, and Singapore. IISS, 2006, p. 258.

[88] Chanlett-Avery, 2005.

"Milan" ("meeting") exercises, together with units from Bangladesh, Indonesia, Singapore, Sri Lanka, and Malaysia.[89] In 2001, Thailand agreed to cooperate with India under the UN framework to tackle terrorism.[90] Anti-Indian terrorists' use of Thai territory caused strains between the two nations, but Bangkok agreed to eradicate the problem in 2003, and the security discussion continued to advance.[91] In June 2005, Prime Minister Thaksin and Prime Minister Manmohan Singh pledged to expand cooperation in trade, political affairs, and security. They agreed to conduct joint naval patrols in the Indian Ocean designed to block smuggling of contraband to insurgent groups in Sri Lanka and India's northeast.[92]

Thailand has also strengthened its military partnerships with its Southeast Asian neighbors. Bangkok's military ties with Singapore have traditionally been the strongest of its relationships in Southeast Asia. For 30 years, Singapore has enjoyed a training relationship with Thailand that enables Singapore's air force pilots to train on and over Thai territory. In November 2004, the two nations expanded their joint training activities under an agreement that will see two or three deployments a year.[93] Historically, concerns about Malaysia and, to a lesser extent, Indonesia have provided at least part of the glue between the two nations. While these concerns have not disappeared entirely, Singapore and Thailand initiated joint naval and air patrols with Malaysia and Indonesia in the Malacca Strait in September 2005. China and Japan have offered to support the operation, but the four Southeast Asian states demurred.[94] Finally, Bangkok proposed creation of the ADMM, bringing together the defense ministers of the ASEAN states for an annual meeting; the first such meeting was held in May 2006.[95]

None of this new activity is directed at or against China; indeed, it is quite possible that China, Japan, and South Korea will be invited to join the ADMM if the forum continues. To the extent these relationships continue to deepen, however, they provide Thailand with additional security options, reduce its reliance on single sources of security, and moderate Thai perceptions of vulnerability to coercion from any single nation. And to the extent Thailand engages with nations that are strategically close to

---

[89] In 2006, Australia and Burma also participated. "Multi-Nation Naval Exercise Begins," *Hindustan Times*, January 9, 2006.

[90] "Thailand to Work with India on Security Cooperation," *Asia Pulse*, November 27, 2001.

[91] "India, Thailand Sign Free Trade Agreement, Four Other Accords," Press Trust of India News Agency, October 9, 2003.

[92] Ministry of Foreign Trade, Public Relations Department, "Trade Expansion as a Result of Thailand-Indian FTA," September 1, 2005; P. S. Suryanarayana, "India Signs Maritime Accord with Thailand," The Hindu, May 21, 2005.

[93] "Singapore and Thailand Sign Agreement on Air Force Training," Channel NewsAsia, November 12, 2004.

[94] "Indonesia, Malaysia, Singapore, Thailand to Safeguard Malacca Strait," Xinhua News Agency, September 11, 2005.

[95] "ASEAN Extends . . . ," 2006.

the United States and employ American military hardware and software (i.e., training and organization), its engagement with these nations further encourages Thailand to maintain extensive security cooperation with the United States.

Conclusions and Implications

Thailand has a long tradition of bending with the wind. In today's East Asia, that means accommodating—and seeking advantage from—China, *as well as the United States*. Thaksin modified Thailand's traditional approach by trying to blow the wind, as well as bend with it, by carving out a leadership role for Thailand, particularly in the subregions centered on the Mekong River to the north and the Malacca Strait to the south. The military-led government's foreign-policy options were constrained; as a result, it did not accomplish much. It remains to be seen whether the foreign policy of the new, democratically elected government will continue in Thaksin's bolder style or become more muted. Future governments may de-emphasize bold initiatives, particularly on the strategic or military front, and refocus Bangkok's diplomatic efforts on ASEAN. Assuming, however, that China continues to grow economically without exhibiting manifestly aggressive behaviors, Bangkok is likely to continue deepening its economic; political; and, to a lesser extent, military relationships with Beijing.

Policy Integration

Thailand's foreign policy, specifically its China policy, is well integrated, although not particularly well or thoroughly implemented. The main integrative mechanism is a widely shared strategic culture and broad elite consensus on foreign policy. Thai elites believe that the nation's position and history provide a powerful guide, one that finds security in omnidirectional diplomacy and, in particular, remaining on good terms with major powers.

Past and looming political changes have increased the possibility that a political leader could emerge who might take the country in new directions and challenge Thai diplomatic traditions. Barring dramatic changes to the constitution, however, businessmen are likely to continue dominating politics, and their business interests in China are growing, not diminishing. Unless a significant group of politicians emerges from outside the business community, politicians are likely to serve as a force for further increasing ties with China, even if they are unlikely to abandon either economic or security cooperation with the United States.

Perhaps because of Thailand's history of military rule, the civilian bureaucracy is relatively pliant. It has its own view of proper diplomacy but is unwilling to cross its political masters (military or civilian), at least directly. The Foreign Ministry scores poorly among non-Thai officials in Bangkok. Thaksin proved that, by making an end run around the bureaucracy, it is possible to provide decisive leadership. But in many cases, the preparatory work and implementation, which often depend on professional administrators, has been weak. The likely weakening of executive authority under a new constitution may further undermine the prospects for policy integration.

Variables and Indicators

China's growth and behavior will be the largest variables in determining Thai perspectives on China's rise. Other important variables include, in the domestic political realm, the development of the Thai political system; in the economic realm, the fate of pending FTA negotiations with the United States; on the diplomatic front, Burma's future course and international reactions to it; and, on the security front, the evolution of military-to-military ties with China and the United States.

Of these, domestic political variables may loom largest. If businessmen continue to dominate parliament in the evolving Thai political system, economic issues will continue to take pride of place in foreign policymaking, and the China relationship will benefit from Beijing's willingness to set aside political issues and focus on the business of business. If, on the other hand, stable political parties and a specialized political class emerge from the new constitutional order, foreign policy priorities may become more diverse. This could potentially rebound to the benefit of the United States, which pursues a moral, as well as material, foreign policy. While this outcome is possible, it would run against the pattern of Thai politics over the last 80 years and the long-standing dominance of business leaders in elected government (except, of course, when parliament has been suspended).

Economically, modest shifts in the balance or composition of winners and losers in the countryside are unlikely to affect China policy as long as Bangkok's interests—particularly those of ethnic Chinese traders and businessmen—retain a privileged political position. More important will be whether Washington and Bangkok can restart and successfully conclude FTA negotiations, which had been suspended after the 2006 coup, and the effects of Thailand's new FTA with Tokyo. Although China is now a larger trade partner for Thailand than the United States, the United States and Japan, which supply far more FDI, are still in many ways more important. FTA negotiations with Washington have been going on for several years, but the Thai side suspended negotiations in April 2006 pending resolution of the political impasse in Bangkok.

Final agreements with the United States would, in principle, boost the status of bilateral relations. More generally, the FTA would, given the terms the United States demands, increase transparency in Thailand's economic (and therefore political) system. Washington's negotiating position will be important in determining the fate of these ongoing negotiations. Many in Thailand see the U.S. demands, particularly on the issues of intellectual property, as more stringent than those under other U.S. foreign agreements. Given the widespread perception of the United States after the 1997 financial crisis as an economically neocolonialist power, the terms of any agreement will be critical in shaping future attitudes. And the expiration of U.S. presidential fast-track authority on FTAs on July 1, 2007, raised the bar on any agreement significantly—possibly decisively—whenever negotiations do resume.

On the diplomatic front, Thailand's rapprochement with Burma and Thailand, India, and China's combined engagement of Burma have mitigated the source of perhaps greatest tension with Beijing. But the Thaksin administration's Burma policy was the most controversial aspect of its foreign policy, with the possible exception of military support for America's war in Iraq. NGOs, the liberal media, and the Democrat Party were all outspoken in their criticism of engagement with Burma. If, however, NGO arguments gain greater traction under a new Thai government, Burma could again become an area of greater contention between Thailand and China. But with India directly involved and with Thailand already committed to several large-scale projects, a course change might be difficult.

In the military realm, the recovery of Thai military budgets, recent additional Chinese military assistance, and improvements in Chinese military manufacturing capabilities have revived the arms relationship. One side effect is an increase in the points of contact between the PLA and Thai military officers and an intensification of other aspects of the military-to-military relationship—all during a time of political transition in Thailand. The military relationship with the United States will be restored (the question being when) and remains important, but whether it regains its former position remains to be seen. In the long run, especially now that civilian rule has resumed, military variables will be important but not decisive in determining Thailand's posture vis-à-vis China.

CHAPTER SEVEN

Singapore

Singapore, as one of the major commercial and financial centers of Asia and as an important security partner of the United States, plays a role disproportionate to its size in maintaining security and stability in Southeast Asia. Of fundamental importance to Singapore is maintenance of the regional and subregional military balances. In this regard, Singapore's overarching national security concerns are

1. the upsurge of Islamic extremism in Southeast Asia
2. the related issue of political stability in neighboring states, particularly Indonesia
3. China's long-term intentions and the U.S.–Chinese relationship
4. relations with Malaysia.

Concerns about the evolution of the balance of power in Northeast Asia, the dangerous situation on the Korean peninsula, and the potential for the remilitarization of Japan, are of secondary concern to Singaporean leaders.

China's rise looms large in Singapore's calculations about its future economic and security environment. Singapore's economy is becoming ever more integrated into an East Asian production chain in which China is a key hub by dint of its role as the point of final assembly. China also plays an important role in Singapore's strategy of becoming the preeminent East Asian hub for financial services. At the same time, Singapore seeks to reduce its economic dependence on any one market by diversifying its economic relationships.

Singaporeans, like most of their neighbors, do not perceive a near-term security threat from China, as long as China does not act coercively and unilaterally, and the mainland's dynamism is channeled into economic engagement with the region. Singaporeans see a weak and dysfunctional China as more worrisome than an assertive and militaristic China. On the other hand, Singaporeans understand that China's growing economic and military capabilities might eventually change Beijing's intentions and thus alter Singapore's calculus regarding China. They worry about the long-term potential threat that a hegemonic China could pose to Singapore's freedom of action and look to the United States as the indispensable power to prevent such an outcome.

Beyond such a role for the United States, Singaporeans see a strong coincidence of other interests with the United States, including combating Islamist terrorism and extremism and maintaining freedom of navigation, access to regional markets, and global financial stability. These missions are the current and constant focus of bilateral security cooperation. The U.S. relationship is also central to Singapore's strategy of strengthening defense technology linkages. Access to U.S. technology, the main source of innovation in defense and information technologies, is critical to Singapore's goal of keeping its armed forces on the technological cutting edge.[1]

Together, these factors have led to a Singaporean regional policy that combines economic engagement with China with closer security ties with the United States and other regional powers with a stake in regional stability and security, such as Australia, Japan, and the United Kingdom. Singaporeans have also struck a balance between Beijing and Taipei, maintaining strong commercial and defense ties with Taiwan, while advising Taipei against actions that might precipitate a Chinese military response.

National Conditions

The Singaporean political system is remarkably stable and not particularly prone to heated public debates about foreign policy and national security issues. Singapore's preeminent political personality, Lee Kuan Yew, and his People's Action Party presided over Singapore's emergence and consolidation as a city-state. After having served more than 30 years as prime minister and head of government, Lee stepped down in 1990 but retained a role in government as senior minister during the administration of Singapore's second prime minister, Goh Chok Tong. Goh, in turn, was succeeded in 2004 by Deputy Prime Minister Lee Hsien Loong, Lee Kuan Yew's son. Goh became senior minister, and Lee Kuan Yew assumed the specially created post of minister mentor.

The fundamental reason for Singapore's political stability is the success of the government's economic and social policies. At the time of independence, Singapore suffered from the widespread poverty, unemployment, and illiteracy that prevailed in Southeast Asia in the 1960s. Prime Minister Lee Kuan Yew and his associates were spectacularly successful in turning an ethnically divided society into one of Asia's most politically stable and economically successful models of development. Elements of this model include a partnership between the government and business, the circulation of senior personnel between government and the private sector, direct government participation in and ownership of companies in key sectors, and a large-scale expansion of the manufacturing and technological base.

At the core of this achievement was the development of a distinct Singaporean identity, which is informed by the social norms and values of the majority of Singa-

---

[1]   For the role of defense technologies in Singapore's defense strategy, see Ministry of Defence (Singapore), *Defending Singapore in the 21st Century*, 2000.

pore's inhabitants but is not exclusive of other identities. Singapore's success as a state ultimately rests on its ability to maintain and strengthen the multiethnic character of its society and to continue to achieve economic growth and prosperity. All state actions are efficiently geared to this end.[2]

At the same time, Singaporean leaders are aware that globalization and rapid technological change are opening up opportunities for Singapore but also intensify competition and increase stress on domestic cohesion. The challenge for Singapore is to continue to spur economic growth while adjusting to changes in its competitive position on global markets. This is not an easy process because new competitors, China being the most recent and in some ways the most daunting, are competing at both the high and low ends of the value chain. To sustain its economy in a more-competitive environment and to maintain social stability, Singapore needs to reinvent itself constantly. This means, in the view of a senior economic official, developing an entrepreneurial culture, attracting and keeping world-class talent, and enhancing the country's global connectivity.[3]

In this system, policymaking is highly centralized, top-down, and seamlessly integrated across the government's political and bureaucratic strata. Until the generational change from Goh Chok Tong to Lee Hsien Loong, the leadership core was composed of senior People's Action Party leaders, most of whom were founding fathers of Singapore. The second echelon was composed of potential successors, who tended to be People's Action Party members of Parliament and senior civil servants, technocrats, administrators, and managers. The style of leadership is by consensus, with the leadership closing ranks once a decision is made. Although there are, of course, policy and bureaucratic differences, they rarely surface in public, and bureaucratic entities rarely pursue parochial agendas at cross-purposes with national policy overtly.[4]

---

[2] For Singapore's transformation after 1965, there is no better book than the second volume of Lee Kuan Yew's autobiography, *From Third World to First: The Singapore Story 1965–2000,* New York: HarperCollins 2000; see also Raj Vasil, *Governing Singapore,* Sydney: Allen & Unwin, 2000.

[3] See the exposition of this vision in Khaw Boon Wan, Senior Minister for Transport and Information, Communications and the Arts, "Singapore Beyond 3G," speech delivered at the Singapore: Future Challenges Conference, Washington, D.C.: Paul H. Nitze School of Advanced International Studies (SAIS), Johns Hopkins University, October 3, 2002.

[4] Another notable aspect of Singapore's governance is the absence of corruption. Transparency International has ranked Singapore fifth out of 158 countries (Transparency International, "Corruption Perceptions Index," Berlin, 2005). A Congressional Research Service country study states that

> The overwhelming majority of the leadership . . . did not appear particularly motivated by profit, gained lawfully or through corruption (which was almost nonexistent), or by the perquisites of their office (which although increasing, remained less than could be achieved in the private sector). Their reward, instead, derived from their access to power and their conviction that they were working for the nation and its long-term survival.

Barbara Leitch Lepoer, *Singapore: A Country Study,* Washington, D.C.: Library of Congress, Federal Research Division, 1989.

The Ethnic Dimension

Seventy-eight percent of Singapore's population is ethnically Chinese, so ethnic affinities have to be factored into Singapore's relations with China, particularly in the cultural and educational spheres.[5] In recent years, Singapore has become a major destination for Chinese studying abroad. According to a 2002 report, 13,000 to 15,000 Chinese nationals were studying in Singapore.[6] Nanjing University (Jiangsu Province) has opened a branch in Singapore.

The important point, however, is that these affinities do not necessarily carry over into state-to-state relations. One reason is that Singapore does not want to be perceived in the region as a stalking horse for China. As a senior Singaporean official stated in an interview, Singapore does not want Chinese influence to predominate in Southeast Asia precisely because its population is predominantly of Chinese origin.[7]

But there is also a historical reason for Singapore's reticence in its relations with China. At its inception as an independent state, Singapore was vulnerable to internal subversion by China-oriented political forces. In the 1963 election, the communist-controlled Socialist Front sought to exploit ethnic Chinese loyalties in its unsuccessful attempt to overturn the ruling People's Action Party. As a result, Singapore's founders sought to develop Singapore as a self-consciously multiethnic state and to attenuate its links with China to reduce the opportunities for Chinese political subversion of the nascent city-state. Singapore was one of the last countries in Southeast Asia to establish diplomatic relations with the People's Republic of China, which it did only in October 1990, after Indonesia resumed diplomatic relations with China in August 1990.[8]

Domestic Politics and Public Opinion

The ruling People's Action Party has governed Singapore since the country achieved self-government in 1959. It has consistently received 60 percent or more of the vote in parliamentary elections.[9] The overwhelming predominance of the People's Action Party and the blurring of boundaries between government, party leaders, and senior civil servants effectively insulates policymaking, especially foreign and defense policy, from politics. To date, there has been no public debate about the government's China policy and few indications that this will change.

---

[5]   Another 15 percent of the population is ethnically Malay, and 6.4 percent Indian.

[6]   "Singapore—New Mecca for Chinese Students," *People's Daily* (online), May 16, 2002.

[7]   Interview with senior official, Singapore, December 2005.

[8]   Indonesia established diplomatic relations with China in 1950, but suspended them after the failed Communist-backed coup of October 1965. Malaysia established diplomatic relations with China in 1974; the Philippines and Thailand did so in 1975.

[9]   In the general elections of May 6, 2006, the People's Action Party won 66.6 percent of the valid votes and 82 out of 84 parliamentary seats. (Actually, this was a decline from the 75.3 percent that the People's Action Party had received in the 2001 parliamentary elections.) The other two parties to win seats were the Workers' Party of Singapore and the Singapore Democratic Alliance, with one seat each.

This is not to say that the Singaporean government is insensitive to public opinion or that there is unanimity about policies. But policy debates, which tend to cover domestic issues, are not channeled through political parties in an adversarial context but through numerous feedback mechanisms and committees. The next few years may bring significant changes in the political environment because the People's Action Party government faces increasing pressures for liberalization and greater accountability from an educated and increasingly engaged young public.[10] Although Singaporeans tend to leave the business of government to the government, the gradual opening of political space will also mean a democratization of policy discourse, including that on China.

Public Perceptions of China

Although China does not play a significant role in Singapore's domestic politics, the Singaporean public has received China's peaceful-rise policy and the deepening of bilateral economic ties well. With 78 percent of the population being ethnic Chinese, students and university faculty are attaching greater importance to Chinese studies. An increasing number of ethnic Chinese students are taking Higher (Mandarin) Chinese (Chinese language at the first-language level) at the primary, secondary, and General Certificate of Education "A" levels.[11] Cultural ties have been deepening since the establishment of diplomatic relations in 1990. Chinese studies centers have been set up at major Singaporean educational institutions—for instance, the Centre for Chinese Language and Culture at Nanyang Technological University, established jointly by Singapore and China. In 2005, the 600th anniversary of Zheng He's first voyage to Southeast Asia, Singapore was chosen as the host location for the world's first "1421 Exhibition," which showcased author Gavin Mantis's best-seller, *1421: The Year China Discovered the World*.[12] The Zheng He commemorations dovetailed with the theme of China's peaceful rise, a centerpiece of China's public diplomacy in Southeast Asia.[13]

While systematic polling data are lacking, anecdotal evidence suggests that the rise in China's prestige and popularity in Singapore and Southeast Asia at large is due in part to successful public relations on the part of the Chinese government and the extraordinary progress China has made in economic development. Singaporean offi-

---

[10] "Singapore: Future Challenges," conference report, Johns Hopkins University, Washington, D.C., October 3, 2002.

[11] Ministry of Education, Singapore, *Education Statistics Digest 2007*, 2007; also see Ministry of Education, Singapore, "Education Statistics Digest: Online Interactive," 2004–2006.

[12] Gavin Menzies, "1421: The Year the Chinese Discovered the World," Web site, 2007.

[13] For instance, they made note of the fact that Zheng did not use naval power to conquer territory or to establish Chinese power in Southeast Asia. The implication is that Southeast Asian countries have nothing to fear from China's military power. See Perdana Global Peace Organisation, "Containing China: A Flawed Agenda," paper presented at Post–9.11 World: Exploring Alternatives for Japan and Australia, Nanzan University, Nagoya, Japan, September 14, 2005.

cials and opinion leaders, who have harbored major reservations about Chinese power and influence, now offer a generally positive view of China's rise but also point out that this is not at the expense of Singapore's relationship with the United States.

Economic Responses

The economic trends of the last decade have resulted in an increasingly closer integration of Singapore's economy with other East Asian economies, with China as the hub of regional integration. Singapore sees the expansion of economic ties with China and the country's fuller integration into an East Asian production zone as inevitable and desirable. In this sense, China is increasingly critical to Singapore's economy because China's development strategy is fueling a process of regional economic integration that Singapore benefits from significantly. For Singapore, increased economic integration around China is not a zero-sum game. The Singaporean elites do not see this expansion taking place at the expense of Singapore's economic ties with the United States and Europe. As with other Southeast Asian economic and business leaders, they promote increased trade as beneficial to all.

Nevertheless, just as Singapore hedges its bets in the security sphere by expanding its security relationship with the United States, it also hedges them in the economic sphere by diversifying its economic relationships. The FTA with the United States is an important step in Singapore's multidimensional economic policy. Singaporeans worry that the United States is not actively countering China's economic diplomacy. According to Singaporean security analyst Evelyn Goh, Singapore's success in getting Japan to agree to a study on a possible FTA in 1999 was part of a strategy to entrench Japan in Southeast Asia. Singapore has sought to expand economic ties to Japan in part because of Tokyo's key role as an anchor for the United States in Asia through the U.S.–Japanese alliance.[14]

In this regard, Singaporean officials see CAFTA as a brilliant political and strategic move on China's part. In contrast, Singaporeans note, Japan has been dragging its feet on the Japan-ASEAN FTA, which is pending the approval of various Japanese agencies. The China-ASEAN FTA, Singaporeans believe, changed the psychological climate in many Southeast Asian countries, leading to more-favorable views of China, particularly since Beijing was generous to less-developed ASEAN countries in the early harvest elements of the agreement.[15]

---

[14] Evelyn Goh, "Singapore's Reaction to a Rising China: Deep Engagement and Strategic Adjustment," in Ho Kai Leong and Samuel C. Y. Ku, eds., *China and Southeast Asia: Global Challenges and Regional Challenges*, Singapore: Institute of Southeast Asian Studies, 2005, pp. 321–322.

[15] Interview with senior official, Singapore, December 2005. The Early Harvest Program is an arrangement under the China-ASEAN FTA that reduces the tariffs on some products, particularly agricultural products, and allows the ASEAN countries access to China's domestic market prior to the establishment of the FTA.

On the negative side, some Southeast Asians believe that China is siphoning off FDI from Southeast Asia (which is important not only as a source of capital but as a means of technology transfer and export-market development). In the last few years, China has been attracting some 50 to 70 percent of FDI in Asia (excluding Japan) with only 20 percent going to Southeast Asia. Some scholars challenge that view. For example, citing a 2005 UNCTAD study, John Wong has argued that China's catalytic role within regional production networks has actually encouraged the inflow of FDI to Southeast Asia.[16]

Singapore's Stake in Regional Economic Integration

Expanded trade with China is an increasingly important part of the economic growth strategies of all Southeast Asian countries, including Singapore. Since 2000, Singapore has been following a strategy of negotiating FTAs to expand trade and diversify its trade and investment opportunities (and, in some cases, to facilitate and consolidate strategic relationships, for instance, with Japan).[17] In the ASEAN context, Singapore has signed FTA framework agreements with India, Japan, South Korea, and now China, among others.[18] Singapore has also concluded bilateral FTAs with New Zealand (2000), Japan (2002),[19] Australia (2002), the United States (2003), Jordan (2004), India (2005), South Korea (2006), and Panama (2006).[20]

China and ASEAN signed a framework agreement on comprehensive economic cooperation in November 2002 in Phnom Penh, setting a target for the China-ASEAN FTA to come into force in 2010 for the six core ASEAN members (Brunei, Indonesia, Malaysia, the Philippines, Singapore, and Thailand) and in 2015 for the other four (Burma, Cambodia, Laos, and Vietnam).[21] As part of the early harvest program, ASEAN countries have benefited from the reduction of Chinese tariffs on 484 seafood and agricultural products, excluding eggs and poultry products, between 2004 and 2006. Tariffs on these products were completely eliminated in January 2006.[22] Of greater interest to Singapore, the deal contains provisions to increase ASEAN market

---

[16] John Wong, "China's Economic Rise and Implications for Southeast Asia: The Big Picture," paper presented at the workshop on Ethnic Chinese Economy and Business in Southeast Asia in the Era of Globalization, Singapore: Institute of Southeast Asian Studies, April 21–22, 2005.

[17] Goh, 2005, p. 322.

[18] Ministry of Trade and Industry, Singapore, free trade agreements, various dates.

[19] Known as the Japan and the Republic of Singapore for a New-Age Economic Partnership.

[20] The Comprehensive Economic Cooperation Agreement Between the Republic of India and the Republic of Singapore, 2005, also known as the India-Singapore Comprehensive Economic Cooperation Agreement.

[21] Framework Agreement on Comprehensive Economic Co-Operation Between ASEAN and the People's Republic of China, Phnom Penh, November 4, 2002.

[22] Singapore, of course, does not have an agricultural sector and so finds Chinese reductions on agricultural tariffs irrelevant.

access in certain service sectors in China and to progressively reduce or eliminate investment regulations and conditions that may impede the investment flows and investment projects of ASEAN investors.[23]

Singaporean officials and academics do not see trade with China in bilateral terms. Rather, they see their country, along with others in East Asia, as part of a complex Asian production network that has sparked a boom in intraregional trade. Multinational corporations manufacture parts and components in a number of Asian countries, taking advantage of their differential production costs and technological capabilities. These parts and components are then exported to China, assembled, and shipped to the United States and other countries as finished exports. Accordingly, China runs a large trade surplus with the United States but a trade deficit with most other Asian countries.[24] Because the value added to products assembled in China for export to the United States and other markets can be quite small, China's trade surplus with the United States is in part an Asian trade surplus.[25]

According to many analysts, competition from China has put great pressure on Singapore's manufacturing sector, which still contributes slightly more than 25 percent of GDP.[26] Since the early 2000s, Singapore has lost large numbers of low–value-added manufacturing jobs and even entire industries, not just to China but also to Malaysia and other Asian countries with lower labor costs. Singaporean officials see the loss of labor-intensive manufacturing as inevitable and have encouraged the economy's shift to services and to economic activities that are more capital intensive.[27] Singapore's government is even facilitating the exit of noncompetitive industries to lower-cost ASEAN economies.[28]

---

[23]   Ministry of Trade and Industry, Singapore, undated.

[24]   Note that, as discussed in Chapter Two, calculations of the magnitude and even the direction of China's bilateral trade balances with other countries depend greatly on which country's data are used. According to Singaporean customs data (but not Chinese customs data), Singapore has run consistent merchandise trade deficits with China since at least 1995. The government does not find these deficits to be of concern because the city-state's overall trade balance has been, on average, in surplus over the same period. In 2005, Singapore's trade surplus with the rest of the world was US$29.6 billion.

[25]   Interview with senior official, Government of Singapore Investment Corporation, Singapore, December 2005.

[26]   Service industries (wholesale and retail trade, transport and communications, financial services, etc.) accounted for more than 60 percent of Singapore's GDP in 2006. Ministry of Trade and Industry, Singapore, *Economic Survey of Singapore 2006*, Singapore: Department of Statistics, February 2007a.

[27]   Daniel Lian has pointed out that manufacturing actually expanded from 24.1 percent of Singapore's GDP in 1994 to 27.1 percent in 2004. In 2006, manufacturing's share of GDP was 27.6 percent. He argues that the government's strategy of promoting diversification into pharmaceuticals and petrochemicals has been highly effective, reducing its dependence on electronics. Daniel Lian, "Singapore Lessons for China," *Asia Pacific Economics*, Morgan Stanley Equity Research, May 6, 2005.

[28]   Interview with Evelyn Goh, Singapore, December 2005.

Singapore's strategy is to become East Asia's equivalent of New York or London. China, of course, is an important part of that strategy, but Singapore's goal is much more ambitious than becoming another hub for China. Singaporeans believe that their city-state is better poised to be such a regional hub than is Hong Kong, Shanghai, or Tokyo because it is less tied to a single national economy. The Singapore government expects to continue to lose manufacturing jobs, but so long as it can retain its dominance in highly profitable service activities, such as stock listings, back-room operations, and other business and financial operations, the country's economy should continue to prosper.[29] Many of these financial services are related to trade and so have benefited from China's emergence as a regional center for manufacturing and assembly.[30] Some Singaporean analysts, however, worry that China will soon become globally competitive in financial and other trade-related services, not just as a low-cost assembler.[31]

Merchandise Trade

Singapore is particularly well positioned to become an East Asian business hub because of its long history as an *entrepôt*.[32] Reexports constitute a significant proportion of Singapore's world trade: In 2005, reexports accounted for almost one-half of Singapore's total exports. Electronic components and parts represented the largest single category of reexports, at almost 36 percent, reflecting Singapore's pivotal role in the electronics production network that dominates much of East Asian trade. A large proportion of these reexports of electronics components and parts is destined for China, which in 2004 surpassed both the United States and the European Union as the single largest exporter of information and communication technology products.[33]

Between 1996 and 2006, the total trade in merchandise (exports plus imports) between Singapore and China grew at an annual average rate of over 20 percent, with growth accelerating to over 30 percent between 2001 and 2006. In 2006, China was Singapore's third-largest trading partner, after Malaysia and the United States. Exports

---

[29] Interviews with senior official, Government of Singapore Investment Corporation, and Simon C. S. Tay, Singapore, December 2005.

[30] In 1997, trade-related services overtook transportation and tourism as the largest component of the services trade account. This transition took place because many multinational corporations have established subsidiaries in Singapore and large numbers of petroleum traders have adopted Singapore as a trading base. Ministry of Trade and Industry, Singapore, Singapore's Trade in Services: New Statistical Estimates and Analysis, Singapore: Department of Statistics, 2000.

[31] Interview with Evelyn Goh, Singapore, December 2005.

[32] Singapore is a highly efficient transport hub and does not levy tariffs on intermediate goods, so processors can import and export items without the hassle of tariffs. The few products that are subject to import duties include motor vehicles, tobacco, alcoholic beverages, and petroleum products, but tariffs are levied only on products for domestic consumption. Inland Revenue Authority of Singapore, "An Overview of the Singapore Tax System," 2005.

[33] OECD, undated.

to China accounted for 9.7 percent of total Singaporean exports, and imports from China were 11.4 percent of total Singaporean imports. As Figures 7.1 and 7.2 show, China surpassed some of Singapore's other important trading partners, such as Taiwan and Japan, between 1996 and 2006. On the Chinese side, Singapore was China's 12th-largest trading partner in 2006, accounting for 2.9 percent of total Chinese exports and 1.8 percent of total Chinese imports.

As Figure 7.3 illustrates, as percentages of the total, the three largest product categories among Singapore's imports from China were electrical and electronic machinery and appliances (at 22 percent); telecommunications equipment, mostly information and communication technology products (at 22 percent); and office machines (at 19 percent). Among exports to China, Figure 7.4 shows that electrical and electronic equipment and appliances dominated (at 45 percent), followed by office equipment (at 13 percent). Unfortunately, these data do not allow us to identify how much of Singapore's imports from China were reexported to other countries or to separate domestic exports to China from exports originating in other countries.

China provides 38 percent of Singapore's imports of parts for telecommunications equipment, 43 percent of Singapore's imports of television and radio transmitters, and 66 percent of Singapore's imports of assembled computers (Table 7.1). Singapore, in turn, provides more than 16 percent of China's imports of memory chips and 35 percent of China's imports of blank recording media (Table 7.2). China is also an

Figure 7.1
Singapore's Major Exports, by Country of Destination, Selected Years

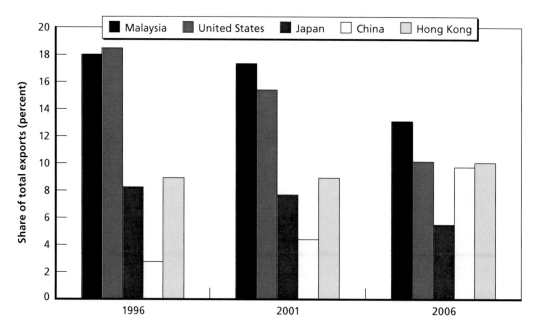

SOURCE: RAND calculations based on UN Statistics Division, 1996, 2001, 2006.
RAND MG736-7.1

Figure 7.2
Singapore's Major Imports, by Country of Origin, Selected Years

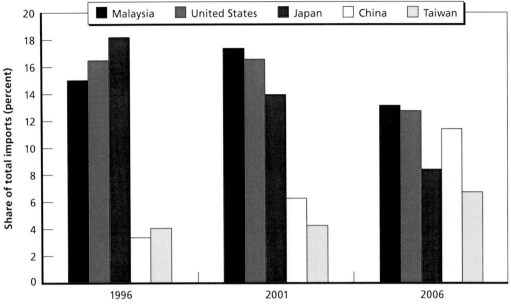

SOURCE: RAND calculations based on UN Statistics Division, 1996, 2001, 2006.
RAND *MG736-7.2*

Figure 7.3
Singapore's Imports from China as a Share of Worldwide Imports, 2006

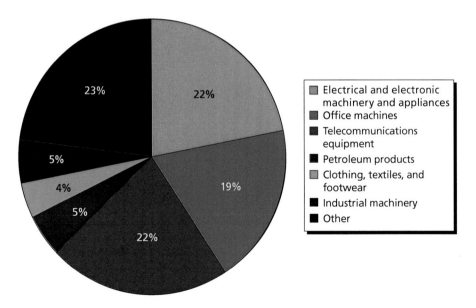

SOURCE: RAND calculations based on UN Statistics Division, 2006.
RAND *MG736-7.3*

Figure 7.4
Singapore's Exports to China as a Share of Worldwide Exports, 2006

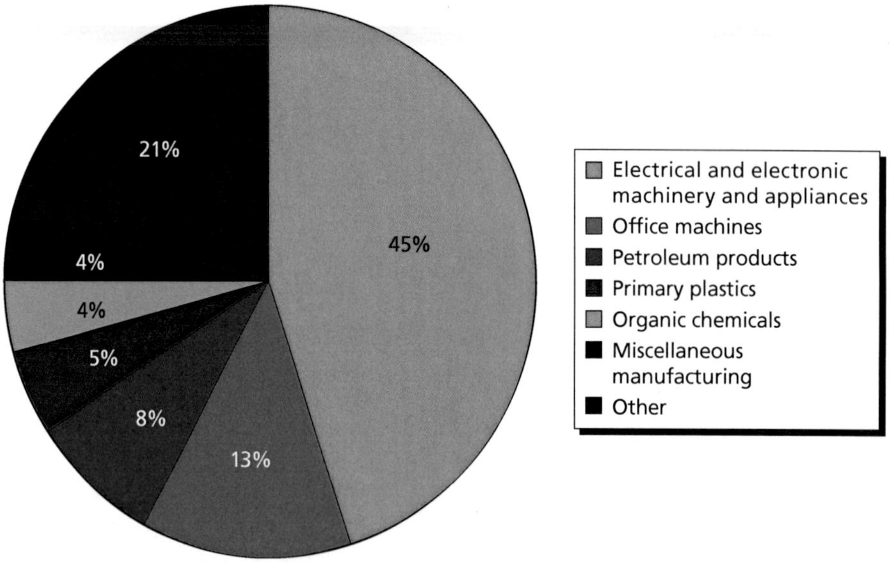

- Electrical and electronic machinery and appliances
- Office machines
- Petroleum products
- Primary plastics
- Organic chemicals
- Miscellaneous manufacturing
- Other

SOURCE: RAND calculations based on UN Statistics Division, 2006.
RAND MG736-7.4

Table 7.1
Top Five Singaporean Imports from China, 2006

Rank	SITC Code[a]	Commodity Name	Value (US$ millions)	Percentage of Singapore's World Imports	Percentage of Chinese World Exports[b]
1	7643	Television and radio transmitters	2,901.9	43.0	5.6
2	7764	Electronic microcircuits	2,803.4	6.6	11.5
3	7599	Computer parts	2,501.7	20.4	3.2
4	7649	Parts for telecommunications equipment	2,202.1	38.3	6.1
5	7522	Computers	756.7	66.3	1.3

SOURCE: RAND calculations based on UN COMTRADE data (UN Statistics Division, various years).
[a] Standard International Trade Classification.
[b] Singaporean import categories measured as Chinese exports to Singapore (free-on-board basis).

extremely important market for Singapore's exports of polyethylene (in 1995, China bought 30 percent of Singapore's exports) and household refrigerators and freezers (in 1995, China purchased over 80 percent of Singapore's exports of these products).[34]

---

[34] See for example International Enterprise Singapore, "Singapore's Bilateral Trade with China," January 23, 2006.

Table 7.2
Top Five Singaporean Exports to China, 2006

Rank	SITC	Commodity Name	Value (US$ millions)	Percentage of Singapore's World Exports	Percentage of Chinese World Imports[a]
1	7764	Electronic microcircuits	9,151.4	16.1	4.2
2	7599	Computer parts	2,064.2	11.0	5.3
3	7527	Computer storage units	1,081.7	13.0	4.1
4	7768	Crystals and electronic components	769.5	11.0	3.0
5	8985	Blank recording media	601.1	35.2	27.2

SOURCE: RAND calculations based on UN COMTRADE data (UN Statistics Division, various years).

[a] Top 20 Singaporean export categories measured as Chinese imports from Singapore (CIF basis).

Foreign Direct Investment

As part of a conscious effort to control production in the face of relatively high domestic manufacturing costs, Singapore's government has encouraged Singaporean investment abroad, particularly in China, India, Southeast Asia, and the United States. Table 7.3 lays out some data on these investments, as well as inward direct investment.

One powerful tool available to the government in the FDI effort is Temasek Holdings, a state-owned investment company established in 1974. Although Temasek has historically focused on domestic investments inside Singapore, it has expanded its international interests in recent years. It is now in the process of reshaping its portfolio to invest one-third of its operating assets in Singapore, one-third in the rest of Asia, and one-third in non-Asian OECD countries. As of March 31, 2007, Temasek's total exposure in Northeast Asia, including China but excluding Japan, constituted 24 percent of its portfolio, compared with 6 percent in 2004.[35]

Direct investment in China by Temasek and others has been particularly strong, with flows growing by an extraordinary 50 percent per year between 1993 and 2001.[36] Since 1997, China has been Singapore's top investment destination. As a result, despite Singapore's relatively small size, in 2005, the most recent year for which data are available, the country was China's sixth-largest foreign investor in terms of actual investment flows, which reached S$3.65 billion (US$2.2 billion).[37] In 2005, Singapore's stock

---

[35] Temasek Holdings, "Our Portfolio by Geography," Web page, March 31, 2007.

[36] Canadian High Commission in Singapore, "Trade, Investment, S&T, and Economic Overview," November 11, 2005; International Enterprise Singapore, 2006.

[37] The actual investment represents an actual cross-border stock or flow of direct investment into China. Contractual investment represents an amount of foreign investment approved by the Chinese authorities but not necessarily realized. In 2005, the value of Singapore's contractual investment in China was US$5.2 billion. "China-Singapore Trade Up in 2005," Xinhua News Agency, February 28, 2006.

Table 7.3
Singapore's Stock of Inward and Outward Direct Investment,
Selected Countries, Year-End 2005

	Value (S$ millions)	Percentage of Total
Inward Direct Investment, Source		
United Kingdom	50,153.8	16.1
United States	42,755.0	13.7
Japan	41,122.5	13.2
Netherlands	31,725.9	10.2
Switzerland	21,650.6	7.0
China	406.6	0.1
Total	311,084.0	
Outward Direct Investment, Destination		
China	25,457.1	13.7
Malaysia	15,895.4	8.6
Indonesia	13,913.5	7.5
Hong Kong	12,250.2	6.6
United States	9,331.1	5.0
United Kingdom	7,327.8	4.0
Total	185,101.4	

SOURCES: Ministry of Trade and Industry, Singapore, *Foreign Equity Investment in Singapore*, Singapore: Department of Statistics, 2005, July 2007b; Ministry of Trade and Industry, Singapore, *Singapore's Investment Abroad*, 2005, Singapore: Department of Statistics, July 2007c.

NOTE: Totals may not sum precisely due to rounding.

of direct investment in China was valued at S$25.5 billion (US$15.3 billion); it was heavily concentrated in manufacturing (62.3 percent).[38] Much of Singapore's manufacturing investment is concentrated in the electronics sector.

Chinese direct investment in Singapore is much smaller than Singaporean investment in China, but it is growing. In 2003 (most recent data available), 1,161 Chinese firms had invested in Singapore, up from 509 in 1999, with a collective investment of S$841.2 million. As of November 2006, 107 Chinese companies were listed on the Singapore stock exchange, many of which were small or midsized companies.[39] According to new Chinese outward FDI data, China's annual investment in Singa-

---

[38] Calculated at the 2005 average exchange rate of S$1.6646 per U.S. dollar. Ministry of Trade and Industry, 2007c.

[39] Larger mainland Chinese firms tend to list in Hong Kong. "Singapore Bourse Woos Mainland Firms," *Shenzhen Daily*, November 6, 2006.

pore has grown significantly since 2004, increasing from US$47.98 million in 2004 to US$132.15 million in 2006. The total stock of Chinese investment in Singapore increased accordingly, from US$164.83 million in 2003 to US$468.01 million in 2006.[40]

Despite the rapid growth in their investments in China, Singaporeans, like others, perceive China as risky because of its murky regulatory and legal environment. Perceptions about investing in China are colored by the debacle over the Suzhou industrial park. In 1993, a consortium of Singaporean and local corporations—the China Singapore Suzhou Industrial Park Development Company—began to invest some $150 million dollars to build an industrial township in Suzhou. Despite working with Singapore to license the project, the Suzhou municipal government shortly thereafter began to develop a rival economic zone, the Suzhou New District, resulting in a contest for investments among multinationals. The Suzhou industrial park did poorly against this competitor.[41] The Singaporean investors sold off a majority of their stake to the Chinese, cutting it to 35 percent and yielding management control. Under the new deal, the Suzhou municipal government agreed to reaffirm the Suzhou industrial park's priority status and avoid disorderly competition between the park and the Suzhou New District; Singapore agreed to train mainland managers for the project.[42]

This experience and others have brought about some reflection in Singapore about the perils, as well as opportunities, of investing in China. The Chinese market, the Singaporeans have learned, is difficult to penetrate, lacks transparency, and lacks a reliable legal regime. Singaporean interlocutors point out that, because most Singaporeans are ethnic Chinese and many speak Mandarin, they think they understand China but that problems persist anyway. Educated Singaporeans are brought up in a British-style educational system and have internalized the Western values of transparency and rule of law, which do not prepare them for the more freewheeling and less rule-bound way of doing business common in today's China, although that is, admittedly, changing.

Singaporeans also bring assumptions about the structure of government that often do not apply to China. While Singapore is a city-state with one layer of government that can make things happen, China is a continental country with many layers of government, not all of which behave consistently. If Beijing blesses a project, that does not mean that all will go well at lower levels, as the Suzhou experience showed.[43]

Singaporean investors, therefore, are proceeding with caution as China opens up its domestic market. Jurong International, which developed the Suzhou industrial park, is advising the Chinese on the development of the Hatachi industrial corridor in Hei-

---

[40] Ministry of Commerce of the People's Republic of China, 2007.

[41] In 1998, the Singapore consortium owned 65 percent of this company and Chinese companies the other 35 percent. "Suzhou Park Problems Can Be Overcome," *Straits Times* (Singapore), January 15, 1998.

[42] Barry Porter, "Singapore Drops Control of Suzhou Park," *South China Morning Post,* June 29, 1999.

[43] Porter, 1999.

longjiang Province, a zone 100 times the size of Singapore. In contrast to the Suzhou experience, Singaporeans are not investing in this project but are acting as consultants and brokers, helping the Chinese look for foreign investors outside Singapore.[44]

A Singaporean-European consortium (Temasek Holdings with UBS AG and the Royal Bank of Scotland) is a leading foreign investor in China's banking sector (consisting of the China Construction Bank; the Bank of China; and Minsheng Bank, China's only privately held bank). Under current Chinese regulation, a single foreign investor may purchase up to 20 percent of the equity of a Chinese bank, and a group of investors may purchase up to 25 percent. The Singaporean partner is taking only a 10-percent share, diluting its risk. Some investors expect the country's stake in the Chinese banking sector will provide Singapore a competitive advantage in investing in Chinese state-owned enterprises or providing consulting services to institutions interested in buying Chinese companies.[45] Some state-owned enterprises are now quite profitable (in part because of price manipulation), and beginning in 2006, state-owned enterprises in some sectors (e.g., tobacco, electricity, coal, petrochemicals) were required to hand over 10 percent of their after-tax profits to the Ministry of Finance.[46]

Portfolios account for roughly 20 percent of Singapore's investment abroad.[47] In 2005, the Government of Singapore Investment Corporation, which manages the government's foreign-currency reserves, had invested less than 5 percent of its portfolio in Chinese equities.[48] The primary reason for the small proportion of portfolio investment in Chinese equities is that capital markets in China are seen as underdeveloped and risky and partially closed to foreign investors.[49] Singaporean investors, including the government's corporation, tend to prefer investments in China over which they have more control, such as controlling stakes in Chinese businesses and purchases of real estate.[50]

---

[44] Interview with Dr. Tan Khee Giap, Asia Research Centre, Singapore, December 2005. Singapore's willingness to participate in the rejuvenation of the old industrial base in Northeast China was announced during the visit of Chinese Vice Premier Wu Yi to Singapore in May 2005. Ministry of Foreign Affairs of the People's Republic of China, "Vice Premier Wu Yi Holds Talks with Her Singaporean Counterpart and the Two Sides Co-Host the Meeting of the Joint Council for Bilateral Cooperation," May 14, 2004.

[45] Interview with Dr. Tan Khee Giap, Asia Research Centre, Singapore, December 2005.

[46] Wu Zhong, "Some of China's SOEs Aren't Such Losers After All," *Asia Times*, September 26, 2007.

[47] Direct investment accounts for slightly less than half of Singapore's investment abroad, while "other foreign assets" (mostly deposits held abroad and loans granted to nonaffiliates) accounted for approximately 30 percent. Ministry of Trade and Industry, 2007c.

[48] Interview with senior official, Government of Singapore Investment Corporation, December 2005. According to Rodan (2004), the corporation does not publish information about its investments. Gary Rodan, "The Coming Challenge to Singapore, Inc.," *Far Eastern Economic Review*, December 2004.

[49] Interview with senior Singaporean investment banker, December 2005.

[50] See, for example, Kelvin Wong, Grace Ng, Fiona Chan, and Gabriel Chen, "Temasek, GIC Now Boast a Stronger Overseas Portfolio," *The Straits Times*, December 30, 2005.

Economic Winners and Losers

Because Singapore is a major *entrepôt* for the world's exports to and imports from all of East Asia, including China, interpreting data on Singaporean imports and exports is difficult: Some Singaporean industrial machinery exports to China, for example, may actually originate in Germany or the United States, while Singaporean telecommunications equipment imports from China may be destined for Saudi Arabia or Brazil.

That said, Singapore is not just a transshipment point: It is still an important manufacturing center for certain products. This allows some assessment of who wins and who loses in trade with China. Two domestic companies, Singapore Petroleum Company Limited and Singapore Refining Company Private Limited, export refined oil products to China. Subsidiaries of Western multinationals, including Total, are also engaged in this industry. An offshoot, petrochemicals, is also a major category of exports. These companies have benefited from China's growing thirst for refined oil products and petrochemicals. Diversified manufacturers and machine builders in Singapore have also benefited from increased demand from China. Pharmaceuticals, a growth industry deriving primarily from the operations of Western multinationals, have also been a booming export.

Exports of electronics, computers, and telecommunications equipment have risen sharply, but so have imports. In the early to mid-2000s, Singapore was still running a hefty surplus with China in electrical and electronic components and parts; even its deficit in office machines was growing. Singaporean firms and subsidiaries of foreign firms have reportedly moved many of their assembly and manufacturing operations to China. Singapore has been trying to keep the higher-end manufacturing of electronic parts and components (e.g., processors and other computer chips) at home. The industry in Singapore has been continually restructuring itself because of the emergence of China as a major assembler and manufacturer of these goods. Singaporean workers who worked in these plants have had to move to other jobs. Some Singaporean managers have also had to find new work.

Repeated shipments of goods to and from China have benefited Singapore's growing service industries, which include ship repair and financial services. Increases in overall volumes of trade, exports, and transshipment contribute to growth in these sectors.

Because so much of Singapore's industry is foreign owned, many exports to and imports from China reflect the actions of companies that may or may not be Singaporean. The Singaporean government heavily influences state-owned firms, but American, European, or Japanese corporations control their own offshoots in Singapore. In this situation, Chinese moves to penalize Singaporean exports may affect firms headquartered outside Singapore more than they do the Singaporean economy.

Diplomatic and Foreign Policy Responses

Regional Policy

Singaporean political leaders are mindful of the rise of China and the implications for regional security and Singapore's interests. This attentiveness to strategic issues is somewhat anomalous in Southeast Asia (with the possible exception of Vietnam), where political elites tend to focus more internally and take a somewhat parochial approach to national-security planning. Singaporean officials and analysts see China as pursuing a consistent long-term strategy toward Southeast Asia that aims to expand Beijing's influence, maintain regional stability, and foster economic and trade relationships that should help ensure China's continued economic growth.

Singapore's regional diplomacy reflects two main priorities: furthering cooperation with the United States and engagement with China. In the view of Singaporean analysts, Beijing is seeking to ensure its place and voice at the table in Southeast Asia but does not necessarily seek to dominate the region—at least such an intention is not yet clearly evident. According to this view, China would like to displace the United States from the center to the side of the stage in East Asia but not to push it off the stage—something the Chinese know they do not have the means to accomplish. Chinese leaders know their nation's limitations, how far China has to go, and what problems it must face before it can become dominant in the region.

Bilateral relations are normal—although there have been tensions over Singapore's relationship with Taiwan—and span the economic, political, educational, cultural, and science and technology spheres. China and Singapore conduct regular high-level exchanges, supplemented by educational and cultural exchanges, such as the Mayors' Study Visit Program, the Senior Chinese Officials Study Visit Program, and the Sino-Singapore Undergraduate Exchange Program.

Over the longer term, Singaporeans are uneasy about China's future course and constantly watch Chinese policies and actual behavior. They worry that a more-powerful China might feel less constrained about aggressively pursuing its interests. China's younger generation is considered assertive and nationalistic and may be less cautious once it comes to power than the current leadership is. China's relatively restrained policy, moreover, could be thrown off course by two potential flashpoints: Taiwan and tensions in Chinese-Japanese relations. Both China and Japan have to cope with nationalism—Japan less so than China—and both have hierarchical worldviews that make it difficult for each to accept the other as the preeminent East Asian power.[51]

Managing the rise of China so that it becomes a stabilizing development in East Asia is, thus, a critical foreign policy challenge for Singapore but one Singapore feels it has, by itself, limited ability to take on. Singaporean diplomacy, therefore, seeks to enmesh China in a network of ASEAN-centric institutions that will make China a

---

[51]   Interview with senior official, Singapore, December 2005.

stakeholder in the international system without, at the same time, allowing Beijing to dominate these institutions. Singapore's position on the participation of non–East Asian countries in the EAS held in Kuala Lumpur in December 2005 reflects this approach. The EAS was originally conceived as an "East Asians only" forum with a view to establishing an East Asian community. China wanted to differentiate the ASEAN Plus Three (China, Japan, and South Korea), as the core of the future East Asian community, from peripheral members. Japan, Singapore, and some other ASEAN states, on the other hand, supported the participation of Australia (therefore ensuring that U.S. interests would be represented), New Zealand, and India as full members of the East Asian community. Singapore's rationale for an inclusive summit was that it did not want the world split into closed blocs or exclusive spheres of influence.[52]

Contrary to China's position, Singapore also supports the candidacies of Japan and India for permanent membership in an expanded UN Security Council.[53] Beijing was upset because it expected the Southeast Asian countries to join it in opposition. China was particularly upset that Singapore, a "Chinese" state, supported Japan's bid. Singapore has also sought to strengthen its relationship with India and paved the way for India's association with the ASEAN Regional Forum.[54]

As part of its overall diplomatic strategy, Singapore also seeks to deepen bilateral cooperation with the United States, especially security cooperation. The close relationship between Singapore and the United States was formalized in the Strategic Framework Agreement President George W. Bush and Prime Minister Lee Hsien Loong signed in Washington in July 2005. The agreement recognizes Singapore's role as a "major security-cooperation partner" and proposes to expand the scope of current cooperation in counterterrorism, counterproliferation, joint military exercises and training, policy dialogues, and defense technology.[55] By the same token, Singapore seeks to involve the United States more deeply in East Asian regional institutions.[56]

---

[52] Mohan Malik, "The East Asia Summit: More Discord than Accord," *YaleGlobal*, December 20, 2005; Bruce Vaughn, *East Asian Summit: Issues for Congress*, Washington, D.C.: Congressional Research Service, December 9, 2005.

[53] China has called for reform of the UN Security Council but has refrained from endorsing the candidacies of Japan and India. China, of course, wants to avoid diluting its influence as the only Asian UN Security Council member, especially by adding peer competitors Japan or India.

[54] Raakhee Suryaprakash, "Singapore-India Relations: CECA and Beyond," South Asia Analysis Group, paper 1493, August 10, 2005.

[55] See George W. Bush, President of the United States, and Lee Hsien Loong, Prime Minister of Singapore, Joint Statement, Washington, D.C.: The White House, July 12, 2005.

[56] Singaporean officials believe that the United States has not taken full advantage of the panoply of formal dialogue mechanisms established between ASEAN and its partners. (Discussion with senior official, Singapore, December 2005.)

Taiwan Policy

Singapore's policy toward Taiwan reflects a balance between its interests in expanding its economic relationship with China and in helping to manage China's rise as a peaceful actor in the Asian security system on the one hand and its important economic and defense equities in Taiwan on the other. From both the Chinese and Taiwanese perspectives, Singapore's policy toward Taiwan appears to be a zero-sum game. Consequently, shifts in this policy are good indicators of changes in Singapore's response to China's rise.

The scope of Singaporean-Taiwanese interactions is fairly extensive, involving an array of reciprocal visits: military vessels and delegations, even high-level politicians (but always privately and informally). Lee Kuan Yew visited Taiwan as senior minister, most recently in September 2002, when he met twice with Taiwanese President Chen Shui-bian. He also visited Taiwan in 1994 and 2000. He has sought to serve as an honest broker by, for example, facilitating the meeting of Chinese and Taiwanese negotiators in Singapore in 1992, which in turn led to several rounds of negotiations on cross-strait issues.[57]

Prime Minister Goh Chok Tong made a transit stop in Taiwan in November 1997 and met with Premier Vincent Siew; in turn, Taiwan's Vice President Lien Chen visited Singapore in January 1998 on what was described as a vacation.[58] Beijing usually reacted to these visits with little more than pro forma protests and démarches.

Yet, China appears to have become more sensitive to such visits. In light of the history of the visits of high-level Singaporean officials to Taiwan, the unexpectedly fierce Chinese reaction to Deputy Prime Minister (and Prime Minister–designate) Lee Hsien Loong's visit to Taiwan in July 2004 surprised the Singaporeans. The Chinese ratcheted up the rhetoric—with a Foreign Ministry spokesman saying that the trip damaged "the political foundations of China-Singapore relations"—and canceled bilateral exchanges. The Singaporean position was that Singapore's policy on Taiwan had not changed.[59]

After assuming the position of prime minister, Lee Hsien Loong paid a high-profile visit to China and was received by President Hu Jintao, National People's Con-

---

[57]   Benjamin Kang Lim and Jonathan Ansfield, "Lee Sr's Visit Taiwan to Annoyance of China," Reuters, September 17, 2002; "Can Singapore's Lee Kuan Yew Kickstart Talks Between China and Taiwan?" *Far Eastern Economic Review*, October 5, 2000.

[58]   "PM Goh Makes Surprise Taiwan Stopover," Reuters, November 28, 1997; "S'pore Press Silent on Taiwan Official's Visit," United Press International, January 1, 1998.

[59]   Barry Wain, "A David-and-Goliath Tussle," *Far Eastern Economic Review*, August 5, 2004. Three explanations have been offered. One was the timing of the visit, during a period of heightened tensions between Beijing and Taipei. A second, one Singaporean officials give credence, was disappointed Chinese expectations, given that former Prime Minister Goh and other officials had made statements in the preceding months warning Taiwan against moving to independence and that Singapore was moving closer to the Chinese position on Taiwan. A third explanation was that the People's Republic of China was testing the resilience of Singapore's relationship with Taiwan and may have been sending a message to the other ASEAN countries to toe the line on Taiwan.

gress Chairman Wu Bangguo, Premier Wen Jiabao, and People's Political Consultative Conference Chairman Jia Qinglin. This marked the end of the controversy. The Chinese may have made their point: There are costs to *not* deferring to Chinese core interests concerning Taiwan. There are reports that members of the Singaporean business community discreetly lobbied the government not to antagonize the People's Republic of China by taking too assertive a position on Taiwan. Singaporean Cabinet–level officers have not traveled to Taiwan since Lee's 2004 visit.[60]

Public warnings that Singaporean leaders have made against Taiwanese officials' movements toward *de jure* independence suggest a high level of concern in Singapore that a Taiwanese miscalculation would likely precipitate Chinese military reaction. At the National Rally Day speech in August 2004, Prime Minister Lee said that, in his talks with the Taiwanese, he was concerned that the Taiwanese did not understand the international strategic environment. "Many Taiwanese believe that China will not use force on Taiwan even if it moves towards independence," Lee said, "They are wrong." He warned that if Taiwan moved to independence, Singapore would not recognize it as an independent nation; China would fight; and Taiwan would be devastated.[61]

Singaporean officials believe that, if Taiwan were to declare independence, Beijing would have no choice but to take action. That said, they also believe that, for the time being, the Taiwan issue appears to have been defused. One somewhat counterintuitive reason is China's Anti-Secession Law. Singapore offered measured support for the law. A short statement on the Ministry of Foreign Affairs' Web site said that Singapore "understands the reason" for the law's enactment and that it appears to restate "China's known position against Taiwan's independence with a strong emphasis on peaceful resolution."[62]

Other reasons Singaporean officials believe the Taiwan issue has receded as a potential source of conflict is the Bush administration's consistent statements that it opposes unilateral changes to the status quo from either China or Taiwan and that, ultimately, the U.S. security commitment to Taiwan has its limits.[63] For Singapore,

---

[60] Interview with Simon S. C. Tay, Director, Singapore Institute of International Affairs, Singapore, December 2005.

[61] Lee said that Taiwanese political leaders do not realize how rapidly China is transforming itself and how major powers in the world are repositioning themselves in response. See Lee Hsien Loong, "National Day Rally 2004 Speech," Prime Minister's speech delivered at the University Cultural Centre, National University of Singapore, August 22, 2004. Foreign Minister George Yeo stressed the same theme at the UN, warning that the "push towards independence by certain groups in Taiwan is most dangerous because it will lead to war with mainland China and drag in other countries." George Yeo, Minister for Foreign Affairs of the Republic of Singapore, statement delivered to the 59th Session of the UN General Assembly, New York, September 24, 2004.

[62] "China–Southeast . . . ," 2005.

[63] Thomas J. Christensen, Deputy Assistant Secretary for East Asian and Pacific Affairs, "A Strong and Moderate Taiwan," speech to U.S.–Taiwan Business Council Defense Industry Conference, Annapolis, Md., September 11, 2007. Also see James A. Kelly, Assistant Secretary of State for East Asian and Pacific Affairs, "Overview of U.S.

other encouraging signs include the opposition KMT leaders' visit to the mainland, for which the KMT did not pay an electoral price, suggesting limited pro-independence sentiments on Taiwan.[64]

Defense Policy Responses

Singapore's defense and security policy operates at two levels: One, at what defense analyst Tim Huxley calls the "grand regional level," Singapore relies on extraregional powers—primarily the United States—to maintain the balance of power and prevent a larger power from dominating the smaller Asian states. Two, in its immediate vicinity, Singapore relies to a much greater extent on its own resources to prevent a neighboring state—primarily Malaysia or Indonesia—from dominating the region.[65] This approach largely bounds how Singapore's military and national security community is responding to the rise of China in regional security affairs.

Concerns about China are not an explicit driver of Singapore's defense policy and military modernization. Rather, the threat of terrorism and rising Islamic extremism in the Muslim majority countries surrounding Singapore, the security of Singapore's sea lanes of communication, and maintenance of the intra-ASEAN balance of power dominate Singapore's defense planning and drive military procurement. One area of external security concern for Singapore is its uneasy relationship with Malaysia. Singapore's relations with Malaysia are in a category by themselves—similar to the tense relations between annoyed relatives living in close quarters. There is a large area of overlap between Singapore's and Malaysia's core security interests.[66] Unlike other Southeast Asian states, Singapore has no conflicting claims with China in the South China Sea. Singapore has also not signed defense treaties with other ASEAN states that could bring it conflict with China over South China Sea disputes.[67]

A brief look at certain capabilities of Singapore's military reveals these priorities. It also indicates that the modern nature of certain Singaporean capabilities provides it with the ability to operate in concert with U.S. forces in a regional contingency, which

---

Policy Toward Taiwan," testimony at a hearing on Taiwan before the House International Relations Committee, Washington, D.C., April 21, 2004.

[64] Interview with senior official, Singapore, December 2005. The Singaporeans hosted KMT chairman Ma Ying-jeou in May 2006; Ma was given high-profile treatment, which probably reflected Singaporean dissatisfaction with Chen Shui-bian's policies.

[65] Tim Huxley, *Defending the Lion City: The Armed Forces of Singapore*, London: Allen & Unwin, 2001, pp. 33–37.

[66] Andrew T. H. Tan, "Singapore's Defence: Capabilities, Trends and Implications," *Contemporary Southeast Asia*, Vol. 21, No. 3, December 1999.

[67] Singapore is part of the Five Power Defence Arrangement with the United Kingdom, Australia, New Zealand, and Malaysia, but this is a consultative arrangement, not a mutual defense treaty. See Huxley, 2001, pp. 38–40.

is a capability that few ASEAN states currently possess. Singapore's future weapon purchases are further facilitating such options, especially joint operations with the U.S. military.

The Republic of Singapore Air Force is the most powerful and capable in Southeast Asia.[68] Its mission is to defend against air threats and to protect Singapore's air and sea lanes of communication. It provides continuous air surveillance and early warning of air threats and is structured to participate in joint operations with the army and the navy. The air force has some 150 combat aircraft and 20 armed helicopters, including two squadrons of F-16s, three squadrons of F-5Es reconfigured for maritime strike and reconnaissance missions, three squadrons of upgraded A-4 Super Skyhawks, and eight maritime patrol aircraft. E-2C patrols have been extended well into the South China Sea, and these aircraft, if deployed at bases in eastern Malaysia, would be able to loiter in the vicinity of the Spratly Islands for a prolonged period. Moreover, the F-5Es and F-16s have a midair refueling capability (accessible via Singapore's KC-130 and KC-135 tanker aircraft), which extends their range and loitering capability well into the South China Sea.[69]

The air force has also taken delivery of a number of Malat Scout remotely piloted vehicles from Israel.[70] In 2005, Singapore selected Boeing's F-15SG Strike Eagle to replace the Skyhawks and signed a contract for 12 aircraft. In 2007, the air force decided to order 12 more of these aircraft.[71] Singapore is also likely to stay closely linked to U.S. air defense systems into the future through its participation in the Joint Strike Fighter program, which may eventually involve purchasing the F-35 multirole aircraft by around 2015.[72]

Defense Cooperation with the United States

Singapore's national security policy reflects the country's fundamental interest in maintaining the regional balance of power to support stability. Although Singaporean officials and analysts do not perceive China to be a security threat on its current course, they do believe that Singapore's—and Southeast Asia's—security and stability are intimately tied to continued U.S. diplomatic involvement and military presence in the region.[73] To this end, Singapore has sought to anchor the U.S. military firmly

---

[68] Jane's, "Singapore," *Jane's World Air Forces*, January 4, 2008b.

[69] Ministry of Defence (Singapore), 2000, pp. 32–33; Sheldon W. Simon, "The Regionalization of Defense in Southeast Asia," *NBR Analysis*, Vol. 3, No. 1, June 1992, p. 116; Huxley, 2001, p. 147.

[70] Tan, 1999, p. 459.

[71] Jane's, "Singapore," *Jane's World Air Forces*, January 4, 2008.

[72] Singapore was the first Asian participant in the F-35 Joint Strike Fighter program, with an option to buy the planes starting in 2012.

[73] For instance, Singaporean security analyst Evelyn Goh does not believe that Southeast Asians see China's expanding military capabilities as changing the balance of power in Southeast Asia because the balance between

in East Asia. In the early 1990s, after U.S. base negotiations with the Philippines had failed, Singapore provided the U.S. military access to facilities in Singapore to fill the security void and to ensure a U.S. presence in the region. The basis of U.S.–Singaporean security cooperation was the MOU of November 1990, as amended, which provided the U.S. military dedicated facilities, including a hangar and operational facilities at Paya Labar air base, supply areas, housing, billets, and recreational facilities, and combined-use facilities, including aircraft parking, a passenger terminal, and the wharves at Sembawang.

Currently, Singapore hosts the U.S. Navy Logistic Group West Pacific (relocated from Subic Bay) and the U.S. Air Force 497th Combat Training Squadron. Changi Naval Base berthing facilities can accommodate a U.S. aircraft carrier.[74] Singapore's close defense relationship with the United States carries relatively few domestic or foreign policy costs for the government. As Evelyn Goh argues, Singapore is probably the only country in ASEAN that can have as close a military relationship with the United States as it does without domestic political problems. While China may be displeased with the high level of Singaporean defense cooperation with the United States, the Chinese have relatively few levers to use on Singapore in this regard.[75]

Singaporean security cooperation with the United States is based on the expectation that the United States will remain engaged in the region. Some Singaporean officials and analysts worry that the United States, preoccupied as it is with Iraq and the Middle East, is not paying enough attention to Asia. Nevertheless, they are confident that the United States will respond appropriately in a crisis.

A 1998 MOU between the United States and Singapore permitted the latter to acquire AIM-120 Advanced Medium-Range Air-to-Air Missiles.[76] Singapore received the training and software to arm its F-16 aircraft with the missiles, but the missiles themselves were kept in the United States, consistent with the U.S. policy of not being the first to introduce sophisticated military technology into the region.[77] Singapore has also taken delivery of eight of 20 AH-64D Apache attack helicopters with the Longbow system, which rapidly and automatically searches, detects, locates, classifies, and prioritizes multiple moving and stationary land, sea, and air targets in clear and adverse

---

China and the ASEAN countries is already asymmetrical. China's growing military strength only increases the existing asymmetry. On the other hand, she argues that Chinese military power is checked by the United States. Discussion with Dr. Evelyn Goh, Institute for Defense and Strategic Studies, Singapore, December 2005.

[74] U.S. Navy vessels are frequent visitors to Singapore, including the aircraft carriers *Kitty Hawk* (CV-63) in April 2004 and *Abraham Lincoln* (CVN-72) in January and April 2006.

[75] Discussion with Dr. Goh, Singapore, December 2005.

[76] The AIM-120 is a high-supersonic, day, night, all-weather, beyond-visual-range, fire-and-forget air-to-air missile.

[77] A similar arrangement exists with Malaysia.

weather conditions. The Apaches are based in Arizona, where the Singaporean crews are training with the Arizona National Guard.

It is not clear to what extent Singapore's air and naval modernization is informed by considerations relating to China's military capabilities and intentions. Certainly, the air force has the capability to deploy high-performance aircraft to potential areas of conflict in the South China Sea. The existence of this capability may contribute to generalized deterrence in the South China Sea, but it does not follow that Singapore contemplates involvement in a conflict with China. Defense analyst Tim Huxley believes that, in a conflict between other ASEAN states and China, Singapore could not easily support its ASEAN partners if they decided to oppose militarily a Chinese attempt to dominate the South China Sea.[78]

Participation in a possible conflict over Taiwan is almost certainly not a driver of Singapore's defense procurement and planning. Singapore is unlikely to become directly involved in a related armed conflict, partly because of its geography and partly because of its force structure. Singapore is some 1,750 nmi from Taipei, but others are closer. From Taipei, it is 1,500 nmi to Guam, 650 nmi to Manila, and 350 nmi to Okinawa (Figure 7.5). However, depending on the circumstances, Singapore might allow the United States to use its facilities for transit and logistics, although it will be reluctant to take such a step. Deciding to become involved in a Taiwan conflict would be very difficult for Singapore's leaders. Singapore highly values its close defense relationship with the United States but, like all other ASEAN states, recognizes that Taiwan is part of China. Singapore's leaders are not likely to risk its vital economic relationship with China by entering an armed conflict with Beijing (particularly if the conflict is seen as having been provoked by the Taiwanese government). Singapore's elite would also likely see such a conflict with China as a failure of U.S. policy and, thus, might begin call into question the degree to which the U.S. role in Asia was a force for stability.

Importance of Technology Cooperation

Because of its small population and personnel constraints, Singapore has to rely on technology as a force multiplier. Since the early 1970s, Singapore has allocated an average of 6 percent of its GDP to defense expenditures and has developed a strong indigenous defense industrial base. For analyzing the responses of U.S. allies and security partners in Asia to the rise of China, the centrality of high technology in Singapore's military procurement and defense industrial policy has powerful implications. It is true that Singapore has prudently diversified its defense procurement precisely to avoid overdependence on any single source. Nevertheless, to the extent that the United States remains the primary source of cutting-edge military technology—and Singapore will settle for nothing less—and that U.S. companies are seen as strategic partners for Sing-

---

[78] Huxley, 2001, p. 37.

Figure 7.5
Distances to Taiwan

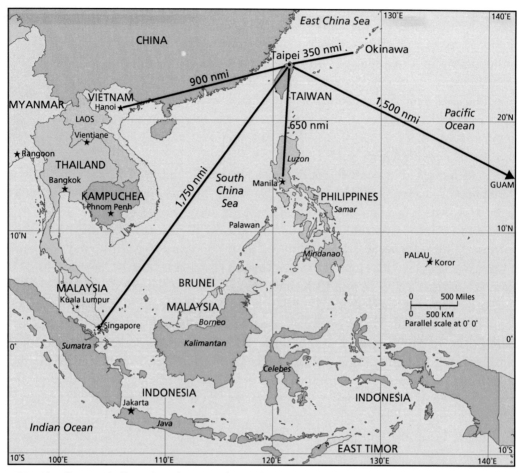

NOTE: The distances indicated are for direct flights from Taipei to the destinations shown.
RAND *MG736-7.5*

apore's defense industries, Singapore will continue to have a strong incentive to maintain its defense relationship with the United States to protect the military's qualitative edge. These considerations are likely to limit Chinese influence in the military sphere.

Defense Relations with ASEAN States and China

Singapore's defense cooperation with other ASEAN states is limited because ASEAN has never been conceived as a defense pact and is not central to Singapore's defense planning. In past years, ASEAN states have indirectly tried to foster greater security cooperation in response to latent concerns about China's growing regional role. The reality, as some Singaporean analysts recognize it, is that the ASEAN states together are not strong enough militarily to balance China.[79] Nonetheless Singapore does see value in expanding the security dialogue within ASEAN. Former Deputy Prime Minister and Coordinating Minister for Security and Defense Tony Tan Keng Yam has stated that the

> ASEAN approach is for each country to raise its capability to defend itself and strengthen national resilience, while at the same time deepening and strengthening bilateral defense cooperation with all other members of the group.

However, little concrete progress has been registered in defense cooperation among ASEAN states.[80]

Singapore's defense relations with China have become closer in recent years. During the visit of Defense Minister Teo Chee Hean to China in November 2005, the two sides agreed to establish an annual defense policy dialogue at the Ministry of Defense Permanent Secretary level and step up high-level military visits and port calls. Singapore and China also agreed to cooperate in international humanitarian assistance and disaster relief and peacekeeping missions. Minister Teo extended an offer of scholarships for PLA officers to attend graduate degree courses in Singapore.[81] From the Singaporean perspective, military engagement with China is part and parcel of its approach of enmeshing China—and its military—into a web of regional relationships that fosters emergence of a China that does not act coercively or otherwise upset regional stability.

Conclusions and Implications

More than many other East Asian countries, Singapore shows little ambivalence in its response to the rise of China. The country's small size, geostrategic vulnerability, and continuing concerns about long-term Chinese intentions propel it toward a close, *strategic* relationship with the United States. Singaporean leaders see the United States as both the principal stabilizer in the event of internal Chinese unrest and the only realistic counterweight to potential Chinese external assertiveness. Keeping the United States actively engaged and forward deployed in the region has thus been a central Singaporean policy objective. China's rise, together with the spread of Islamic extremism

---

[79]   Discussion with Dr. Goh, Singapore, December 2005.

[80]   An annual meeting of defense officials—the Senior Officials Meeting—has been instituted to exchange views on regional security matters. Minister Tan allowed that there could be other forms of defense cooperation in the future, but it was "too early at this stage to elaborate on what forms these could take." ("The View from Singapore: ASEAN Has a Role to Play in Keeping the Peace," *Asiaweek,* March 22, 1996.)

[81]   Ministry of Defence, Singapore, "Singapore and China Agree to Enhance Bilateral Defence Exchanges," November 16, 2005.

and heightened concerns about stability in neighboring states, has prompted Singapore to further strengthen security cooperation with the United States. At the same time, Singapore has sought to expand security ties with the United Kingdom, Japan, Australia, and other states with stakes in regional stability.

This core component of Singapore's response to the rise of China is coupled with efforts to further develop bilateral economic relations, as with other pairs in this book. The benefits Singapore receives from increasing trade and investment with China, as well as from China's broader economic integration in the region, underpin efforts to expand bilateral economic ties. These efforts are balanced, however, by an attempt to diversify Singapore's economic relationships as a means of avoiding excessive dependence on the Chinese market. They are also balanced by efforts to negotiate a range of FTAs, in particular with Japan and the United States, as a means of countering China's active economic diplomacy and entrenching these key countries economically in Southeast Asia.

Because of the relative lack of ambivalence about China and the clarity of Singapore's long-term vision, the future of Singapore's relationship with China is arguably less murky than that of any other Southeast Asian nation. Singapore has adjusted well through the years to changes in the distribution of economic and military power in Asia and has successfully protected its political independence. If or as China becomes more powerful, Singaporean leaders will make further adjustments to maintain the country's independence, growth, and room for maneuver. Toward these ends, they will do everything they can to ensure a continued balance of power in the region, so that China does not and cannot dominate.

This effort will almost surely guarantee continued close security relations with the United States (assuming continued U.S. interest and effort). To be sure, Singapore has no interest in heightened tensions in Asia, including those resulting from U.S. diplomacy. In the absence of unprovoked Chinese aggression, Singapore will neither encourage nor support a containment or explicitly anti-China balancing coalition. But Singaporean leaders understand that their own security and well-being are inextricably connected to the stability of the international system. They will thus seek to build on the U.S.–Singapore Strategic Framework Agreement in measured ways to expand bilateral security cooperation with the United States on a range of shared security interests. They will try to ensure that the United States remains active, relevant, and influential in East Asian political and economic affairs more broadly. Singapore will reinforce this effort by encouraging expanded roles for Japan, Australia, and other like-minded states in regional economics and security affairs. Singapore will continue to try to enmesh China further in a network of ASEAN-centric institutions as a means of increasing its stakes in the regional and international orders, while working to prevent Beijing from dominating these institutions.

Along with these efforts, Singapore will continue to develop its economic relationship with China and foster broader regional economic integration. Singapore will seek to implement the ASEAN-Chinese FTA, for example, while striving to maintain Singapore's lead over China in such areas as financial services, in which Singapore retains a comparative advantage. Economic ties will be somewhat constrained, however, by Singapore's caution about the risks of investment in China and concern over excessive dependence on the Chinese market.

Singapore's enduring anxieties about China's future course will similarly constrain radical departures in the political relationship. Bilateral exchanges, including military-to-military exchanges, will continue to grow modestly as Singapore seeks to foster improved communication and understanding. But the thrust of these activities will be toward shaping Chinese intentions and folding China into a network of relationships that minimizes prospects for aggressive Chinese actions—rather than toward realigning Singaporean policy or adopting a new accommodationist stance vis-à-vis Beijing. Singapore will remain wary of China's attempts to expand its influence in the region and will strive to counter potential Chinese efforts to dominate, however gradually and subtly, key regional organizations.

At least two implications may be drawn from the analysis in this chapter. First, Singapore will remain an important U.S. security partner—both in the global war on terrorism and on key issues affecting Asian security affairs. Singapore's fundamental interest in regional stability, which is essential to both its economic and its military interests, ensures a continued focus on maintaining an equitable balance of power in the region. For the foreseeable future, the United States will remain the only country able to help maintain this power balance. Moreover, countering potential Chinese domination of the region and/or heavy-handed efforts to expand China's influence is only one among many interests Singapore shares with the United States. Singapore's growing ability to cooperate operationally with the United States in regional contingencies increases not only its importance to U.S. regional policy but also its attractiveness as a security partner.

Second, the actions of both China and the United States will affect the nature and degree of Singaporean-U.S. security cooperation. For China, much hinges on a continuation of its current emphasis on internal development and external stability. Singapore has no interest in heightened tensions with China but a strong interest in China's emergence as a peaceful actor in international and regional affairs. With no claims of its own to territories in the South China Sea or formal defense treaties with its ASEAN partners, Singapore will try to avoid involvement in any military conflict with China in this area. It is even more likely to avoid entering an armed conflict with China over Taiwan in the absence of unprovoked Chinese aggression. A Chinese shift toward expansive, coercive, and unilateral measures, on the other hand, would jack up Singaporean threat perceptions—including those related to Singapore's economic and defense equities in Taiwan—and broaden consideration of cooperative measures with the United States.

The key for Singapore with regard to the United States role is the latter's continued and high-quality engagement in Southeast Asia. Expectations of an active U.S. regional diplomacy and forward-deployed military presence underpin virtually all Singaporean foreign and security policies, including those relating to China. Absent such U.S. involvement (or even a perception of it), Singapore's policies could look significantly different. Singapore could seek alternative means of balancing Chinese power, for example, or could move closer to the positions of other ASEAN states that are warier of a U.S. military presence in the region.

Asian perceptions that the United States is not paying enough attention to Asia are worrisome in this context. Singaporeans, more than most Asians, understand the global challenges the United States faces and Washington's inability to focus exclusively on any single region. But they need to be confident that maintaining stability in Asia is a key part of America's strategic agenda—and that the United States has the staying power to achieve this objective. The U.S. ability to expand security cooperation with Singapore will hinge on its ability to sustain such confidence. Unfortunately, the United States keeps missing opportunities to send such important signals. In 2007, Secretary of State Condoleezza Rice missed her second ASEAN Regional Forum meeting, and President Bush canceled the first full United States–ASEAN summit arranged by Singapore to be held in Singapore after the 2007 Asia-Pacific Economic Cooperation summit in Australia.

CHAPTER EIGHT

Australia

Australia's strategic interests have become increasingly defined by the major security challenges the international community is confronting: Islamic extremism, failed states, Asian regionalism, nascent democratization, and the rise of China. Australia, beginning in the early 1990s, has gradually emerged as an active and influential player in managing these challenges and has done so to secure its own immediate periphery, bolster its alliance with the United States,[1] and ensure continued stability and prosperity in Asia. Canberra has pursued these three goals through extensive cooperation with the United States, occasional and growing military deployments abroad, and robust diplomacy in Asia. The scale and pace of Australia's alliance activities and its regional involvements have grown over the past decade—trends that are likely to continue. This has facilitated Australia's growing influence in the Asia-Pacific *and globally*.[2] This evolution in Australia's regional and global roles entered an important new phase with the November 2007 election of Prime Minister Kevin Rudd.

One of the most immediate and consequential challenges Australia faces is how it will manage the rise of China. It has become trite and obvious to point out that Australia's relationship with China is changing and to great consequence for its core economic and security interests. Canberra rightly sees China as assuming greater strategic weight in East Asia—at the very time that Australia's security and prosperity ties to the region are increasing. For its part, China is seeking more influence over Australian policymaking.

Furthermore, the Australia-China nexus raises questions in U.S. minds about the consequences for the Australian-U.S. alliance and the scope of Australia's commitments. Differences (or perceptions of them) over how to manage China's growing regional and global profile could strain the alliance and complicate the evolution of

---

[1] Unless otherwise indicated, the U.S.–Australian alliance is the one meant in all later references to "the alliance" in this chapter.

[2] Hugh White, "Australian Strategic Policy," in Ashley J. Tellis and Michael Wills, *Strategic Asia: 2005–06: Military Modernization in an Era of Uncertainty*, Seattle, Wash.: National Bureau of Asian Research, 2005; Peter Chalk, *Australian Foreign and Defense Policy in the Wake of the 1999/2000 East Timor Intervention*, Santa Monica, Calif.: RAND Corporation, MR-1409-SRF, 2001.

the regional security architecture. At the same time, if the views of Washington and Beijing converge further and policy coordination improves, it may be possible to shape the emerging East Asian order to the best interests of the United States and its regional allies and partners.

To sharpen an appreciation for these challenges for Australia and their implications, this chapter identifies the manner, mechanisms, and degree to which Australia has been responding to the rise of China. It elucidates the scope of growing interactions between Australia and China and assesses their influence on Australia's foreign and security policymaking. We begin with a description of the national political and economic context in Australia that is shaping its responses to China. We then assess Australian responses in the areas of politics and public opinion, economic affairs, foreign and security policy, and defense policy. The conclusion assesses the main forces driving Australia's responses to China and suggests possible future reactions to China's growing power and influence.

Much of the research and writing for this chapter took place before Prime Minister Rudd was elected in November 2007. Given that this chapter examines long-term trends in Australian views and policymaking on China, many of the arguments are based on the empirical record of former Prime Minister John Howard's policymaking, dating back to 1996. The material also covers Rudd's recent statements and policy actions regarding China policy and the alliance. We do not, however, see a dramatic change in China policy between the past and current leadership in Canberra. While Rudd's foreign policy is admittedly evolving (and with some important differences already emerging, related to such issues as climate change, Iraq, and nonproliferation), greater continuity than change appears to be the order of the day on Australian policy toward China.

National Conditions

Several broad political, economic, and foreign policy trends provide the context for Australia's responses to the rise of China. Most important is that Australia has been undergoing a major leadership transition, its biggest in over a decade. In the November 2007 parliamentary election, the Australian Labour Party (ALP), led by Kevin Rudd, summarily defeated the Liberal-National coalition government, led by Prime Minister Howard. Howard had been in power for 11 years, having won six successive elections. His reign was historic: He had served as prime minister longer than all but one of Australia's former prime ministers (Robert Gordon Menzies, who served for 18 years but not consecutively).[3] Despite Howard's impressive record, the ALP's victory was a land-

---

[3]   The last 11 years of the conservative coalition's tenure (1996–2007) afforded Howard the time and political space to develop and implement a variety of unique foreign and defense policies; prior to becoming prime minister, his experience with these issues had been modest. Since 1996, Howard had forged and solidified many

slide, winning 89 of 150 parliamentary seats; this provided Kevin Rudd with a strong initial governing mandate.

Following the 2007 election, Australia's domestic political scene has become far more fluid and dynamic than earlier in the decade. The Labour leadership confronts myriad new challenges, both those unique to being a new ruling party and those specific to managing the leadership of the ALP. Prime Minister Rudd is in the process of consolidating his election mandate by following through on campaign promises, mainly related to domestic reforms, and the ALP is coming to grips with its new responsibility after serving as the opposition for more than a decade. A defining aspect of the political scene in Australia will be Rudd's and the broader ALP's immediate efforts to ensure their credibility in the eyes of the Australian public. Doing so will require following through on some major domestic initiatives, such as ensuring continued economic growth even under the ALP's industrial relations policy. Some of Rudd's most proximate political challenges include managing a senate that now lacks an ALP majority and managing an assertive union movement, which has traditionally been the ALP's core. As a social and economic conservative within the ALP, Rudd faces a major challenge in dealing with ALP's left wing, which seeks to undermine the social and cultural legacy of the Howard administration. This situation could worsen left-right tension in the ALP, frustrating Rudd's ability to pursue both his domestic and foreign policy agendas.

The election brought with it new policies on foreign and defense issues and, more generally, changes in the domestic context in which these issues are debated. The latter factor could place unforeseen constraints on Rudd's foreign and defense policymaking. A key difference for Rudd (in contrast to Howard in 1996) is that he has extensive foreign policy expertise and experience, especially on China, having served as a diplomat for many years. This brings knowledge and experience that will help facilitate this transition. In addition, making these postelection challenges for Rudd somewhat less difficult is the fact that, at least in the months just following the election, the Liberal Party was arguably in shambles and lacking strong leadership.[4] ALP's broad election win thus provided some political space in the near term for the party to solidify its mandate and establish itself as a capable steward of Australia's domestic, foreign, and defense policy needs.

Beyond politics, Australia is in the longest period of economic growth in its history. As of early 2008, Australia is in its 18th year of uninterrupted economic expan-

---

personal relationships with key foreign leaders, in Asia as well as with Australia's allies. Howard leveraged these ties to pursue foreign policy strategies that have simultaneously enhanced Australia's engagement with Asia and expanded the Australian-U.S. alliance. Also, his domestic economic successes afforded him the political space to pursue a conservative foreign policy agenda.

[4]   In fact, former Prime Minister Howard even lost his parliament seat in the election—something that last happened to an outgoing Australian prime minister in the 1920s. Interestingly, Howard's loss was reportedly abetted by Rudd's courting of the growing Chinese immigrant population in Howard's district of Benelong.

sion, although, recently, rising inflation and interest rates have begun to threaten that record. A prominent Australian analyst called this past record of expansion a quiet boom:

> In the last fifteen years [1991–2006] wealth has more than doubled, output has increased by nearly two thirds, the capital stock by more than half, labour productivity by a little under half, and the number of jobs by a quarter. The growth of income per person has been faster in Australia over the period than in Canada, the United States, the United Kingdom or New Zealand. The Australian economy has become more closely integrated into the global economy, with exports and imports increasing as a share of GDP, and Australian businesses often now investing more in the rest of the world than foreign businesses invest in Australia. The performance of the economy since 1991 is all the more remarkable because during the previous twenty years it experienced five recessions, two of them very severe.[5]

The deepest roots of this expansion lie in the economic policy reforms of the 1980s and early 1990s: Australia floated its exchange rate, cut tariffs, broke with its trade union legacy, legislated a dynamic retirement fund, deregulated banking, privatized large state-owned assets, and shifted from national wage arbitration to wage bargaining at the company level. As a result, the Australian economy became more efficient, productive, and competitive. It also became more integrated into the global economy in the 1990s, being nicely positioned to benefit from the rise in world trade and economic integration. The fruits of these policy changes largely explain the second decade of economic expansion, the 1990s. John Edwards has stated that

> Australia's economic success has been grounded on its closer integration into a global economy which has become bigger, more diverse, and more congenial as Australia has become more completely a part of it . . . . Australia's increasing participation in the global economy . . . is now helping to sustain a robust expansion of indefinite duration.[6]

The challenge for the Australian economy is to sustain consistent growth. This will be difficult. The benefits of past policy reforms and greater integration into the world economy are diminishing. Productivity growth has declined in recent years. Australia has benefited from the global boom in commodity sales, especially to East Asian nations, but it is not clear how long these high commodity volumes and high prices will continue. Macroeconomic imbalances could also threaten growth; the current account deficit has reached an all-time high between 2006 and 2008. In 2008, inflation and interest rates are rising. To sustain growth, the Australian economy will

---

[5]   John Edwards, *Quiet Boom: How the Long Economic Upswing Is Changing Australia and Its Place in the World*, Sydney: Lowy Institute for International Policy, paper 14, 2006, pp. vii–viii.

[6]   Edwards, 2006, pp. vii–viii.

need to continue to increase exports and attract foreign investment. The importance of Australia's trade with Asia, which accounts for over 50 percent of its total trade, is growing.

On foreign and defense policy issues, Howard established an important legacy that persists today.[7] He forged an identity for Australia that affirmed its position not only as a regional power but also one with a distinctly global vision, interests, and responsibilities—trends arguably begun by Gareth Evans in the late 1980s. Veteran Australian journalist Paul Kelly summarized Howard's distinctive beliefs in a 2006 study:

> the bond with America was our special national asset, that Japan was our best friend in Asia and China was our greatest opportunity, that Australia's success originated in its British heritage, that our national values were beyond compromise and that national identity was beyond political engineering, that Indonesia was a flawed giant that should not monopolise our attention, that Europe cared little for Australia and had entered its afternoon twilight, that Israel must be defended for its values and its history, that nationalism not regionalism was the main driver of global affairs, that globalization was a golden opportunity for Australia's advancement, that Australia's prestige in the world would be determined by the quality of its economy and society and not by moral edicts from the human rights industry and, finally, that Australia's tradition of overseas military deployment reflected a timeless appreciation of its national interest.[8]

A defining element of Howard's approach was his effort to simultaneously embrace the two traditional (and often competing) pillars of Australian foreign policy: alliance relations and engagement with Asia. Howard rejected the notions that Australia had to choose between its geography and its history, between the United States and Asia, or between regional and global interests or that, in each case, either choice had to be subordinate to the other.[9] Indeed, the Howard administration maintained that these two pillars are not only mutually compatible but mutually reinforcing.[10]

Howard reenergized and expanded the alliance, particularly after September 11. Howard aligned Australia closely with the Bush administration's war against Islamic extremism. Australia contributed military forces to Operation Enduring Freedom in Afghanistan and Operation Iraqi Freedom; these were the Australian government's most controversial deployments since the Vietnam conflict. Operational military coop-

---

[7] For an insightful study on this see Paul Kelly, *Howard's Decade: An Australian Foreign Policy Reappraisal*, Sydney: Lowy Institute for International Policy, paper 15, 2006.

[8] Kelly, 2006, pp. 3–4.

[9] This is one of the main arguments in Kelly, 2006.

[10] John Howard, "Australia in the World," address to the Lowy Institute for International Studies, March 31, 2005a; Dennis Richardson, Australian Ambassador to the United States, "Australia and a Rising China," address at The Nixon Center, Washington, D.C., June 6, 2006.

eration, intelligence sharing, and arms sales between the United States and Australia have continued to expand as well.

Howard's engagement with Asia was equally extensive; Australia's regional involvements and responsibilities grew under Howard. Prominent examples include Australia's military deployments in East Timor and the South Pacific; joining the EAS; and expanding bilateral relations with China, Indonesia, Japan, and now India. In contrast to earlier governments, Howard took these actions while strongly identifying Australia as a staunch ally of the United States. At one point, the Howard administration seemed to be positioning itself to act as a bridge connecting the United States, Asia, and Europe but eventually backed away from this aspiration.[11]

Rudd's foreign and defense policies are evolving—which is probably their most defining aspect as of this writing. There are strong indications that Rudd will continue, in broad terms, key aspects of Howard's approach. Before, during, and after the election, Rudd consistently stated that the alliance is the centerpiece of Australia's foreign and defense policy and the context in which Australia will engage Asia.[12] In December 2007, Rudd's new foreign minister, Steve Smith, explained that Rudd's foreign policy would be based on three pillars: the alliance with the United States, the UN, and engagement with Asia (without listing or prioritizing which countries in Asia).[13] This suggests a substantial degree of continuity with Howard's approach: the alliance as the foundation of Australian national security policy, the simultaneous engagement of the United States and Asian powers, and an effort to keep the United States fully engaged and influential in Asia. As with Howard, unforeseen global events and domestic politics will shape and mold Rudd's and the ALP's positions on key international questions. But Rudd's own experience and substantive expertise in this arena of national policy bodes well for a sober, centrist approach to foreign and defense policymaking.

At the same time, Rudd has already begun to distinguish himself from the policies of his predecessor and the Bush administration but only in limited ways and mostly on global, as opposed to Asian, affairs. Two of Rudd's initial policy shifts by early 2008 were indicated by his attendance at the UN Climate Change Conference in Bali in December 2007, complete with ratification of the Kyoto Protocol and a pledge to support a Kyoto II accord, and his call for a limited troop withdrawal from Iraq. These events should not be overinterpreted as indicating a growing divide with Washington or a radical shift away from Howard's policies.

All America's other allies in the industrialized world have signed Kyoto, and the Kyoto effort is being driven, in part, by Japan, one of America's leading allies in Asia.

---

[11]   See Howard, 2005a; White, 2005; and Kelly, 2006.

[12]   Kevin Michael Rudd, "The Rise of China and the Strategic Implications for U.S.–Australia Relations," speech to the Brookings Institution, Washington, D.C., April 20, 2007.

[13]   Stephen Smith, Minister for Foreign Affairs, "Speech Notes for the Annual Diplomatic Corps Christmas Party," Canberra, December 3, 2007.

Rudd strongly agrees with Washington that China and India have to be involved in a successor to the Kyoto Protocol, and he has pledged to work with the United States to make that happen.

Although Rudd has called for withdrawal of *combat* troops from Iraq, he has pledged to continue (and possibly increase) Australia's noncombat support in Iraq. Rudd will also almost certainly maintain current troop contributions to Operation Iraqi Freedom command elements to ensure high-quality alliance coordination. Australian noncombat forces in Iraq could total 1,000 troops even after combat forces return to Australia in mid-2008. Rudd has strongly and publicly committed to keeping Australian combat forces in Afghanistan.[14]

Rudd's approach to foreign policy may diverge further from Howard's legacy, but not in core beliefs or policy objectives. Possible policy changes include increasing support for practical engagement with the UN, cooperation with multilateral organizations in Asia, and support for multilateral arms control. These emerging differences are likely driven by Rudd's own views, his desire to make a definitive mark on Australian foreign policy, and the ALP's traditional foreign policy inclinations (toward multilateralism, for example). Rudd's evolving ability to manage the internal debates about party identity that may result from his foreign policy positions could affect Australian policymaking, such as ALP calls for a greater commitment to multilateral forums in Asia. Under the Labour government, foreign policy debates will likely play out differently from past years under Howard; the media, trade unions, and NGOs will be more influential in shaping the domestic context for deliberations of diplomacy and national security questions. This altered context could conceivably constrain Rudd's centrist approach to foreign policy.[15]

Domestic Politics and Public Opinion

Domestic Politics
The most striking aspect of assessing the role of China in Australia's domestic politics is that it is not a partisan issue. Australia's China policy did not arise in the 2007 election, except as an area of Rudd's expertise that redounded to his benefit. Indeed, foreign policy and national defense issues, more generally, were not major topics of debate in the 2007 election, aside from discussions of the need for action on global climate change and reducing Australia's involvement in Iraq. China policy had also not been an issue in the 2004 election. Since 1997, the Labour Party had seldom criti-

[14]   Robert Ayson, "Kevin Rudd and Asia's Security," *PacNet*, No. 49, November 28, 2007; and Ralph A. Cossa, "U.S.–Australia: Still Mates!," *PacNet*, No. 49A, December 17, 2007.

[15]   On the latter point, see Michael Fullilove, "Don't Be Fooled—There'll Be More Change Than Continuity in Foreign Policy," *Sydney Morning Herald*, December 20, 2007.

cized Howard's approach to China, which—in practice, if not in theory—mirrored the China policy of such former ALP luminaries as Paul Keating. There is a strong, consistent bipartisan consensus, spanning all the major Australian political parties, about the value of economic and political engagement with China. Conservative and liberal policymakers in Australia share many of the same views about China, about both the opportunities it presents and the challenges it poses to Australia's economic and security interests.

Very few Australian policymakers or commentators promote a China-threat school of thought, especially in comparison to debate in the United States. To the extent that such views exist, they do not have much political resonance and thus do not influence public discussion of China. Australian policymakers do have concerns about China's growing economic and military power, but these concerns do not enter into partisan debates. For example, concerns about Chinese exports to Australia did not prevent Howard from initiating FTA negotiations with China in 2005, a decision that engendered minimal criticism. Few political leaders and few members of the Australian public make a major issue out of China's political system; for them, the fact that mainland China is under communist rule does not invalidate Australia's interests in maintaining a positive relationship with the country.

That said, under a Labour government, China's poor human rights record could figure more prominently in media and public discussion of China policy. Still, political debates were far more rancorous over and disagreements were much sharper about Howard's efforts to strengthen the alliance and Australia's military deployments to Iraq and Afghanistan.

Public Opinion

The Australian public's views of China have evolved substantially since the end of World War II. Throughout most of the Cold War, especially the 1950s and 1960s, Australian leaders and the public viewed China with outright fear and hostility. These sentiments were motivated by a concern that China sought to dominate Asia and that the Chinese could actually make their way down to Australia. These extreme fears of Chinese aspirations and capabilities have now largely vanished from public discourse about China, broadly as a consequence of reforms in Australia immigration policy in recent decades. As of 2007, the Australian public now views China and Australia-China relations in a positive light, punctuated by much optimism about the future. The level of Australian amity for China has been similar to the level for the United States. The Australian public has expressed some skepticism about China as a trusted international partner and some modest concern about China as a security threat. However, the public has not expressed a marked preference for relations with Japan and India over China.

A 2006 Lowy Institute poll of Australian views on international relations provides the most recent basis for assessing popular views of China. The Lowy study began by observing that "the great majority of Australians appear to be outward looking and interested in Australia's international relationships" and that 82 percent felt "it would be best for the future of Australia if we take an active part in world affairs rather than 'stay out of world affairs.'"[16]

The Australian public expressed consistently positive views about China and Australian-Chinese relations. On a 100-point scale of "feelings toward other countries" (with 100 as a "very warm, favorable feeling"), Australians ranked China at 61, Indonesia at 50, India and the United States at 62, Japan at 64, Singapore at 65, and Great Britain at 74. On the direction of Australia's bilateral relationships, 59 percent of Australians felt that relations with China were improving, and 51 percent felt the same about those with the United States. In contrast, majorities felt that ties with the European Union, Japan, and India were "staying about the same."

Australians also ranked China as the most influential country in Asia, putting it ahead of (in order) the United States, Japan, India, Australia, and Indonesia. This ranking did not, however, indicate confidence that these countries would act responsibly. Sixty percent of Australians surveyed said they trusted China "a great deal" or "somewhat," which was the same amount of trust they felt toward the United States. Yet, when asked whether they trusted a country "a great deal," more Australians said they did so of the United States (19 percent) than of China (7 percent). Interestingly, the amounts of distrust for China and for the United States were about equal, at 37 percent and 39 percent, respectively. Japan was the country most widely trusted to act responsibly, with an aggregate trust level of 73 percent. On a 10-point scale, Australians wanted the European Union and the United States to be most influential in global affairs, with rankings of 6.6 and 6.1, followed by Japan (5.7), China (5.5), and India (5.2).[17]

China did not rank as a major and immediate security threat in the Lowy poll, but there was some concern. The poll offered a list of 13 "possible threats to the vital interest of Australia in the next ten years," from which 33 percent of the respondents chose a U.S.–China conflict over Taiwan, ranking it ninth among perceived threats. Twenty-five percent of respondents chose "the development of China as a world power," ranking it as 13th and last in the list of threats to Australia's vital interests.[18]

Economic Responses

The trends in Australia-China economic relations are clear and robust. Growth in bilateral trade has been strong, averaging approximately 20 percent per year since 1996,

---

[16]   Ivan Cook, *Australia, Indonesia and the World: Public Opinion and Foreign Policy*, Sydney: Lowy Institute for International Policy, 2006, p. 6.

[17]   Cook, 2006, pp. 8–10.

[18]   Cook, 2006, pp. 11–12.

compared worldwide. In 2007, for the first time, China became Australia' largest two-way trading partner (Japan is now the second largest but remains Australia's biggest export destination). Trade relations with China are highly complementary, and this pattern is unlikely to change. Australia and China are currently negotiating an FTA that may expand their already extensive trade relationship, although negotiations have been slow and may eventually slip from the bilateral agenda. Australian business and political leaders largely see trade with China as key to Australia's future prosperity.

However, these trends need to be kept in context. China's actual contribution to overall Australian growth in GDP, trade, and aggregate output has been limited. About 70 percent of the Australian economy consists of services, not merchandise. The service sector employs four out of five Australian workers.[19] According to one Australian study, "by 2005, [merchandise] exports to China accounted for just 2 percent of Australian GDP."[20] Further, despite the rapid growth in commodity exports to China, the markets for Australia's exports of raw materials are more diversified today than they were 20 years ago, lessening its aggregate dependency on any single foreign market. Until quite recently, increases in Australia's merchandise exports overall kept pace with its increases in commodity exports.

These facts, especially the structure of the Australian economy, suggest that Australia's very impressive growth in GDP over the last two decades has not been driven by trade with China. Rather, Australian productivity and incomes have increased because, beginning in the 1980s, it adopted numerous policy reforms that integrated it with the global economy.

Trade

Australia's bilateral trade ties with China are strong and growing stronger. From 1996 to 2006, total merchandise trade between the two countries grew at an annual average rate of about 20 percent, with growth accelerating particularly rapidly from 2000 to 2006. From 2000 to 2006, exports to China more than tripled. In 2004, China surpassed the United States to become Australia's second-largest export market after Japan (Figure 8.1); in 2006, China surpassed the United States to become Australia's largest source of imports (Figure 8.2). In 2007, China became Australia's largest overall trade partner (imports and exports of goods and services), with total two-way trade reaching US$47.5 billion.[21]

---

[19] Mark Vaile, Member of Parliament, Minister for Trade, "Unlocking China's Services Sector," speech delivered at the launch of the Economic Analytical Unit report, Sydney, February 9, 2006. For the report, see DFAT, Economic Analysis Unit, *Unlocking China's Services Sector*, Canberra: Commonwealth of Australia, 2005.

[20] Edwards, 2006, pp. 60–61.

[21] Simon Crean, Australian Minister for Trade, "Trade Figures Confirm China and Japan as Top Trade Partners," Department of Foreign Affairs and Trade Web Site, May 6, 2008.

Figure 8.1
Australian Exports, by Country of Destination, Selected Years

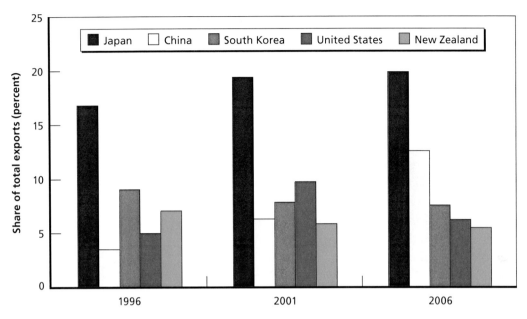

SOURCE: Authors' calculations UN Statistics Division, 1996, 2001, 2006.
RAND *MG736-8.1*

Figure 8.2
Australian Imports, by Country of Origin, Selected Years

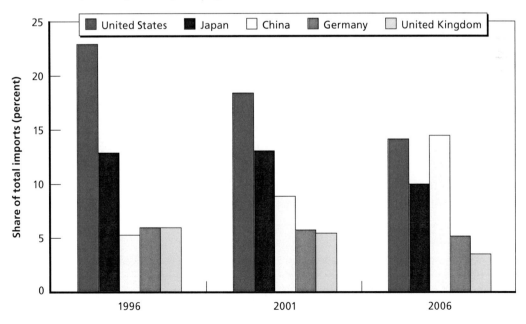

SOURCE: Authors' calculations based on UN Statistics Division, 1996, 2001, 2006.
RAND *MG736-8.2*

In 2006, Australia exported US$15.4 billion worth of goods to China (12.5 percent of total exports), while its imports from China were US$19.2 billion (14.5 percent of imports). Australia was China's 15-largest export destination, accounting for 1.7 percent of total Chinese exports, and its eighth-largest import source, accounting for 2.0 percent of total Chinese imports. Australia's top export to China, iron ore, accounted for almost 40 percent of Chinese iron ore imports and more than 50 percent of all Australian iron ore exports. The trade in iron ore shows no sign of slowing: Between 2004 and 2006, the dollar value of Australian exports of iron ore to China grew by over 225 percent.

Australian exports to China are slated to grow in the energy sector. In September 2007, Australian firm Woodside Petroleum signed a landmark 30-year deal with PetroChina to sell up to 3 million tons of liquefied natural gas (LNG) annually to PetroChina. Woodside estimates that the contract will be worth up to US$37 billion, making it Australia's largest ever export contract. Also in September 2007, Royal Dutch Shell signed a large, 20-year deal with PetroChina for LNG from a field in Western Australia to China.[22]

Despite the increase in aggregate trade between China and Australia, Japan remained Australia's top export destination in 2007 and will likely keep that position for the foreseeable future. In 2006, Australia exported half again as much to Japan as it did to China. Also, Australia's total trade with China in 2007 was only about US$3 billion less than its total trade with Japan, at US$44.6 billion.

In assessing the future of China-Australia trade (especially relative to Japan-Australia trade), three considerations are worth bearing in mind. First, the growth in the value of Australia's exports to China is being driven by growth in the *price* not just in the *quantity* of key exports, such as iron ore. Commodity prices are determined on world markets and are notoriously volatile. Even if Chinese demand remains strong, there is no guarantee that *the value of* Australian commodity exports to China will continue to expand at the current rapid rate, which may mean a net decline in export value. Second, the calculation assumes that growth in the Chinese economy, and hence Chinese demand for Australian exports, will not decline. Third, until 2005, Japan suffered a prolonged recession beginning in the early 1990s. Japan's economy has strengthened considerably since then: The average annual rate of growth of Japan's trade with Australia for 2000–2006 was more than three times that for 1996–2006.

Trade in merchandise is not the only area in which Australia's economic relations with China are expanding. Trade in services is also growing, albeit from a smaller base. According to the Australian Department of Foreign Affairs and Trade (DFAT), China was Australia's third-largest export market for services in 2006, up from 13th in

[22]   Virginia Marsh and Richard McGregor, "Woodside Seals China LNG Deal," *Financial Times* (London), September 6, 2007.

1995.[23] According to 2008 DFAT data, "services exports [to China] in 2007 grew 18 per cent to US$3.9 billion on the back of strong growth in Chinese student enrolments [sic]."[24] Rising consumer incomes and service-sector reforms in China helped spur a 10-percent increase in Australian exports of services to China between 2005 and 2006 (to A$3.6 billion), led by education and tourism (which account for 80 percent of service exports).[25] At just under 24 percent of the total, China is the largest source of international student enrollments in Australian universities (this rises to almost 30 percent if Hong Kong is included), and Chinese visitors now make up over 5 percent of the 5.5 million people who visit Australia annually. However, Australian access to China's tightly controlled service sector is a major point of contention in ongoing negotiations over an FTA between the two countries.[26]

The Composition of Trade

Trade between Australia and China is highly complementary, reflecting China's comparative advantage in labor-intensive manufacturing and Australia's comparative advantage in natural resources and agriculture. Figure 8.3 illustrates the distribution of Australia's top four exports to China in 2006:

1. ferrous metal ores and scrap, predominantly iron ore
2. textile fibers, predominantly wool
3. coal, oil, and gas products, predominantly crude petroleum
4. nonferrous metals, predominantly copper ore and scrap.

Australia began exporting LNG to China in 2006 and uranium in 2007. These commodities are becoming important exports to other countries as well, thereby further entrenching the pattern of complementarity in bilateral trade relations.

Figure 8.4 illustrates the distribution of Australia's top five imports from China in 2006:

1. clothing, textiles, and footwear, predominantly clothing
2. office machines, predominantly computers
3. telecommunications equipment, predominantly audio and video recorders
4. miscellaneous manufactured goods, predominantly toys
5. electrical and electronic equipment, predominantly household appliances.

---

[23] DFAT, 2005.

[24] Crean, 2008.

[25] DFAT, 2007b.

[26] Emma-Kate Symons, "Howard Raises Stake on Trade Pact with China," *The Australian*, January 15, 2007.

Figure 8.3
Composition of Australian Exports to China, 2006

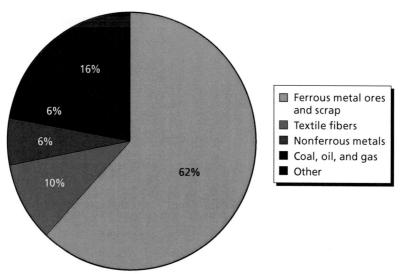

SOURCE: Authors' calculations based on UN Statistics Division, 2006.
RAND MG736-8.3

Figure 8.4
Composition of Australian Imports from China, 2006

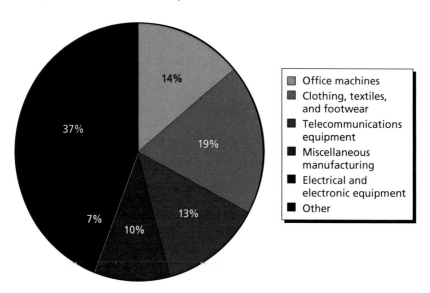

SOURCE: Authors' calculations based on UN Statistics Division, 2006.
RAND MG736-8.4

Although Chinese data show Australia running a surplus in the merchandise trade in every year since 1996, Australian figures show a relatively small but growing bilateral trade deficit. One reason for the discrepancy is that Australian and Chinese statistical authorities treat goods transshipped through Hong Kong differently: China includes Hong Kong in its counting, but Australia does not.[27] Australia's deficit appears to be driven primarily by Australian demand for cheap Chinese clothes and computers, although it is Chinese inroads into such industries as plastics and chemicals that have spurred Australia to take some protectionist actions.[28] Between 1995 and 2005, China was the number one focus of Australian antidumping investigations, but only a relatively narrow range of industries was involved, mostly chemicals, petroleum, and associated products.[29]

Australia's trade deficits with China have *not* been a major concern in bilateral economic relations or in the domestic debate about China policy—in stark contrast with the debates in the United States. For the most part, Australian leaders and the public see China as a source of current and future prosperity. To be sure, some Australian manufacturers are concerned about growing competition from Chinese imports, but so far, such concerns have not heavily shaped government policy. One such example was the Howard government's 2005 decision to launch FTA negotiations with China.

Gaining access to China's heavily protected service sector appears to be a greater priority for the Australian government than the merchandise trade balance. To address this issue and to further expand merchandise trade ties, Canberra and Beijing first discussed the possibility of concluding an FTA in October 2003.[30] As a precondition, China demanded that Australia formally grant it market economy status, which, under World Trade Organization rules, would help protect it from antidumping actions.[31] In April 2005, Canberra agreed, and the two countries initiated formal negotiations for an FTA. As of early 2008, these negotiations continue, with Rudd trying to inject greater momentum into the talks.[32]

---

[27] Other sources of the discrepancy are explained by differences in methods of accounting for costs of insurance and freight that create discrepancies in the bilateral trade statistics of all countries.

[28] "Cheap Chinese Goods Take Toll on Deficit," Australian Associated Press, January 11, 2005.

[29] Michael Priestly, "Anti-Dumping Rules and the Australia-China Free Trade Agreement," Canberra: Parliament of Australia, Department of Parliamentary Services, Research Note 38, March 14, 2005.

[30] Australia currently has FTAs with New Zealand, Singapore, Thailand, and the United States. Negotiations on an FTA with Japan commenced in December 2006.

[31] The U.S. government was opposed to Australia's decision to grant China market economy status. Antidumping actions are a primary tool of U.S. trade policy, and the United States did not wish Australia to push China farther along the path to this level of recognition around the world. However, it is probably already too late: According to *People's Daily*, as of February 2006, 51 countries had given China market economy status. So far, the world's "big three" trading entities—the European Union, Japan, and the United States itself—are still refusing China market economy status.

[32] Priestly, 2005.

Now that negotiations have begun, the key issues to be resolved on the Chinese side include better protection of intellectual property rights, Chinese observation of Australian product standards and testing regimes, and better access to Chinese service and agricultural product markets.[33] China would like Australia to lower its tariffs on imported clothing, textiles, and automobile components, and to liberalize rules governing Chinese investment in Australian businesses, such as automotive manufacturing.

Foreign Direct Investment

Investment ties between the two countries are much weaker than trade ties; growth in FDI over the past decade has been uneven.[34] Nevertheless, by 2005, China was Australia's 20th-largest investment destination; China, in turn, was the 17th-largest investor in Australia. The total stock of Australian investment in China (portfolio plus direct investment) reached A$2,043 million (US$1,560 million) in 2005, representing 0.3 percent of Australia's total stock of investment abroad.[35] The total stock of Chinese investment in Australia was A$2,275 million (US$1,737 million) in 2005, representing 0.2 percent of the total stock of foreign investment in Australia.[36]

According to DFAT, China's investment in Australia is largely concentrated in the extractive industries, minerals processing, real estate, and agriculture. China's largest and most high-profile investments are in China National Offshore Oil Corporation's recent purchase of a 5-percent stake in North West Shelf LNG production (worth A$460 million, or US$351 million); Sinosteel and Midwest Corporation's A$1.5 billion (US$1.15 billion) iron ore investment deal in Western Australia; Yanzhou Coal Mining's A$23 million (US$17.6 million) investment in a Hunter Valley coal mine; and Shougang's 50-percent interest (worth A$120 million, or US$92 million) in the Mt. Gibson iron mine.[37] In mid-2007, Anshan Iron and Steel and Australia's Gindalbie Metals signed a joint venture agreement to invest A$1.8 billion (US$1.38 billion) in an iron ore project in Western Australia. All these investments are in the extractive industries. In early 2008, China Aluminum Corporation, a state-owned entity, teamed up with the American company Alcoa to acquire a 12-percent stake in Australia's Rio-

---

[33] "Real Deal Is in the Fine Print," *The Age*, October 19, 2005.

[34] For data-collection purposes, FDI has been defined as involving an equity stake of 10 percent or more in a foreign enterprise. See for example, IMF and OECD, *Foreign Direct Investment Statistics: How Countries Measure FDI 2001*, Washington, D.C., 2003.

[35] DFAT, 2007b. These were the most recent calculations available; our currency conversion used the 2005 average of 1.30947 Australian dollars per U.S. dollar.

[36] Australian Government, Department of Innovation, Industry, Science, and Research, "China Investment Fact Sheet," Country Snapshots, Canberra, undated, but data last accessed in January 2008. For the sake of confidentiality, the Australian government has reported only total investment numbers for China, not direct investment numbers, since 2005.

[37] DFAT, 2007b; Department of Innovation, Industry, Science, and Research, undated.

Tinto, a major mineral exporter. The success of this effort was unknown as of this writing.

Australian direct investment in China has remained relatively flat in recent years. A DFAT survey conducted in 2000 suggested that two-thirds of the Australian companies in China were involved in manufacturing or property and business services, while the rest were located in a wide range of sectors including finance, insurance, education, mineral exploration, information services, and energy supply.[38]

Winners and Losers

Winners. Australia has the most complementary pattern of trade with China of the six countries we examined. Its exports are heavily concentrated in primary products, such as ores, wool, and energy, and the large increases in these exports since 1995 are raising demand from China (Figure 8.5). Other exports include such products as technologically sophisticated machinery, which China still does not manufacture itself.

Australia's extractive (ores and oil) industries are expanding capacity on the assumption that China will continue to import more primary products as its economy grows. Despite press accounts, however, expectations for the long-run growth in

Figure 8.5
Trends in Australian Winning World Exports, 1996–2006

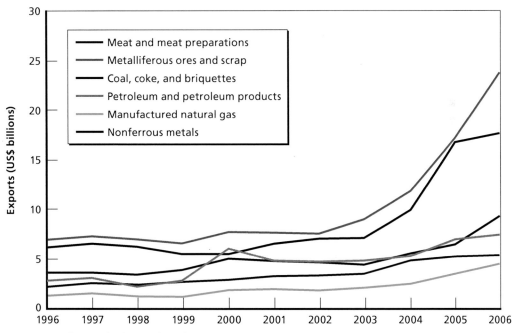

SOURCE: Authors' calculations based on UN Statistics Division, 2006.
RAND MG736-8.5

---

[38] DFAT, 2007b; Department of Innovation, Industry, Science, and Research, undated.

Chinese demand for these commodities are tempered. One economist expects growth in Chinese demand for primary products to run roughly the same as that for industrial output, which he projects will run less than 10 percent per year. Although Chinese demand is rising, Japan continues to import almost twice as much as China from Australia. Australia's extractive companies see China as an important, expanding market but actually have a more-diversified set of markets than in the past, when Japan and South Korea accounted for a disproportionate share of foreign purchases of ores, energy, and wool.

The large Australian companies in the extractive industries have a strong interest in China's markets. BHP Billington, headquartered in Australia, is an important exporter. Rio Tinto, although headquartered in the United Kingdom, has major subsidiaries in Western Australia that export much of their output to China. These companies have predicated their investments in expanded capacity on increased exports to China. If denied access to Chinese markets, these exporters would be hard pressed to find alternative markets quickly.[39]

These companies are politically influential. They are important sources of tax revenues, and their large revenues give them substantial political clout. Although not major employers in Australia as a whole, they are key employers in mining localities, mainly around Perth in Western Australia. There is a perception among the Australian general public that the financial success of these mining firms has been driven by exports to China and that their profitability, in turn, has been a major contributor to Australia's overall economic health, as well as the government's ability to cut taxes. The robust business of these firms has also driven Australia's capital markets in recent years. On the other hand, because these firms are large, wealthy, and often foreign-owned, they have to tread carefully when pushing political positions.

Agricultural interests do not need to be as reticent. Farmers with large wool operations, in particular, have strong interests in good relations with China. Historically, farmers have been an important political constituency: They formed the core of the National Party in Howard's former ruling coalition. (The former leader of the National Party was also Howard's minister for trade.) Farmers are popular with most of the rest of the electorate, something that cannot usually be said about the large mining companies, and their views on Chinese export markets are and will remain politically important.

Although a number of larger Australian companies have tested the waters, their investments in China are much smaller than those of Japanese and South Korean firms. These companies have not invested in integrated assembly operations that connect plants throughout Asia with operations in China. Most of the investment tends to be in Chinese real estate or in expanding operations of Australian service companies

---

[39] But then, China also relies heavily on minerals imported from Australia, and finding replacement suppliers quickly would also be difficult.

into the Chinese market, such as investments Australian banks have made in China's financial services sector. These investments are growing, and investors have a significant interest in improving the investment environment in China. However, Australian companies have not yet located significant parts of their operations in China, unlike Japanese and Korean electronics manufacturers, which now do most of their final assembly in China. This difference contributes to the fact that the business communities of Japan and South Korea feel a greater sense of dependency than does that of Australia.

Losers. Losers from trade with China tend to be concentrated in just a few sectors: textiles and clothing manufacturers, auto parts and tire manufacturers, and producers of some fruits and vegetables. Chinese exports of these goods to Australia have eaten away at the domestic market shares of Australian producers. Aside from automotive components, these industries are generally not politically important; textile production is no longer a major industry in Australia. Not surprisingly, domestic opposition to expanding trade with China has been relatively muted and has not emerged as a potent political force.

As the composition of Chinese exports shifts, more-powerful industries may feel challenged and could mobilize politically. There is some concern about competition from imports of Chinese-brand vehicles; Australia's vehicle assemblers have strong political backers in parliament and the executive from the states in which the plants are located. Although China is not yet a major exporter of cars, several domestic Chinese manufacturers (such as Cheri) are planning on exporting. To date, most major foreign vehicle manufacturers who have invested in China are focused on the Chinese market, but this is gradually changing.

Despite articles in the Australian media and growth in public perceptions of China as the engine of economic growth, the economic importance of China to Australia in the last two decades of impressive growth should not be exaggerated. Although policymakers and the public widely perceive growing trade with China as a major driver of prosperity, China is just one of several large export markets for Australian goods, with bilateral trade heavily tilted toward mineral exports during this period of unusually high global commodity prices. Japan remains Australia's dominant foreign trade market. Australia has enjoyed close to 20 years of growth, most of which has been driven by major policy reforms in its domestic economy. Thus, from the perspective of the last two decades, trade with China has been the icing on Australia's growing economic cake.

Australia's economy is gravitating more toward Asia, which will further increase the economic importance of trade with China over time. Eventually, Australia's bilateral trade with China may surpass that with Japan. China will not, however, be the main determinant of Australian growth and its macroeconomic health. About 70 percent of Australia's GDP comes from the service sector, in which bilateral trade remains limited. Australia's growth will continue to depend on productivity improvements.

Domestic economic policies will continue to be a major determinant of productivity improvements and hence the pace of growth. Australian export markets are more diversified than ever before. If commodity prices fall, the revenue from trade with China would fall as well, perhaps dramatically. Thus, economic relations with China will continue to expand, but China will not determine the overall health of Australia's national economy. To be sure, policymakers and business leaders continue to see China as increasingly central to the health of Australia's economy, a perception that will shape bilateral trade relations and broader China policy.

Diplomatic and Foreign Policy Responses

Over the last decade, Australia has pursued a complex and nuanced approach toward China, so its foreign policy responses to China have been mixed. Canberra has actively and successfully expanded all levels of bilateral interactions with China. Australian policymakers publicly praise China's economic successes and have sought to enhance economic and diplomatic cooperation, with much success. Canberra has also downplayed—*publicly*—the differences in political values and its concerns about Chinese diplomatic behavior and military activities. Australia's China policy—especially its public statements—reflects a growing sensitivity to Chinese views and interests. At the same time, Canberra has been willing to confront Beijing to a limited degree and to communicate the limits to bilateral rapprochement. Canberra's real and enduring concerns about China's growing power and influence in East Asia have been reflected in its broader Asia policy and alliance activities. Australia has sought to ensure that the United States remains engaged and influential in Asia and has expanded its own cooperation with Japan and India—with China in mind. The country has sought to foster a regional security order in East Asia in which China will be unable to dominate and in which the United States and its allies retain substantial, and arguably predominant, influence.

There are many indications this approach to China will continue under Prime Minister Rudd. His policy statements about China before, during, and after the election have largely been consistent with these approaches and goals. Rudd has gone out of his way to emphasize the importance of the alliance to Australia's approach to East Asia. To the extent that Rudd pursues policy shifts relevant to China, they may be related to Australia's broader Asia policy, such as the degree of Australia's embrace of Japan and India as possible counterweights to China and the degree of Australia's engagement with multilateral organizations in East Asia. Rudd may be lukewarm about *some* U.S.–led initiatives in Asia that Howard had embraced (such as developing a limited alliance with Japan)—and he has opposed some initiatives that the United States and others pushed for and Howard supported, such as developing an alliance of democracies among India, Japan, Australia, and the United States in Asia.

Perceptions of China in Regional Security Affairs

Australia's foreign policymakers and analysts share several widely held beliefs about the challenges of a rising China, the nation's ability to influence Asia-Pacific affairs, and the type of regional order in Asia that advances national security interests.[40] These views are shaping Australia's foreign policy responses to China's rise.

Australian policymakers and analysts see China as a nation of growing global influence and key to the future stability and prosperity of Asia. Australian policymakers note that China has become the hub of a regional production chain of trade and investment connections among Asian countries. The country has become a core driver of regional growth. China's Asian diplomacy is expanding its regional influence and has benefited from a period of relative U.S. inattention to the region in the early 2000s. China's military is engaged in a comprehensive modernization effort that could disrupt regional military balances.

Australia's stake in Asian stability and prosperity is growing at the very time that China's ability to affect both is increasing. Australian policymakers also point out that China is not alone in its influence in Asia: Japan continues to have the region's largest economy, and India's influence is expanding. China's status as an increasingly influential regional power is not unique—or at least, Australia does not want it to be. Rudd has gone out of his way to note that India is Asia's second rising power.[41]

These views motivate nagging concerns about China's emergence as a regional power and global actor. Official statements seldom emphasize these views, and they do not dominate the national discourse, which currently emphasizes economic opportunities over security challenges. Yet Australian policymakers and strategists do ask: How will China use its expanding power and influence, and will it be a force for regional stability and security in Asia?

Australian responses to this question reflect neither alarm nor acute anxiety. Policymakers and analysts argue that China generally acts as a status quo power, albeit one that is dissatisfied with certain aspects of the status quo (such as the status of Taiwan). China is focused on economic growth and political stability; these goals principally drive Chinese foreign policy, at least currently. Australians see few indications that China seeks fundamental changes in the regional order in Asia or globally. China has as much at stake, if not more, as other regional powers in the continued maintenance of the prevailing economic and security dynamics in Asia. Chinese leaders view regional stability as necessary for China's continued growth and political stability and, therefore, for the preservation of the CCP's power.

---

[40] This collection of views is a distillation based on interviews and documentary sources. The author interviewed over 30 officials, analysts, and scholars in Sydney and Canberra in 2006. For key government documents, see Rudd, 2007; Howard, 2005a; Richardson, 2006. A good summary of government and nongovernmental views on Chinese foreign policy can be found in Parliament of Australia, *China's Emergence: Implications for Australia*, Canberra: Senate Foreign Affairs, Defense and Trade References Committee, March 28, 2006b.

[41] Ayson, 2007.

Australian policymakers are concerned about China's growing diplomatic influence within Southeast Asia and its activities in the South Pacific, which have at times undermined Australia's regional security interests. Australian policymakers and analysts express equal, if not greater, concern about China's internal stability and the possibility of domestic breakdown. The fear of a weak, unstable, chaotic China receives as much attention from Australian analysts and policymakers as a strong China that throws its weight around in Asia.

Australian policymakers and strategists have mixed views about their nation's ability to influence these regional trends. Some argue that Australia has limited capability to shape the rise of China as an economic, diplomatic, and military power, except on the margins. Many argue that Australia has far more to lose from an unstable and acrimonious relationship with China than does the United States, so Canberra needs to tread carefully. Yet many Australian policymakers and analysts continue to believe that the regional influence Australia does possess (including in shaping Chinese behavior) is only enhanced by a robust alliance with the United States. Moreover, neither Canberra nor its U.S. or other Asian allies can contain or restrain China's rise, and attempting to do so would be neither desirable nor feasible. They maintain this is not the goal of alliance coordination on Asia policy.

These perceptions and beliefs collectively motivate Australia's conception of the regional security order that would best serve its interests. That order would have the following attributes:

- a United States that is deeply engaged in regional affairs
- a China that does not dominate but has a voice
- multiple regional power centers
- a U.S. alliance structure that remains the foundation of regional security interactions.

Some Australian policymakers add that these beliefs do not diminish the value of multilateral organizations in contributing to Asia stability and prosperity. But these organizations only supplement—and do not replace—the networks of U.S.-based bilateral alliances and security cooperation. Debates about the relative value of multilateralism are somewhat partisan, with the ALP as the traditional proponents. Rudd's regional diplomacy will likely increase emphasis on these beliefs.

These views have led Australia to pursue a variety of responses to China in its bilateral interactions, in its regional diplomacy, and within the alliance.

Australia's Embrace of China

In the last decade, largely under Howard, Australia has pursued a consistent strategy of broadening and deepening Australia's political and economic relations with China. This will continue under Rudd.

After an early spike in tensions precipitated by the 1996 Taiwan Strait missile crisis, a visit by the Dalai Lama, and other problems, Howard revitalized bilateral relations. He expanded the scope and content of Australia-China ties and built a multifaceted relationship that operates on many levels, from frequent meetings between leaders to robust people-to-people interactions.

Building strong economic relations has been one of Australia's top priorities; as a result, economic relations are now a driving force in bilateral relations. Perhaps they have been *the* driving force, because economic cooperation has served as a foundation for gradually growing political ties. Howard effectively portrayed China to the Australian public as a huge economic opportunity and as important to Australia's future prosperity. Rudd has continued this line.

Australia's political relations with China have matured and expanded as economic ties have grown. During his tenure, Howard visited China eight times and welcomed multiple visits to Australia from China's senior leaders, including Jiang Zemin, Zhu Rongji, Hu Jintao, and Wen Jiabao. Howard and his foreign minister, Alexander Downer, also met Chinese leaders abroad many times. Rudd made his first trip to China in spring 2008, after his state visit to the United States.

Intergovernmental communications have increased since the mid-1990s to include senior-level exchanges, regional security and arms-control talks, consular talks, a human-rights dialogue, joint ministerial economic consultations, FTA negotiations, a new high-level economic dialogue, bilateral aid talks, and annual defense consultations. In 1997, Howard established the interagency China Policy Group, which meets two to three times a year, to provide "strategic planning and coordination to Australia's China policy."[42] Higher-level policy coordination mechanisms also exist—at the minister, secretary, and deputy secretary levels—to coordinate China and other foreign and national security policy decisions.[43]

According to accounts from Australians in and out of government, the quality of these dialogues has improved in the last decade. In the aggregate, the degree of interaction has increased, and the results are more tangible. Still, Australians have criticized some of these, notably those on human rights, for being perfunctory. There is little indication that the Howard administration really pressed human rights in its diplomacy with China; such an approach would have undercut the conceptual foundation of its China policy. This could change under Rudd because the pressure from traditional ALP constituencies to address China's human rights behavior will likely grow. A prominent symbol of the improving political relationship was Australia's invitation to Hu Jintao to address parliament during an October 2003 trip to Canberra—just one

---

[42] Parliament of Australia, Senate, *Government Response to the Senate Foreign Affairs, Defence and Trade Inquiry into Australia's Relations with China*, Canberra, 2006a, pp. 1–44, esp. 27.

[43] These equate to the secretary, deputy secretary, and undersecretary levels in the U.S. bureaucracy. Interview with Australian official, Washington, D.C., 2007.

day after President Bush's address to parliament. At that time, this privilege had not been given to leaders of the United Kingdom or Japan. By many accounts, Hu Jintao received a far warmer response than George W. Bush.

Beyond the high politics of bilateral relations, interactions among people have grown as well. The total number of Chinese visitors traveling to Australia annually had grown from 9,000 in 1991 and 1992 to over 50,000 as of late 2007. More mainland Chinese students study in Australian educational and training institutions than any other nationality, accounting for 24 percent of total foreign students in 2005. From 2002 to 2005, enrollments of Chinese students in Australian schools increased 70 percent. China is Australia's fastest growing market for inbound tourism. Air travel services are being liberalized to double the number of seats available per week between China and major Australian cities.[44] Some Australian policymakers claim that the Chinese language (both Mandarin and Cantonese dialects) is the most commonly spoken foreign language in Australia.[45]

Australia's steady expansion of bilateral relations with China has been based on a conceptual foundation that Howard articulated at the beginning of his tenure and that persists today. At his first meeting with Jiang Zemin in fall 1996 and then again during his initial trip to China in 1997, Howard stated that the relationship would be built on the twin pillars of "mutual interest and mutual respect." He noted that although Australia and China were different societies and have different political systems with vastly different values, these differences were not a barrier to practical cooperation. Australia's diplomacy would not "hector and lecture and moralise" but rather focus on expanding shared interests, with economic ties at the forefront of that effort.[46] In John Howard's words, "we seek to build on shared goals and not become obsessed with those things that make us different."[47]

Howard's drive to expand bilateral relations with China was assisted by history and circumstance.[48] The 1997 Asian financial crises provided China and Australia with an opportunity to cooperate in forging assistance packages for Southeast Asian economies. The post–September 11 expansion of alliance cooperation provided a political environment (in Australia's relations with the United States and other allies in Asia) conducive to further expansion of Australian-Chinese ties, both symbolic and sub-

---

[44] See Parliament of Australia, 2006a, pp. 2–17.

[45] John Howard, "Address to AsiaLink Conversations Gala Dinner," Park Hyatt Hotel, Ho Chi Minh City, November 20, 2006b.

[46] John Howard, "Address at the Reception to Mark the 25th Anniversary of Diplomatic Relations Between Australia and China," Sydney, December 17, 1997; also see John Howard, press conference, Beijing, April 1, 1997, as noted in Kelly, 2006, p. 67.

[47] John Howard, "Address to the Asia Society Lunch," speech delivered to the Asia Society, New York City, September 12, 2005b.

[48] Kelly, 2006a, pp. 63–70.

stantive. Australia has no defense relations with or security commitments to Taiwan that would complicate bilateral relations. Australia's internationally oriented economy was poised to benefit from China's booming economy, providing further reason for policymakers and the populace to see China as an opportunity rather than a threat.

Australia's Asia Diplomacy

Australia's regional diplomacy in Asia offers another window into its response to China. On the one hand, Canberra has sought to integrate China further into regional institutions and has sought to avoid confronting Beijing and initiatives intended to do so. On the other hand, it has focused a great deal of diplomatic effort on ensuring that China does not dominate regional affairs, that other power centers emerge in Asia, and that the United States remains highly engaged and influential in the region. Australia's Asian diplomacy accords with mainstream U.S. perceptions and is extensively coordinated with Washington and other U.S. allies. Under Howard, there was also a domestic political element to Australia's Asia policy; he sought to demonstrate his party's strong credentials in engaging Asia to counter traditional Labour party criticisms of conservatives.[49]

Australia, like the United States, has significantly expanded its diplomatic and security ties with Japan. Australia has been encouraging Japan to play a larger and more normal role in both regional and global security affairs. Canberra supported the 2002 creation of the Trilateral Security Dialogue (TSD), which institutionalized annual security consultations among the United States, Japan, and Australia.[50] This has been a key channel for sharing regional security assessments and coordinating regional security cooperation, about China and other international issues. Australian troops in Iraq are providing security for the Japanese contribution to Iraqi reconstruction. In 2006, Australian and Japanese policymakers began calling their ties a "comprehensive strategic relationship," and Howard stated that "Japan has no closer partner or friend in the region than Australia."[51] In March 2007, Australia and Japan took a major step by formalizing and expanding bilateral diplomatic and defense cooperation as prime ministers Howard and Abe signed a joint declaration on security cooperation in Tokyo. While this was not a formal defense treaty, it represented a qualitative increase in defense links. The document established annual meetings between the nations' defense and foreign ministers; the United States and Australia have a similar arrangement. They also pledged to expand bilateral military cooperation (e.g., personnel exchanges

---

[49] On the latter point, see Kelly, 2006, p. 66.

[50] The formal name of the TSD was changed to Trilateral *Strategic* Dialogue in March 2006 when the meeting was elevated to the secretary of state or ministerial level.

[51] Leigh Sales, "PM Hails Japan's Friendship," transcript, *Lateline*, Australian Broadcasting Corporation, June 15, 2006. Interestingly, this formulation was a slight evolution from past statements about Japan; see Howard, 2005a.

and joint training and exercises) and to apply such bilateral security cooperation to addressing regional security threats. Australia pledged support for Japan's bid for permanent membership in the UN Security Council.[52]

Rudd has avoided making categorical Howard-esque statements about the primacy of Australia's ties with Japan, but he has, to date, supported the slowly evolving defense and diplomatic cooperation with Japan.[53] Rudd will be less aggressive in expanding this defense relationship than Howard was and will almost certainly not push for a full defense alliance with Japan. To avoid provoking Beijing, Rudd will likely calibrate his defense cooperation with Japan against his China policy. In early 2008, during the first visit of China's foreign minister following the 2007 election, the Rudd administration publicly opposed Japan's effort to develop a coalition of democracies around China that would include Japan, India, the United States, and Australia.

The Howard administration gradually expanded Australia's security and defense ties with India, a further reflection of Australia's support for the U.S.–led effort to create multiple power centers in Asia. Howard endorsed the U.S.–Indian strategic rapprochement, especially the growing defense and security links. In 2006, Howard began to expand Australia's own defense links with India, with the signing of an MOU on defense cooperation.[54] Furthermore, Canberra supported the politically controversial U.S.–Indian nuclear deal. In summer 2007, the Howard government took a major and controversial step by agreeing to sell uranium to India to support the U.S.–Indian nuclear deal. This decision constituted a major policy shift for Australia because India is not a signatory to the Nuclear Nonproliferation Treaty (NPT), historically a requirement for access to nuclear materials and assistance from NPT members. As of early 2008, the Rudd administration is strongly predisposed *against* approving uranium sales to India but is not going to oppose the broader U.S.–Indian deal in the multilateral Nuclear Suppliers Group. The Rudd administration will likely continue to increase relations with India, including defense ties, but will avoid actions that make it appear as though the United States, Australia, Japan, and India are working together to constrain Chinese power.

Australia succeeded, with assistance from Japan and Singapore, in joining the inaugural EAS in 2005 (along with India and New Zealand). Australia's membership ensured that the summit would not be an exclusive, Asia-only grouping. Australia, like the United States, regularly reiterates support for an open and inclusive regionalism in Asia, as a signal to China concerning Beijing's subtle promotion of exclusively Asian membership. To join the EAS, Canberra took the necessary and somewhat controversial step of signing ASEAN's Treaty of Amity and Cooperation, which required some

---

[52]   The document can be found on the Ministry of Foreign Affairs of Japan's Web site; for Australian commentary on agreement, see Paul Kelly, "Security Accord Flags New Japan," *The Australian*, March 14, 2007.

[53]   On the latter point, see Rudd, 2007.

[54]   Mark Dodd, "India Defence Ties to Be Tightened," *The Australian*, June 4, 2007.

deft legal maneuvering.[55] Despite joining the EAS, Canberra publicly maintains that its existing system of alliances remains central to regional security affairs, with multilateral organizations only supplementing these alliances. Canberra also continues to view the Asia-Pacific Economic Cooperation organization as the premier multilateral organization in Asia—a view identical with that of the Bush administration.

Australia has been pursuing active security dialogues and security cooperation with many Southeast Asian states. In November 2006, Australia signed a major framework agreement on security cooperation with Indonesia to facilitate greater cooperation on counterterrorism, defense policy, and policing. While Australia has many longstanding motivations for security cooperation with Southeast Asia, one of them is to provide these nations with the confidence and capabilities to resist predation by larger powers, of which China is a major candidate.[56] This goal drives Australia's efforts to promote good governance and democracy among Asian nations.

The U.S. Factor in Australian-Chinese Relations

When assessing Australia's responses to China, the effects on alliance relations are a key factor. The alliance has both *shaped and been shaped by* Australia's relations with China. Several dynamics are relevant here.

Howard managed to expand ties with Beijing without pulling away from the United States or creating serious, permanent tensions in alliance relations (or the perception of doing either). This is perhaps one of Howard's greatest foreign policy successes: He managed to simultaneously expand bilateral relations with both the United States and China. He pulled both China and the United States closer at the same time, rejecting the notion that he had to choose between them.[57] Howard accomplished this impressive diplomatic feat mainly by dint of the good will that he gained from the United States with his expansion of alliance activities. As Paul Kelly noted in his 2006 study,

> Howard incorporated into the US alliance framework a more independent discretion for Australia's China policy. There is no doubt his close ties with the Bush Administration purchased him a political immunity in this task. Indeed, the same China policy followed by another Australian government without Howard's level of trust with Washington (such as a Labor government that opposed the Iraq War) would likely have prompted US concerns.[58]

---

[55] The United States did not join the EAS for several reasons. For one, it was unwilling to sign the Treaty of Amity and Cooperation because the treaty might limit U.S. policy options on Burma. Other concerns related to the treaty's possible restrictions on military activities in Southeast Asia.

[56] Interview with Australian officials, Canberra, March 2006.

[57] Howard, 2005a.

[58] Kelly, 2006, p. 69.

Australia's engagement with China has resulted in differences with the United States. Some concern the form of Australia's diplomacy and others its substance. None have caused permanent damage to alliance relations, but they are indicative of shifting sensitivities toward China and some differences with the United States.

Canberra has taken a few actions in an effort to put distance between Canberra's and Washington's approaches to China. Regardless of the fact that none caused lasting damage to alliance relations *and* some were often reversed or clarified, they indicate that such views exist and could reemerge in the future. First, in 2003 and 2004, Australia was reluctant to participate in an informal organization, known as the Halibut Group, consisting of the United States, the United Kingdom, New Zealand, Japan, and Canada. This organization was originally established to coordinate policies on the 1997 return of Hong Kong to China. It was reborn to coordinate policy and operational aspects of these nations' bilateral relations with China. Some Australian senior diplomats reportedly feared that the group was an effort to contain China by stealth or that Beijing would see it as such. Canberra opted out of the first two rounds of consultations. Following U.S. complaints and Howard's intervention in 2005, Australia began attending the group's meetings.[59]

The possibility of a U.S.–China conflict over Taiwan and Australia's possible involvement remains a point of uncertainty—and occasional tension—in the alliance. The issue came to the fore in August 2004 when then–Foreign Minister Alexander Downer, during a press conference in Beijing, publicly questioned whether Australia is automatically committed, under the Australia, New Zealand, and United States Security Treaty (ANZUS Treaty), 1951, to assist the U.S. military in the event of a U.S.–China conflict over Taiwan.[60] In March 2005 Downer stated:

> We would be bound to consult with the Americans and the ANZUS Treaty could be invoked, but that is a very different thing from saying that we would make a decision to go to war. We would make a decision on the basis of the circumstances on which this arose . . . . We have no circumstances where we pre-commit ourselves to participating in a war which is entirely hypothetical. We don't know what the situation would precisely be nor is it terribly productive to continually speculate on what we would or wouldn't do—we don't know what we would do.[61]

This generated immediate concern in Washington about a looming policy shift in Canberra. This incident resulted in clarifications at multiple levels, including among top leaders, about Australia's interpretations of its alliance commitments.[62] It is unclear

---

[59] Interviews with current and former U.S. officials, Washington, D.C., 2006, 2007.

[60] Specifically, Downer stated, "some military activity elsewhere in the world . . . does not automatically invoke the ANZUS Treaty."

[61] Alexander Downer, interview with Fran Kelly, Radio National IV, March 14, 2005.

[62] Interview with former senior U.S. officials, Washington, D.C., 2006.

what prompted Downer's 2004 and 2005 statements. Some Australia officials claim that Downer sought to put some distance between Canberra and Washington on China, reflecting one school of thought about Australia's China policy. The resulting bilateral tensions were moderated following both private and public clarifications Howard made to senior U.S. officials.[63] Publicly, Australian officials continue to be circumspect about this specific issue, as do most Asian countries.

Public statements aside, Australia policymakers and strategists commonly argue (though seldom publicly) that the reason Australia has assisted the United States in every major military conflict over the last 100 years is a calculation that doing so supported Australia's national interests. Australian strategists then ask, "What leader would want to be the first to break that record?"[64] Australia's defense planning and procurement are consistent with both an Australian willingness and capability to assist the United States in a Taiwan-related contingency, even though few talk publicly in these terms. Australia possesses both the political will and the operational capability to aid the United States but does not want to commit in advance. Australian defense planners and strategists say they are focused on developing such capabilities to deter conflict rather than commit to its inevitability.

Moreover, Australian government officials under Howard did distinguish their public rhetoric about China from that of U.S. officials, especially regarding China's military capabilities and its regional diplomacy. Australian officials publicly downplayed their concerns about Chinese military modernization. This was evident during the first ministerial-level TSD meeting, involving Australia, Japan, and the United States in Sydney in March 2006. At the start of the meeting, Foreign Minister Alexander Downer publicly stated that Australia, in hosting the TSD, did not seek to contain China. This was a straw man argument; neither Downer's U.S. nor his Japanese counterparts before or during the TSD made such claims. Prior to the meeting, U.S. Secretary of State Condoleezza Rice stated that she hoped China would emerge as a force for stability in the region. Similar patterns of public commentary about China were repeated during the December 2006 U.S.–Australia Ministerial Consultations in Washington.[65]

Interpreting Australian-Chinese Relations

As ties with China have expanded, certain questions are often asked: "Has this process significantly altered Australia's policies toward China? Is Australia increasingly accom-

---

[63] Interviews with Australian officials, Canberra, March 2006.

[64] Peter Jennings, "Getting China Right: Australia's Policy Options for Dealing with China," Barton, Australian Capital Terr.: Australian Strategic Policy Institute, Strategic Insights 19, October 2005, pp. 6–8.

[65] Steven R. Weisman, "Rice and Australian Counterpart Differ About China," *New York Times*, March 17, 2006; Janaki Kremmer, "Once Lock Step Australia Tunes Out U.S. Drumbeat on China," *Christian Science Monitor*, March 17, 2006.

modating Chinese interests?" On balance, the evidence suggests greater Australian sensitivity to certain Chinese views and limited accommodation of them—but not categorically so.

Australia, like the others among our six case-study nations, is struggling with the growing complexity of its relations with China and is striving for the right balance of national interests. The *substance* of Australia's China policy, its regional diplomacy, and its alliance cooperation indicates shared threat perceptions and a willingness to forge a regional order in which China cannot throw its weight around, currently or in the future. On major issues of strategic importance to Australia, Canberra has resisted Chinese pressure and communicated to Beijing the limits of Australian-Chinese relations.

Canberra has restrained aspects of its China policy, for fear of unnecessarily alienating Beijing. Canberra approaches the Taiwan issue and interactions with Taipei very gingerly, especially in comparison to Washington's approach.[66] Casual deviations or slips from the government's official One-China policy seldom occur. While Australia maintains a representative office in Taiwan, Australian-Taiwanese government-to-government interactions are highly restricted, especially for defense and intelligence officials. The last visit of a senior Australian minister to Taiwan was in 2001.[67] Such visits are often carefully limited to economic affairs to avoid giving any hint of change in relations; years have passed without a ministerial-level visit to Taiwan. Australia, like other nations, has been unsupportive of U.S. efforts to expand Taiwan's international space and profile. Australia did not support Taiwan's bid to join the World Health Organization but did make efforts to improve Taiwan's access to the organization's activities and capabilities.[68]

Howard did not meet with the Dalai Lama after their 1996 meeting, which exacerbated already tense relations with Beijing at the beginning of his administration. Rudd met with him in 2002, but has been unwilling to do so in recent years. The Australian media often criticize bilateral human rights dialogues as meaningless and producing few results. Canberra did not comment publicly on the European Union's decision to lift its arms embargo on China, believing that, because Australia does not embargo arms to China, it should not comment on a European Union decision. As noted above, the Australian government invited Hu Jintao to address parliament in 2003. And Australia granted China market economy status in 2005 in exchange for initiating FTA talks, a major and controversial political concession at the time.

---

[66] To be fair, this is also a function of the fact that Australia simply does not share the U.S. security commitments to Taiwan. Thus, Australia is not uniquely reluctant in this regard.

[67] The last minister-level visit was from Gary Hargrave, Minister for Technical and Vocational Education in 2005.

[68] Interview with former senior official of the U.S. Department of State, Washington, D.C., February 2006; interview with Australian diplomat, Canberra, March 2006.

On the other hand, Australian leaders have also dealt frankly with Beijing on disagreements and communicated the limits to bilateral relations. Canberra, importantly, has done so on issues of strong national interest. Australia has, to date, resisted China's consistent efforts to establish a strategic partnership between Canberra and Beijing.

Australia also resisted China's diplomatic harangue in 2002 opposing the initial formation of the TSD, which not only went forward but expanded in 2006. During high-profile political asylum cases involving Chinese citizens, such as in 2005 when Chinese diplomat Chen Yonglin requested asylum, Australia has refused to repatriate the asylum seekers.[69] During 2006 and 2007 negotiations on a large contract for long-term LNG sales to China (concluded in fall 2007), the Howard government resisted pressures from Beijing for the government to intervene in commercial negotiations because Beijing felt the Australian asking price was too high. Howard steadily maintained that governments should not intervene in commercial transactions. At the groundbreaking ceremony for an LNG terminal in southern China tied to an earlier LNG contract with China, Howard reminded Beijing that Australia has other LNG customers in Asia.

Moreover, Howard has *publicly* remonstrated both mainland China and Taiwan about their destabilizing foreign-assistance offers in the South Pacific in their contest for diplomatic recognition. He argued that Beijing's and Taipei's actions have contributed to poor governance, political instability, and social chaos in Papua New Guinea, Fiji, and the Solomon Islands.[70] Canberra was one of the first nations in Asia (along with Japan) to voice strong public concern following China's January 2007 test of a ground-based antisatellite weapon, calling for an explanation and a halt to further tests.[71]

More recently, Rudd has been willing to confront Chinese leaders with Australian concerns about China's human rights and internal governance practices. For example, during his 2008 visit to China, Rudd publicly raised the issue of the March 2008 Chinese crackdown on violence in Tibet and the cultural rights of ethnic Tibetans.

Defense Policy Responses

Australia's defense policy responses to China have been motivated by persistent but limited concerns about its growing military power (especially in power projection) and a desire not to confront China and trigger a regional military competition. Canberra

---

[69] Interviews with former U.S. officials, Washington, D.C., 2006 and 2007; Interviews with Australian officials, Canberra, 2006.

[70] Graeme Doebell, *China and Taiwan in the South Pacific: Diplomatic Chess Versus Pacific Political Rugby*, Policy Brief, Sydney: Lowy Institute for International Policy, January 2007.

[71] Cynthia Banham and Mark Coultan, "Canberra Tackles China on Space War," *Sydney Morning Herald*, January 20, 2007.

has adopted defense policies to ensure that Australia's military capabilities are equal to or exceed those of major Asian militaries, like China's, and that Australia possesses the military capability to contribute to high-intensity regional conflicts, such as a U.S.–China conflict over Taiwan, one involving China and Japan, or a Korean war.

Australia's defense policy responses to China should be viewed in the context of a major and ongoing transformation in Australian defense policy that began with the publication of the 2000 defense white paper known as *Defence 2000: Our Future Defence Force* (with corresponding updates in 2003, 2005, and 2007).[72] This document spurred the renovation of Australia's defense policy for the first time since the end of the Cold War. It outlined a wider conception of Australia's strategic interests and, in doing so, motivated a major boost in defense procurement. China was one of a number of strategic interests that motivated such a major change in defense policy.

The new Rudd administration will likely publish a new defense white paper that will serve as an important indicator of the future direction in Australian defense policy. Based on Rudd's statements and actions as of this writing, his administration is not likely to pursue a major reorientation of defense policy, despite debates within his Labour Party.

The 2000 white paper outlined four broad defense objectives, including building a resilient regional defense community in Southeast Asia, bolstering strategic stability in the Asia-Pacific, fostering stability among weak or failed states on Australia's periphery, and supporting global security by contributing to U.S.–led operations and UN-led peacekeeping ones.[73] The first two objectives are directly related to China and, under Howard, motivated planning and procurement accordingly. One of the most significant consequences of this document was the Howard administration's subsequent commitment to increasing annual defense spending by an average of 3 percent annually from 2001 to 2011 to build a force to pursue these interests.

Defense Community Perceptions of China

Australian defense planners see China's rise as a dynamic and increasingly important factor shaping their regional security environment. China is not, however, an immediate military concern.[74] According to Australia's 2007 *Defence Update*,

> At present Australia does not face any conventional military threat to our territory nor, on current trends, is this likely in the foreseeable future. But we cannot be complacent. Defence must plan for a full range of possibilities even if they seem remote right now.

---

[72] Australian Government, Department of Defence, *Defence 2000: Our Future Defence Force*, Canberra, 2000.

[73] For an excellent discussion of Australia's defense policy, this white paper, and China issues, see White, 2005.

[74] Australian Government, Department of Defence, "Inquiry into Australia's Defence Relations with China," submission to Senate Foreign Affairs, Defence, and Trade References Committee, Canberra, March 2005.

Australia's future strategic landscape will be shaped by how the world's major powers—the United States, Japan and China in particular—deal with each other in the Asia-Pacific. Thus far the prospects are good. The Asia-Pacific has benefited from a status quo where the United States has been the predominant military power for over 50 years. This has underpinned the region's remarkable economic growth for decades. We do not believe that any regional power is eager to see fundamental geo-strategic change.

Still, as China and India grow, and the United States re-balances its global commitments, power relations will change, and as this happens there is always a possibility of strategic miscalculation.[75]

Australian defense planners' concerns about China's military have grown in recent years.[76] Planners and analysts argue that China's military modernization has accelerated, is comprehensive, and has achieved surprising successes in key areas, especially related to regional power projection. They highlight the consistent rises in China's defense budget, its deployments of new and highly capable naval and air-combat platforms, its 2007 antisatellite test, and its growing conventional missile arsenal with longer-range systems.[77] Australia's 2007 *Defence Update* expressed far more concern about Chinese military modernization than past versions and is a stark break from past policy. The 2007 report noted that

the pace and scope of its military modernisation, particularly the development of new and disruptive capabilities such as the antisatellite (ASAT) missile (tested in January 2007), could create misunderstandings and instability in the region.[78]

Few Australian defense planners or analysts are concerned about a direct Chinese military strike on the Australian homeland. Australian defense planners do worry that the pace and scale of PLA modernization could spark a rivalry with the United States, into which Australia might get drawn, or that it would spark a regional competition between China and Japan or India. Defense planners are also concerned that China might use its military forces to coerce its neighbors to support Beijing's regional policy goals.[79]

---

[75] Australian Government, Department of Defence, "Australia's Strategic Environment," in *Australia's National Security: A Defence Update*, Canberra, 2007.

[76] See the China-related sections of Australian Government, Department of Defence, 2007, pp. 6–7.

[77] The information in this paragraph is drawn from Australian Government, Department of Defence, 2007, and interviews with officials from the Department of Defence, Office of National Assessments and Defense Intelligence Organization, Canberra, March 2006.

[78] Australian Government, Department of Defence, 2007.

[79] The information in this paragraph is drawn from interviews with officials from the Department of Defence, Office of National Assessments and Defense Intelligence Organization, Canberra, March 2006.

These concerns are matched by more-hopeful views about China's future. In general, the Australian defense establishment to date does not believe China is undertaking a crash military modernization program focused on dominating East Asia. China's interests lie in continued economic development and political stability. Australian defense planners frequently note that China faces numerous internal challenges that, if not managed, could weaken and destabilize China, equally threatening regional stability. Defense policymakers maintain that a military confrontation with China is not inevitable and that it is not in Australia's interests to confront China over its military modernization. In June 2005, former Defense Minister Robert Hill stated, "we accept that it is perfectly legitimate that China modernise its defence force . . . ."[80] The Rudd administration's public comments on PLA modernization will be an important indicator of its defense policy.

Defense Planning and Procurement

The defense establishment's nagging concerns about China's regional security policy and defense modernization have been clearly reflected in defense planning and procurement.[81] Australian defense *planners* make two calculations when thinking about the challenges China presents. First, defense planners talk about ensuring that their military forces possess a regional capability edge, in which China's modernizing military increasingly serves as an important technological baseline. China's sophisticated and growing air and naval forces are of particular concern for defense policymakers in ensuring such an edge.

Second, defense planners explain that a central tenet guiding planning is being able to participate in a range of coalition military operations with the United States. They explain that this includes the ability to contribute to high-intensity regional operations, such as a U.S.–China conflict over Taiwan or a conflict in Korea. Defense planners seldom discuss (publicly or privately with foreigners) plans for a Taiwan contingency because much depends on how the conflict begins and the level of U.S. involvement. Yet, when asked, they make three points: ANZUS could be invoked; the Australian military possesses the capability to make a variety of air and naval contributions (and is procuring capabilities to sustain and, in some cases, grow such contributions); and Australia has contributed to every major U.S. military operation since the alliance treaty was signed in 1951.[82]

---

[80] Stephen Wyatt, "Hill Shows His Moderate Side to a Bristling China," *Australian Financial Review*, June 17, 2005, p. 28.

[81] This subsection draws on a range of sources, including interviews with defense policymakers and planners, as well as defense intelligence analysts in Canberra in March 2006; Raspal Khosa, *Australian Defence Almanac 2006–2007*, Canberra: Australian Strategic Policy Institute, 2006; and White, 2005, pp. 312–317.

[82] Interviews with defense policymakers and planners, as well as defense intelligence analysts, Canberra, March 2006.

This planning guidance is reflected in procurement. As military spending began to grow in 2001, the Australian military has purchased or is planning to buy a variety of new systems and upgrades to bolster its air combat and naval warfare capabilities. Almost all the main platforms and technological upgrades Australia purchases are U.S.–built and are compatible with U.S. military equipment, a further indication of Australia's emphasis on maximizing interoperability with U.S. forces for future coalition operations.

Australia has upgraded the avionics and missile capabilities of its F/A-18s and F-111s, the backbone of the Royal Australian Air Force (RAAF). The multipurpose F/A-18 is equipped with the beyond-visual-range Advanced Medium-Range Air-to-Air Missile, making this aircraft one of the most capable in Asia. Both the F/A-18 and F-111 can be optimized for antisurface, maritime strike missions using Harpoon missiles or possibly even the Joint Air-to-Surface Standoff Missile, which the RAAF plans to purchase. The F-111 provides Australia with an airborne medium-range precision-strike capability unmatched among Asian militaries. Yet the F-111 is aging.[83] Consequently, the RAAF plans to purchase some 80 to 100 F-35 Joint Strike Fighters by around 2010 to replace all its F-111s and some F/A-18s.[84] The F-35 will offer improved survivability and sustainability over the F-111. The addition of this multimission platform to the RAAF's inventory will also enhance the operational flexibility of Australia's combat aircraft fleet. On deployment, it will likely be the most capable ground-attack aircraft in Asia.

To support integrated air combat and distance operations, Australia possesses five air-refueling aircraft and six airborne early warning and control aircraft. The RAAF has also ordered four new C-17 transport aircraft to boost its strategic lift capability. Canberra is also investing in air defense capabilities by integrating ground-based radar, command systems, and airborne early warning and control systems.

The Royal Australian Navy is upgrading and replacing much of its fleet over the next decade in one of its largest naval procurement efforts since the 1950s. It already has the capability to operate over long distances in true blue-water environments. It is acquiring systems to enhance its area air-defense and amphibious lift capabilities. Many of its new or enhanced capabilities would significantly contribute to coalition operations in a high-intensity conflict with a well-armed regional adversary, such as China.

The navy is upgrading the combat systems on its two main classes of frigates and plans to acquire three Aegis-capable air warfare destroyers beginning in 2013; some of these destroyers may possess theater missile defense capabilities as well, akin to those of Japan's *Konga*-class air warfare destroyers. The navy is expanding its amphibious lift

---

[83] The U.S. Air Force first deployed it in 1967, the RAAF in 1973.

[84] Because some F-111s will have to be retired before the F-35s are ready, Australia plans to purchase some 25 F/A-18Fs to fill the gap.

capability with acquisition of two new, large amphibious vessels beginning in 2012 (each is three times the size of its predecessors). These platforms will be capable of multiple functions, including air support, amphibious assault, transport, and command center roles. Depending on the ultimate configuration of these vessels, they may support a small number of naval fixed-wing aircraft.

The navy currently operates six *Collin*-class diesel submarines, which possess the highly capable successor to the Mk-48 torpedo and the capability to fire Harpoon antiship missiles. Once all upgrades are complete, these submarines will be among the most capable and quiet in Asia and, thus, could significantly assist antisubmarine warfare in the East Asia littoral, a notoriously difficult operating environment. Complementing the antisubmarine warfare role of the submarines are AP-3C long-range maritime patrol craft, with extended surface search radar and improved submarine strike capabilities. These may remain in service for at least another decade and could be further aided by Australia's possible acquisition of unmanned aerial vehicles. These antisubmarine warfare capabilities combined with the RAAF's antiship capability provide Australia with a range of options for participating in a high-intensity conflict against a capable adversary.

Military-to-Military Relations with China

Australia has consistently pursued a modest defense relationship with China's military, beginning as far back as the 1980s. The scope of these military-to-military interactions is wide but shallow. The Howard government strongly supported military-to-military exchanges, which have not been politically controversial in Australia. The Australian government stated in 2005 that such dialogues had already moved from "expansion to consolidation."[85]

Australian-Chinese defense exchanges encompass senior-level visits, strategic dialogues, intelligence exchanges, staff college and student exchanges, language training, functional working-level exchanges, and ship visits.[86] According to Australia's Defence Department, enhancing senior officer exchanges is the centerpiece of the bilateral defense dialogue and will remain so in the future. Australian defense officials note that they only infrequently receive high-level PLA officials and are seldom invited to be among the first to visit key PLA facilities to which foreign militaries have not previously had access.[87] These are often reserved for the U.S.–China defense exchanges. The Australian navy conducted two low-level exercises with the Chinese navy in 2002 and 2004, a passage exercise and a search-and-rescue exchange. The United States conducted both types of activities with China in 2006. While Australia does not have an

---

[85] Australian Government, Department of Defence, 2005, p. 4.

[86] Australian Government, Department of Defence, 2005.

[87] For example, in 2005, then–U.S. Secretary of Defense Rumsfeld was, according to the PLA, the first foreigner to visit the headquarters of China's Second Artillery, which controls its nuclear and conventional missile forces.

embargo on arms sales to China, it keeps defense exports at a modest level. From 2002 through 2005, Australia exported a little over A$500,000 of military items to China and A$15 million worth of dual-use items.[88]

Exchanges with China's military are premised on a logic common to Australia's military diplomacy throughout Asia: Regular defense dialogues, even if very limited, and frequent personal interactions among military officers are critical to managing sensitive relationships with militaries of developing nations. Australians point to the extensive ties built with the Indonesian military in past decades and the critical role such relations played in managing past regional crises, such as the one in East Timor in 1999.

Canberra views defense exchanges with Beijing as a natural complement to the bilateral political relationship. These exchanges provide an opportunity to exchange views to reduce misperception and miscommunication. According to an Australian Defence Department statement,

> Our defence engagement with China is focused on strategic activities designed to generate mutual goodwill, trust, and understanding between our respective defence organizations while providing opportunity for personal contacts to develop, especially at the senior level.[89]

Australian defense officials use this channel to communicate views on the ANZUS alliance and to explain key alliance activities of concern to China, such as joint training and missile defense cooperation. Australian defense officials stress that they seek to dispel the PLA's frequent misimpressions about Australian and U.S. intentions and to reinforce messages about Australia's strong and enduring commitment to the alliance. Deterrence is a consistent and subtle message in such exchanges; defense officials state they do not want to provoke China but also seek to communicate the costs of provocative PLA actions. This is also one channel that was used to reinforce Howard's political message to China that Australia will not be Finlandized as China's power and influence in East Asia grows.

Australian defense officials are realistic about the limits of the defense dialogues with China and do not expect them to have the same levels of success as those with Indonesia. Canberra and Beijing are unwilling to share much information about operational military capabilities. Australia seeks to avoid any bilateral activities that could aid the modernization of the PLA's capabilities.

---

[88] Australian Government, Department of Defence, 2005.

[89] Australian Government, Department of Defence, 2005, p. 7.

Conclusions and Implications

Key Findings

Three forces are driving Australia's responses to the rise of China. First, rapidly growing economic relations and the resulting perception that China is key to Australia's future prosperity have been propelling bilateral relations forward. The pattern of highly complementary trade relations provides a rationale and engine for Australia-China relations, from which all types of bilateral interactions have expanded over the last decade.

Second, few in Australia see China as a growing security threat or view conflict with China as inevitable or even likely. Australia wants to avoid being drawn into a major power rivalry in East Asia involving China. As a trans-Pacific nation whose pan-Asian links are growing, Australia would find rivalry with China very costly—and far more costly for Australia than such a rivalry would be for the United States. The Howard administration often reiterated that political, cultural, and historical differences with China do not predispose Australia and China to acrimony and confrontation. Rudd has stressed an identical message, during and since the election. Public opinion data indicate that Australians hold relatively benign views of China and see it as a large economic opportunity. Thus, elite and popular opinion are in sync on this point.

Third, some Australian policymakers and analysts, especially foreign and defense policy specialists, see uncertainty mixed with a nagging concern about China's growing power and influence. These policymakers and analysts remain wary of the possibility that a more-powerful China could, in the future, become coercive and destabilizing. Linked with that view is the belief that the ANZUS alliance and U.S. security commitments throughout Asia are central to ensuring regional stability and protecting Australia's strategic interests. Rudd has stressed this point on multiple occasions, especially during his first state visit to the United States in spring 2008.

Thus, Australian-Chinese relations are feeling distinct cross pressures, many propelling relations with China forward, some constraining the two nations. These pressures exist in the context of a changing U.S.–Australian alliance and a rapidly modernizing China. How will these various pressures manifest themselves? Where are they pushing Australia?

Canberra has improved and will continue to improve its bilateral relations with Beijing, with trade ties clearly leading the charge. Bilateral trade will remain highly complementary: China will continue to need Australia's raw materials, with uranium and natural gas exports poised to grow substantially. The successful conclusion of FTA talks would further deepen economic relations and send an important political signal to Beijing. As with the others among our six case-study nations, China looms larger in Australia's foreign policy and, as a result, Canberra will continue to take Beijing's interests and possible reactions increasingly into account. Canberra will also likely continue to eschew public rhetoric critical of Beijing (such as regarding military modernization) and stress areas of bilateral cooperation—an approach not unlike many others in Asia. Canberra will remain sensitive to Beijing's views on hot-button issues that could complicate relations, such as Taiwan and human rights. To be sure, on issues of direct Australian national interest, such as the South Pacific, Canberra will deal forthrightly with Beijing in an effort to change its behavior. Debates within the Australian government about the relative importance of China to Australia's national interests, the appropriate degree of Australian sensitivity to Chinese preferences, and the role of alliance relations in Australia-China ties will continue—albeit with varying degrees of expression in public and in policy.

Australia's concerns about China's growing influence and behavior will persist as well. These concerns have motivated a series of foreign and defense policies that seek to ensure that the United States remains highly engaged and increasingly influential in Asia, that the U.S.–led bilateral alliances in Asia remain the centerpiece of the regional security order, that multilateral organizations do not replace alliance relations, that Japan and India assume greater regional roles, that Southeast Asian states have the confidence and capabilities to resist coercion from larger states, and that Australia possesses the requisite military capability to assist the United States in a major regional contingency.

Recent history indicates that Canberra will deal frankly with Beijing when the two countries disagree on issues touching Australia's core security interests, although the intensity and manifestation of Australia's responses is subject to variation. Nonetheless, the views of Prime Minister Rudd and the health of the ANZUS alliance will be central to sustaining such an approach.

On balance, Australia's policies toward China have broadly benefited the Australian-U.S. alliance. For the most part, the Howard and Bush administrations shared similar views on the economic and security challenges China's rise poses, the proper regional order in Asia, and the role of the alliance in addressing the former two challenges. Howard's approach of simultaneously engaging key Asian nations (mainly China and Japan) and broadening alliance relations (and thereby rejecting the need to choose between the United States and China) helped Canberra manage and mitigate the cross pressures inherent in its China policy. Rudd will face a formidable challenge in maintaining this balance, in particular in maintaining the perception of such a balance.

Australia's China policy has been a source of occasional tensions in alliance relations, with the most acute tensions revolving around the question of Australia's involvement in a possible Taiwan conflict. None of the resulting problems were long lasting but raised latent questions among American policymakers about the Australian commitment to the alliance and the effect of growing Australian-Chinese ties on alliance relations. These latent questions linger in the United States and occasionally manifest themselves in Australian-U.S. relations.

Most differences between U.S. and Australian policy on China have been more of tone than substance. Australian policymakers avoid stark characterizations of China's internal or external behavior, such as publicly using the term *threat* to describe Chinese actions. American policymakers have been far more willing to talk tough about China, in part because of domestic debates in the United States. Past Australian ambiguity about its alliance commitments and the corresponding implications for a military conflict over Taiwan have been the most serious policy differences between Washington and Canberra. Some U.S. policymakers want an explicit, private commitment that Australia will be with the United States in the event of a conflict. Canberra wants to avoid having to choose between Beijing and Washington at all costs, for fear that such a choice would shape U.S. policy in a certain direction. When such differences have come to the fore, they have not severely damaged alliance relations. Policymakers either tolerated the policy differences or intervened to clarify them, but such intervention needed to occur between top leaders. Although both nations have gotten past such incidents, concerns linger in Washington, and frustrations persist in Canberra.

These past tensions and problems over China policy provided both the United States and Australia with opportunities to identify differences and to develop a policy framework for managing them. It is unclear how robust and enduring this framework is, however. It will be tested under the Rudd government as its Asia policy, relations with China, and alliance cooperation take shape. For some Americans, these bilateral debates suggest possible future trends in Australia's China policy. Howard's push to deepen the alliance on all fronts purchased much political good will in Washington, making it easier for Canberra to develop an extensive relationship with Beijing without raising concerns in Washington. Rudd's decision to withdraw troops from Iraq created some but not a great deal of distance from the Bush administration. In the future, Rudd will need to take this and other foreign and defense policy actions into account as he builds a relationship with the next American president.

Future Trends and Indicators

Four variables will influence Australia's future responses to China: the political leadership in Australia, alliance relations, bilateral economic relations, and China's regional behavior. Australian views of China are a balance of optimism and limited and latent concerns about China's future direction. These four variables will affect the balance between optimism and concern in Australia's China policy.

Howard's concurrent expansion of the alliance and ties with Asian nations was central to his successful broadening of Australian-Chinese ties. Howard possessed the domestic political space and American confidence in his commitment to the alliance to expand ties with China. Kevin Rudd will need to pull off a similar balancing act and do so consistently. He will need to sustain the political latitude—at home *and* in the alliance—to pursue a similar policy toward China. Rudd's current statements on China policy, the alliance, and strategic stability in Asia suggest substantial continuity with Howard's approach. Rudd has gone out of his way to make the ANZUS alliance a priority in his overall foreign policy, as well as in his approach to Asia. Washington has recognized these core elements of his foreign and defense policymaking, deferring immediate concerns following the 2007 election. Actual policy behavior will need to reflect these policies consistently.

But Rudd's own priorities and the changed domestic political context after the 2007 election may evolve in such a way that limits his ability to sustain such political space at home and in the alliance. This is at least a possibility worthy of consideration. Some Australians, in both parties, believe the nation should distance itself from U.S. Asia policy for fear of getting dragged into an avoidable and costly confrontation with China. They fear that the United States ultimately wants to contain China. Other Australian policymakers, specifically in the ALP, favor increasing emphasis on multi-lateral organizations in Asia policy (as opposed to the alliance) and want Canberra to become a balancer between Washington and Beijing. As the domestic political landscape under Rudd develops, these views could nudge Australia's China policy toward greater accommodation. This is an issue to be watched. Moreover, even if Rudd's Asia policy does not vary much from Howard's, a *perception* that Australia is distancing itself from the alliance could create perceptions in the United States that Australia is moving closer to China. This could result in alliance tensions over China policy.

Another variable affecting the future of Australian-Chinese relations is their economic relationship. As Australia's trade with China grows, Australia's leadership is likely to feel greater pressure from the growing political constituencies that favor good relations with China and seek to avoid creating unnecessary tensions in bilateral relations. Howard's strong coalition government was able to withstand such pressures. Rudd will have to manage similar pressures, which could be more difficult if the economy began to slow or the governing coalition began to weaken (neither condition appears imminent as of this writing).

Several factors suggest these pressures can be managed in the coming years. Although exports to China will continue to grow, the Australian economy and its export markets are becoming more, not less, diversified. China's ability to threaten Australia's national economy seriously will remain modest and focused on certain sectors. At the same time, Chinese reliance on imports from Australia is high in certain categories, such as iron ore and, eventually, LNG. Bilateral investment is very thin, so Australian businesses are not tied to a production chain that creates structural dependencies on factories in China. Despite recent, very large increases in trade volumes, Canberra has not pulled many punches with Beijing on its core strategic concerns; indeed, Howard substantially expanded the scope of alliance cooperation, including controversial items, such as missile defense cooperation and the strategic embrace of Japan. Australia's diplomatic coordination with the United States and its Asian allies has been extensive and continues to grow, even as China became Australia's second-largest trading partner in 2007. Also, Australia's defense establishment will remain so closely and structurally tied to the U.S. defense community that no single Australian leader could easily alter the deep links among intelligence analysts, defense planners, and warfighters.

China's behavior in the region will exert a strong influence on the future of Australian-Chinese relations. Barring a major change in China's regional diplomacy, Australia will likely continue to expand economic ties with Beijing while strengthening the alliance and expanding its regional security relationships to hedge against a revisionist China. A more-aggressive China could lead Australia to adopt more-confrontational policies to limit Chinese activism, or at least to become more public about its concerns. Also, if China tried to probe and test the strength of the alliance regularly, Australia's China policy could become more combative. Given the latent concerns in Australia about China's growing economic and military power, China could do little to *force* Australia to become more accommodating of Chinese interests in Asia. The only way Australia would be likely to become more accommodating would be through a dramatic change in its own political leadership or a crisis in alliance relations. Looking from the vantage point of mid-2008, neither of these is likely.

CHAPTER NINE

Conclusions

We began with two central questions: How are U.S. allies and major security partners in East Asia responding to China's rise in regional economic and security affairs? What are the implications for U.S. security interests in the region? China's growing weight in the Asia-Pacific is one of the most recent, rapid, and consequential trends shaping the regional order. The responses of U.S. allies and major security partners to China may well affect U.S. regional security cooperation; U.S. basing and access agreements; and ultimately, the U.S. ability to deter and defeat regional threats. Drawing on the data and analysis in our six case studies, this final chapter offers several types of conclusions: general and specific, practical and theoretical. We begin with an overview of our main conclusions, then provide more-detailed findings. Finally, we assess the implications for U.S. regional security policy and U.S. Air Force planning and activities in Asia.

Overall Conclusions

Currently, China's growing involvement and influence in East Asian economic and security affairs is not fundamentally eroding the foundation of U.S. alliances and security partnerships in the Asia-Pacific. As of this writing, none of our six case-study nations see China as a viable strategic alternative to the United States; thus, the United States remains the security partner of choice in the region.

China *is* changing some U.S. Asian alliances and security partnerships. In many cases, China makes U.S. security commitments even more relevant: Nations feel they can more confidently engage China precisely because U.S. security commitments endure. However, U.S. Asian allies and partners are increasingly seeking to maximize their room to maneuver by positioning themselves to benefit from ties with both China and the United States. On balance, U.S. Asian allies and security partners want continued U.S. involvement in the region but sometimes only in certain ways, at certain times, and on particular issues.

All six nations whose policies we assessed in the preceding chapters uniformly view China as an economic opportunity and are rapidly expanding their economic links with China. There is a pervasive and compelling economic logic to these bilateral relationships. However, for some, trade with China is not an unqualified good; it has damaged certain sectors of their economies, producing both economic winners and losers. Nevertheless, there is little sign that these nations will come to see trade with China as a net loss at any time in the foreseeable future. In fact, many of their political and business leaders view China as key to their nations' future prosperity. In some instances, that perception appears to be out of step with the reality of an individual nation's economy and bilateral trade and investment with China.

What is *not* occurring in Asia in response to China's rise is as important as what is occurring. Contrary to media reporting, East Asia is not gradually falling under China's hegemony, at least not our six case-study nations. China is not gradually pushing the United States out of the region or otherwise making it irrelevant. Regional states are not trying to ingratiate themselves in the expectation of an eventual Chinese hegemony. The United States and China are jockeying for power and influence, but theirs is not a zero-sum game.

While the six nations and other regional governments are watching Chinese military modernization with varying degrees of attention and concern, they are not rushing out en masse to modernize their militaries or to expand their military budgets or force structures as a result. Rather, these governments have tightened existing alliances and diversified security ties by expanding cooperation with other Asian states.

As China's role in Asian affairs has expanded, the six nations' desire to keep the United States engaged in the region has not diminished; in some important cases, this desire has grown. Most East Asian nations welcome positive and mutually beneficial interactions with both the United States and China, on a range of traditional and nontraditional security issues.

China is undoubtedly gaining influence among all six nations, but in a limited way and of a certain type, and China has become more important in their policy decisions. These nations have become more sensitive to Chinese preferences and interests, often on sovereignty-related questions that already resonate. Also, many Asian nations are censoring their own China policy more frequently. However, the influence China has gained is most effective at preventing efforts at anti-China containment. This passive variety of influence involves nations not taking certain actions deemed to be provocative. We assess that China has not gained offensive influence, which it could use to attenuate alliance relationships or otherwise marginalize U.S. influence. When China has tried to assert itself in such ways, its efforts have often been counterproductive. China's diplomatic overreaches in Asia in recent years have prompted occasional backlashes and a further embrace of the United States.

Several East Asian nations are now moving out of what might be called a honeymoon in their multidimensional relationships with China, coming to recognize the costs and complexities involved. Many view stable relations with China as, on balance, central to their livelihoods, but not everyone sees China as a reliable or predictable actor or partner.

None of America's East Asian allies wants to have to choose between the United States and China. Being forced to do so is considered a worst-case scenario, one to be avoided at all costs. In fact, most reject the need for such a choice, often arguing that they do not view interactions between the United States and China in Asia in zero-sum terms. This makes the possibility of a U.S.–Chinese conflict over Taiwan a matter of particular and acute sensitivity because it could force such an unwanted choice.

The six nations are uniformly expanding their bilateral interactions with China. To varying degrees, they are accommodating some Chinese interests, such as those regarding Taiwan and human rights, in both bilateral and multilateral forums. None is in favor of appeasing China, and most are aware of the dangers of appearing to do so. And even though these nations are more sensitive to China's preferences and increasingly take China's reactions into account in policymaking, they have not shown themselves willing to capitulate to China's demands on issues related to their core national interests, specifically including their security ties with the United States.

There is little to suggest that the growing economic links between China and U.S. allies will yield direct political influence that China can effectively leverage to shape the allies' foreign policy or military affairs. Indeed, China would find it difficult to translate economic ties into that kind of influence. While the six case-study nations practice some self-censorship and self-restraint in areas of key interest to China, commonly on Taiwan-related issues, they also remain highly sensitive and resistant to Chinese actions that appear to be open attempts at manipulation.

U.S. allies in Asia expressed differing levels of concern about the uncertainty of China's future and its potential to affect regional stability and prosperity. This was due, in part, to how much emphasis national policymaking placed on domestic priorities relative to external security threats. The six nations fear both a strong and a weak China because both possibilities could threaten regional security and development.

The six case-study nations support a robust role for the United States in regional security affairs. To varying degrees, they have strengthened their security relationships with the United States (often for reasons having little to do with China) and have engaged China at the same time. While these nations need to expand certain interactions with China to foster economic development, they want to ensure that the United States remains the principal security guarantor in the region as insurance against a destabilizing China.

None of the six nations favors or expects China to supplant the United States as the predominant power in Asia. At the same time, none supports an explicit or implicit U.S.–led effort to contain China's rise. None considers such a strategy desirable or feasible because it would precipitate unnecessary strategic rivalry.

The U.S. security partners constituting our six case-study nations all believe that U.S. policy toward China and toward Asia as a whole will have a strong and determining influence on whether China's rise is stabilizing or destabilizing in the region. In short, U.S. policy remains a key variable in the six nations' reactions to China's growing regional influence. As long as the United States remains a major economic actor and security guarantor to the region, countries there will respond to China's rise with confidence and moderation.

On one side of the balance, the six U.S. allies and security partners are relatively optimistic about China's current and potential contributions to Asian and global economic affairs. They want Washington to remain a key economic actor and security guarantor in the region so that the benefits of China's growing economy can be harvested. On the other side, they share some general discomfort about U.S. foreign policy in the Middle East and the current U.S. approach to countering global terrorism (both of which appearing coercive and unilateral). Also of concern are Washington's level of engagement in the regional issues of primary interest to the six nations and the perceived insensitivity of U.S. Asia policy to the desire these countries have for stable relations with China.

Evaluating Regional Responses to China

Beyond these common responses to China, there are also important variations as well. The six nations fall along a continuum in their views about and responses to China. Roughly speaking, the six can be divided into three groupings, each sharing similar orientations regarding responses to China. The differences among the groups add a layer of complexity to the commonalities in national responses noted above.

Australia, Japan, and Singapore

In overall terms (and acknowledging the myriad differences among these three nations), the views about and responses to China's rise that Australia, Japan, and Singapore share have common qualities. For these three nations, the rise of China in Asian economic and security affairs is salient for their policymakers and debated among their strategists. These nations think strategically about regional affairs and are concerned about maintaining a balance of power in Asia. All want to benefit from continued trade with and investment from China and are engaging China to shape its emergence and to deter it from provocative actions. Australian, Japanese, and Singaporean policymakers recognize that a China that is either too strong or too weak could undermine regional stability. In particular, all three share concerns about China's growing power and influence in Asia and keep a keen eye on China's diplomatic influence in Asia and its military modernization. Of the three, Japan's concerns are the most acute.

All three nations have actively responded to China's rise by taking distinct actions to protect their own national interests. To ensure that the United States remains engaged and relevant to Asian security and economic affairs, they have expanded their cooperation in alliances with the United States to pull their ties closer. They share the American view that regional stability and prosperity require the United States and its network of alliances to remain central to the evolving Asian security order—but not the only means of stabilizing it. None want China to replace the United States in Asia, even gradually.

These three nations have made sustained efforts to translate their views into reality in Asia. Their expanded alliance cooperation with the United States and among each other, such as expanding EAS membership, is part of this effort. These nations have also begun to diversify their security and diplomatic relations with other regional powers, as an implicit bulwark against the emergence of a coercive regional actor. None, however, has pursued this approach in a way that appears to challenge or confront China. These three nations have also accommodated Chinese interests to some degree, such as on the Taiwan question and on certain trade issues. To be sure, Japan is more forward leaning than the others and is thus a partial exception. Its policies have added to Chinese-Japanese tensions (for which China shares responsibility), distinguishing Japan's reactions somewhat from those of Australia and Singapore. This is largely a function of historical animosities, political appeals to nationalist sentiments, and a nascent sense of competition for regional status between Tokyo and Beijing.

The Philippines and Thailand

While the Philippines and Thailand are very different countries by any measure, their responses to China have many common attributes. China, as a strategic concern (especially in the military sense), does not factor nearly as heavily in the minds of policymakers or the public in these two nations as it does in Australia, Japan, and Singapore. The leaders and publics in these two nations focus intensely on domestic challenges. The governments of Thailand and the Philippines are heavily preoccupied with frequent political instability, economic problems, and internal insurgencies. Their national weaknesses influence their policymaking toward China more than any strategic vision would. This internal focus militates against China becoming a major driver of national policymaking.

This strong emphasis on internal affairs heavily shapes their diplomatic and military responses to China. Foreign policy remains the purview of the elite; the public has minimal, if any, real direct influence. Their diplomacy tends not to reflect a strategic view of Asia. Foreign policy challenges beyond their immediate neighborhood garner limited attention. When China does register with these countries, it is as an economic opportunity and as a source of potential leverage with other regional powers. The military establishments in these two nations focus mostly on internal insurgencies and to a lesser extent regional security environments. China seldom factors into their military planning, except perhaps as a long-term issue of potential concern—or when the Taiwan issue is raised.

These two nations each have a sense of domestic vulnerability and a legacy born of their developmental histories. So, to the extent that they do think strategically about China, it is in political-economic rather than military terms. All six of our case-study nations care deeply about economic growth and well-being, but Thailand and the Philippines have a greater tendency to define security in economic terms. Economic development, for them, equals not just national strength (reflected in GDP and defense potential) but also national resilience. Partly for this reason, each of these two nations uses its relationship with the United States to manage its relations with China, and its relationship with China to manage relations with the United States. Thus, Thailand and the Philippines create leverage and opportunities by playing one large power off the other—an expected and common feature of small-nation diplomacy when facing two larger powers vying for influence.

Although their interest in ties with China continues to grow, these smaller nations have also become more sensitive to the complications and disadvantages of China's growing economic influence and regional involvements. Whether it is China-induced environmental problems in the Mekong Delta or the spread of severe acute respiratory syndrome (SARS) in 2003, both nations appear to be moving beyond their initial delight and fascination with the economic potential of China. They have seen the different dimensions of China's internal challenges and external behavior up close, including the costly ones. The two nations continue to view China as indispensable but not as highly reliable. They are settling into a more-variegated pattern of bilateral relations with China, informed by an awareness of both the costs and benefits of China's growing weight in Asian affairs.

Although the two nations want the United States to remain engaged and active in Asia, this sentiment is not always as strong among the nations' publics as among their policy elites. It is not clear how much Thailand and the Philippines are willing to do to support their alliances when they bump up against Chinese preferences, prerogatives, and interests. These nations are reluctant to participate in certain alliance activities that Beijing could perceive as challenging or confrontational.

South Korea

South Korea is in a group of its own because it straddles the prior two groupings, possessing attributes of both. As is true in many democracies, South Korean leaders and the public focus primarily on domestic issues. Unlike Thailand and the Philippines, this insularity is not due to internal weaknesses or instability but rather because of South Korea's economic prosperity and vibrant democracy. Relatively low public threat perceptions and the generally positive role China has been perceived to have played (at least until recently) on North Korea issues reinforce this inward focus. As a result, China does not factor as a strategic concern for South Korea as much as it does for the first grouping of states. When China does factor into the popular and elite consciousness, it is on economic questions. China is looming larger in South Korea's economy but in a complex and evolving dynamic that is seen as both an opportunity and a challenge. Using China as a production platform has been an enormous source of leverage that has helped South Korean consumer electronics firms overtake their Japanese competitors. At the same time, key South Korean industries, such as steel production and shipbuilding, face threats from Chinese companies. Also, as South Korean investment continues to pour into China, it has the potential of hollowing out South Korean manufacturing industries.

Foreign and defense policies remain focused principally on North Korea and South Korea's alliance with the United States, limiting the extent to which regional strategy questions are debated in Seoul or reflected in its foreign policy. Concerns about China do not drive military planning or procurement, which retain their traditional orientation on North Korea as a threat and the U.S. alliance as a bulwark against it. When national security elites think about the region, Japan is often the subject of long-term security concern, not China. Indeed, Seoul has publicly taken some actions to distance itself from U.S. and Japanese positions on North Korea policy and, to a lesser extent, from the alliance (e.g., the Proliferation Security Initiative and missile defense). Yet, anxieties about China have begun creeping onto South Korean diplomatic and security policy agendas, forcing the nation's policymakers and the public to consider and debate the regional implications of China's rise. China's position that, during the Koguryo Empire (37 BCE to 668 CE), Korea was part of China has inflamed Korean popular sentiments; also, South Korean policymakers view China's expanding economic influence in North Korea with concern. In this sense, Korea's responses to China are highly dynamic and may gradually look more like the activism of the nations in the first grouping than the passive approaches of those in the second.

Understanding Regional Responses to China

This section steps back from the broader conclusion to disaggregate our main findings. Here, we look across the six case studies and draw conclusions from them for each of four response categories.

Domestic Politics and Public Opinion

Our six nations produced highly similar domestic politics and public opinion responses. China was not a high-profile issue in the domestic politics of any of these nations. In most cases, China policy was not a political football manipulated for partisan purposes. In at least five of the six nations (Japan being the partial exception), there was very little disagreement among the major political parties about policymaking toward China. Political leaders in all the nations viewed China's rise as inevitable and generally positive, given its contributions to economic development. Accordingly, they seek to engage China and to expand bilateral relations with China. To be sure, these sentiments are partly a function of the fact that foreign policy issues do not loom particularly large in most of these nations. In many of them, foreign policy remains the purview of the elite. Interestingly, we found that relations with the United States and U.S. foreign policy were almost always more politically contentious than China policy.

Public opinions about China in five of the six nations were positive, expressing high levels of amity toward China. Japan was the glaring exception. Asian publics are increasingly aware of China's importance to the region's economic future and regional stability. While popular opinion data indicate some concerns about China as a security threat, these views did not dominate. Rather, polling data indicate that China is widely viewed as an increasingly important source of national prosperity. Not surprisingly, a variety of domestic actors have influenced national debates about China, including the media, business associations, labor and trade unions, educational institutions, and numerous NGOs. As China has expanded its economic, diplomatic, and cultural outreach to East Asia, the number of national stakeholders with views on China has proliferated. Their views are generally in favor of engaging China and growing bilateral interactions.

However, these pro-China trends in domestic politics and public opinion have not led the six nations to alter their national interests significantly. There is little indication that China has been able to manipulate ethnic Chinese or pro-China domestic constituencies in these nations to pursue Chinese objectives. While it is not clear that China has tried to do so, it is far clearer that the general affinity for China and growing bilateral economic relations would be difficult to mobilize into a force for shaping national policy on China. In some cases, the benefits of trade with China are diffuse, while the costs are more focused and evident. In other cases, such as in the mature democracies of Australia and Japan, supporters of trade and investment with China can be vocal but are not a dominant voice (at least not yet) in shaping China policy.

Moreover, the patterns of investment and trade in Asia are not particularly conducive to China operationalizing its influence. The key traders with China in Asia are foreign multinational corporations (e.g., Japanese, Korean, Taiwanese) operating in other Asian countries, producing goods for export to China, or importing from it as part of larger regional production chains. These actors, however, have limited political influence over their host-nations' governments. In the Philippines, for example, most trade with China is conducted through Japanese firms, not local ones.

To be sure, China's role in Japanese politics and public opinion was a distinct outlier in our work. As politics in Japan have become more transparent and competitive, China policy has become increasingly politicized. Despite former Prime Minister Abe's successful efforts to improve bilateral relations, concerns about China as a looming security threat have hardened within both major political parties, and the influence of traditional supporters of Chinese-Japanese relations has lessened. Recent stability in these relations notwithstanding, Japanese public opinion about China has hit a nadir in recent years, and China has become a lightening rod issue for a vocal nationalist minority. At the same time, there is a lively and polarized debate within and between the parties about a range of China-related issues, especially in the context of the debate about the controversial Yasukuni shrine (which commemorates Japanese soldiers, including some war criminals).

Economic Relations

The core of China's increasing engagement with the six nations is economic. All continue to expand trade with China, doubling, tripling, or quadrupling it over the last decade. Japan, Korea, and Singapore have invested heavily in China. All six nations view trade and other economic interactions with China as central to their continued economic development and national prosperity.

Australia and Japan enjoy a high degree of complementarity in trade relations with China, which is fueling an ongoing expansion in aggregate bilateral trade volumes. Manufacturers in Thailand, the Philippines, and South Korea have had to contend with more head-to-head competition with Chinese firms, both domestically and in export markets. Some companies in all six nations have been driven out of business because of competition from China; many manufacturers face tough competition. Thus, in all six nations, trade with China has generated political frictions. In South Korea's case, competition between South Korean and Chinese manufacturers has ended the honeymoon in Chinese–South Korean relations. Despite these frictions, all these nations view China as the center of a regional production chain in which intermediate goods are produced domestically, shipped to China for final assembly, then reexported, usually to the United States, Europe, or Japan. In short, while economic relations between China and U.S. allies and security partners will continue to expand, increased competition from Chinese exporters is already creating mixed reviews of the expansion of economic relations and China's status as an economic opportunity.

Our six case-study nations are among China's largest trading partners. However, their share of China's total trade has fallen, primarily because of slower-than-average growth in trade with Japan. China has also not invested much in these nations. Rather, the bulk of Chinese FDI has gone to Europe and the United States to purchase established brands and to the Middle East and Africa to invest in oil, minerals, infrastructure, transportation, and telecommunications.

Over time, can China translate this economic interdependence into political influence? China is unlikely to appease its major Asian trading partners through economic inducements. First, high levels of economic interactions and positive views of China are not strongly correlated. The two U.S. allies with the most complementary trade relations with China, Australia and Japan, have deep concerns about China as a regional security threat. Both are responding by buttressing regional alliances. In contrast, Thailand and the Philippines have suffered more from competition from Chinese exporters than has Australia or Japan yet hold relatively benign views of China and have welcomed greater diplomatic rapprochement with Beijing. Second, to date, China does not appear to have had much success in translating economic interactions into political influence. In some countries, the economic losers from trade with China have been a vocal minority. The winners, such as local consumers, are often a diffuse political force.

Third, the six nations' investments in China remain limited, although South Korea's investment in China is growing substantially. This reduces the sense of dependence that can come from having fixed infrastructure in China that cannot be repatriated easily. Fourth, the patterns of regional trade with China do not lend themselves to Chinese manipulation for strategic ends. Much of the growth in interregional trade has been driven by Japanese, Taiwanese, South Korean, and Western firms operating manufacturing facilities abroad, such as in the Philippines or Thailand, where they produce intermediate goods for export to China for final assembly. The real controllers of East Asian trade are the non-Chinese owners of these companies. These firms are not closely linked to the Chinese government and have little influence on the governments of the host nations in which they have set up plants. Third-country ownership of these companies greatly reduces China's ability to leverage economic relations for political purposes. Last, many East Asian exports to China are sold to foreign-owned factories that are producing goods for reexport, not necessarily for sale to Chinese consumers, although this is changing in some instances. Thus, Thailand and the Philippines depend more on multinational firms with operations in China than on the Chinese market per se. This attenuates the mechanisms through which China could try to exert pressure because the owners of most of the integrated production facilities reside outside China.

Diplomacy and Foreign Policy

We found three major foreign policy responses to China among the six nations analyzed. First, all six nations have actively engaged China in an effort to broaden bilateral diplomatic relations. They all view China's rise as a major Asian power as inevitable and are expanding their interactions both to help ensure that this is a stabilizing development and to benefit from China's booming economy. All view China as indispensable to the region's economic development and stability. Among the six nations, the stronger nations are engaging China in the hopes of shaping its preferences and, if necessary, to deter it from provocative or coercive actions. The weaker nations have embraced relations with China to create a political relationship conducive to resolving existing disputes. Most of the six nations have sought to avoid confronting or even challenging China, in particular to avoid being seen as part of a coalition to constrain or ultimately contain Chinese power. Interestingly, these views are largely consistent with current U.S. policy toward China and the evolving security order in East Asia.

Japan remains a partial outlier. Tokyo and Beijing see one another as a long-term rival for regional influence. Neither Tokyo nor Beijing has eschewed confrontation over emotionally charged issues, such as the Yasukuni Shrine or competing territorial claims in the East China Sea. These competitive tendencies will likely dominate Japanese perceptions of China and Japanese responses to China for decades.

As a result of their deepening bilateral interactions, China is looming larger in the foreign policy and foreign relations of our six nations—to the extent that foreign policy garners the attention of their leaders. Especially in public rhetoric, policymakers in these nations are paying more attention to Chinese perceptions and interests. They have all, to varying degrees, become more sensitive to Chinese views on foreign policy questions, in particular the status of Taiwan and China's human rights record. Thus, there has been some accommodation of China, but its scope has been fairly narrow to date. Many of our six nations continue to deal frankly with Beijing, for example, on issues of core national interest. This response is motivated by an acute awareness of China's efforts to expand its regional influence. Australia, for example, assumes a very low-key approach to Taiwan and China's human rights record. However, Canberra also continues to deal forthrightly with Beijing in trade and commercial negotiations and, most recently, the effects of its aid policies and practices in the South Pacific. Singapore bristled at China's 2004 effort to prevent its prime minister designate from visiting Taiwan. Regional reactions to China's initial proposal for the EAS in 2005 are another case in point. Japan and Singapore worked to expand the summit's member-ship, which now includes Australia, India, and New Zealand. Southeast Asian states acted to ensure that the summit would always take place in their subregion, not in Beijing. In addition, both Northeast and Southeast Asian states worked to prevent China from dominating the summit's agenda. While some Chinese interests have been accommodated, there is little evidence of even a creeping capitulation to Chinese inter-ests in response to an assumption that its status as a rising power will eventually lead to hegemony over East Asia.

Moreover, a common theme among the foreign policy elites was that the initial exuberance for relations with China has begun to wane. Many U.S. allies and partners in East Asia have begun to move beyond their most idealistic and naïve expectations about China and are replacing them with sober assessments of the uncertain implica-tions of China's rise as a strategic actor in Asia. As these nations become more tied to China and as China looms larger in Asian stability and economic development, these nations have become more sensitive to uncertainties about China's future. In particu-lar, many Asian leaders have realized that the destabilizing consequences of a fractured, politically unstable, and weak China would be as much a matter of concern as the pros-pect of an economically and militarily strong China.

A second major response to China has been to diversify regional relations by enhancing ties with other Asian power centers. This is most evident in the behavior of Japan; Australia; and, to a lesser extent, Singapore and Thailand. All four nations have sought to expand their diplomatic coordination and security ties with each other and with India and have extended this coordination to non-Asian affairs, such as in UN deliberations. The motivation here is a desire to forge a regional order in which nei-ther China nor any other regional power can dominate or otherwise act coercively. In addition, the six nations all support regional institutions that are open and inclusive, in which neither China nor other major powers can dominate. Regional responses to China's initial EAS proposal are a prominent example.

A third prominent response has been a tighter embrace of the United States as a regional actor. The six nations have sought to expand political and security relations with the United States to ensure that it remains engaged in Asia. To varying degrees, all see this engagement as critical to regional stability in Asia and as an implicit counterbalance to China's growing influence. While none wants to be part of any explicit or implicit effort to contain Chinese power, all welcome the United States remaining the principal security guarantor to the region. Again, none sees China as a viable strategic alternative to the United States. Moreover, none wants to choose between the United States and China, and all vocally reject the need for such a choice, which is why most Asian nations are reluctant to address the Taiwan issue. Suggestions that such a choice be made over the Taiwan issue have been a source of friction in U.S.–Australian relations. The six nations view their dual engagement of the United States and China as mutually supportive. In some cases, their ties with the United States help facilitate their engagement of China; at the same time, their ties to China give them leverage and options in dealing with the United States. Smaller Asian nations, such as Thailand and the Philippines, can use their ties with China to make Washington better appreciate their needs. These are the sentiments that motivate much of the pro-China diplomatic rhetoric coming from some Asian capitals.

Defense Policy Responses

In assessing regional defense policy responses to China, what is most notable is what is *not* occurring among the six nations surveyed. None of them has initiated major military modernization programs driven by concerns about growing Chinese military power and the need to balance it. No systematic internal balancing has been occurring in response to concerns about the Chinese military. The Philippines, for example, has a long-standing offshore territorial dispute with China but has devoted very few resources to resuscitating its crumbling air and naval forces.

So how have the six Asian militaries responded to China? The nations varied in how or whether they perceived a threat and in their military responses to any threat perceived. In all cases, however, the concerns about China and associated military responses have been limited. Chinese military modernization has not sparked a regional military buildup.

Of the six, Japan has, by far, been the most concerned about PLA modernization and the potential consequences for regional stability. As a result, PLA activities are increasingly informing Japanese defense planning and procurement, although this has still not prompted a buildup in overall funding or force levels. Australian policymakers are closely watching the rapid improvements in PLA capabilities and take the PLA's emerging capabilities, especially those related to regional power projection, into account when considering their own modernization efforts. Canberra's concerns do not, however, dominate either its defense modernization plans or its diplomacy with Beijing. Australian defense planners instead highlight the destabilizing consequences of a weak

China. South Korean, Thai, and Filipino policymakers all hold very sanguine views about the Chinese military. Their defense establishments are more intensely focused on either their immediate security environment (North Korea, in South Korea's case) or their internal security threats (for Thailand and the Philippines). Thus, in some cases, concerns about the Chinese military play almost no role in military modernization. In others, PLA modernization has been only one of many security concerns influencing defense planning and procurement. It has not been an exclusive consideration in any of the six nations.

Although the six nations have not been modernizing or increasing their force structures in response to China's activities, all have expanded the scope of alliance cooperation with the United States. While this is partly due to concerns about China, it is also part of joint efforts to combat Islamic extremism in Asia and to participate in military operations in Iraq and Afghanistan. The growing coordination among the United States, Australia, and Japan reflects a desire to forge a regional security order in which China cannot throw its weight around. Also, none of the six nations sees China as a viable security alternative to the Unites States as the principal guarantor of regional security. Defense and security ties with the United States provide the smaller operational capabilities, via joint training, exercises, and procurement, that will allow them to address internal security challenges and to interact with Beijing more confidently. However, concerns about potential Chinese reactions have also, in some instances, constrained these nations' security cooperation with the United States. None of them wants to be seen as part of an anti-China coalition. For example, these concerns have led South Korea to limit its security cooperation by refusing to participate in U.S.–led programs on theater missile defense.

A major concern for all U.S. allies and major security partners in Asia is the status of Taiwan and the possibility of a U.S.–Chinese conflict over Taiwan's status. All six of our case-study nations want to avoid such a conflict because it would likely force a choice between Washington and Beijing. Policymakers and military officials in these countries are highly reticent about declaring how they would respond in such a situation, although Japan has at least hinted publicly that it would, under some circumstances, support U.S. operations. Most simply do not know, given the numerous uncertainties regarding the initiation of such a conflict. The Taiwan question is therefore not a useful litmus test of the quality of U.S. alliance relations or the relative balance of influence between the United States and China in particular countries. The responses of even the United States' closest allies are unknowable, and raising the issue—especially publicly—would put unnecessary stress on the relationship and could send counterproductive signals to Beijing or Taipei.

Some of the six nations have also been expanding their security cooperation with each other and with other Asian powers. These intra-Asian security relationships are an extension of the diplomatic diversification strategy noted above. The increasingly formal and institutionalized security relationship between Japan and Australia is perhaps the most prominent example. Singapore has begun to broaden its security ties with Japan and Australia. All three are building security ties with India. Policymakers in these Asian nations state that they seek a regional security order in which no single power can dominate and in which all play an active role in managing emerging challenges to regional stability and prosperity.

Bilateral military relations are the final dimension, and all six nations have gradually expanded their military-to-military ties with China, albeit starting from a very low baseline. In most cases, these exchanges began in response to PLA initiatives, but most nations involved welcomed the opportunity they presented. These interactions remain quite thin and often highly symbolic, such as those with Japan, but the level of actual cooperation is gradually growing. Currently, these interactions are limited to educational exchanges and small-scale joint exercises. China has also invited U.S. allies to observe Chinese military exercises. China has sold a small amount of weapons to Thailand and the Philippines and holds out the possibility of future deals. While the reliability of Chinese-made weapons remains a concern, their relative affordability contributes to the creation of a high-low mixture in the small force structures of these Asian nations. China is pushing for greater military-to-military cooperation with many U.S. allies as a means of reassuring them and of sensitizing them to Chinese views on regional security questions, notably Taiwan. Given the value China places on military diplomacy and expanding the scope of its activities, the responses U.S. allies make to Chinese outreach are worth watching.

Implications for U.S. Regional Security Policy

Understanding the policy implications of this monograph begins with a statement about U.S. objectives in the Asia-Pacific.[1] We posit two core objectives for U.S. security policy in Asia:

1. to ensure that the United States is in no way denied major and sustained economic, political, or military access to the Asia-Pacific
2. to prevent one nation or a coalition of nations from concentrating sufficient resources to support or otherwise constitute a regional or global challenge to U.S. interests in the Asia-Pacific.

These two objectives contribute to the larger goal of ensuring that Asia is stable and prosperous; such an Asia is one in which the United States can best protect and promote its numerous and growing security and economic stakes in the region.

---

[1]   For a useful assessment of U.S. strategic interests in Asia, see Khalilzad et al., 2001, pp. 43–45.

To accomplish these objectives, the United States will need to use its entire toolbox of national statecraft and military power for two purposes: to shape the regional security environment and to respond to regional crises. U.S. policy should use incentives and disincentives to affect the preferences of allies, security partners, competitors, and potential adversaries to ensure continued U.S. access to Asia; to prevent highly competitive forces from amassing influence; and to bolster regional and international rules, norms, and institutions. It is also critical to reinforce the perception in East Asia that the United States will remain involved and active and that Asian nations can count on it to meet critical external security needs. This will serve as an enduring foundation for the region's continuing security and stability.

The regional responses to China we have identified suggest several implications for U.S. Asia-Pacific policy. First, the United States remains well positioned to continue to achieve its core objectives in the Asia-Pacific. In contrast to some headlines, the United States does not face a crisis in Asia in which an ascendant China gradually replaces U.S. influence. Our six case-study nations are simply not reacting to China that way, and none of them desires that outcome. In fact, the rise of China has made the United States even more relevant in some ways; active American involvement fosters a regional security context in which East Asian states can confidently engage and set limits to bilateral relations with China. Moreover, the apparent regional consensus favoring engaging and cooperating with China is largely driven by economic logic: to benefit from China's growing economy. But this consensus also has a tentative quality.

Several East Asian nations have their own concerns about how China might use its growing power, such as reasserting its historical and domineering patterns of bilateral relations. Others fear the emergence of a stagnating and socially volatile China that inadvertently exports instability abroad. In short, among U.S. allies and security partners, definite concerns exist about China, and the degree of concern tends to vary depending on each nation's ability to focus on foreign policy and regional security issues. Thus, the United States still has abundant geopolitical space in which to nurture its regional relationships and, thus, to further entrench its traditional role as the region's preeminent power.

Second, it is still early days in East Asia's responses to China's rise. The region is still coming to terms with China's expanding involvement in Asian political, social, economic, and security affairs. The United States has a good amount of time to shape the direction of regional responses to China or at least to shape the context in which these responses evolve (e.g., U.S. policy toward East Asia). China also faces its own constraints in influencing Asian perceptions and policies. China will likely face difficulties translating its growing economic interactions with East Asian states into political influence over them—a likely goal on Beijing's part. Therefore, given the centrality of the United States to Asian security affairs (over the last 50 years) and its status as a provider of critical public goods to the region, the United States has both the time and space to respond effectively to the emerging challenges of regional reactions to China's rise.

Third, it is not in U.S. interests to take a highly competitive approach to China (or to China's regional policy) when interacting with allies and security partners in East Asia. U.S. policy should continue to be sensitive to the changing constellations of national interests of its allies and partners in the region, none of whom wants to provoke China into becoming a strategic adversary, and all of whom want to benefit from China's growing economy. U.S. policy should respect China's legitimate rights and responsibilities in Asia and be willing to address some of them. To be sure, no U.S. Asian allies want it to depart the region, even gradually; fear of abandonment and even detachment is just as strong a motivation as the concern about becoming entrapped in a U.S. regional policy that confronts China.

Fourth, as China becomes more relevant to U.S. allies and partners in East Asia, America's relationships with many of the individual nations are changing and will continue to evolve. Our six case-study nations are increasingly calculating Chinese preferences and possible reactions into their foreign and defense policy decisions. Most obviously, the United States should tread carefully on issues that might force a choice between Washington and Beijing. The United States should pursue a finely calibrated policy that seeks to meet the individual needs and national interests of its allies and security partners. This represents a distinct challenge for the United States, especially in its dealings with its smaller, internally focused allies, such as Thailand and the Philippines. The United States must remain cognizant of their internal economic and security needs and seek to be relevant to them. The United States has much to bring to these relationships, including trade and investment opportunities, extensive security cooperation, cooperation in multilateral forums, and politically salient high-level bilateral interactions. Thus, the United States should craft a tailored and differentiated strategy for interacting with regional allies and security partners in East Asia. It is incumbent on the United States to calibrate the right mix of policy tools to ensure that, as China becomes more relevant to U.S. allies and partners in East Asia, the balance of influence stays in America's favor.

Fifth, our conclusions bear on the types of security architectures and related security strategies the United States could pursue toward the Asia-Pacific.[2] The United States will be most successful pursuing a regional strategy that is conceptually somewhere between two ideal types. One ideal type is the United States actively coordinating and cooperating with a small number of Asia's major powers (e.g., Japan, India, or China), in which burdens are shared and the interests of the participating powers are balanced; this model would approximate a concert of powers in Asia but one in which there is an implicit hierarchy, with the United States on the top. A second, less-

---

[2]   These ideal types are drawn from Khalilzad et al., 2001, pp. 45–48; also see Robert J. Art, "A Defensible Defense: America's Grand Strategy After the Cold War," *International Security*, Spring 1991, pp. 5–53.

ambitious model would have the United States assuming a balancing role among several major regional powers (China, Japan, India, Russia, a unified Korea, Indonesia, potentially Vietnam); in this model, Asia evolves into a multipolar system in which numerous nations compete for power, influence, status, and relative gains and geopolitical advantage. The United States would play the detached role of balancer among these competing states, enjoying the freedom to make and shift alliances as needed. Our analysis suggests that either of these two strategic approaches would be generally consistent with the preferences of U.S. allies and security partners. Two other potential security strategies, which are more extreme, do not appear to be feasible: One would be the U.S. pursuit of ultimate and uncontested hegemony in Asia in which the interests of the nation's regional partners would not constrain the exclusive pursuit of its interests and values (i.e., "we can do it all") in regional affairs. The other model would be the U.S. pursuit of a non-*Reapolitik* strategy involving the creation of a collective security system in the region.

Implications for the U.S. Air Force

Assuming that U.S. policy toward East Asia will continue to pursue the objectives described above, U.S. policymakers will require the armed forces in the Asia-Pacific necessary to (1) maintain and strengthen relationships with the militaries of allied and partner states in Asia and (2) sustain, in the face of improving Chinese military capabilities, the abilities to deter and defeat aggression, offset regional imbalances, and defend allies and security partners. This implies that the U.S. Air Force and other services will be called on to do the following:

- maintain vibrant and extensive programs of security assistance, joint training and exercises, and other military-to-military interactions tailored to the needs and circumstances of each partner nation
- ensure that the U.S. posture in and around the Asia-Pacific is adequate to support all plausible military contingencies
- modernize their own forces so that they have the requisite capabilities to deter and defeat aggression in the region.

These missions present U.S. defense strategists and the U.S. Air Force with both opportunities and constraints in the U.S. maintenance of a robust regional force posture. The opportunities stem from the fact that all six allied and partner states will remain open—and in some cases quite eager—to continue a range of alliance activities with the United States. Our six case-study nations continue to see bilateral security cooperation—as well as alliance relations more broadly—as enhancing their national capabilities to address a range of national security concerns, which for them importantly include both internal security challenges (insurgencies) and external threats. These nations appear to be quite willing to embrace the United States when China's diplomacy overreaches and appears coercive. However, the six nations' views about China are only one part of that calculation; their views about U.S. foreign and defense policies (within Asia and beyond) are equally, if not more, important.

Japan and Australia have already demonstrated a pronounced readiness to expand the full complement of alliance activities with the United States and to leverage these to expand cooperation between each other. These intentions and activities are likely to continue. The Philippines remains eager to maintain security cooperation with the United States, even though this has become politically sensitive at times for its political leaders. Sensitivities about China do not appear to have substantially constrained bilateral security cooperation. The defense relationship between the United States and the Philippines will likely have further opportunities to expand when the Filipino military turns to rebuilding its highly atrophied naval and air force capabilities. Security assistance and arms sales from the United States could play a critical role in that process.

There are also constraints on the U.S. military's efforts to maintain a robust regional force posture. Most East Asian states view the United States—specifically, U.S. regional security policy—with some trepidation and occasional derision, which affects the scope of bilateral security cooperation. Some of this is unavoidable because it stems from the unparalleled global power of the United States and the high degree of dependency these nations have on the United States. However, two dynamics are more controllable and relevant to U.S. interests in Asia.

First, many East Asian leaders are averse to being seen as too close to America when elites and the public in their countries see U.S. foreign and security policymaking in East Asia or other regions as being unilateral and coercive. The U.S. invasion of Iraq in 2003 and certain aspects of U.S. counterterrorism policy elicited many of these very concerns. The anticolonial sensitivities of many East Asian states continue to inform their views of the U.S. role in international security affairs. In addition, Asian governments occasionally perceive U.S. security policymaking toward Asia as simply detached from or even inconsistent with their own economic security interests, broadly conceived. These sentiments foster a political dynamic in alliance relations that is not conducive to broadening cooperation. Allies or partners could limit the scope of their security cooperation, perhaps permitting only certain deployments, participating only in certain multilateral exercises, or limiting participation in out-of-area U.S. military operations. These views could also limit U.S. opportunities to develop ad hoc contingency agreements for occasional access to local facilities.

Second, concerns about being drawn into a regional rivalry between the United States and China or into a protocontainment of China could also constrain the scope and pace of security cooperation the six nations are willing to engage in with allies and partners. Even the United States' closest allies and partners want to retain sufficient room to maneuver in their relations with China so that they can maximize their benefits from its economic opportunities. None wants to feel locked into a U.S. regional strategy that could eventually move toward overt confrontation and eventual containment of China. Such sensitivities vary by nation. Among our six nations, the governments of Thailand and South Korea appear to be most concerned about maintaining maximum maneuvering room for their relations with China. This has—at times— restrained their security cooperation with the United States. But the sentiments in these nations are also linked to their specific government leaders, who are subject to change.

Last, and on a different note, the U.S. Air Force faces consistent and growing challenges to its posture in the Asia-Pacific. Chinese military modernization (especially its growing conventional missile capabilities) and the related risk of a U.S.–Chinese conflict over Taiwan currently pose direct threats to U.S. Air Force and overall U.S. military interests in the region. We recommend two possible responses for U.S. Air Force planners: dispersal and hardening. First, the Air Force should consider dispersing its aviation assets in the region, including, when possible, taking them out of range of China's current conventional missile arsenal. In doing so, the Air Force should ensure that these assets remain available to prosecute a Taiwan conflict effectively, an admittedly onerous task, given the region's geography. Dispersing some of the Air Force's regional strike and intelligence, surveillance, and reconnaissance assets to bases in the northern Philippines and to Guam may be appropriate. However, these are likely to be short-term fixes. As the range, precision, and destructiveness of Chinese missiles improve, China's ability to hold U.S. Air Force assets in the region at risk will increase. A second possible solution is increasing the robustness of U.S. bases in the region, specifically on Okinawa. This hardening effort would include deploying more theater missile defense capabilities. China's growing arsenal of short- and medium-range ballistic missiles increases China's ability to credibly threaten U.S. aviation assets in the East and South China Seas, potentially limiting the value of U.S. deployments in these locations. Dispersal, hardening, and theater missile defenses offer important responses to these challenges and would assist the United States in prosecuting a conflict against China over Taiwan.

Prospects for Future Security Cooperation

The above analysis suggests several possibilities for the Department of Defense and for the U.S. Air Force, in particular, to expand current security cooperation activities with the six case-study nations.

Australia

U.S. security cooperation with Australia is already quite extensive (see Chapter Eight). This is a function of the long-standing ANZUS alliance; the high quality of Australia's military and the broader national security establishment (which has the capacity to both contribute to and absorb security cooperation); and the interests, values, and perceptions about stability and security in Asia that the United States and Australia share.

The highly mature security cooperation between the United States and Australia encompasses joint military training, education, and exercises; extensive access and support arrangements; wide-ranging intelligence cooperation; defense trade; joint efforts to prevent proliferation of weapons of mass destruction; joint theater security cooperation planning and execution; and joint operations, including stabilization and humanitarian assistance operations. Moreover, U.S.–Australian security cooperation has consistently expanded since September 11, led by John Howard's efforts to further broaden alliance relations. Australia has contributed combat forces to military operations in both Afghanistan and Iraq, has led stabilization operations in failing states in the South Pacific (as part of an effort to combat terrorism), and coordinates its theater security cooperation toward Asia with the United States to maximize the value for Asian militaries. Australia is an active participant both in the U.S.–led Proliferation Security Initiative and in missile defense cooperation with the United States, unlike the other U.S. allies in Asia, except Japan.

Given the comprehensiveness of their existing relationship, the two militaries have no new major areas into which they could expand security cooperation. Indeed, because of resource limitations on both sides, merely maintaining the current extensive level of defense cooperation is a challenge. That said, there is always room to improve and refine existing activities, and bilateral security cooperation has not been problem free. Also, modernization in both militaries will create new needs and opportunities for further cooperation.

U.S.–Australian defense relations would benefit from improving the interoperability of their respective armed forces. Interoperability, especially as it concerns secure communications, logistics, and information sharing, remains a major challenge as the U.S. and Australian militaries develop and deploy advanced technologies linked to the Revolution in Military Affairs. Both militaries would also benefit from a greater integration of the Australian Defence Force's logistics support requirements into U.S. contingency planning, as well as more efforts to improve the ability to communicate and share information across secure channels during coalition operations.

Furthermore, the U.S. Air Force could contribute to bilateral security cooperation in certain specific areas:

- helping the RAAF
  - improve and eventually expand its strategic transport capability
  - transition to a more-modern combat force, eventually replacing the F-111 with the F-35
  - modernize its aerial refueling capability

- acquire airborne early warning and control systems and modernize maritime patrol aircraft
- coordinating with the RAAF on theater security cooperation activities in Asia to assist the modernization of the air force capabilities of such regional partners as the Philippines.[3]

Japan

Security cooperation with Japan is already mature, well developed, and increasingly well rounded. It continues to progress as Japan's force structure evolves and as Japanese forces become more capable of absorbing the benefits. Increasingly, U.S. units are also able to gain from combined training. Viewed primarily from the Japanese perspective, there are several particularly promising areas for further development.

One is in joint operations. The SDF has recently strengthened the position of the chairman of its equivalent of the Joint Chiefs of Staff and is emphasizing jointness more heavily. This, however, is a new development for the SDF, and Japanese military officers and civilian defense officials are aware that they have much to learn about joint operations from their American counterparts.[4] The most useful combined U.S.–Japan exercises will, then, be those that involve more than one service.

As far as the individual services are concerned, all are likely to seek intensified cooperation with their U.S. counterparts. The biggest relative change will be among the ground forces—in the relationship between the Japanese army and the U.S. Army and Marine Corps. Traditionally, U.S. and Japanese ground forces have interacted less with one another than have the air forces and navies. This is already changing as Japanese and American armies have increased the pace and scale of exercises and the I Corps headquarters moves to Japan. As the Japanese army force structure transitions to become more conventional, mobile, and high-tech (and at an accelerating pace), the need and desire for joint training with U.S. forces will increase.

U.S. military realignment, particularly the collocation of U.S. and Japanese units, will provide significant new opportunities for units to work and train together.[5] Discussions with U.S. military officers suggest that some of the most meaningful combined training with the Japanese military is relatively spontaneous, growing out of personal relationships between units and commanders. Collocation will significantly strengthen the existing web of relationships. To the extent that specific decisions about collocation are taken with such secondary effects in mind, the opportunities for combined training will be maximized.

---

[3] The authors are grateful to RAND colleague Peter Chalk for some of these suggestions.

[4] True jointness, of course, remains a continuing challenge for U.S. forces. Nevertheless, the U.S. military is still ahead of Japan on this score.

[5] This will primarily affect ground and air force elements because they will be the first to collocate.

From the U.S. perspective, the vast preponderance of new training opportunities will be highly desirable from both the strategic and operational perspectives. Some specific types of cooperation, however, will carry strategic baggage that will have to be weighed against other considerations. The government of Japan (or the SDF) may wish to involve the United States in exercises on or near disputed territory that may, apart from the U.S. legal and alliance positions on these disputes, send signals to China (and conceivably South Korea or Russia) that might or might not be desirable from the larger U.S. strategic perspective. Hence, planning and decisionmaking about combined military training and exercises should include diplomatic input.

The Philippines

Since September 11, defense and security cooperation between the United States and the Philippines has been greatly enhanced because the latter was initially perceived as the second front in the global war on terrorism. That role has since been overshadowed by the war in Iraq and terrorist threats in other parts of the world. The Philippines was designated a major non-NATO ally on October 6, 2003, and has become the largest recipient of U.S. security assistance in the Asia-Pacific region and one of the largest recipients in the world. The United States and the Philippines also conduct a series of annual combined military exercises (called Balikatan) that are keyed to the counterterrorism campaign in the southern Philippines against Abu Sayyaf. Through the Philippine Defense Reform Program, the United States helped overhaul the Philippines' defense planning process, focusing on combating terrorism, assisting national development, and responding to man-made or natural disasters. Yet U.S. arms sales to the Philippines have remained limited, especially to Philippine air and naval forces.

Despite the enhancement of U.S.–Philippine security cooperation since 2001, there may be some room for further improvements in maritime security and the rebuilding of Philippine external defense capabilities. Maritime security is an area of growing concern in Southeast Asia, but multilateral efforts so far have focused on the Malacca Strait. The waters between the southern Philippines, eastern Malaysia, and Indonesia are known for piracy and constitute an important logistical and mobility corridor for regional terrorists. Improving these nations' naval and maritime air patrol capabilities could be an area for expanded security cooperation, as a way to combat piracy and bolster regional maritime security. A related problem is that the Philippine focus on defense against internal threats means that its external defense capabilities (the air and naval forces) have continued to decay. A decision to rebuild these capabilities will require substantial external assistance—from the United States or elsewhere.

The United States would do well to fill these needs to prevent the Philippines from turning to other potential suppliers. In the context of expanded security cooperation, the United States benefits from Manila's willingness to allow U.S. overflight of Philippine airspace, use of airfields in support of military operations (as for Operation Enduring Freedom), and continued cooperation in the global war on terrorism.

That said, U.S.–Philippine defense cooperation faces some natural limits, largely defined by domestic politics in the Philippines and by constitutional restraints. Despite the steady improvement in U.S.–Philippine security cooperation, a considerable slice of Philippine political opinion opposes closer security cooperation with the United States. The Macapagal-Arroyo government's weakness also constrains its ability to cooperate on issues that could incur domestic political costs. A clear example of this was the Philippine government's decision to accelerate the withdrawal of Philippine personnel from Iraq after the kidnapping of a Filipino driver in July 2004, despite the negative U.S. reaction and the resulting concerns about the reliability of the Philippines as a security partner.

Singapore

As with the Philippines, although for different reasons, Singapore has significantly strengthened its security cooperation with the United States over the past few years. This was formalized via a July 2005 strategic framework agreement signed in Washington that recognized Singapore's role as a major security cooperation partner. Unlike the Philippines, Singapore has few domestic barriers to closer security cooperation with the United States. From the Singaporean perspective, greater closeness would be most welcome in areas that involve advanced defense technology, maritime security, and counterterrorism. A key U.S. interest, access to military facilities in Singapore, is already optimal.

Advanced Defense Technology. Access to U.S. technology is critical to Singapore's goal of keeping its armed forces on the technological cutting edge. Opportunities to expand security cooperation in defense technology (and, beyond technology, in the military's ability to wage network-centric warfare) arise in the context of the ongoing organizational transformation of the Singapore Air Force and its acquisition of advanced U.S. aircraft, such as the F-15SG, and related systems.[6]

Maritime Security. Singapore sees maritime security as an existential issue and has cooperated closely with the United States on related matters. Singapore was the first country in Asia to sign the Container Security Initiative and maintains a high level of vigilance over its port and sea lanes of communication. The United States should continue to work with Singapore to improve its situational awareness of maritime threats, encourage multilateral cooperation among Southeast Asian littoral states, enhance interoperability with U.S. forces, and facilitate the ability of the United States to respond in a crisis.

Counterterrorism. This is another high priority to both the United States and Singapore. Singapore is highly concerned about the spread of radical Islam throughout

---

[6] Adrian W. J. Kuah, "The Transformation of the RSAF: The Organizational Dimension," Singapore: S. Rajaratnam School of International Studies, Nanyang Technological University, RSIS Commentaries 6, January 31, 2007.

the region and its potential effects on Indonesia. Enhanced information sharing would be valuable for both countries. The United States could benefit from Singapore's analytical capabilities and sources in the region, while Singapore could benefit from timelier release of classified information bearing on terrorism issues relevant to Singapore.

South Korea

The United States and South Korea are currently in the midst of an intensive effort to reconfigure the U.S.–South Korean alliance. Under the Security Policy Initiative, ongoing consultations are addressing the full range of issues affecting the bilateral security relationship. Agreements reached thus far include measures to enhance combined U.S.–South Korean deterrence and defense capabilities, realign and redeploy U.S. forces stationed in South Korea, and transfer wartime operational control of South Korean forces from the Combined Forces Command to South Korea. South Korea has committed significant resources to these initiatives—including majority funding of U.S. restationing and new-facility construction costs associated with the move of U.S. forces into two hubs south of Seoul—while agreeing to increase its share of the nonpersonnel stationing costs for U.S. forces in South Korea from 38 percent in 2006 to 41 percent in 2007 (below the U.S. goal of 50 percent but still among the highest for U.S. allies).

At the same time, South Korea has agreed to support the strategic flexibility of U.S. forces in South Korea. It has enhanced its own military capabilities in ways that reinforce U.S. power-projection potential.[7] It has continued to actively support global security issues of strategic importance to the United States. A short list of this support includes both reconstruction aid and troop contingents to support U.S. efforts in Afghanistan and Iraq;[8] the deployment of South Korean troops as part of the UN peacekeeping operation in Lebanon; and South Korean participation in a range of other UN-based peacekeeping, humanitarian assistance, and disaster relief missions. In short, the U.S.–South Korean security cooperation plate is quite full. Implementing the full range of South Korean assistance activities either already agreed on or actively being discussed may be more important for the U.S. Air Force—and for U.S.–South Korean security relations more broadly—than identifying new initiatives or potential opportunities for further expanding bilateral security cooperation.

Having said that, there are certainly areas in which more might be done. In addition to those already being addressed in the Security Policy Initiative talks and identified in Chapter Four, three broad areas offer room for improvement. One relates to the Proliferation Security Initiative, which South Korea has publicly endorsed but

---

[7] For example, South Korea recently completed a new naval pier capable of handling U.S. nuclear-powered aircraft carriers.

[8] In December 2006, South Korea's National Assembly approved a third, one-year extension of the South Korean military force commitment to Iraq.

not yet fully participated in. If there is further progress in the Six-Party Talks, South Korea's reluctance to participate because of concerns about damaging prospects for inter-Korean dialogue could diminish, which would provide an opportunity for greater South Korean participation.

Another area is theater missile defense. South Korea has had something of a blind spot about the regional threat North Korean missiles pose, but concern has been growing within the South Korean military over South Korea's vulnerability since North Korea's nuclear test. This concern could increase support for acquiring a theater missile defense system, such as the ones developed in the United States.

A third area has to do with contingency planning. The transfer of wartime operational control is likely to provide opportunities for the United States and South Korea to reexamine their respective approaches to planning for unexpected developments in North Korea and to see whether modifications might improve their cooperation in preparing for such contingencies. To be sure, South Korean sensitivities in these areas are not likely to change overnight. However, as the United States transitions to a supporting security role on the peninsula, a patient approach predicated on a clearly communicated desire to be helpful could improve South Korean receptivity.

Thailand

In the long term, the prospects for intensified U.S.–Thai military cooperation are good, although not without obstacles. In the short term, the diplomatic impasse over military rule and transition to a democratically elected government represents a significant hurdle. Shortly after the 2006 military coup d'état, the United States suspended $24 million in security-related assistance. Some counterterrorism assistance was continued, as were military-to-military contacts at the working level, but high-level contacts were suspended along with the bulk of military assistance. The process of resuming normal bilateral military relations began in early 2008, when democracy was restored. The door is now open to expand U.S.–Thai cooperation, during a period in which Thailand's defense budget is growing.

The Thai government clearly hopes to further strengthen security cooperation with the United States. The primary motivation is to improve the Thai military's competence in all areas and is not aimed at security against an immediate perceived threat. Counterinsurgency and the situation in southern Thailand (see Chapter Six) provide motivations for certain types of exchange, such as special forces training and intelligence exchanges. Long-term trends and middle-term plans, however, call for evolution away from the emphasis on counterinsurgency doctrines and force structure toward a greater mobility, high technology, and a conventional force structure. Hence, the Thai military will be looking for security cooperation and military assistance from the United States across the spectrum of capabilities.

Among the Thai services, the army remains dominant (with a larger share of the budget than the air force and navy combined) and may continue to generate the heaviest demands for defense cooperation, although not necessarily defense purchases. The navy and air force are, nevertheless, gradually gaining in importance. Naval cooperation with the United States is already significant and will become more so as the military's budgetary prospects continue to improve.[9] Prospects for enhanced air force cooperation are also positive, now that the air force is buying aircraft again and has refocused on force structure modernization.

Although Thailand is likely to welcome greater military cooperation with the United States, it will also seek to strike a balance in its defense relationships, and this may limit the pace and scope of future security cooperation with the U.S. military. Bangkok will look to further develop ties with other local nations, particularly Singapore. It will also likely continue to pursue closer military-to-military ties with China, which received a significant boost when Beijing moved to fill the void left by the suspension of U.S. military assistance with a package of $49 million worth of military aid and training. Thai political and military officers will be reluctant to participate in exercises or other activities with the United States that appear directed at challenging China. They will, on the other hand, welcome efforts to engage China by, for example, including Chinese military elements in some portion of the Cobra Gold exercises.

---

[9]   The 1997 financial crisis affected the navy disproportionately because of its outstanding, dollar-denominated, loans.

Bibliography

"50 Percent of Japanese Support Koizumi's Visit to Yasukuni Shrine," *Mainichi Shimbun*, August 17, 2006.

"Abe for 'Arc of Freedom' in Asia-Pacific," *Hindustan Times*, August 22, 2007.

"Abe Off to Impressive Start," *Japan Times*, October 16, 2006.

Abe Shinzo, Prime Minister of Japan, and John Howard, Prime Minister of Australia, "Japan-Australia Joint Declaration on Security Cooperation," March 13, 2007. As of March 14, 2008: http://www.mofa.go.jp/region/asia-paci/australia/joint0703.html

"Admiral Calls for Adjustment of Combat Forces," Bangkok Army Television, November 2, 1993, tr., Foreign Broadcast Information Service, FBIS-EAS-1993-1102, November 2, 1993.

Akkarasriprapai, Benjaprut, "Free-Trade Deal with China Leaves Growers at a Loss," *The Nation* (Bangkok), February 12, 2004.

Akiyama Jyoji and Ko Bunyu, *Chugoku Nyumon* [*Introduction to China*], Asuka Shinsha, 2005.

"Amata, PTT and EGAT Trying to Lure Chinese Firms Here," Global News Wire, September 30, 2005.

Amnesty International, "Philippines: Human Rights Need to Be Respected as Election Campaign Intensifies," London, May 6, 2004. As of March 13, 2008: http://web.amnesty.org/library/Index/ENGASA350072004?open&of=ENG-PHL

Amyx, Jennifer, and Peter Drysdale, eds., *Japanese Governance: Beyond Japan, Inc.*, New York: RoutledgeCurzon, 2003.

Ang Cheng Guan, "The South China Sea Dispute Revisited," working paper, Singapore: Institute of Defence and Strategic Studies, Nanyang Technological University, August 1999.

Armitage, Richard L., and Joseph S. Nye, *The U.S.–Japan Alliance: Getting Asia Right Through 2020*, Washington, D.C.: Center for Strategic and International Studies, 2007.

Art, Robert J., "A Defensible Defense: America's Grand Strategy After the Cold War," *International Security*, Spring 1991, pp. 5–53.

ASEAN—*See* Association of Southeast Asian Nations.

"Aso Shooting from the Lip: Minister's Sound Bites Boost Profile but Raise Hackles," *Yomiuri Shimbun*, February 20, 2006.

Aso Taro, Foreign Minister, statement at press conference, Ministry of Foreign Affairs, Japan, December 22, 2005. As of March 17, 2008: http://www.mofa.go.jp/announce/fm_press/2005/12/1222.html

Association of Southeast Asian Nations, Declaration on the Conduct of Parties in the South China Sea, 2002. As of April 7, 2008:
http://www.aseansec.org/13163.htm

Association of Southeast Asian Nations and the People's Republic of China, Framework Agreement on Comprehensive Economic Co-Operation, Phnom Penh, Cambodia, November 5, 2002.

Australia, New Zealand, and the United States (ANZUS), Security Treaty, 1952.

Australian Government, Department of Defence, *Defence 2000: Our Future Defence Force*, Canberra, 2000.

———, "Inquiry into Australia's Defence Relations with China," submission to Senate Foreign Affairs, Defence, and Trade References Committee, Canberra, March 2005. As of March 13, 2008:
http://www.aph.gov.au/senate/committee/fadt_ctte/china/submissions/sub09.pdf

———, *Australia's National Security: A Defence Update*, Canberra, 2007. As of March 13, 2008:
http://www.defence.gov.au/ans/2007/chapter_1.htm

Australian Government, Department of Foreign Affairs and Trade (DFAT), Economic Analysis Unit, *Unlocking China's Services Sector*, Canberra: Commonwealth of Australia, 2005. As of March 13, 2008:
http://www.dfat.gov.au/publications/eau_unlocking_china/index.html

———, "Trade in Services," Canberra, June 2007a.

———, "People's Republic of China," country brief, Canberra, December 2007b. As of March 13, 2008:
http://www.dfat.gov.au/geo/china/cb_index.html

———, "Republic of the Philippines," country brief, Canberra, December 2007c. As of March 13, 2008:
http://www.dfat.gov.au/geo/philippines/philippines_brief.html

Australian Government, Department of Innovation, Industry, Science and Research, "China Investment Fact Sheet," Country Snapshots, Canberra, undated. As of January 2008:
http://www.investaustralia.gov.au/NR/rdonlyres/96CD81B4-5A2D-4907-A541-DF9F2964ACF1/0/CFS_China.pdf

Ayson, Robert, "Kevin Rudd and Asia's Security," *PacNet*, No. 49, November 28, 2007. As of March 13, 2008:
http://www.csis.org/media/csis/pubs/pac0749.pdf

Backman, Michael, "Burmese Junta Not in the Least Put Out by Western Sanctions," *The Age* (Melbourne), April 13, 2007.

Bangko Sentral ng Pilipinas [Central Bank of the Philippines], Web site. As of April 7, 2008:
http://www.bsp.gov.ph

———, "Philippines: Balance of Payments," statistical database, 2006. As of April 22, 2008:
http://www.bsp.gov.ph/statistics/statistics_bop.asp

Banham, Cynthia, and Mark Coultan, "Canberra Tackles China on Space War," *Sydney Morning Herald*, January 20, 2007.

Bank of Thailand, International Investment Position Team, Data Management Department, "Thailand's International Investment Position at the End of December 2006," 2007. As of March 13, 2008:
http://www.bot.or.th/bothomepage/databank/EconData/Surveys/IIPSurvey_49E.pdf

Baruah, Amit, "Thais 'Vague' About ACD Process," *The Hindu*, June 17, 2002. As of April 7, 2008:
http://www.hinduonnet.com/2002/06/18/stories/2002061802251200.htm

Bennett, Bruce W., *A Brief Analysis of the Republic of Korea's Defense Reform Plan*, Santa Monica, Calif.: RAND Corporation, OP-165-OSD, 2006. As of March 17, 2008:
http://www.rand.org/pubs/occasional_papers/OP165/

Bitzinger, Richard A., and Curie Maharani, "Arms, Money, and Security: Southeast Asia's Growing Importance as an Arms Market," RSIS Commentaries, Singapore: S. Rajaratnam School of International Studies, Nanyang Technological University, April 8, 2008. As of June 5, 2008:
http://www.ntu.edu.sg/rsis/publications/perspective/rsis0432008.pdf

Block, Ryan, "New Songdo, the South Korean 'Ubiquitous City' of the Future," *Engadget*, October 5, 2005. As of March 13, 2008:
http://www.engadget.com/2005/10/05/new-songdo-the-south-korean-ubiquitous-city-of-the-future

BOI Investment Review, September 2005: BOI Mid-Year Investment Promotion Update, Business-in-Asia.com, September 2005. As of March 13, 2008:
http://www.business-in-asia.com/automotive/japan_fdi.htm

Boucher, Richard, "Joint Statement of the U.S.–Japan Security Consultative Committee," Washington, D.C., February 19, 2005. As of March 13, 2008:
http://www.state.gov/r/pa/prs/ps/2005/42490.htm

Boyd, J. Patrick, and Richard J. Samuels, *Nine Lives? The Politics of Constitutional Reform in Japan*, Policy Studies 19, Washington, D.C.: East-West Center, 2005.

"Breaking Ice with Japan," *Indian Express*, December 9, 1999.

Brooke, James, "Japanese Island Tries to Evade Flight Path," *New York Times*, September 20, 2004.

Bryant, Ashleigh, "F-2 Makes Live Bomb Debut During Exercise," Air Force Link, June 15, 2007. As of March 14, 2008:
http://www.af.mil/news/story.asp?id=123057339

Bush, George W., President of the United States, and Lee Hsien Loong, Prime Minister of Singapore, Joint Statement, Washington, D.C.: The White House, July 12, 2005. As of March 17, 2008:
http://www.whitehouse.gov/news/releases/2005/07/20050712.html

"Business Leaders Wary of Negative Fallout from Yasukuni Visit," Japan Economic Newswire, October 17, 2005.

Cabinet Office, Government of Japan, public opinion statistics, 1987–2006. As of April 22, 2008:
http://www.cao.go.jp/index-e.html

"Can Singapore's Lee Kuan Yew Kickstart Talks Between China and Taiwan?" *Far Eastern Economic Review*, October 5, 2000.

Canadian High Commission in Singapore, "Trade, Investment, S&T, and Economic Overview," November 11, 2005. As of March 13, 2008:
http://www.dfait-maeci.gc.ca/asia/singapore/trade/overview-en.asp

"CASS Survey Says Chinese Residents Have Feelings of 'Not Being Close' to Japan," *Zhongguo Qingnian Bao*, November 24, 2004.

Central Intelligence Agency, *The World Factbook*, 2006. As of January 28, 2008:
https://www.cia.gov/cia/publications/factbook/print/rp.html

Chaibong, Hahm, "The Two South Koreas: A House Divided," *The Washington Quarterly*, Summer 2005.

Chaipipat, Kulachada, "China and the Delicate Task," *The Nation* (Bangkok), May 21, 2001.

Chalk, Peter, *Australian Foreign and Defense Policy in the Wake of the 1999/2000 East Timor Intervention*, Santa Monica, Calif.: RAND Corporation, MR-1409-SRF, 2001. As of March 17, 2008:
http://www.rand.org/pubs/monograph_reports/MR1409/

Chambers, Michael R., "Rising China: The Search for Power and Plenty," in Ashley J. Tellis and Michael Wills, *Strategic Asia 2006–07: Trade, Interdependence and Security*, Seattle: National Bureau of Asian Research, 2006, pp. 65–104.

Chang Noi, "The Board, the Management, and the Lollipops," *The Nation* (Bangkok), February 20, 2001.

———, "Reimagining the Thai Nation," *The Nation* (Bangkok), August 19, 2002.

Chang, Yihong, and Robert Karniol, "China Tempts Thailand with Modified MBT," *Jane's Defence Weekly*, February 15, 2006.

Chanlett-Avery, Emma, "Thailand: Background and U.S. Relations," Washington, D.C.: Congressional Research Service, January 13, 2005.

"Cheap Chinese Goods Take Toll on Trade Deficit," Australian Associated Press, January 11, 2005.

"China Bid to Join Inter-American Devt Bank Exposes Divisions—Report," AFX–Asia, April 11, 2005.

"China Cancels Meetings with Japan, S. Korea in Shrine Row," Agence France Presse, December 9, 2005.

"China Goes All Out to Woo Southeast Asia," *The Korea Herald*, August 6, 2001.

"China-Japan Economic Ties Glow Amid Political Chill," *Los Angeles Times*, April 17, 2006.

"China Opportunity, Not Threat, for Southeast Asia: Arroyo," Agence France Presse, October 31, 2006. As of March 14, 2008:
http://www.channelnewsasia.com/stories/afp_asiapacific/view/238561/1/.html

"China Puts off Japan, China, S. Korea Ministerial Telecom Meeting," Kyodo World News Service, December 21, 2005. As of March 14, 2008:
http://www.highbeam.com/doc/1P1-116597770.html

"China-Singapore Trade Up in 2005," Xinhua News Agency, February 28, 2006. As of March 14, 2008:
http://english.sina.com/business/1/2006/0228/67467.html

"China–Southeast Asia: Limited Regional Enthusiasm for Anti-Secession Law," Open Source Center, SEP20050318000098, March 18, 2005.

"China, the Philippines Hold Defense Consultations in Beijing," *People's Daily* (Beijing), October 10, 2006. As of March 14, 2008:
http://english.people.com.cn/200610/10/eng20061010_310514.html

Chinese Academy of Social Sciences, "Disanci Zhongri Yulun Diaocha (2006 Nian 9–10 Yue)" ["Third Chinese-Japanese Public Opinion Survey (September–October 2006)"], *Riben Xuekan*, December 2006.

"Chinese, South Korean Leaders Blame Japan for Cancelled Trilateral Summit," BBC, December 12, 2005.

Choe Sang-Hun, "Shift GIs in Korea to Taiwan? Never, China Envoy Says," *International Herald Tribune*, March 22, 2006.

Chongkittavorn, Kavi, "Strategic Value of Thai-Chinese Relations," *The Nation* (Bangkok), January 9, 2006a.

———, "Relations with Asian Giants Hampered by Lack of Realism," *The Nation* (Bangkok), May 8, 2006b.

———, "Burma: Thai Diplomacy's Biggest Travesty," *The Nation* (Bangkok), December 4, 2006c.

Christensen, Thomas J., Deputy Assistant Secretary for East Asian and Pacific Affairs, "A Strong and Moderate Taiwan," speech to U.S.–Taiwan Business Council Defense Industry Conference, Annapolis, Md., September 11, 2007. As of March 14, 2008:
http://www.state.gov/p/eap/rls/rm/2007/91979.htm

Chua, Amy, interview with Harry Kreisler, Conversations with History series, Institute of International Studies, University of California at Berkeley, posted February 2, 2004. As of March 14, 2008:
http://globetrotter.berkeley.edu/people4/Chua/chua-con2.html

Chun Su-jin and Bae Young-dae, "Postwar History Gets Makeover from a 'New Right' Perspective," *JoongAng Daily*, February 4, 2006.

Comprehensive Economic Cooperation Agreement Between the Republic of India and the Republic of Singapore, 2005. As of April 7, 2008:
http://commerce.nic.in/ceca/toc.htm

Cook, Ivan, *Australia, Indonesia and the World: Public Opinion and Foreign Policy*, Sydney: Lowy Institute for International Policy, 2006.

Cossa, Ralph A., "U.S.–Australia: Still Mates!," *PacNet*, No. 49A, December 17, 2007. As of March 14, 2008:
http://www.csis.org/media/csis/pubs/pac0749a.pdf

"CPC to Conduct Various Exchanges, Cooperation with Philippine Parties, Says Wu Guanzheng," 3rd International Conference of Asian Political Parties, Xinhua News Agency, September 4, 2004. As of March 14, 2008:
http://www.idcpc.org.cn/icapp3/2004-09/04/content_2807722.htm

Crean, Simon, Australian Minister for Trade, "Trade Figures Confirm China and Japan as Top Trade Partners," Department of Foreign Affairs and Trade Web site, May 6, 2008. As of June 5, 2008:
http://www.trademinister.gov.au/releases/2008/sc_033.html

Cutler, Wendy, U.S. Trade Representative, "United States–Korea Free Trade Agreement: A Win-Win Proposition," speech, Seoul: American Chamber of Commerce, March 7, 2006. As of March 14, 2008:
http://seoul.usembassy.gov/rok20060307.html

de Dios, Emmanuel S., "Philippine Economic Growth: Can It Last?" in David G. Timberman, ed., *The Philippines: New Directions in Domestic Policy and Foreign Relations*, New York: The Asia Society, 1998.

"Defense Agency to Upgrade Fighter Jets at Naha Base," *The Daily Yomiuri*, March 4, 2005.

DFAT—*See* Australian Government, Department of Foreign Affairs and Trade.

Dodd, Mark, "India Defence Ties to Be Tightened," *The Australian*, June 4, 2007.

Doebele, Justin, Chaniga Vorasarun, and Cristina Von Zeppelin, "Thailand's Top 40," *Forbes.com*, July 24, 2006. As of March 17, 2008:
http://www.forbes.com/global/2006/0724/045.html

Doebell, Graeme, *China and Taiwan in the South Pacific: Diplomatic Chess Versus Pacific Political Rugby*, Policy Brief, Sydney: Lowy Institute for International Policy, January 2007.

Dolan, Ronald E., ed., *Philippines: A Country Study*, Washington, D.C.: Library of Congress, Federal Research Division, 1991. As of March 17, 2008: http://countrystudies.us/philippines/1.htm

Dolor, Beting Laygo, "China Gives Military Aid to Philippines," *Philippine News*, March 14, 2005. As of March 14, 2008: http://news.pacificnews.org/news/view_article.html?article_id=4b11fc54b8df81a42b376c22bedf719a

Donelley, Eric, "The United States–China EP-3 Incident: Legality and Realpolitik," *Journal of Conflict & Security Law*, Vol. 9, No. 1, 2004, pp. 25–42.

Downer, Alexander, interview with Fran Kelly, Radio National IV, March 14, 2005.

Edwards, John, *Quiet Boom: How the Long Economic Upswing Is Changing Australia and Its Place in the World*, Sydney: Lowy Institute for International Policy, paper 14, 2006.

Embassy of the Philippines, "Philippines-China Relations," Beijing, 2005. As of March 14, 2008: http://www.philembassy-china.org/relations/update1.html

Embassy of the United States, Web site, Seoul, undated. As of April 21, 2008: http://seoul.usembassy.gov

Engardio, Pete, Dexter Roberts, and Catherine Belton, "Chinese Oil Giants Grow Up Fast: They're Finally Becoming Serious Global Players," *Business Week On-Line*, March 31, 2003. As of March 14, 2008: http://www.businessweek.com/magazine/content/03_13/b3826036_mz014.htm

"Estrada Says China Does Not Pose a Threat to the Philippines," *Asian Political News*, May 22, 2000. As of March 14, 2008: http://www.findarticles.com/p/articles/mi_m0WDQ/is_2000_May_22/ai_62242972

Faiola, Anthony, "Japan-Taiwan Ties Blossom as Regional Rivalry Grows: Tokyo, Wary of China, Tilts Toward Taipei," *Washington Post*, March 24, 2006a, p. A12.

———, "When Escape Seems Just a Mouse-Click Away," *Washington Post*, May 27, 2006b.

Fifield, Anna, "Beijing's Rising Influence in Pyongyang Raises Fears in Seoul," *Financial Times*, February 3, 2006.

"Foreign Policy Set to Take Center Stage in Election," *The Nation* (Bangkok), October 17, 2000.

Framework Agreement on Comprehensive Economic Co-Operation Between the Association of South East Asian Nations and the People's Republic of China, November 4, 2002. As of March 14, 2008: http://www.bilaterals.org/article.php3?id_article=2488

Fullilove, Michael, "Don't Be Fooled—There'll Be More Change Than Continuity in Foreign Policy," *Sydney Morning Herald*, December 20, 2007, p. 13.

"The Future of Asia 2002: Mr. Dhanin Chearavanont: Chairman & CEO, Charoen Pokphand Group (Thailand)," curriculum vitae, Nikkei Net Interactive. As of March 14, 2008: http://www.nni.nikkei.co.jp/FR/NIKKEI/inasia/future/2002/2002pro_chearavanont.html

Gates, Robert M., U.S. Secretary of Defense, and Kim Jang-soo, Republic of Korea Minister of National Defense, transcript of joint press conference, Seoul, November 7, 2007. As of March 17, 2008: http://www.defenselink.mil/transcripts/transcript.aspx?transcriptid=4083

George, Alexander L., and Andrew Bennett, *Case Studies and Theory Development in the Social Sciences*, Boston: MIT Press, 2005.

GlobalSecurity.org, "DDH '13,500-ton' Ton Class," August 29, 2006a. As of March 14, 2008: http://www.globalsecurity.org/military/world/japan/ddh-x.htm

————, "LST Osumi Class," November 14, 2006b. As of March 14, 2008: http://www.globalsecurity.org/military/world/japan/osumi.htm

Glosserman, Brad, Michael McDevitt, Laura Peterson, James Przystup, Brad Roberts, and Phillip Saunders, "Sino-Japan Rivalry: A CNA, IDA, NDU/INSS, and Pacific Forum CSIS Project Report," *Issues and Insights*, Vol. 7, No. 2, March 2007.

Go, Marianne V., "JPEPA: More Japanese Investments, Trade Opportunities Seen," *The Philippine Star*, February 24, 2005. As of March 17, 2008: http://www.bilaterals.org/article.php3?id_article=1356

Goh, Evelyn, "Singapore's Reaction to a Rising China: Deep Engagement and Strategic Adjustment," in Ho Kai Leong and Samuel C. Y. Ku, eds., *China and Southeast Asia: Global Challenges and Regional Challenges*, Singapore: Institute of Southeast Asian Studies, 2005.

Government Information Office, *Taiwan 2005 Yearbook: Foreign Relations*, Taipei, Taiwan, 2005.

————, *Taiwan 2007 Yearbook: Foreign Relations*, Taipei, Taiwan, 2007. As of April 7, 2008: http://www.gio.gov.tw/taiwan-website/5-gp/yearbook/

"Ground Unit in Okinawa to Be Beefed Up to Defend Islands," *Kyodo News Service*, September 20, 2004.

Halloran, Richard, "S. Korea Looks to the Open Seas for Regional Military Strength," *Taipei Times*, July 3, 2007.

Han Yong-sup, "Analyzing South Korea's Defense Reform 2020," *The Korean Journal of Defense Analysis*, Spring 2006.

Harden, Blaine, "Japan Warns U.S. House Against Resolution on WWII Sex Slaves," *Washington Post*, July 18, 2007, p. A15.

Harrison, Selig S., ed., *Seabed Petroleum in Northeast Asia: Conflict or Cooperation?* working paper, Washington, D.C.: Woodrow Wilson International Center for Scholars, 2005.

Heginbotham, Eric, and Richard J. Samuels, "Mercantile Realism and Japanese Foreign Policy," *International Security*, Vol. 22, No. 4, Spring 1998, pp. 171–203.

Hong Kyu-dok, "The Strategic Linkage Between the Republic of Korea's Defense Reform 2020 and Changing Security Environment," *Korea Focus*, April 2006.

Howard, John, "Address at the Reception to Mark the 25th Anniversary of Diplomatic Relations Between Australia and China," Sydney, December 17, 1997. As of March 14, 2008: http://pandora.nla.gov.au/pan/10052/20030821-0000/www.pm.gov.au/news/speeches/1997/china.htm

————, "Australia in the World," address to the Lowy Institute for International Studies, March 31, 2005a.

————, "Address to the Asia Society Lunch," speech delivered to the Asia Society, New York, September 12, 2005b.

————, press conference, Beijing, April, 1, 1997, as recorded in Kelly, 2006a, p. 67.

————, "Address to AsiaLink Conversations Gala Dinner," Park Hyatt Hotel, Ho Chi Minh City, November 20, 2006b.

Hsu-Su-Fen, "A Short Report on the Migrant Fishworkers in Taiwan," Asian Human Rights Commission—Asian Charter, November 9, 2001. As of March 14, 2008: http://material.ahrchk.net/charter/mainfile.php/east/5/

Huxley, Tim, *Defending the Lion City: The Armed Forces of Singapore,* London: Allen & Unwin, 2001.

IISS—*See* International Institute for Strategic Studies.

"India, Thailand Sign Free Trade Agreement, Four Other Accords," Press Trust of India News Agency, October 9, 2003.

"Indonesia, Malaysia, Singapore, Thailand to Safeguard Malacca Strait," Xinhua News Agency, September 11, 2005.

Inland Revenue Authority of Singapore, "An Overview of the Singapore Tax System," 2005. As of March 14, 2008: http://www.iras.gov.sg/irasHome/page03a.aspx?id=5676

International Enterprise Singapore, "Singapore's Bilateral Trade with China," January 23, 2006. As of March 14, 2008: http://www.iesingapore.gov.sg/wps/portal/MI_NorthAsia_China

International Institute for Strategic Studies, *The Military Balance,* London, 2005–2007.

International Monetary Fund, International Financial Statistics, database, various dates. As of April 22, 2008: http://www.imfstatistics.org/imf/

International Monetary Fund and Organisation for Economic Co-Operation and Development (IMF/OECD), *Foreign Direct Investment Statistics: How Countries Measure FDI 2001*, Washington, D.C., 2003.

Ishiba Shegeru, *Kokubou* [*National Defense*], Tokyo: Shinchousha, 2005.

Jagan, Larry, "Farmers Devastated by Free Trade Deal with China," Inter Press Service, February 7, 2006.

Jamaluddin, J. M., "Thailand's Force Modernization Efforts," *Asian Defence Journal*, November 2005.

Jane's, "South Korea at a Glance, Jane's Sentinel Security Assessment—China and Northeast Asia," January 13, 2006a.

————, "Procurement, Japan," January 27, 2006b.

————, "Frigates, Thailand," *Jane's Fighting Ship*s, May 2, 2006c.

————, "Corvettes, Thailand," *Jane's Fighting Ships*, December 6, 2007.

————, "Navy, Japan: Jane's Sentinel Security Assessment—China and Northeast Asia," *Jane's Sentinel Country Risk Assessments*, January 3, 2008a.

————, "Singapore," *Jane's World Air Forces*, January 4, 2008b.

————, "Army, Thailand: Jane's Sentinel Security Assessment—Southeast Asia," *Jane's Sentinel Country Risk Assessments,* January 7, 2008c.

————, "Procurement, Japan: Jane's Sentinel Security Assessment—China and Northeast Asia," *Jane's Sentinel Country Risk Assessments*, February 21, 2008d.

————, "Political Leadership, Korea, South: Jane's Sentinel Security Assessment—China and Northeast Asia," *Jane's Sentinel Country Risk Assessments,* March 11, 2008e.

Japan Bank for International Cooperation, *Wagakuni Seizogyo no Kaigai Jigyo Tenkai ni Kan Suru Chosa Hokoku* [*Survey Report on Our Nation's Manufacturing Industries' Development Overseas*], Tokyo, November 2005.

Japan Defense Agency, *Boei Hyakusho Heisei 12 Nenpan* [*Defense of Japan 2000*], Tokyo, August 28, 2000.

————, "Jieitai, Boei Mondai ni kan Suru Yoron Chosa [Public Opinion Survey on Self-Defense Force and Defense Issues]," 2006. As of 2006:
http://www8.cao.go.jp/survey/h17/h17-bouei/index.html

————, "Survey of Lower House Members," *Aera*, August 5, 2004. As of June 3, 2008:
http://www8.cao.go.jp/survey/h17/h17-bouei/index.html

————, *Nihon no Boei Heisei 15 Nenpan* [*Defense of Japan 2003*], Tokyo, 2003.

————, *Nihon no Boei Heisei 17 Nenpan* [*Defense of Japan 2005*], Tokyo, August 2, 2005.

————, *Nihon no Boei Heisei 19 Nenpan* [*Defense of Japan 2007*], Tokyo, 2007.

"Japan Dismisses Chinese Protest over Taiwan General's Visit," BBC, August 28, 2006.

Japan External Trade Organization, trade data, 1994–2006.

"Japan Gets Good Marks in Poll," *Daily Yomiuri*, September 5, 2006.

"Japan Links Lifting of Curbs to CTBT Signing," *The Statesman*, November 24, 1999.

"Japan Plans to Boost Patrols of Gas Field Disputed with China," AFX News Ltd., December 2, 2005.

"Japan Prepares Defence Plan for Islands Disputed with China," *Asia Africa Intelligence Wire*, BBC Monitoring International Reports, January 16, 2005.

"Japan to Set Up Aid and Trade Plan for ASEAN Amid China Rift," Agence France Presse, May 30, 2005.

Japanese Government, Ministry of Defense, *National Defense Program Guidelines FY 2005*, December 10, 2004. As of March 14, 2008:
http://www.us.emb-japan.go.jp/english/html/pressreleases/2004/NDPG.pdf

"Japan's Abe Running for PM," Reuters, September 1, 2006.

"Japan's New Defense Posture: Towards Power Projection," *IISS Strategic Comments*, Vol. 10, No. 8, October 2004.

Japan-Singapore Economic Partnership Agreement, January 2007. As of April 7, 2008:
http://www.mofa.go.jp/region/asia-paci/singapore/jsepa.html

JBIC—*See* Japan Bank for International Cooperation.

JDA—*See* Japan Defense Agency.

Jennings, Peter, "Getting China Right: Australia's Policy Options for Dealing with China," Barton, Australian Capital Terr.: Australian Strategic Policy Institute, Strategic Insights 19, October 2005.

Jin Dae-woong, "Junior Officials Blamed for Secrets Leak," *The Korea Herald*, January 12, 2006.

————, "South Korea Eyes High-Tech Navy," *The Korea Herald*, June 4, 2007.

Jin-hyun Kim, "Finding a New Center or a Zigzag? Elections and FTA Negotiations with the U.S.," *PacNet Newsletter*, No. 9A, March 10, 2006.

"Joint Venture of Thai and Chinese Companies to Make Automobiles in Thailand," Global News Wire, December 26, 2005.

Jory, Patrick, "Multiculturalism in Thailand? Cultural and Regional Resurgence in a Diverse Kingdom," *Harvard Asia Pacific Review*, Winter 2000.

Jung Sung-ki, "New Ideological Groups to Gain Momentum, *The Korea Times*, January 8, 2006a.

————, "'Peace Island' in Dilemma over Naval Base," *The Korea Times*, July 17, 2006b.

Kang, David C., *China Rising: Peace, Power, and Order in East Asia*, New York: Columbia University Press, 2007.

Karniol, Robert, "ASEAN Extends Its Remit to Cover Regional Security," *Jane's Defence Weekly*, May 10, 2006. As of June 3, 2008:
http://www.iiss.org/whats-new/iiss-in-the-press/press-coverage-2006/may-2006/asean-extends-its-remit/ (reprint)

Keizai Doyukai, *Heiwa to Han'ei no Nijuyi Seiji wo Mezashite* [*Aiming Toward a Peaceful and Prosperous Twenty-First Century*], Tokyo, April 25, 2001. As of March 17, 2008:
http://www.doyukai.or.jp/policyproposals/articles/2000/010425a.html

Kelly, James A., Assistant Secretary of State for East Asian and Pacific Affairs, "Overview of U.S. Policy Toward Taiwan," testimony at a hearing on Taiwan before the House International Relations Committee, Washington, D.C., April 21, 2004.

Kelly, Paul, *Howard's Decade: An Australian Foreign Policy Reappraisal*, Sydney: Lowy Institute for International Policy, paper 15, 2006.

————, "Security Accord Flags New Japan," *The Australian*, March 14, 2007.

Khalilzad, Zalmay, David T. Orletsky, Jonathan D. Pollack, Kevin L. Pollpeter, Angel Rabasa, David A. Shlapak, Abram N. Shulsky, and Ashley J. Tellis, *The United States and Asia: Toward a New U.S. Strategy and Force Posture*, Santa Monica, Calif.: RAND Corporation, MR-1315-AF, 2001. As of March 17, 2008:
http://www.rand.org/pubs/monograph_reports/MR1315/

Khaw Boon Wan, Senior Minister for Transport and Information, Communications and the Arts, "Singapore Beyond 3G," speech delivered at the Singapore: Future Challenges Conference, Washington, D.C.: Paul H. Nitze School of Advanced International Studies (SAIS), Johns Hopkins University, October 3, 2002.

Khosa, Raspal, *Australian Defence Almanac 2006–2007*, Canberra: Australian Strategic Policy Institute, 2006.

Kim Hyun-cheol, "Inchon Rises as New Far East Hub," *The Korea Times*, March 31, 2006.

Kim, Jack, "Seoul Says Wartime Command Shift Won't Harm U.S. Ties," *Washington Post*, August 9, 2006.

Kim Kwi-ku'n, "Military Keeps Watchful Eye on How China-Russia Joint Exercise Proceeds—'No Information on Military Exercise Provided to South Korea,'" Yonhap News Agency, August 17, 2005.

Kim So Young, "New Conservative Groups Band Against Roh, Uri Party," *The Korea Herald*, November 30, 2004.

Kim Sue-young, "South Koreans Insensible to Missile Tests," *The Korea Times*, July 9, 2006.

Kim Sung-jin, "Finance Minister Warns Against China Threat," *The Korea Times*, March 21, 2006.

Klingner, Bruce, "China Shock for South Korea," *Asia Times* (online), September 11, 2004.

Kohara Masahiro, *Higashi Ajia Kyodotai* [*The East Asian Community*], Tokyo: Nihon Keizai Shimbunsha, 2005.

Koizumi Junichiro, Prime Minister of Japan, and Manmohan Singh, Prime Minister of the Republic of India, "Japan-India Partnership in a New Asian Era: Strategic Orientation of Japan-India Global Partnership," New Delhi, April 29, 2005. As of January 28, 2008: http://www.mofa.go.jp/region/asia-paci/india/partner0504.html

"Koreas Jointly Counter Chinese Moves to Lay Claims to Ancient Koguryo Kingdom," Yonhap News Agency, February 22, 2004.

Kremmer, Janaki, "Once Lock Step Australia Tunes Out U.S. Drumbeat on China," *Christian Science Monitor*, March 17, 2006.

Kuah, Adrian W. J., "The Transformation of the RSAF: The Organizational Dimension," Singapore: S. Rajaratnam School of International Studies, Nanyang Technological University, RSIS Commentaries 6, January 31, 2007. As of March 17, 2008: http://www.ntu.edu.sg/rsis/publications/Perspective/RSIS0062007.pdf

Kurlantzick, Joshua, "China's Charm Offensive in Southeast Asia," *Current History*, September 2006, pp. 270–276.

―――, *Charm Offensive: How China's Soft Power Is Transforming the World*, New Haven: Yale University Press, 2007.

Kwan, C. H., *Kyozon Kyoei no Nicchu Keizai* [*Coexistence and Coprosperity of the Japanese and Chinese Economies*], Tokyo: Toyo Keizai Shinposha, 2005.

Lankov, Andrei, "China Raises Its Stake in North Korea," *Asia Times*, December 17, 2005.

Larson, Eric V., Norman D. Levin, Seonhae Baik, and Bogdan Savych, *Ambivalent Allies? A Study of South Korean Attitudes Toward the U.S.*, Santa Monica, Calif.: RAND Corporation, TR-141-SRF, 2004. As of March 17, 2008: http://www.rand.org/pubs/technical_reports/TR141/

Lee Chi-dong, "Would-Be Moderates Roll Up Sleeves to Tackle Ideological Conflict," Yonhap News Agency, November 29, 2005.

Lee Hsien Loong, "National Day Rally 2004 Speech," Prime Minister's speech delivered at the University Cultural Centre, National University of Singapore, August 22, 2004. As of March 17, 2008: http://www.gov.sg/nd/ND04.htm

Lee Kuan Yew, *From Third World to First: The Singapore Story 1965–2000*, Vol. II, New York: HarperCollins, 2000.

Lee Nae-Young, "South Korea and the U.S.–ROK Alliance—Public Opinion About ROK–U.S. Relations," in Korea Economic Institute, *Challenges Posed by the DPRK for the Alliance and the Region*, Washington, D.C., 2006.

Lee Tae-sik, Ambassador of the Republic of Korea to the United States, "The Korea–U.S. Alliance—A Partnership for the Future," speech delivered at the St. Regis Hotel, Washington, D.C., February 7, 2006. As of March 17, 2008: http://www.dynamic-korea.com

Lepoer, Barbara Leitch, *Singapore: A Country Study,* Washington, D.C.: Library of Congress, Federal Research Division, 1989. As of March 17, 2008: http://countrystudies.us/singapore/

Levin, Norman D., *Do the Ties Still Bind? The U.S.–ROK Security Relationship After 9/11*, Santa Monica, Calif.: RAND Corporation, MG-115-AF/KF, 2004. As of March 17, 2008: http://www.rand.org/pubs/monographs/MG115/

Levin, Norman D., and Yong-Sup Han, *The Shape of Korea's Future: South Korean Attitudes Toward Unification and Long-Term Security Issues*, Santa Monica, Calif.: RAND Corporation, MR-1092-CAPP, 1999. As of March 17, 2008: http://www.rand.org/pubs/monograph_reports/MR1092/

———, *Sunshine in Korea: The South Korean Debate over Policies Toward North Korea*, Santa Monica, Calif.: RAND Corporation, MR-1555-CAPP, 2002. As of March 17, 2008: http://www.rand.org/pubs/monograph_reports/MR1555/

Lian, Daniel, "Singapore Lessons for China," *Asia Pacific Economics*, Morgan Stanley Equity Research, May 6, 2005.

Ligang, Lieu, Kevin Chow, and Unias Li, "Has China Crowded Out Foreign Direct Investment from Its Developing East Asian Neighbors?" *World Economy*, Vol. 15, No. 3, May–June 2007, pp. 70–88.

Lim, Benito, "The Political Economy of Philippines-China Relations," Philippine APEC Study Center Network, Discussion Paper 99-16, 1999. As of March 17, 2008: http://pascn.pids.gov.ph/DiscList/d99/s99-16.pdf

Lim, Benjamin Kang, and Jonathan Ansfield, "Lee Sr's Visit Taiwan to Annoyance of China," *Reuters,* September 17, 2002. As of March 17, 2008: http://www.singapore-window.org/sw02/020917re.htm

Lim Hua Sing, "Settlement of Japan-China Trade Dispute Vital," *Asahi Shimbun*, August 31, 2001. As of March 17, 2007: http://www.asahi.com/english/asianet/column/eng_010831.html

Lim, Robyn, "East Asia Summit: China Checkmated," Alexandria, Va.: International Assessment and Strategy Center, January 8, 2006. As of March 17, 2008: http://www.strategycenter.net/research/pubID.88/pub_detail.asp

Linantud, John L., "The 2004 Philippine Elections," *Contemporary Southeast Asia,* Vol. 27, No. 1, April 2005.

Lin Li, "China, Thailand Stage Combined Training of Special Troops," GOV.cn, Xinhua News Agency, July 16, 2007. As of April 7, 2008: http://www.gov.cn/misc/2007-07/16/content_686577.htm

Lopez, Antonio, and Sangwon Suh, "The Troubleshooters," *Asiaweek*, March 19, 1999.

Macapagal-Arroyo, Gloria, "Arrival Statement by President Gloria Macapagal-Arroyo," October 31, 2001. As of March 13, 2008: http://www.ops.gov.ph/china2001/speeches.htm

Maehara Seiji, "Make Them Trigger Revitalization of Party," remarks, *Mainichi Shimbun*, December 14, 2005, tr., Foreign Broadcast Information Service, FBIS-JPP20051214026004, December 14, 2005.

"Maehara Stands Firm on China Warning," *The Daily Yomiuri*, December 15, 2005.

Malik, Mohan, "The East Asia Summit: More Discord Than Accord," *YaleGlobal*, December 20, 2005. As of March 17, 2008:
http://yaleglobal.yale.edu/display.article?id=6645

Mangahas, Malou, "Despite Hard Times, GMA Hires Pricey Foreign Consultants for Charter Change," Philippine Center for Investigative Journalism, September 13, 2005. As of March 17, 2008:
http://www.pcij.org/stories/2005/chacha.html

The Maureen and Mike Mansfield Foundation, tr., "*Monthly JoongAng* Survey Research on US-Korea Alliance," June 30–July 8, 2005. As of April 29, 2008:
http://www.mansfieldfdn.org/polls/poll-05-5.htm

—————, tr., "November 2005 *Dong-A Ilbo* Opinion Poll on the Roh Administration's Performance and Potential Presidential Candidates," Mansfield Asian Opinion Poll Database, November 5, 2005. As of April 29, 2008:
http://www.mansfieldfdn.org/polls/poll-05-14.htm

Marquardt, Erich, "The Price of Japanese Nationalism," *Asia Times* (online), April 14, 2005. As of March 17, 2008:
http://www.atimes.com/atimes/Japan/GD14Dh05.html

Marsh, Virginia, and Richard McGregor, "Woodside Seals China LNG Deal," *Financial Times* (London), September 6, 2007. As of March 17, 2008:
http://www.ft.com/cms/s/0/42850d14-5c69-11dc-9cc9-0000779fd2ac.html

Marshall, Tyler, "Image Wars: China Versus the United States," *The National Interest*, September–October 2006, pp. 119–124.

Medeiros, Evan S., Roger Cliff, Keith Crane, and James C. Mulvenon, *A New Direction for China's Defense Industry*, Santa Monica, Calif.: RAND Corporation, MG-334-AF, 2005. As of March 17, 2008:
http://www.rand.org/pubs/monographs/MG334/

Menzies, Gavin, "1421: The Year the Chinese Discovered the World," Web site, 2007. As of March 13, 2008:
http://www.1421.tv/pages/content/index.asp?PageID=116

METI—*See* Ministry of Economy, Trade, and Industry (Japan).

Min Seong-jae, "The 'New Right': How New Is It?" *JoongAng Daily*, March 14, 2005.

Ministry of Commerce, Industry, and Environment (South Korea), foreign direct investment data, 1995–2005.

Ministry of Commerce of the People's Republic of China, "2005 Statistical Bulletin of China's Outward Foreign Direct Investment," September 30, 2006.

—————, "2006 Statistical Bulletin of China's Outward Foreign Direct Investment," September 30, 2007. As of March 17, 2008:
http://preview.hzs2.mofcom.gov.cn/

Ministry of Defence (Singapore), *Defending Singapore in the 21st Century*, 2000.

—————, "Singapore and China Agree to Enhance Bilateral Defence Exchanges," November 16, 2005. As of January 28, 2008:
http://www.mindef.gov.sg/imindef/news_and_events/nr/2005/nov/16nov05_nr2.html

Ministry of Defense (Thailand), "The Defense of Thailand," Bangkok: Thailand Ministry of Defense, 1996.

Ministry of Economy, Trade, and Industry (Japan), "East Asia as the Hub of a MegaCompetition Era," white paper, Tokyo, 2001.

———, "White Paper on International Economy and Trade 2005," Tokyo, July 2005.

———, "Tsusho Hyakusho [White Paper]," Tokyo, 2006. As of March 17, 2008:
http://www.meti.go.jp/report/tsuhaku2006/index.html

Ministry of Education, Singapore, "Education Statistics Digest: Online Interactive," 2004–2006. As of June 5, 2008:
http://www.moe.gov.sg/education/education-statistics-digest/online-interactive/

———, *Education Statistics Digest 2007*, 2007. As of June 5, 2008:
http://www.moe.gov.sg/education/education-statistics-digest/

Ministry of Foreign Affairs of Japan, Web site, undated. As of January 28, 2008:
http://www.mofa.go.jp/region/asia-paci/india/partner0504.html

Ministry of Foreign Affairs of the People's Republic of China, "Vice Premier Wu Yi Holds Talks with Her Singaporean Counterpart and the Two Sides Co-Host the Meeting of the Joint Council for Bilateral Cooperation," May 14, 2004. As of March 14, 2008:
http://www.mfa.gov.cn/eng/zxxx/t108506.htm

Ministry of Foreign Trade, Public Relations Department, "Trade Expansion as a Result of Thailand-India FTA," September 1, 2005.

Ministry of Trade and Industry, Singapore, free trade agreements, various dates. As of March 17, 2008:
http://www.iesingapore.gov.sg/wps/portal/FTA

———, *Singapore's Trade in Services: New Statistical Estimates and Analysis*, Singapore: Department of Statistics, 2000.

———, *Economic Survey of Singapore 2005*, Singapore: Department of Statistics, February 2006. As of March 17, 2008
http://app.mti.gov.sg/default.asp?id=148&articleID=1962

———, *Economic Survey of Singapore 2006*, Singapore: Department of Statistics, February 2007a.

———, *Foreign Equity Investment in Singapore,* Singapore: Department of Statistics, 2005, July 2007b.

———, *Singapore's Investment Abroad, 2005,* Singapore: Department of Statistics, July 2007c.

Mitchell, Derek J., *Strategy and Sentiment: South Korean Views of the United States and the U.S.–ROK Alliance*, Washington, D.C.: Center for Strategic and International Studies, 2004.

MOFAT—*See* Republic of Korea, Ministry of Foreign Affairs and Trade.

"Molotov Cocktails Found Outside Home of Fuji Xerox Chairman," *Mainichi Shimbun*, January 11, 2005.

Montaperto, Ronald N., "China Shows Its Sensitivity to SE Asia," *Asia Times,* April 27, 2005. As of March 17, 2008:
http://www.atimes.com/atimes/Southeast_Asia/GD27Ae03.html

Montreevat, Sakulrat, "Prospect of Thailand's Bilateral Trade Pacts," *Viewpoints*, December 10, 2003.

"MPs Urge PM: 'Be Cautious,'" *The Nation* (Bangkok), September 18, 2001.

"Multi-Nation Naval Exercise Begins," *Hindustan Times*, January 9, 2006.

Murphy, James, "Chickens Could Fuel Thai Modernization Plans," *Jane's Defence Weekly*, December 7, 2005.

"Myanmar, Thailand to Build Deep Seaport," Xinhua News Agency, January 12, 2004.

Nam Sung Wook, "North Korea Invites China into the Inner Room of Its Economy," *Korea Focus*, May–June 2005.

Nanto, Dick K., and Emma Chanlett-Avery, *The Rise of China and Its Effect on Taiwan, Japan and South Korea*: U.S. Policy Choices, Congressional Research Service, Washington, D.C.: Library of Congress, April 12, 2005.

Nathan, John, *Japan Unbound: A Volatile Nation's Quest for Pride and Purpose*, Boston: Houghton Mifflin Company, 2004.

National Bureau of Statistics of China, *China Statistical Yearbook*, Beijing: China Statistics Press, various dates.

———, Web site, undated. As of March 17, 2008:
http://www.stats.gov.cn/english/statisticaldata

National Institute of Defense Studies, *East Asian Strategic Review 2006*, Tokyo, March 2006. As of March 17, 2008:
http://www.nids.go.jp/english/index.html

———, *East Asian Strategic Review 2007*, Tokyo, April 2007. As of March 17, 2008:
http://www.nids.go.jp/english/index.html

"Navy Chief on Budget Cut, Foreign Threat," *Bangkok Post*, January 2, 1999.

"Navy Chief on Modernization, PRC Technology," *The Nation* (Bangkok), December 26, 1993.

New Right, Web site (in Japanese), 2007. As of April 21, 2008:
http://www.newright.net

"Nichibei Shikisho Enshu Hajimaru–Hajime no Tosho Boei Sotei [Japanese-U.S. Command Post Exercise Begins: The First to Envision Small Island Defense]," *Sankei Shimbun*, January 27, 2006.

NIDS—*See* National Institute of Defense Studies.

Nikkei Net Interactive, The Future of Asia 2002, Bio/CV of Dhanin Chearavanont, Chairman & CEO, Charoen Pokphand Group (Thailand), 2002. As of March 17, 2008:
http://www.nni.nikkei.co.jp/FR/NIKKEI/inasia/future/2002/2002pro_chearavanont.html

Nippon Keidanren [Japan Federation of Economic Organizations], "Japan-China Relations in the 21st Century," Tokyo, February 20, 2001. As of March 14, 2008:
http://www.keidanren.or.jp/english/policy/2001/006.html

Nukaga Fukushiro, "Japan's Defence Policy and International Peace Cooperation Activities," speech delivered to the Royal United Service Institute for Defence and Security Studies, London, January 11, 2006. As of March 8, 2007:
http://www.mod.go.jp/e/rusi.pdf

Office of the Cabinet Secretary, Japan, Yoron Chosa [Public Opinion Surveys], various dates. As of March 17, 2008:
http://www8.cao.go.jp/survey/y-index.html

Ohashi, Hideo, "China's Regional Trade and Investment Profile," in Shambaugh, 2006.

Onishi, Norimitsu, "Ugly Images of Asian Rivals Become Best Sellers in Japan," *New York Times*, November 14, 2005.

————, "In a Wired South Korea, Robots Will Feel Right at Home," *The New York Times*, April 2, 2006.

Open Source Center, *OSC Analysis 08 June: ROKAF Upgrade, Modernization Continues Despite Challenges,* June 8, 2007.

Organisation for Economic Co-Operation and Development (OECD), "OECD Finds That China Is Biggest Exporter of Information Technology Goods in 2004, Surpassing US and EU," undated. As of March 17, 2008:
http://www.oecd.org/document/8/0,2340,en_2649_201185_35833096_1_1_1_1,00.html

OSC—*See* Open Source Center.

"Paradaimu wa kawatta no ka? [Paradigm Shift?]," *Gaiko Foramu*, January 2002.

Park Doo-Bok, "History of Goguryeo Calls for Fact-Based Approach," *Korea Focus*, January–February 2004.

Park Song-wu, "Korea Can Take Wartime Control Now," *The Korea Times*, August 9, 2006.

Parliament of Australia, *Government Response to the Senate Foreign Affairs, Defence and Trade Inquiry into Australia's Relations with China*, Canberra: Senate, 2006a. As of March 17, 2008:
http://www.aph.gov.au/senate/committee/fadt_ctte/china/govt_response.pdf

————, *China's Emergence: Implications for Australia*, Canberra: Senate Foreign Affairs, Defense and Trade References Committee, March 28, 2006b. As of March 17, 2008:
http://www.aph.gov.au/senate/committee/fadt_ctte/china/report02/

Pathan, Don, "Is the World Getting an Accurate Image of Thailand?" *The Nation* (Bangkok), February 10, 2003.

"Patrol Ships, Planes to Be Stationed in East China Sea; Japan Coast Guard to Spend 350 Billion Yen to Upgrade Equipment," *Sankei Shimbun*, December 2, 2005.

People's Republic of China, *Chinese National Defence in 2004*, white paper, Information Office of the State Council of the People's Republic of China, Beijing, December 27, 2004.

People's Republic of China and the Government of the Republic of the Philippines, "Joint Statement on the Framework of Bilateral Cooperation in the Twenty-First Century," May 16, 2000.

Perdana Global Peace Organisation, "Containing China: A Flawed Agenda," paper presented at Post–9.11 World: Exploring Alternatives for Japan and Australia, Nanzan University, Nagoya, Japan, September 14, 2005. As of March 14, 2008:
http://www.perdana4peace.org/press2.aspx?t=chinaagenda

Perlez, Jane, "China Is Romping with the Neighbors (U.S. Is Distracted), *New York Times*, December 3, 2003.

————, "Across Asia, Beijing's Star Is in Ascendance," *New York Times*, August 24, 2004a.

————, "Chinese Move to Eclipse U.S. Appeal in Southeast Asia," *New York Times*, November 18, 2004b.

————, "China's Role Emerges as Major Issue for Southeast Asia," *New York Times*, March 14, 2006a.

————, "U.S. Competes with China for Vietnam's Allegiance," *New York Times*, June 19, 2006b.

————, "China Competes with West in Aid to Its Neighbors," *New York Times*, September 18, 2006c.

Perry, Tony, and Bruce Wallace, "Japanese Troops Shore Up Skills," *Los Angeles Times*, January 13, 2006, p. A3.

"Philippine Leader Heralds 'Golden Age' with China Ahead of Visit," *Asia Pacific News*, October 27, 2006. As of March 17, 2008:
http://www.channelnewsasia.com/stories/afp_asiapacific/view/237810/1/.html

Phongpaichit, Pasuk, and Chris Baker, *Thaksin: The Business of Politics in Thailand*, Bangkok: Silkworm Books, 2005.

Plastics and Chemicals Industries Association, "China—Market Economy Status—Implications for Anti-Dumping Remedies," supplementary submission to the Department of Foreign Affairs and Trade feasibility study on an Australia-China Free Trade Agreement, July, 2004. As of March 13, 2008:
http://www.pacia.org.au/_uploaditems/docs/10.china_fta_sup.pdf

"PM Clarifies Push for Closer Links in Asia," *Bangkok Post*, December 17, 2001, p. 2.

"PM Goh Makes Surprise Taiwan Stopover," Reuters, November 28, 1997. As of March 17, 2008:
http://www.singapore-window.org/1127reut.htm

Porter, Barry, "Singapore Drops Control of Suzhou Park," *South China Morning Post*, June 29, 1999. As of March 17, 2008:
http://www.singapore-window.org/sw99/90629sc.htm

"Post-Coup Thailand in the Eyes of the U.S. and China," *The Nation* (Bangkok), February 12, 2007.

Priestly, Michael, "Anti-Dumping Rules and the Australia-China Free Trade Agreement," Canberra: Parliament of Australia, Department of Parliamentary Services, Research Note 38, March 14, 2005.

The Program on International Policy Attitudes, "22-Nation Poll Shows China Viewed Positively by Most Countries Including Its Asian Neighbors," March 5, 2005. As of March 17, 2008:
http://www.pipa.org/OnlineReports/China/China_Mar05/China_Mar05_rpt.pdf

"Protecting Japan—Part IV: Meeting New Threats to the Realm," *Yomiuri Shimbun*, September 18, 2004.

Quilop, Raymund, "Philippines Lists Equipment Priorities," *Jane's Defence Weekly*, April 11, 2007. As of March 17, 2008:
http://www4.janes.com/subscribe/jdw/doc_view.jsp?K2DocKey=/content1/janesdata/mags/jdw/history/jdw2007/jdw32430.htm@current&Prod_Name=JDW&QueryText=Philippines

"Radios, Helicopters for the Philippines," *Defense Industry Daily*, June 12, 2007. As of March 17, 2008:
http://www.defenseindustrydaily.com/radios-helicopters-for-the-philippines-03366/

Rank, Michael, "Minerals, Railways Draw China to North Korea," *Asia Times*, November 18, 2005.

"Real Deal Is in the Fine Print," *The Age*, October 19, 2005. As of March 17, 2008:
http://www.theage.com.au/articles/2005/10/18/1129401255194.html

"Regional Role Possible for Baht," *The Nation* (Bangkok), January 26, 2004.

Republic of Korea, Ministry of Foreign Affairs and Trade (MOFAT), Web site, undated. As of March 17, 2008:
http://www.mofat.go.kr

Republic of Korea, Ministry of National Defense (MND), Web site, undated a. As of March 17, 2008:
http://www.mnd.go.kr/mndEng/main/index.jsp

————, *Defense Reform 2020*, Eng. undated b. As of April 29, 2008:
http://www.mnd.go.kr/mndEng/DefensePolicy/DefenseReform2020/overview/index.jsp

Richardson, Dennis, Australian Ambassador to the United States, "Australia and a Rising China," speech delivered at The Nixon Center, Washington, D.C., June 6, 2006.

Rocamora, Joel, "Philippine Political Parties, Electoral System and Political Reform," *Philippines International Review,* Vol. 1, No. 1, Spring 1998. As of March 17, 2008:
http://www.philsol.nl/pir/JR-98a.htm

Rodan, Gary, "The Coming Challenge to Singapore, Inc.," *Far Eastern Economic Review*, December 2004.

Roy, Denny, "Southeast Asia and China: Balancing or Bandwagoning?" *Contemporary Southeast Asia*, Vol. 27, No. 2, August 2005, pp. 305–322.

Royal Danish Ministry of Foreign Affairs, Danish Trade Council, "Sector Overview: The Electronics Industry in Thailand," Copenhagen, July 9, 2005.

Rudd, Kevin Michael, "The Rise of China and the Strategic Implications for U.S.–Australia Relations," speech to the Brookings Institution, Washington, D.C., April 20, 2007. As of March 17, 2008:
http://www.brookings.edu/events/2007/0420china.aspx

Runckel and Associates, Inc., "Table of Comparison: Asian Countries' Foreign Direct Investment: Asian Development Outlook 2007," 2007. As of March 17, 2008:
http://www.business-in-asia.com/asia/asia_fdi.html

"S. Korea, China to Stage Joint Naval Training," Yonhap News Agency, April 24, 2007.

Sales, Leigh, "PM Hails Japan's Friendship," *Lateline*, Australian Broadcasting Corporation, June 15, 2006. As of March 17, 2008:
http://www.abc.net.au/lateline/content/2006/s1664304.htm

Schlesinger, Jacob M., *Shadow Shoguns*, Stanford, Calif.: Stanford University Press, 1997.

Schuman, Michael, "Families Under Fire," *TimeAsia*, February 16, 2004. As of March 14, 2008:
http://www.time.com/time/asia/covers/501040223/sy.html

"Security Pact to Deepen Japan Ties," *Weekend Australian*, August 12, 2006.

Sekai Nippo, "Korea in Crisis: Is N. Korea Becoming a Chinese Colony?" February 11, 2006.

"Senior Chinese Leader Meets Philippine Congress Leaders," *People's Daily* (online), October 20, 2004. As of January 28, 2008:
http://english.people.com.cn/200410/20/eng20041020_160841.html

Seo Hyun-jin, "Nationalism Fuels Asian History Row," *The Korea Herald*, September 8, 2004.

Ser Myo-ja and Bae Young-dae, "'New Right' Group Launched," *JoongAng Daily*, November 8, 2005.

Shambaugh, David, ed., *Power Shift: China and Asia's New Dynamics*, Berkeley: University of California Press, 2006.

Shinawatra, Thaksin, Prime Minister of Thailand, "Policy of the Government," statement, delivered to the National Assembly, March 23, 2005. As of March 17, 2008:
http://www.thaiembdc.org/politics/govtment/policy/55thpolicy/index_e.html

Shinoda Tomohito, "Koizumi's Top-Down Leadership in the Anti-Terrorism Legislation: The Impact of Political Institutional Changes," *SAIS Review*, Vol. 23, No. 1, Winter–Spring 2003, pp. 19–34.

————, 官邸外交：政治リーダーシップの行方 (*Kantei Gaik: Seiji Ridashippu no Yukue*) [*Kantei Foreign Policy: Political Leadership Direction*], Tokyo: Asahi Shimbunsha, 2004.

Simon, Sheldon W., "The Regionalization of Defense in Southeast Asia," *NBR Analysis*, Vol. 3, No. 1, June 1992.

"Singapore and Thailand Sign Agreement on Air Force Training," Channel NewsAsia, November 12, 2004.

"Singapore Bourse Woos Mainland Firms," *Shenzhen Daily*, November 6, 2006. As of January 28, 2008:
http://previewchina.tdctrade.com

"Singapore: Future Challenges," conference report, Washington, D.C.: Johns Hopkins University, October 3, 2002. As of March 17, 2008:
http://saisauth.nts.jhu.edu/programs/asia/sea/seasiapublications.html

"Singapore—New Mecca for Chinese Students," *People's Daily* (online), May 16, 2002. As of January 28, 2008:
http://english.people.com.cn/200205/16/eng20020516_95807.shtml

"Sino-Thai Joint Communiqué," Xinhua News Agency, April 30, 1999.

Smith, Stephen, Minister for Foreign Affairs, "Speech Notes for the Annual Diplomatic Corps Christmas Party," Canberra, December 3, 2007. As of March 17, 2008:
http://www.foreignminister.gov.au/speeches/2007/071203.html

Snyder, Scott, "All Eyes on Beijing: Raising the Stakes," *Comparative Connections*, January–March 2005.

"South Koreans See China as Threat Later, Not North—Poll," Reuters, March 20, 2006.

Southeast Asia Treaty Organization, Manila pact, 1954.

"S'pore Press Silent on Taiwan Official's Visit," United Press International, January 1, 1998. As of March 17, 2008:
http://www.singapore-window.org/980101up.htm

State Council Information Office, *China's National Defense: 2004*, Beijing, December 2004.

Storey, Ian, "Creeping Assertiveness: China, the Philippines, and the South China Sea Dispute," *Contemporary Southeast Asia*, Vol. 21, No. 1, April 1999, pp. 98–107.

————, "China and the Philippines: Moving Beyond the South China Sea Dispute," *China Brief*, Vol. 6, No. 17, August 16, 2006a. As of April 7, 2008:
http://www.jamestown.org/china_brief/article.php?issue_id=3837

————, "A Hiatus in the Sino-Thai 'Special Relationship,'" *China Brief*, Vol. 6, No. 19, September 20, 2006b. As of April 7, 2008:
http://www.jamestown.org/china_brief/article.php?issue_id=3861

Sugawa Kiyoshi, "Time to Pop the Cork: Three Scenarios to Redefine Japanese Use of Force," working paper, Washington, D.C.: Brookings Institution, Center for Northeast Asian Policy Studies, June 2000.

"Summaries of Seminar Presentations and Core Group Discussions," China in Asia Seminar Series, Washington, D.C.: American Enterprise Institute and National Defense University, 2006.

Sung-Joo Han, *The Failure of Democracy in South Korea*, University of California Press, 1974.

Suryanarayana, P. S., "India Signs Maritime Accord with Thailand," *The Hindu*, May 21, 2005.

Suryaprakash, Raakhee, "Singapore-India Relations: CECA and Beyond," South Asia Analysis Group, paper 1493, August 10, 2005. As of March 17, 2008:
http://www.southasiaanalysis.org/%5Cpapers15%5Cpaper1493.html

Sutter, Robert G., *China's Rise in Asia: Promises and Perils*, Boulder, Colo.: Rowman and Littlefield Publishers, 2005.

"Suzhou Park Problems Can Be Overcome," *Straits Times* (Singapore), January 15, 1998. As of March 17, 2008:
http://www.singapore-window.org/80115st1.htm

Symons, Emma-Kate, "Howard Raises Stake on Trade Pact with China," *The Australian*, January 15, 2007.

Tai no Kajin Zaibatsu 57 Ke [*57 Great (Ethnic) Chinese Thai Business Families*], Tokyo: NNA, September 2005.

"Taidan: Yasukuni wo Kataru, Gaiko wo Kataru, Watanabe Tsuneo x Wakamiya Yoshibumi [Interview: Watanabe Tsuneo and Wakamiya Yoshibumi Discuss Yasukuni and Foreign Policy]," *Ronza*, February 2006.

Taik-young Hamm, "The Self-Reliant National Defense of South Korea and the Future of the U.S.–ROK Alliance," Nautilus Institute for Security and Sustainable Development Northeast Asia Peace and Security Project, Policy Forum Online 06-49A, June 20, 2006. As of March 17, 2008:
http://www.nautilus.org/fora/security/0649Hamm.html

"Taiwan Opposition Leader to Visit Japan War Shrine Amid Criticism," Agence France Presse, April 4, 2005.

Tan, Andrew T. H., "Singapore's Defence: Capabilities, Trends and Implications," *Contemporary Southeast Asia*, Vol. 21, No. 3, December 1999.

Tarrazona, Noel, "US, China Vie for Philippine Military Influence," *Asia Times* (online), September 20, 2007. As of March 17, 2008:
http://www.atimes.com/atimes/Southeast_Asia/II20Ae01.html

Tasker, Rodney, "Silent Service: Navy Reaps Rewards of Steering Clear of Politics," *Far Eastern Economic Review*, October 21, 1993, pp. 30–31.

Tellis, Ashley J., and Michael Wills, *Strategic Asia: 2005–06: Military Modernization in and Era of Uncertainty*, Seattle, Wash.: National Bureau of Asian Research, 2005.

———, *Strategic Asia 2006–07: Trade, Interdependence and Security*, Seattle, Wash.: National Bureau of Asian Research, 2006.

Temasek Holdings, "Our Portfolio by Geography," Web page, March 31, 2007. As of June 13, 2008:
http://www.temasekholdings.com.sg/our_portfolio_portfolio_highlights_geography.htm

"Thai PM Concludes China Tour," Xinhua News Agency, July 3, 2005.

"Thai Prime Minister Interviewed on Eve of China Visit," Xinhua News Agency, August 26, 2001.

"Thai Princess Calls for More Exchanges Between Chinese, Thai Students" Xinhua News Agency, April 4, 2006.

Thailand Board of Investment, Foreign Investment Web page, 2008. As of March 17, 2008:
http://www.boi.go.th/english/about/statistics_investment.asp

"Thailand Mulls Loan Repayment Extension After Burma Visit," BBC Monitoring Asia Pacific, November 26, 2006.

"Thailand Signs Four Agreements in Move Towards Becoming Regional Energy Center," Global News Wire, November 13, 2003.

"Thailand to Offer Baht Denominated Loans to Neighboring Countries," Global News Wire, November 12, 2003.

"Thailand to Work with India on Security Cooperation," *Asia Pulse*, November 27, 2001.

"Thaksin Willing to Mediate to Repair Sino-US Relations," *South China Morning Post*, May 11, 2001.

Thanat-Rusk communiqué of 1962.

"Three Thai-Involved Myanmar Industrial Zone Projects to Start Sooner," Xinhua News Agency, June 3, 2004.

"Top Legislator Appreciates Philippines' One-China Policy," *People's Daily* (online), September 4, 2004. As of March 17, 2008:
http://english.people.com.cn/200409/04/eng20040904_155876.html

Torrijos, Elena R., "Doing Business in China," *Newsbreak*, May 27, 2002.

"Tosho Boei Nado Sotei—Nichibei Shikisho Enshu Hajimaru [Envisioning Small Island Defense: U.S.–Japanese Command Post Exercise Begins]," *Kyodo Tsushin*, January 27, 2006.

"Toyota Shuts India Plant After Strike by Workers," Reuters, January 8, 2006.

Transparency International, "Corruption Perceptions Index," Berlin, 2005. As of April 29, 2008:
http://www.transparency.org/policy_research/surveys_indices/cpi/2005

"Two Years of Thaksin: All the PM's Men," *The Nation* (Bangkok), February 10, 2003.

UNCTAD—*See* United Nations Conference on Trade and Development.

United Nations Conference on Trade and Development, Division on Investment and Enterprise, Foreign Direct Investment Statistics, Country Profile on Australia, updated periodically. As of January 28, 2008:
http://www.unctad.org/Templates/StartPage.asp?intItemID=2921&lang=1

————, Country Profile on Japan, updated periodically. As of January 28, 2008:
http://www.unctad.org/Templates/StartPage.asp?intItemID=2921&lang=1

United Nations Statistics Division, United Nations Commodity Trade Statistics Database (UN COMTRADE), various years. As of March 17, 2008:
http://unstats.un.org/unsd/comtrade

United States and Japan, Mutual Defense Treaty, 1960.

United States and the Republic of Korea, Mutual Defense Treaty, 1954.

United States and the Republic of the Philippines, Mutual Defense Treaty, 1952.

U.S. Department of Defense, "U.S. Military Support to Tsunami Relief Efforts," news release, No. 1325-04, December 28, 2004. As of March 17, 2008:
http://www.defenselink.mil/releases/release.aspx?releaseid=8090

U.S. Department of State, Bureau of East Asian and Pacific Affairs, "Background Note: Philippines," October 2007. As of April 4, 2008:
http://www.state.gov/r/pa/ei/bgn/2794.htm

U.S. Department of State, Bureau of Intelligence and Research, "INR Poll: Asian Views of China," Opinion Analysis, Washington, D.C., November 9, 2005.

U.S. House of Representatives, "Whereas the Government of Japan . . . ," H.R. 121, 110 Cong., 2nd Sess., July 30, 2007.

U.S.–Japan Security Consultative Committee, Joint Statement, February 19, 2005. As of March 17, 2008:
http://www.state.gov/r/pa/prs/ps/2005/42490.htm

Vaile, Mark, Member of Parliament, Minister for Trade, "Unlocking China's Services Sector," speech delivered at the launch of the Economic Analytical Unit report, Sydney, February 9, 2006. As of March 17, 2008:
http://www.trademinister.gov.au/speeches/2006/060209_eau_report.html

Vasil, Raj, *Governing Singapore,* Sydney: Allen & Unwin, 2000.

Vaughn, Bruce, *East Asian Summit: Issues for Congress*, Washington, D.C.: Congressional Research Service, December 9, 2005. As of March 17, 2008:
http://fpc.state.gov/documents/organization/58236.pdf

Vershbow, Alexander, U.S. Ambassador to the Republic of Korea, "U.S.–Korea Free Trade Agreement: A Path to Sustainable Growth," speech, Seoul: Institute for Global Economics, February 14, 2006. As of January 28, 2008:
http://americancorners.or.kr/e-infousa/wwwh3307.html

"Veteran Diplomat Asada Slams Thaksin's Foreign Policy in New Book," *The Nation* (Bangkok), August 17, 2004.

"The View from Singapore: ASEAN Has a Role to Play in Keeping the Peace," *Asiaweek,* March 22, 1996.

Vinyaratn, Pansak, *Facing the Challenge: Economic Policy and Strategy*, Hong Kong: CLSA Books, August 2004.

Viotti, Paul R., and Mark V. Kauppi, eds., *International Relations Theory: Realism Pluralism, Globalism, and Beyond*, New York: Macmillan, 1999.

Virola, Romulo A., Marriel M. Remulla, Lea H. Amoro, and Milagros Y. Say, "Measuring the Contribution of Tourism to the Economy: The Philippine Tourism Satellite Account," paper prepared for the 8th National Convention on Statistics, Manila, October 1–2, 2001. As of April 7, 2008:
http://www.nscb.gov.ph/stats/ptsa/papers.asp

Wain, Barry, "A David-and-Goliath Tussle," *Far Eastern Economic Review*, August 5, 2004. As of March 14, 2008, 2008:
http://www.singapore-window.org/sw04/040805fe.htm

Walker, Martin, "Asia's New Map Lacks U.S.," United Press International, December 8, 2005. As of March 13, 2008:
http://www.upi.com/International_Intelligence/Analysis/2005/12/08/
walkers_world_asias_new_map_lacks_us/4817/

Watanabe Osamu, "Chugoku Purasu 1 to Chiiki Keizai [China Plus One and the Regional Economy]," October 27, 2004.

———, "Higashi Ajia Bijinesu Keizaiken wo Misueta Chugoku Bijinesu Tenbo [Developing China Business with Eyes on the East Asian Business Economic Zone]," September 21, 2005. As of March 17, 2008:
http://www.jetro.go.jp/jetro/profile/speech/

————, "Economic Integration of East Asia and Japan's Future," speech delivered at the Foreign Press Center, Tokyo, March 10, 2004.

Wattanayagorn, Panitan, "Thailand: The Elite's Shifting Conceptions of Security," in Muthiah Alagappa, ed., *Asian Security Practice*, Stanford: Stanford University Press, 1998.

Weisman, Steven R., "Rice and Australian Counterpart Differ About China," *New York Times*, March 17, 2006.

White, Hugh, "Australian Strategic Policy," in Ashley J. Tellis and Michael Wills, *Strategic Asia: 2005–06: Military Modernization in and Era of Uncertainty*, Seattle, Wash.: National Bureau of Asian Research, 2005, pp. 305–331.

Wijers-Hasegawa, Yumi, "Time for Japan to Shut Up and Drill: Energy Expert," *The Japan Times*, April 11, 2006.

Wilson, Dominic, and Roopa Purushothaman, *Dreaming with the BRICs: The Path to 2050*, New York: Goldman Sachs Group Inc., Global Economics Paper No. 99, October 1, 2003.

Wong, John, "China's Economic Rise and Implications for Southeast Asia: The Big Picture," paper presented at the workshop on Ethnic Chinese Economy and Business in Southeast Asia in the Era of Globalization, Singapore: Institute of Southeast Asian Studies, April 21–22, 2005.

Wong, Kelvin, Grace Ng, Fiona Chan, and Gabriel Chen, "Temasek, GIC Now Boast a Stronger Overseas Portfolio," *The Straits Times*, December 30, 2005.

World Public Opinion, "World Opinion on China More Positive Than on US, But Slipping," Washington, D.C., April 17, 2006. As of March 17, 2008: http://www.worldpublicopinion.org/pipa/articles/views_on_countriesregions_bt/190. php?nid=&id=&pnt=190

Wu Zhong, "Some of China's SOEs Aren't Such Losers After All," *Asia Times*, September 26, 2007. As of March 17, 2008: http://www.atimes.com/atimes/China_Business/II26Cb02.html

Wyatt, David K., *Thailand: A Short History*, New Haven, Conn.: Yale University Press, 1982.

Wyatt, Stephen, "Hill Shows His Moderate Side to a Bristling China," *Australian Financial Review*, June 17, 2005.

Yamagiwa Sumio, Asahi Shimbun *ga Chugoku wo Ogoraseru* [*The* Asahi Shimbun *Makes China Arrogant*], Tokyo: Nisshin Hodo, 2005.

Yamano Sharin, *Kenkanryu* [*Hating the Korea Wave*], Tokyo: Shinyusha, September 2005.

Yeo, George, Minister for Foreign Affairs of the Republic of Singapore, statement delivered to the 59th Session of the United Nations General Assembly, New York, September 24, 2004. As of January 28, 2008: http://app.mfa.gov.sg/internet/press/view_press.asp?post_id=1076

York, Geoffrey, "The Junta's Enablers: Thailand, India, China," *The Globe and Mail* (Toronto), October 6, 2007.

Yu Jae-Dong and Min Dong-Yong, "New Right Movement Finds Supporters," *Dong-A Ilbo*, November 22, 2004.

Zhang Yunling and Tang Shiping, "China's Regional Strategy," in David Shambaugh, ed., 2006, pp. 48–70.